PERSONALITY
AND
INDIVIDUAL
DIFFERENCES
CURRENT DIRECTIONS

EDITED BY RICHARD E. HICKS

www.
AUSTRALIANACADEMIC**PRESS**
.com.au

First published in 2010
Australian Academic Press
32 Jeays Street
Bowen Hills Qld 4006
Australia
www.australianacademicpress.com.au

National Library of Australia Cataloguing-in-Publication entry

Title:	Personality and individual differences : current directions / edited by Richard Hicks.
Edition:	1st ed.
ISBN:	9781921513664 (pbk.)
	9781921513671 : (ebook : pdf)
Subjects:	Personality.
	Individual differences.
Other Authors/ Contributors:	Hicks, Richard.
Dewey Number:	155.22

Cover illustration by ©istockphoto.com/velusariot. Cover designed by Maria Biaggini.

Contents

Section 1.2
Education, personality and emotional intelligence

Section 1.3
Moral, social and individual aspects in personality psychology

Section 1.4
Performance aspects and personality influences

PART TWO:
On Professional Context and Applications
of Personality Knowledge

Section 2.1
*Applications in organisational psychology: Wellbeing and distress,
'role stress' and reputation at work*

Preface

Personality and individual differences are areas central to our understanding of human behaviour. This book reflects current directions in our research in these areas and covers both theory and application across work, leisure, health and community. Research into positive and negative behaviours in a variety of fields extends our understanding of personality and individual differences — the two main sections in this book clearly indicate the importance of the topic areas as the table of contents demonstrates. Part 1 is entitled 'On Personality Theory', covering areas such as personality theory and context, goal-setting and cognitive issues, questionnaires and their development and use, emotional intelligence and moral judgement and decision making. Part 2 is entitled 'On Professional Context and Applications of Personality Knowledge', covering such areas as educational, school and university studies, personality and organisations, stress, health and wellbeing, cross-cultural studies and clinical, forensic and general studies.

Every chapter in this book has undergone stringent peer reviews, and been rewritten as required, before final acceptance for inclusion. The origin of most of the papers was their presentation at the Seventh Australian Conference on Personality and Individual Differences held at Bond University, Queensland, in November 2008. All of the written papers finally accepted were submitted during 2009, assessed by two anonymous reviewers (double-blind reviews), resubmitted with corrections if the paper was suitable for publication at this point, and then given a final review. The best of these peer-reviewed papers are included in this book, thus giving an overview of current directions in personality and individual differences at this time.

There were many original submitted papers and this book would not have been possible without the help of expert academic and professional reviewers in the review and selection process. All reviewers completed three to six or more reviews with attention to current suitability for publication, improvements needed if suitable, and advice to the authors and to the editor. Thanks are gratefully extended to the reviewers for the time and care taken; they share in the standard and quality of this book. They are listed below. These reviewers included leading national and international researchers and academics, mainly from throughout Australasia.

This book is the second produced as a result of the sharing of ideas at conferences held in Australia on personality and individual differences research in our region. The first was edited by Simon Boag (2008; Personality Down Under: Perspectives from Australia. New York: Nova Science). The series of books will continue as a result of the growing interest and the quality of research being conducted by Australasian academics and practitioners.

I have enjoyed the stimulation and challenge from editing this book and have learned much — including that book editing can also be frustrating, demanding and time consuming, but in the end rewarding. I hope you enjoy dipping into this book and can make good use of its many chapters for your own knowledge and purposes. Lastly, I dedicate this book to Carol, my partner and wife, for her valuable support and understanding throughout this period.

Richard E. Hicks
Professor of Psychology, Bond University

List of Reviewers

Thanks are due to the reviewers listed below, all of whom reviewed independently at least three manuscripts; most reviewed five or six papers.

Mark Bahr, School of Social Sciences, Bond University, Australia.

Simon Boag, Department of Psychology, Macquarie University, Australia.

Douglas Boer, Department of Psychology, University of Waikato, New Zealand.

Miles Bore, School of Psychology, University of Newcastle, Australia.

Rebekah Doley, School of Social Sciences, Bond University, Australia.

Mark Edwards, School of Social Sciences, Bond University, Australia.

Gerard Fogarty, University of Southern Queensland, Australia.

Katarina Fritzon, School of Social Sciences, Bond University, Australia.

Richard Hicks, School of Social Sciences, Bond University, Australia.

Carolyn MacCann, School of Psychology, University of Sydney, Australia.

John O'Gorman, School of Psychology, Griffith University, Australia.

Gerry Pallier, School of Psychology, The University of Sydney, Australia.

Aileen M. Pidgeon, School of Social Sciences, Bond University, Australia.

Richard D. Roberts, Center for New Constructs, Educational Testing Services, Princeton, New Jersey, United States of America.

David Robinson, Central Queensland University, Australia.

Bruce D. Watt, School of Social Sciences, Bond University, Australia.

As can be seen reviewers came from a cross-section of Australian and international universities, professional institutions and authorities. A thank you to all, on my behalf and on behalf of the chapter writers themselves. And a special thank you to staff of Bond University's Department of Psychology, School of Social Sciences, who provided strong reviewer and back-up support.

List of Contributors

Authors of the chapters to this book are listed below with an indication of the workplace and position, or study institution, at the time of the conference presentation and paper submission, and the current appointment where known.

Lisa M. Abel, Assistant Professor, School of Social Sciences, Bond University, Australia.

Mattias Allard, School of Social Sciences, Bond University, Australia.

Vidya Sagar Athota, University of New South Wales, Australia.

Mark Bahr, Assistant Professor, School of Social Sciences, Bond University, Australia.

Norman Barling, Private Practice, Gold Coast; formerly Bond University, Australia.

Erica Begelhole, Child and Youth Mental Health Service, Gold Coast Health Service District, Australia.

Navjot Bhullar, University of New England, Armidale, Australia.

Janine Blacker, Centre for Forensic & Family Psychology, University of Birmingham, United Kingdom.

Simon Boag, Lecturer, Department of Psychology, Macquarie University, Australia.

Douglas Boer, Associate Professor of Psychology, University of Waikato, New Zealand.

Gregory Boyle, Professor of Psychology, School of Social Sciences, Bond University, Australia.

Elise Brown, School of Psychology, University of Tasmania, Australia.

Edmond Chiu, School of Psychology, University of Tasmania, Australia.

Carla Ferrari, School of Social Sciences, Bond University, Australia.

Laura Fleming, School of Social Sciences, Bond University, Australia.

Gerard Fogarty, Professor of Psychology, University of Southern Queensland, Australia.

Katarina Fritzon, Associate Professor of Psychology, School of Social Sciences, Bond University, Australia.

Natalie Games, University of Southern Queensland, Australia.

Jonathan P. Gerber, Associate Lecturer, Department of Psychology, Macquarie University, Australia.

A. Ian Glendon, Associate Professor of Psychology, Griffith University, Australia.

Nicole Guse, Queensland Corrective Services, Australia.

Tasneem Hasan, Queensland Health, Australia.

Richard E. Hicks, Professor of Psychology, School of Social Sciences, Bond University, Australia.

Donald W. Hine, University of New England, Australia.

Matthew Hornsey, Associate Professor, School of Psychology, The University of Queensland.

Zahra Isadikhah, The University of Queensland, Australia.

Chris J. Jackson, Professor of Business Psychology, School of Organisation and Management, University of New South Wales, Australia.

Sarang Kim, Centre for Mental Health Research, Australian National University; formerly School of Social Sciences, Bond University, Australia.

Poppy Liossis, Senior Lecturer, School of Psychology & Counselling, Queensland University of Technology, Australia.

Carolyn MacCann, School of Psychology, University of Sydney, Australia.

Timothy Marsh, Department of Psychology, Macquarie University, Australia.

Trishita Mathew, School of Social Sciences, Bond University, Australia.

Maryke R. Mead, School of Social Sciences, Bond University, Australia.

Prudence Millear, School of Psychology & Counselling, Queensland University of Technology, Australia.

Bronwen R. Myall, University of New England, Armidale, Australia.

Lloyd Neill, School of Psychology, University of Tasmania, Australia.

Peter J. O'Connor, University of Notre Dame, Australia.

John O'Gorman, Professor of Psychology, Griffith University, Australia.

Gerry Pallier, Research Assistant and Tutor, School of Psychology, The University of Sydney, Australia.

Tanya Paspaliaris, School of Social Sciences, Bond University, Australia.

Michelle Perrin, School of Social Sciences, Bond University, Australia.

John Reid, Associate Lecturer, School of Psychology, University of Tasmania, Australia.

Richard D. Roberts, Center for New Constructs, Educational Testing Services, Princeton, New Jersey, United States of America.

David Robinson, Adjunct Professor of Management Studies, Central Queensland University, Australia (formerly Associate Professor of Entrepreneurship, Bond University)

Mary E. Rogers, Research Fellow, School of Psychology, Griffith University, Australia.

Margaret Shapiro, Associate Professor, School of Social Work and Human Services, The University of Queensland, Australia.

Mona Taouk, School of Social Sciences, Bond University, Australia.

Niko Tiliopoulos, Lecturer, School of Psychology, The University of Sydney, Australia.

Juliet Tobin, School of Psychology, University of Tasmania, Australia.

Yolande van Gellecum, School of Social Sciences, The University Of Queensland, Australia.

Wendy Wan, Associate Professor of Marketing, SunYat-Sen University, Guangshou, China; formerly Assistant Professor, School of Social Sciences, Bond University.

Jeni Warburton, Adjunct Associate Professor, School of Social Work and Human Services, The University of Queensland, Australia.

Wayne Warburton, Lecturer; Deputy Director, Children and Families Research Centre, Macquarie University, Australia.

Bruce D. Watt, Assistant Professor of Psychology, School of Social Sciences, Bond University, Australia.

Jacqueline Yoxall, School of Social Sciences, Bond University, Australia.

Context and Background to Australian Research in Personality and Individual Differences

Richard E. Hicks

Interest and research in personality and individual differences, in why people behave the way they do and the implications for life and living, remain unabated around the world. Human beings are fascinated by how they are similar to one another and how they are different. The similarities and differences underpin many implicit and espoused theories of behaviour and of personal and professional practice, informing the decisions that we all make on what we will do and when.

That the understanding of personality and individual differences has long been of interest to us all, and not only researchers, is evident every day in the news events reported around the world and indeed from what we see of romance, and fear and concern and many other aspects of our daily lives — from our attempts to understand the well-springs of behaviour and the actions we should take for ourselves and for others. These areas of interest include whether personality traits are inborn or learned; the impacts of family environment and culture and ideology; the impacts of the alignment of the earth and the planets, or the 'greening' of the world or worse the polluting of the world through greenhouse gases, or of the influence of the Internet or of television; how children can learn most effectively; the stresses and strains of life whether in leisure, at home, at work or driving, flying or just getting to work or home or business; why at different times conformity and obedience or aggression and violence occur; and how to assess and measure and control in some way these elements, as needed ... the list of interest is extensive as is the list of researchers and professionals involved in these areas.

This book, on current directions on research in personality and individual differences, is an example of and a snapshot of where we are currently in research and practical applications, as reflected by leading researchers, writers and practitioners from Australia, New Zealand and Asia in the main. But no researcher or practitioner or country is today isolated from others — even more so today than ever, 'no man is an island, entire to itself' (John Donne); massive increases have occurred in the ability to communicate events and ideas immediately to large numbers of people through the electronic media, through the Internet, through Facebook or Twitter or Google and its competitors — and we maintain contact now with loved ones and others through mobile phones, and video-phone or computer-based links such as Skype. We can also be located, or at least our mobile phones can be located, via the technology available (if we are lost, or if there is reason to search for us), and we use satellite technology to guide us on the roads to our destinations — mostly without too much error; although sometimes things do go wrong and roads are no longer operating as on the 'map'. How to make sense of all these changes and how we react to them, and to relate them to 'personality and individual differences'? We live in a fast-changing world, an observation that has been made regularly over the centuries, but we seem to be moving and changing at an even more exponential rate in this 21st century. In the event, with change all around us, of wars and rumours of wars, with pressures and delights around us, at base, human beings are the same as ever. We are driven or influenced by our personalities, by the circumstances in which we have found and now find ourselves, and by the interactions between personality and circumstance. This book reflects the continued attempts to come to terms with and make sense of 'personality and individual differences' and how we respond to change.

Burgeoning Research in Personality and Individual Differences

That research in personality and individual differences remains of high interest and importance is reflected by the number of journals, books and handbooks devoted to the area from around the world, and the number of specialist groups that have formed to share information, run conferences, develop workshops and otherwise extend knowledge in the area, including among academic and practitioner groups as well as the general community.

Journals covering the area include *Personality and Individual Differences*, the *Journal of Research in Personality*, and many others; examples of recent handbooks on personality include those by Boyle, Matthews, and Saklofske (2008), and by Coor and Mathews (2009); examples of handbooks on 'individual differences' include those in forensic psychology (e.g., Weiner & Hess, 2006), organisational psychology (e.g., Anderson,

Ones, Sinangil, & Viswesvaran, 2002; Borman, Ilgen, & Klimoski, 2003); and vocational, clinical and cross-cultural psychology, among many. Not only do we have hardcopy and electronic forms of sharing of information, but we still have numerous groups especially set up to examine personality and individual differences, in a face to face environment and over cups of coffee, ensuring lively interactive debate and learning. These groups include the Australasian Personality and Individual Differences interest group of the Australian Psychological Society that grew out of the early group of Australian researchers interested in the area and responsible for the first of the Australian Conferences on Personality and Individual Differences. This is the body of researchers, practitioners and colleagues from the Australasian region and beyond that are behind the papers presented in this volume.

Background and Context for the Chapters in *Personality and Individual Differences: Current Directions*

There has recently been an exponential growth in the research and literature on personality and individual differences as reflected in part by the journals and handbooks referred to already. In the early 1900s the first of the volumes on individual differences and personality emphasised school and education, and suitability for different careers. This current 2000s volume shows continued emphases on education and individual differences/personal qualities, with much of the work of the 20th century being developed further (e.g., through identifying the Big Five personality factors, although there is still controversy over 'the correct basic number'), and researching how related attributes influence educational outcomes (cf., in this volume papers by MacCann & Roberts, 2010; and Games, Fogarty, MacCann, & Roberts, 2010). Exploration of aspects 'beyond the Big Five' is reflected in work by Jackson (2010) on how personality is related to functional and dysfunctional learning, in Boag's (2010) examination of description and explanation in personality psychology research, and in a variety of papers published by members in recent years.

Much of the history of personality and individual differences has also been tied up with implications for wellbeing and performance at work and in careers (cf., Walsh & Savickas, 2005), on work–life balance (e.g., Millear & Liossis, 2010) and on aspects related to performance (cf., Izadikhah & Jackson, 2010; Mathew & Hicks, 2010; Pallier & Tiliopoulos, 2010). The current moves towards an emphasis on wellbeing personally and at work reflect the professional applied origins of psychology combined with scientific rigor. Much of the earlier work on describing and explaining personality attributes led to Cattell's monumental contributions via trait-factor assessments of personality (e.g., through Cattell's Sixteen Personality Factor Questionnaire and Handbook); and to extensive reviews and handbooks dealing with trait approaches to personality and individual differences generally (cf., Boyle, 2010; Boyle, Matthews, & Saklofski, 2008; Saklofske & Zeidner, 1995). But the Cattellian approach and the 16PF have never been enough to meet all needs. Examples of recent personality questionnaires, among many, that have been developed towards meeting needs related to personal concerns, career guidance and planning, selection and placement, and organisational needs include the NEO-PI-R with five main factors of personality each with six subscales (giving a total of 30 subscales or facets of personality); the Occupational Personality Questionnaires of the Saville and Holdsworth UK-based group; the Zuckerman-Kuhlman Personality Questionnaire and the Millon Clinical Multiaxial Inventory (cf., Aluja, Cuevas, Garcia, & Garcia, 2007) ; the Apollo Profile (Hicks & Bowden, 1996, 2008); and integration and realignment of personality variables, scales and models that yield more predictive results at school or work (e.g., Jackson's hybrid model: Jackson, 2008, 2010). The search for appropriate assessment and selection devices and processes goes on unabated, indicating there is still much to learn.

Another area in personality assessment in practice has to do with mental health and personality including personality disorders. This has been and still is a central aspect in professional psychology in clinical, counseling and health areas. One longstanding research interest with theoretical and practical implications has emphasised understanding and management ·of stress. An example is O'Gorman's (2010) chapter in this book on the Type A personality, especially on the correlates of the Achievement Striving and the Impatience–Irritability subscales, updating earlier studies on this Type. However, the relationship of personality to health and related issues has been tackled in many fields relating findings to depression, anxiety, general mental health and wellbeing. The current directions in research in the 2000s continue the earlier trends as reflected by papers in this volume on aged care (Bhullar, Hine, & Myall, 2010), on depression and its incidence and assessment (e.g., Mead & Hicks, 2010; Paspaliaris & Hicks, 2010; Taouk & Bahr, 2010), on emotional intelligence (Athota, O'Connor, & Jackson, 2010; Brown, Chiu, Neill, Tobin, & Reid, 2010) and on aggression, violence and risk assessment especially in relation to clinical and forensic psychology (cf., Boer & Blacker, 2010; Fritzon, Ferrari, & Fleming, 2010; Perrin, Watt, & Hasan, 2010; Watt & Allard, 2010; Watt, Guse, & Begelhole, 2010).

Environmental and social correlates of personality and personal differences also continue to be areas of special interest, both in positive terms and in negative terms. In positive or neutral terms, attention to moral judgements and social behaviour has been evidenced in a variety of social contexts (cf., Abel, 2010; Gerber & Warburton, 2010; Kim & Wan, 2010; Marsh & Boag, 2010). Also the studies of Rogers and Glendon (2010a, 2010b) on effects of date and season of birth fall into this category. In more negative terms (of behaviour), such interest is also reflected in the growing need for detection of potentially fraudulent or anti-social behaviour either in a health-personal context (see Yoxall, Bahr, & Barling, 2010) or in organisational contexts (cf., Bahr, Warburton, MacFarlane, & van Gellecum, 2010; Robinson, 2010). There is overlapping interest in integrity and its correlates, and the management in questionnaires of associated social desirability or distortion propensities of some respondents, to help make the questionnaires less susceptible to these effects (cf., Boyle, 2010; Hicks, 2008; Yoxall, Bahr, & Barling, 2010).

In the chapters presented in this volume there is clear evidence of new trends and understanding, with development building on the shoulders of the researchers of the 20th century. This volume of papers, and the many other studies and groups showing interest in the area, demonstrate that the 21st century research in personality and individual differences is alive and well. The current directions in personality research at least in the antipodes, in Australasian research, are clearly multi-faceted but involve both theoretical and professional applications of the knowledge being gleaned through our research processes. The studies will range from examining the stars (or the seasons and dates of birth) and their effects on us; they will come through clinical and professional needs driving aspects of research (aimed at expansion of our understanding of traits, emotions, moral processes and bio-social responses to drugs and alcohol) and they will be related to efforts to make a difference for the wellbeing and survival of our world, whether as individuals or as the human race. Hence the emphases on theoretical models and on clinical, forensic, organisational, cross-cultural and cross-ideological studies that are in part examined or reflected in some way in this volume. There will be no shortage of research topics and needs in personality and individual differences in the decades ahead.

References

Abel, L.M., & Hornsey, M. (2010). Social identity and moral judgement: The impact of political affiliation on the evaluation of government policy. In R.E. Hicks (Ed.), *Personality and individual differences: Current directions* (pp. 113–122). Brisbane, Australia: Australian Academic Press.

Aluja, A., Cuevas, L., García, L.F.., & García, O. (2007). Zuckerman's personality model predicts MCMI-III personality disorders. *Personality and Individual Differences, 42,* 1311–1321.

Anderson, N., Ones, D.S., Sinangil, H.K., & Viswesvaran, C. (Eds.). (2002). *Handbook of industrial, work and organizational psychology, Volume 2: Organizational psychology.* Thousand Oaks, CA: Sage Publications Ltd.

Athota, V.S., O'Connor, P.J., & Jackson, C.J. (2010). The role of emotional intelligence in moral judgement: The impact of political affiliation on the evaluation of government policy. In R.E. Hicks (Ed.), *Personality and individual differences: Current directions* (pp. 105–112). Brisbane, Australia: Australian Academic Press.

Bahr, M., Warburton, J., MacFarlane, M., van Gellecum, Y., & Shapiro, M. (2010). Stakeholder perceptions of organisational reputation. In R.E. Hicks (Ed.), *Personality and individual differences: Current directions* (pp. 214–223). Brisbane, Australia: Australian Academic Press.

Bhullar, N., Hine, D.W., & Myall, B.R.. (2010). Physical decline and psychological wellbeing in older adults: A longitudinal investigation of several potential buffering factors. In R.E. Hicks (Ed.), *Personality and individual differences: Current directions* (pp. 237–247). Brisbane, Australia: Australian Academic Press.

Boag, S. (2010). Description and explanation within personality psychology research. In R.E. Hicks (Ed.), *Personality and individual differences: Current directions* (pp. 21–29). Brisbane, Australia: Australian Academic Press.

Boer, D., & Blacker, J. (2010). The importance of ecological validity for risk assessment. In R.E. Hicks (Ed.), *Personality and individual differences: Current directions* (pp. 271–282). Brisbane, Australia: Australian Academic Press.

Borman, W.C., Ilgen, D.R., & Klimoski, R.J. (Eds.). (2003). *Handbook of psychology: Vol 12 Industrial and organizational psychology.* Hoboken, NJ: John Wiley & Sons.

Boyle, G.J. (2010). Current research in personality traits and individual differences. In R.E. Hicks (Ed.), *Personality and individual differences: Current directions* (pp. 13–20). Brisbane: Australian Academic Press.

Boyle, G.J., Matthews, G., & Saklofske, D.H. (Eds.). (2008). *The Sage handbook of personality theory and assessment* (Vols 1–2). Los Angeles, CA: Sage.

Brown, E., Chiu, E., Neill, L., Tobin, J., & Reid, J. (2010). Is low emotional intelligence a primary causal factor in drug and alcohol addiction? In R.E. Hicks (Ed.), *Personality and individual differences: Current directions* (pp. 91–101). Brisbane, Australia: Australian Academic Press.

Chiu, C.-Y., Kim, Y.-H., & Wan, W.W. (2008). Personality: Cross-Cultural perspectives. In G.J. Boyle, G. Matthews, & D.H. Saklofske (Eds.), *The Sage handbook of personality theory and assessment* (Vols. 1–2). Los Angeles, CA: Sage.

Coor, P.J., & Mathews, G. (Eds.). (2009). *The Cambridge handbook of personality psychology.* Cambridge: Cambridge University.

Fritzon, K., Ferrari, C., & Fleming, L. (2010). Personality and social risk factors for dangerous driving. In R.E. Hicks (Ed.), *Personality and individual differences: Current directions* (pp. 327–339). Brisbane, Australia: Australian Academic Press.

Games, N., Fogarty, G., MacCann, C., & Roberts, R.D. (2010). Emotional intelligence, coping, and school performance In R.E. Hicks (Ed.), *Personality and individual differences: Current directions* (pp. 69–78). Brisbane, Australia: Australian Academic Press.

Gerber, J.P., & Warburton, W. (2010). The rejection alarm: Person and situation moderators of rejection effects. In R.E. Hicks (Ed.), *Personality and individual differences: Current directions* (pp. 135–142). Brisbane, Australia: Australian Academic Press.

Hicks, R.E. (2008). Item formats and social desirability in personality assessment: a review of the place of forced choice items. In S. Boag (Ed.), *Personality down under: Perspectives from Australia.* New York: Nova Science Publishers.

Hicks, R.E., & Bowden, J. (1996, 2008). *The Apollo Profile (Questionnaire).* Brisbane, Australia: Apollonean Institute.

Izadikhah, Z., & Jackson, C.J. (2010). The significance of different viewpoints in self-regulation studies: Similarities and differences between mastery and performance approach orientation. In R.E. Hicks (Ed.), *Personality and individual differences: Current directions* (pp. 153–164). Brisbane, Australia: Australian Academic Press.

Jackson, C.J. (2008). Measurement issues concerning a personality model spanning temperament, character, and experience. In G. Boyle, G. Matthews, & D. Saklofske (Eds.), *The Sage handbook of personality theory and assessment* (Vols. 1–2). Los Angeles, CA: Sage Publications.

Jackson, C.J. (2010). Functional and dysfunctional learning. In R.E. Hicks (Ed.), *Personality and individual differences: Current directions* (pp. 58–65). Brisbane, Australia: Australian Academic Press.

Kim, S., & Wan, W. (2010). Creativity and individual differences among people with different sexual orientation. In R.E. Hicks (Ed.), *Personality and individual differences: Current directions* (pp. 143–233). Brisbane, Australia: Australian Academic Press.

MacCann, C., & Roberts, R. (2010). Do time management, grit, and self-control relate to academic achievement independently of conscientiousness? In R.E. Hicks (Ed.), *Personality and individual differences: Current directions* (pp. 79–90). Brisbane, Australia: Australian Academic Press.

Marsh, T., & Boag, S. (2010). Applying evolutionary theory to individual differences: Insights from moral psychology. In R.E. Hicks (Ed.), *Personality and individual differences: Current directions* (pp. 21–29). Brisbane, Australia: Australian Academic Press.

Mathew, T., & Hicks, R.E. (2010). Personality and task performance. In R.E. Hicks (Ed.), *Personality and individual differences: Current directions* (pp. 165–173). Brisbane: Australian Academic Press.

Mead, M.R., & Hicks, R.E. (2010). Are you a perfectionist and does it matter? Depression and perfectionism in Australian university students. In R.E. Hicks (Ed.), *Personality and individual differences: Current directions* (pp. 248–257). Brisbane: Australian Academic Press.

Millear, P., & Liossis, P. (2010). Longitudinal modelling of the influence of individual differences and the workplace on wellbeing and work engagement. In R.E. Hicks (Ed.), *Personality and individual differences: Current directions* (pp. 189–199). Brisbane, Australia: Australian Academic Press.

O'Gorman, J. (2010). Construct validity of two components of the Type A behaviour pattern. In R.E. Hicks (Ed.), *Personality and individual differences: Current directions* (pp. 30–38). Brisbane, Australia: Australian Academic Press.

Pallier, G., & Tiliopoulos, N. (2010). Taking a break increases visual creativity more than verbal creativity. In R.E. Hicks (Ed.), *Personality and individual differences: Current directions* (pp. 174–184). Brisbane, Australia: Australian Academic Press.

Paspaliaris, T., & Hicks, R.E. (2010). Coping strategies employed by university students in handling their occupational role stress. In R.E. Hicks (Ed.), *Personality and individual differences: Current directions* (pp. 224–233). Brisbane, Australia: Australian Academic Press.

Perrin, M., Watt, B., & Hasan, T. (2010). The validation of a screening tool for the assessment of violence risk among juvenile offenders. In R.E. Hicks (Ed.), *Personality and individual differences: Current directions* (pp. 305–314). Brisbane, Australia: Australian Academic Press.

Robinson, D. (2010). Sad, bad or mad: Common personality disorders in firms. In R.E. Hicks (Ed.), *Personality and individual differences: Current directions* (pp. 200–213). Brisbane, Australia: Australian Academic Press.

Rogers, M. & Glendon, I. (2010a). Personality and birth date: Taurus, Year of the Ox, or complete bull? In R.E. Hicks (Ed.), *Personality and individual differences: Current directions* (pp. 39–49). Brisbane, Australia: Australian Academic Press.

Rogers, M., & Glendon, I. (2010b). Personality and season of birth: Evidence from Oceania and Northern Hemisphere samples. In R.E. Hicks (Ed.), *Personality and individual differences: Current directions* (pp. 50–57). Brisbane, Australia: Australian Academic Press.

Saklofske, D.H., & & Zeidner, M. (Eds.). (1995). *International handbook of personality and intelligence.* New York: Jossey Bass.

Taouk, M., & Bahr, M. (2010). Measuring adolescent depression: The Adolescent Depression Scale. In R.E. Hicks (Ed.), *Personality and individual differences: Current directions* (pp. 258–268). Brisbane, Australia: Australian Academic Press.

Walsh, W.B., & Savickas, M.L. (2005). *Handbook of vocational psychology* (3rd ed.). Mahwah, NJ: Erlbaum.

Watt, B., & Allard, M. (2010). The virus of violence. In R.E. Hicks (Ed.), *Personality and individual differences: Current directions* (pp. 293–304). Brisbane, Australia: Australian Academic Press.

Watt, B., Begelhole, E., & Guse, N. (2010). Explaining individual differences in physical aggression among a community sample In R.E. Hicks (Ed.), *Personality and individual differences: Current directions* (pp. 283–292). Brisbane, Australia: Australian Academic Press.

Weiner, I.B., & Hess, A.K.. (Eds.). (2006). *The handbook of forensic psychology* (3rd ed). Hoboken, NJ: John Wiley & Sons.

Yoxall, J., Bahr, M., & Barling, N. (2010). Australian psychologists' beliefs and practice in the detection of malingering. In R.E. Hicks (Ed.), *Personality and individual differences: Current directions* (pp. 315–326). Brisbane, Australia: Australian Academic Press.

Part 1:

On Personality Theory

Personality theory and context:

Descriptions and explanation

Type A components

Birth and personality influences

Effective learning

Current Research in Personality Traits and Individual Differences

Gregory J. Boyle

Personality traits have been a central part of the study of personality for 70 years or more, from early studies by personologists to more recent studies by Cattell and Eysenck, and their associates. Most of the research has used data from self-report inventories and rating scales and these have posed problems, such as response distortion, that have become the focus of further research. Currently, there are attempts to assess personality traits through other means than self-report inventories, such as through genetic-biological analyses and from computer-generated approaches. A review of the history of personality traits, the recent attempt to define and limit personality structure to the 'Big Five', and the influence of these and related traits on behaviour is given in this chapter, which also details the theoretical emphases associated with the various approaches, especially in the current century.

Personality trait constructs are typically viewed as enduring dispositions that persist and remain relatively stable over time (see Boyle & Saklofske, 2004; Boyle, Matthews, & Saklofske, 2008). Historically, trait constructs were proposed by personologists such as Allport, Cattell and Eysenck. Allport (1937) defined a trait as 'a generalised neuropsychic structure'. Personality traits are believed to filter incoming stimuli such that, for example, a high A-Trait (Anxiety Trait) individual may interpret a multitude of diverse stimuli as threatening. Personality trait research has stimulated much controversy as to the optimal measurement framework, the causal effects of traits on behaviour, as well as the influences of sociocultural factors on traits (Boyle et al., 2008). Nomothetic approaches that seek to identify common personality traits have become predominant (see the works of Cattell, Comrey, and Eysenck).

Cattell was an early proponent of the nomothetic approach that described personality in terms of discrete common factors (Cattell, 1978, 1980). The Cattellian psychometric model (Cattell, Boyle, & Chant, 2002; cf. Boyle, 2006, 2008b) was derived from a programmatic series of factor analyses of data from self-report questionnaires and rating-scales (e.g., Cattell's 16 Personality Factor [16PF] Questionnaire). Cattell (1973, 1980) viewed traits as causal latent constructs (source traits) to be distinguished from more superficial surface traits. In Cattell's hierarchical personality trait model, higher-stratum factors were defined by combinations of primary traits. In Cattell's model (also see Nesselroade & Cattell, 1988), the variance explained by the personality sphere is regarded as being mostly discrete from that accounted for by ability, motivation and mood-state domains. As well, situational influences on behaviour are believed to be moderated by traits. These features of Cattellian theory remain as central tenets of contemporary trait theory in the 21st century.

Historically, personality trait measures have consisted mainly of intro-spective self-report questionnaires (Q-data), or subjective reports of others via rating scales (L-data), which have been limited by problems of item transparency, motivational/response distortion, outright dissimula-tion, conscious/unconscious faking (good/bad), inadequate self-insight, and/or distorted perceptions of others. Use of objective (T-data) person-ality tests, where it is not possible for the respondent to detect what traits are being measured, would certainly help to minimise motivational/response distortion (see compendium of objective personality tests com-piled by Cattell & Warburton, 1967). While the objective–analytic test battery (OATB) (Schuerger, 1986, 2008) comprises such objective tests, nevertheless, a major deterrent to its use is the length of time needed for administration (taking longer than 5 hours). Thus, construction of truly objective, computer-interactive T-data personality tests will be a major challenge for personality research in the years ahead.

In contrast to Cattell's hierarchical trait model (e.g., 16 obliquely-rotated primary factors and 5–6 second-order 16PF factors), Eysenck focused on just three broad dimensions of extraversion, neuroticism and psychoticism as measured in the Eysenck Personality Questionnaire or EPQ-R (see Eysenck, 1981; Eysenck & Eysenck, 1985; O'Connor, 2008). At the second-order 16PF level, the Cattellian and Eysenckian factors were similar, prompting Eysenck to acknowledge that 'The Cattell and Eysenck constructs and theories should be seen, not as mutually contradictory, but as complementary and mutually supportive' (1984, p. 336). However, whereas Eysenck (1994) suggested a gradation from normal to abnormal personality (e.g., EPQ-R Psychoticism scale), Cattell (1995) maintained that abnormal traits extend beyond the normal trait sphere into the abnormal personality trait domain. In the factor-analytically constructed clinical analysis questionnaire (CAQ), Part A measures the 16 normal personality trait dimensions. In addition, Part B measures 12 abnormal trait factors. Unlike other personality instruments (such as the California Psychological Inventory [CPI], the 16PF, the Revised NEO Personality Inventory [NEO-PI-R], the Minnesota Multiphasic Personality Inventory [MMPI], or the Personality Assessment Inventory [PAI]), administration of both Parts A and B of the CAQ provides coverage of both the normal and abnormal personality trait spheres.

Two broad strategies for investigating personality structure have been employed (Matthews, 2004). First, biological reductionism attempts to explain trait constructs in terms of underlying brain function. Thus, genetic variation is believed to impact directly on brain systems such as Eysenck's Reticulo-Cortical Activation Model (cf. Gray's Reinforcement Sensitivity Theory [RST]), which in turn influences behaviour (Pickering & Corr, 2008). While traits are presumed to modulate the processing of incoming stimuli, Gray's RST model attributes traits to motivational rather than arousal systems. Second, the cognitive science approach relates personality traits to brain function (hardware), virtual symbolic software (information-processing), and self-knowledge (intentions, motives, goals; see Matthews, 2008). Progress in understanding traits is signaled by (1) greater understanding of the biological bases of traits, (2) increased integration of trait research within mainstream psychology, and (3) increased use of trait assessment in real-life contexts (e.g., measurement of traits in occupational selection; Matthews, Deary, & Whiteman, 2003).

Models of the Structure of Personality

Although the five-factor model (FFM) has been promoted strongly (see McCrae & Costa, 2008), a slightly different five-factor structure has been discovered empirically from factor analyses of 16PF data on over 17 000 respondents (Krug & Johns, 1986). This 16PF data has been verified across males and females separately, providing solid evidence that the higher-stratum 16PF factors are robust. In addition, Zuckerman's five-factor model (Zuckerman, 1995, 2005) incorporates biological, comparative, experimental, and trait approaches extending beyond mere descriptive accounts of traits as, for example, in the currently popular lexical FFM (cf. Fraley & Roberts, 2005). Thus, Zuckerman argued that personality traits arise from multiple underlying neurophysiological and biochemical processes. In addition, Boyle, Stankov, and Cattell (1995) suggested that the currently popular FFM was derived from methodologically flawed factor-analytic analyses. They also reported empirical evidence suggesting that the FFM does not provide coverage of more than 40% of the known trait variance within the normal personality sphere alone, let alone the abnormal trait sphere, which is virtually ignored. Further limitations of the FFM relate to the validity of dimensional models generally (McAdams, 1992; Roberts, 2006), the presumed stability of traits over the lifespan (Roberts, Walton, & Viechtbauer, 2006a, 2006b), and associated psychometric limitations (Block, 1995; Boyle, 2008a). Since theoretically, the personality sphere can be divided into any number of factors, it remains to be seen whether or not a consensus can be reached as to a universally accepted taxonomy of personality traits.

Genetic Factors and Culture in Personality

Johnson, Vernon, and Feiler (2008) concluded that genetic factors appear to play a critical role in shaping interactions with the environment (also see Rutter, Moffitt, & Caspi, 2006). If personality traits reflect universal brain physiology, then they should emerge as common factors across diverse cultures. It is hoped, new brain-imaging studies using functional Magnetic Resonance Imaging (fMRI; Congdon & Canli, 2008) may permit mappings of traits onto specific brain structures, enabling better theories of personality traits to emerge (Pickering & Corr, 2008). On the other hand, if personality structure is a function of cultural variations, then trait structures found within different cultures should differ significantly (see Chiu, Kim, & Wan, 2008).

Abnormal Personality Traits

Abnormal personality traits are receiving increased attention (Malik, Johannsen, & Beutler, 2008). Constructs underlying cognitive–behaviour therapy (e.g., see Fernandez, 2008; Fernandez & Boyle, 2008) such as the self-schema, attentional and memory bias, and dysfunctional coping appear to be related to traits such as neuroticism (Matthews, 2008). Likewise, personality trait measurement is central to children's psycho-educational assessment (Andrews, Saklofske, & Janzen, 2001). Trait psychology has also played a prominent role in the area of 'emotional intelligence' (EI; e.g., Rivers, Brackett, & Salovey, 2008; Roberts & Schulze, 2008). However, it is important to note that some uncertainty remains as to the construct validity of currently available EI measures (see Matthews, Zeidner, & Roberts, 2002).

Conclusion

In conclusion, the notion of personality traits has received widespread acceptance in light of the universal consistencies shown in individuals' behaviours and responsivities to situational stimuli. In terms of the peer-reviewed journal literature, both Cattell and Eysenck were listed among the top 10 most highly cited psychologists of the 20th century (Haggbloom et al., 2002, p. 142), leaving little doubt as to the prominence and influence of both these giants of personality research. Debates about factor analytic methodology have often served to obscure the fact that both Cattell and Eysenck were in much agreement in relation to their taxonomic findings into human personality structure. More recently, the FFM has become prominent as a putative framework for organising personality trait data. Although the FFM has generated much empirical data, substantive objections to the FFM have been raised in relation both to the validity of dimensional models generally (and to the psychometric evidence more specifically). However, progress in understanding traits is evidenced by a better understanding of the biological bases of traits, an increased integration of trait research within mainstream psychology, and an increased focus on assessing traits. Although the major focus to-date has been on introspective (subjective) self-report questionnaires and rating scales, there are indications that research into the construction of computer-interactive objective personality tests will become more prominent during the 21st century.

References

Allport, G.W. (1937). *Personality: A psychological interpretation.* New York: Holt.

Andrews, J.J.W., Saklofske, D.H., & Janzen, H.L. (Eds.) (2001). *Handbook of psychoeducational assessment: Ability, achievement, and behavior in children.* San Diego, CA: Academic.

Block, J. (1995). A contrarian view of the five-factor approach to personality description. *Psychological Bulletin, 117,* 187–215.

Block, J. (2001). Millennial contrarianism: The five-factor approach to personality description 5 years later. *Journal of Research in Personality, 35,* 98–107.

Boyle, G.J. (2006). Scientific analysis of personality and individual differences (Doctor of Science thesis). University of Queensland, St Lucia, Queensland.

Boyle, G.J. (2008a). Critique of the Five-Factor Model of personality. In G.J. Boyle, G. Matthews, & D.H. Saklofske (Eds.), *Handbook of personality theory and assessment. Vol. 1. Personality theories and models* (pp. 295–312). Los Angeles: Sage.

Boyle, G.J. (2008b). Simplifying the Cattellian psychometric model. In G.J. Boyle, G. Matthews, & D.H. Saklofske (Eds.), *Handbook of personality theory and assessment. Vol. 1. Personality theories and models* (pp. 257–272). Los Angeles: Sage.

Boyle, G.J., Matthews, G., & Saklofske, D.H. (2008). (Eds.), *The Sage handbook of personality theory and assessment* (Vols. 1–2). Los Angeles: Sage.

Boyle, G.J., & Saklofske, D.H. (2004). (Eds.), *Sage benchmarks in psychology: The psychology of individual differences* (Vols. 1–4). London: Sage.

Boyle, G.J., Stankov, L., & Cattell, R.B. (1995). Measurement and statistical models in the study of personality and intelligence. In D.H. Saklofske & M. Zeidner (Eds.), *International handbook of personality and intelligence.* New York: Plenum.

Cattell, R.B. (1973). *Personality and mood by questionnaire.* New York: Jossey-Bass.

Cattell, R.B. (1978). *The scientific use of factor analysis in behavioral and life sciences.* New York: Plenum.

Cattell, R.B. (1980). *Personality and learning theory, Vol. 2: A systems theory of maturation and learning.* New York: Springer.

Cattell, R.B. (1995). The fallacy of five factors in the personality sphere. *The Psychologist,* May, 207–208.

Cattell, R.B., & Nesselroade, J.R. (Eds.) (1988). *Handbook of multivariate experimental psychology* (Rev. 2nd ed.). New York: Plenum.

Cattell, R.B., & Warburton, F.W. (1967). *Objective personality and motivation tests: A theoretical introduction and practical compendium.* Champaign, IL: University of Illinois Press.

Cattell, R.B., Boyle, G.J., & Chant, D. (2002). The enriched behavioral prediction equation and its impact on structured learning and the dynamic calculus. *Psychological Review,* 109, 202–205.

Chiu, C.-Y., Kim, Y.-H., & Wan, W.W.N. (2008). Personality: Cross-cultural perspectives. In G.J. Boyle, G. Matthews, & D.H. Saklofske (Eds.), *Handbook of personality theory and assessment. Vol. 1. Personality theories and models* (pp. 124–144). Los Angeles: Sage.

Congdon, E., & Canli, T. (2008). Genomic imaging of personality: Towards a molecular neurobiology of impulsivity. In G.J. Boyle, G. Matthews, & D.H. Saklofske (Eds.), *Handbook of personality theory and assessment: Vol. 2. Personality measurement and testing* (pp. 334–351). Los Angeles: Sage.

Eysenck, H.J. (1981). General features of the model. In H.J. Eysenck (Ed.), *A model for personality,* pp. 1–37. Berlin: Springer.

Eysenck, H.J. (1984). Cattell and the theory of personality. *Multivariate Behavioral Research,* 19, 323–336.

Eysenck, H.J., & Eysenck, M.W. (1985). *Personality and individual differences: A natural science approach.* New York: Plenum.

Fernandez, E. (2008). The angry personality: A representation on six dimensions of anger expression. In G.J. Boyle, G. Matthews, & D.H. Saklofske (Eds.), *Handbook of personality theory and assessment: Vol. 2. Personality measurement and testing* (pp. 402–419). Los Angeles, CA: Sage.

Fernandez, E., & Boyle, G.J (2009, October). *An expanded cognitive behavioral program for treatment of dysfunctional anger.* Paper presented at Faculty of Psychology, Gadjah Mada University, Yogyakarta, Indonesia.

Fraley, R.C., & Roberts, B.W. (2005). Patterns of continuity: A dynamic model for conceptualizing the stability of individual differences in psychological constructs across the life course. *Psychological Review, 112*, 60–74.

Gray, J.A. (1991). Neural systems, emotion and personality. In J. Madden IV (Ed.), *Neurobiology of learning, emotion and affect*, pp. 273–306. New York: Raven.

Haggbloom, S.J., Warnick, R., Warnick, J.E., Jones, V.K., Yarbrough, G.L., Russell, T.M. et al. (2002). The 100 most eminent psychologists of the 20th century. *Review of General Psychology, 6*, 139–152.

Johnson, A.M., Vernon, P.A., & Feiler, A.R. (2008). Behavioral genetic studies of personality: An introduction and review of the results of 50+ years of research. In G.J. Boyle, G. Matthews, & D.H. Saklofske (Eds.), *Handbook of personality theory and assessment: Vol. 1. Personality theories and models* (pp. 145–173). Los Angeles: Sage.

Krug, S.E., & Johns, E.F. (1986). A large scale cross-validation of second-order personality structure defined by the 16PF. *Psychological Reports, 59*, 683–93.

Malik, M.L., Johannsen, B.E., & Beutler, L.E. (2008). Personality disorders and the DSM: A critical review. In G.J. Boyle, G. Matthews, & D.H. Saklofske (Eds.), *Handbook of personality theory and assessment: Vol. 1. Personality theories and models* (pp. 599–619). Los Angeles: Sage.

Matthews, G. (2004). *Designing personality: Cognitive architectures and beyond.* Proceedings of the American Artificial Intelligence Society Symposium on Architectures for Modeling Emotion: Cross-Disciplinary Foundations, pp. 83–91. Menlo Park, CA: AAIS.

Matthews, G. (2008). Personality and information processing: A cognitive-adaptive theory. In G.J. Boyle, G. Matthews, & D.H. Saklofske (Eds.), *Handbook of personality theory and assessment: Vol. 1. Personality theories and models* (pp. 56–79). Los Angeles: Sage.

Matthews, G., Deary, I.J., & Whiteman, M.C. (2003). *Personality traits* (2nd edn.). New York: Cambridge.

Matthews, G., Zeidner, M., & Roberts, R. (2002). *Emotional intelligence: Science and myth.* Cambridge, MA: MIT Press.

McAdams, D.P. (1992). The five-factor model in personality: A critical appraisal. *Journal of Personality, 60*, 329–361.

McCrae, R.R., & Costa, P.T. (2008). Empirical and theoretical status of the Five-Factor Model of personality traits. In G.J. Boyle, G. Matthews, & D.H. Saklofske (Eds.), *Handbook of personality theory and assessment: Vol. 1. Personality theories and models* (pp. 273–294). Los Angeles: Sage.

O'Connor, K.P. (2008). Eysenck's model of individual differences. In G.J. Boyle, G. Matthews, & D.H. Saklofske (Eds.), *Handbook of personality theory and assessment: Vol. 1. Personality theories and models* (pp. 215–238). Los Angeles: Sage.

Pickering, A.D., & Corr, P.J. (2008). J.A. Gray's Reinforcement Sensitivity Theory (RST) of personality. In G.J. Boyle, G. Matthews, & D.H. Saklofske (Eds.), *Handbook of personality theory and assessment: Vol. 1. Personality theories and models* (pp. 239–256). Los Angeles: Sage.

Rivers, S.E., Brackett, M.A., & Salovey, P. (2008). Measuring emotional intelligence as a mental ability in adults and children. In G.J. Boyle, G. Matthews, & D.H. Saklofske (Eds.), *Handbook of personality theory and assessment: Vol. 2. Personality measurement and testing* (pp. 440–460). Los Angeles: Sage.

Roberts, B.W. (2006). Personal communication. October 21.

Roberts, B.W., Walton, K.E., & Viechtbauer, W. (2006a). Patterns of mean-level change in personality traits across the life course: A meta-analysis of longitudinal studies. *Psychological Bulletin, 132*, 1–25.

Roberts, B.W., Walton, K.E., & Viechtbauer, W. (2006b). Personality traits change in adulthood: Reply to Costa and McCrae (2006). *Psychological Bulletin, 132*, 29–32.

Roberts, R.D., Schulze, R., & MacCann, C. (2008). The measurement of emotional intelligence: A decade of progress? In G.J. Boyle, G. Matthews, & D.H. Saklofske (Eds.), *Handbook of personality theory and assessment: Vol. 2. Personality measurement and testing* (pp. 461–482). Los Angeles: Sage.

Rutter, M., Moffitt, T.E., & Caspi, A. (2006). Gene-environment interplay and psychopathology: Multiple varieties but real effects. *Journal of Child Psychology and Psychiatry, 47*, 226–261.

Schuerger, J.M. (1986). Personality assessment by objective tests. In R.B. Cattell & R.C. Johnson (Eds.), *Functional psychological testing: Principles and instruments*. New York: Brunner/Mazel.

Schuerger, J.M. (2008). The Objective-Analytic Test Battery. In G.J. Boyle, G. Matthews, & D.H. Saklofske (Eds.), *Handbook of personality theory and assessment: Vol. 2. Personality measurement and testing* (pp. 529–546). Los Angeles: Sage.

Zuckerman, M. (1995). Good and bad humors: Biochemical bases of personality and its disorders. *Psychological Science, 6*, 325–32.

Zuckerman, M. (2005). *Psychobiology of personality* (2nd Rev. ed.). New York: Cambridge University Press.

Description and Explanation Within Personality Psychology Research

Simon Boag

Personality psychology generally involves both describing personality factors and explaining how such factors arise and go on to influence other things. However, since there are various meanings of the term 'personality', and the causal role of personality is often ambiguous, there are numerous theoretical and practical problems involved in both of these pursuits. This chapter proposes a theoretical framework for clarifying both the descriptive and explanatory tasks within personality psychology. The work of description is discussed here with respect to classifying personality factors in terms of intrinsic properties and relationships. The importance of causal antecedents and mechanisms for explanation in personality psychology is then addressed, and problems with teleology and constitutive relations identified. The 'self' is used to illustrate problems in both personality description and explanation and suggestions for avoiding potential theoretical and conceptual problems within personality research are discussed.

Although the meaning of the term 'science' has undergone extensive revision over the last century (Machamer, 2002), a traditional position proposes that science entails both description and explanation within any particular field of interest. Description typically involves identification and classification, whereas explanation involves providing an account of origins, development and causal relationships. In personality psychology, for example, a person might be described as a psychopath, and this may be explained in terms of emotional deficiency and specific biological functioning (e.g., Blair, Peschardt, Budhani, Mitchell, & Pine, 2006; Herpertz & Sass, 2000). Description precedes explanation, insofar as it provides an indication of the phenomena that are yet to be understood (cf. Eysenck, 1997), although the relationship between description and explanation becomes blurred given that any explanation involves describing parts and processes.

Errors can emerge at either the descriptive or explanatory phase of the scientific endeavour, and this underscores the fundamental need for critical examination of concepts and theories when both describing and explaining any phenomenon of interest (Michell, 2000). The aim of this chapter is to propose a first step towards general criteria for clarifying both description and explanation within personality psychology. This involves discussing the distinction between relations, and terms standing within relations, before developing some logical requirements for understanding satisfactory explanatory accounts. Problems with certain constructs found within personality research, both in terms of description and explanation, are addressed.

Description in Personality Psychology

Disputes in personality theory often reflect the fundamental differences found concerning the nature of personality. Funder (2001) refers to the rival paradigms of personality theories — to use one of Kuhn's (1962/ 1970) senses of the word — and such paradigmatic differences consist of basic theoretical disagreements about the nature of persons and indeed reality generally (e.g., free will vs. determinism). This is not simply empty philosophical speculation, since the inherent assumptions of any given paradigm consequently guide and limit what terms are considered appropriate descriptions and explanations of personality. Consequently, there is a critical need for clarifying the basic issues and determining the accuracy of any given position. In particular, there is a critical need for greater theoretical and conceptual clarification. If, for instance, personality is described as something 'inner' there needs to be some clear explication as to in what sense 'inner' is actually meant (e.g., internal to the body or the mind, however conceived). On the other hand, if personality is not separate from the environment, then how should it specifically be conceptualised? Furthermore, accurate description necessitates some approach for distinguishing any given element or aspect from another.

The path of analysis proposed here can be described as a *realist* approach, which appreciates a distinction between *relationships* and *terms* standing within relationships (Anderson, 1927/1962; Maze, 1983). Any relation (e.g., spatial, logical) involves at least two or more distinct terms that must have their own intrinsic properties (to constitute what stands in the relation):

Anything that can stand ... in any relation at all, must have at least some intrinsic properties. If that were not the case ... then we could not understand what it was that was said to have those relationships. A relation can only hold between two or more terms, and a part of what is involved in seeing those terms as related is being able to see them as distinct, that is, as each having its own intrinsic properties, so that we can say what the terms are that are related. This means that each term of the relation must in principle be able to be described without the need to include any reference to its relation to the other. (Maze, 1983, p. 24; cf. Michell, 1988, p. 234)

Appreciating relationships and their terms helps clarify at least the ontological status of the matter in question by attempting to identify intrinsic properties or features of things, and also the relationships that things and properties enter into. For instance, since knowing involves a knower and something known, the act of knowing can be considered a relationship between a knowing *subject (S)* and an *object (x)* known (i.e., *S* knows *x*, where *x* is a situation; Anderson, 1927/1962). Similarly, 'experience', which involves a subject *S* experiencing something (*x*), can also be considered a relationship between a subject and object of experience. Appreciating this means that knowing and experience cannot be reduced to either term of the relationship (e.g., knowing cannot be reduced to brain states; see Boag, 2008), and further allows asking appropriate questions concerning the terms standing in the knowing or experiencing relationship (e.g., what are the characteristics of the 'knower' or what is the 'object' of experience?).

Self and Identity

Concepts such as 'self', 'ego', and 'identity' are all fairly common within personality psychology, and while it is true that some personality approaches downplay reference to the 'self' (e.g., trait approaches examining the question of which attributes best typify 'global tendencies'), one can still find references to the self and identity in these accounts (e.g., Allport, 1961). There are also, of course, many different accounts of the 'self' — William James (1890) described the 'material' self, 'social self', 'spiritual self', and 'pure ego' (p. 292), while the psychoanalytic conception of the 'ego' or 'Ich' also captures some sense of self as well (e.g., Bornstein, 2006; Freud, 1923). In fact, Sleeth (2006) recently notes that the enormous prevalence of self and self-related terms means that the 'self has come to mean so many things that it hardly means anything at all' (p. 243). Deciding which account of the self best describes personality is difficult, and not helped by the proposal that views of 'self' may differ between cultures (Hall, 2003), or even between different time periods (McAdams, 1996).

The first question we might ask of any account is 'what exactly is this self?' Is the self an agent that engages in knowing and other activities, or is it something known (e.g., self-concept)? Such basic questions are often inadequately addressed. For instance, Lambie and Marcel (2002, p. 231) confusingly treat the 'self' as both the subject and object of experience, without recognising the distinction (see Dalgleish & Power, 2004, pp. 813–814; cf. Boag, 2005). A similar analysis can be extended to the issue of 'identity'. McAdams (1996), for instance, writes:

> If the psychologist seeks to describe and explain the personality of a typical adult living in *modern* society, then the answer to this question is *identity*. The answer stems from the characteristic mind set of modernity, within which individuals are expected to create, discover, explore, control, and 'work on' personalised *selves* as reflexive projects that define who they are over time and how they are similar to as well as different from other individuals. (p. 381)

McAdams (1996, 2001) divides personality into 'traits' and 'personal concerns' (e.g., motives, defenses, strategies), as well as 'life stories', which 'provide the person with a purposeful self-history that explains how the self of yesterday became the self of today and will become the anticipated self of tomorrow' (McAdams, 1996, p. 381). But what is precisely meant by identity and self here? If identity is a relationship (*S* identifies with *x* but not *y*) then describing the person in terms of identity is to tell us what the person is doing (i.e., identifying) but not what actually stands as the subject term in the identifying relationship. Consequently, McAdams's personality account does not tell us what *has* the identity (or identifying relations), and so must remain an incomplete account of persons. Having said this, relations exist objectively (as features of situations), and are worthy objects of scientific inquiry; the point simply here is that a *complete* account must recognise the relational nature of such terms (and hence look for the terms involved in the relationship).

The distinction between relationships, and terms standing within relationships, also helps clarify issues to do with the relationship between personality and environment. Markus (2004) questions the claim that the 'person' is separate from the (social) environment (cf. Gergen, 2001; Hall, 2003), arguing that theories of personality are rooted in Western philosophical and religious assumptions about persons (which are then imposed upon different cultures). Instead, she wants to say that 'personality is an ongoing social process, as something people do, and to see ways to go beyond the false dichotomy between person and situation' (p. 76),

That is, Markus is saying that personality is constructed in relationship to others and is therefore not a property of persons. Nevertheless, viewing personality as simply social relationships ignores the fact that social relationships are made up of individuals standing within those relationships. While our relationships with others influence who we are or what we become, nevertheless we exist independently of social relations (i.e., each individual is a separate term of the social relation). Accordingly, Markus' position ignores, then, the individual characteristics that individuals must consist of, and which contribute to 'society'. To say otherwise would be to deny individual differences (i.e., to say that a person is without characteristics), which is tantamount to saying that individuals have no characteristics at all (and so literally do not exist). Again, this is not to say that Markus' claim does not have merit, but only that clearly distinguishing terms and relationships is necessary for providing a coherent account of social relationships.

Explanation in Personality Psychology

The concept of explanation is complex, involving questions of reductionism and interactions between biological-neural properties and psychological acts (see de Jong, 2002, 2003). However, explanation typically involves a causal analysis, and while 'causality' is by no means, itself, a simple issue (see Mackie, 1974; Psillos, 2002), of relevance here to this discussion is the position that explaining an event entails providing a causal account of the factors that give rise to the effects in question, which implicates *determinism* (viz. all events arise out of causal antecedents and go on to cause other events). Without a deterministic outlook, the scientific study of behaviour, or any phenomenon, would not be possible, since random, noncausal fluctuations could pervade any field of research (see Maze, 1983, 1987). Furthermore, since to make sense of the world is to understand its workings, then '[t]hose who are interested in mind's workings will naturally take up a determinist position' (Anderson, 1936/1962, p. 125). The concept of *mechanism* is also important here because it provides intelligibility for understanding how certain antecedent conditions give rise to certain effects (Bechtel, 2005; Machamer, Darden, & Craver, 2000; Maze, 1983). A mechanism is a system of both entities and their relationships and interactions that produce certain outcomes, and we can recognise biological mechanisms, social mechanisms, and so on. We can talk, for instance, about the mechanism of 'natural selection', which explains the continuity and discontinuity of species in terms of the interaction between certain biological and environmental factors.

Agency in Personality Theory

While the issue of causality and determinism is arguably fundamental to explanation and science generally, the thesis that all events are caused is often disputed when it comes to explaining the actions of 'persons'. Part of the issue here is the tension between explanations of human behaviour in terms of either mechanistic operations or in terms of agency and 'persons'. Some maintain (notably humanistic theorists) that human beings are *agents*, choosing outcomes rather than being driven into various courses of action via causal antecedents (e.g., Rychlak, 2000). However, 'explaining' behaviour in terms of an internal agent or 'person' simply defers actual explanation of 'choice' or proposes that agents 'freely choose' to act, making behaviour literally inexplicable (cf. Maze, 1983, 1987).

Turning again to the 'self', this construct is sometimes postulated as the agency within the organism responsible for action and decision. Mid-20th century behaviourism, however, was rightfully skeptical of the 'self as agent' (e.g., Skinner, 1953) as the 'self' is not typically discussed in terms of what it is but only in terms of what it *does* (see McMullen, 1982). If the 'self' is defined only in relation to other things then it should not be construed as a separate subject term from which acts proceed, since relationships cannot be reduced to the terms standing within the relationships (Boag, 2005). Similarly, if we are to treat personality factors as agencies (or *doers*) then these features need to be ascribed features or properties separate from the activity supposedly being performed by the agent. Allport (1961), for instance, explicitly ascribes such agency to personality:

> Personality is something and *does* something ... All the systems that comprise personality are to be regarded as *determining tendencies*. They exert a directive influence upon all adjustive and expressive acts by which the personality comes to be known. (p. 29)

While in Allport's account 'personality' is proposed as a 'doer', the basic appeal to 'tendencies' as such doers is difficult to sustain, since a tendency is a relationship (S tends to do x), a description (if anything) of an activity, and so cannot also be the 'doing subject' itself (see also Boag, in press). On the earlier analysis, whatever is posited as a 'doer' (a subject term) should be identifiable in terms of intrinsic properties and qualities, and not simply in terms of activities engaged in. To reify an agent from activities is to commit the *fallacy of constitutive relations* (i.e., the fallacy of constituting an entity solely in terms of its activities rather than in terms of intrinsic properties; Boag, 2005; Maze, 1954; McMullen, 1982).

Causes, Effects and Teleology

To avoid both teleological reasoning (Mackay, 1996) and circularity (Boag, in press), causes and effects should be distinct events with the former preceding the latter. As distinct events, causes and effects should be describable without reference to the other. For instance, we can explain 'psychopathy' in terms of the relationship between genetics and biological processes (e.g., amygdala dysfunction) causing 'deficient emotional responsiveness', which leads to psychopathic personality traits (Blair et al., 2006; Herpertz & Sass, 2000). While perhaps not a complete explanation of psychopathy (if, for instance, not everyone with such biological features becomes psychopathic), the causal factors (biology) are distinct from the effects (psychopathic behaviour), and so such an approach is consistent with deterministic reasoning. On the other hand, teleological explanations of behaviour rest upon the premise that an end-state (an effect) is causally efficacious, so that, for example, P does A *in order to bring about B* (some future state of affairs; see Rychlak, 2000). While it is clear that the river does not flow down stream 'in order to get to the sea', we might claim that 'the heart beats in order to circulate blood', or explain someone's behaviour in terms of what they wish to achieve (e.g., John studies in order to fulfil his potential). However, if every event is caused by antecedent conditions, then the outcome or purpose is irrelevant to explanation (Mackay, 1996; Maze, 1983). For example, we can explain the heart's beating in terms of electrical impulses and muscle properties, and the effect (circulation) is simply that, an effect, even if past instances of that effect contributed to the form that the heart (and its workings) take now (cf. Maze, 1983, p. 19). Similarly, a person's behaviour can be explained in terms of causal antecedents (e.g., drives or 'biological engines' guided by beliefs — Maze, 1983), without reference to any future events. Accordingly, teleological accounts add nothing but confusion to explanation in personality psychology.

References

Allport, G.W. & Vernon, P.E. (1930). The field of personality. *Psychological Bulletin, 27,* 677–730.

Allport, G.W. (1961). *Pattern and growth in personality.* New York: Holt, Rinehart & Winston.

Anderson, J. (1927/1962). The knower and the known. In *Studies in empirical philosophy* (pp. 27–40). Sydney, Australia: Angus & Robertson.

Anderson, J. (1936/1962). Causality and logic. In *Studies in empirical philosophy* (pp. 122–125). Sydney, Australia: Angus & Robertson.

Bechtel, W. (2005). The challenge of characterising operations in the mechanisms underlying behavior. *Journal of the Experimental Analysis of Behavior, 84*, 313–325.

Blair, R.J.R., Peschardt, K.S., Budhani, S., Mitchell, D.G.V., & Pine, D.S. (2006). The development of psychopathy. *Journal of Child Psychology & Psychiatry, 47*, 262–275.

Boag, S. (2005). Addressing mental plurality: Justification, objections & logical requirements of strongly partitive accounts of mind. *Theory & Psychology, 15*, 747–767.

Boag, S. (2007). 'Real processes' and the explanatory status of repression and inhibition. *Philosophical Psychology, 20*, 375–392.

Boag, S. (2008). 'Mind as feeling' or affective relations? A contribution to the School of Andersonian Realism. *Theory & Psychology, 18*, 505–525.

Boag, S. (in press). Explanation in personality psychology: 'Verbal magic' and the Five-Factor Model. *Philosophical Psychology*.

Bornstein, R.F. (2006). A Freudian construct lost and reclaimed. *Psychoanalytic Psychology, 23*, 339–353.

Dalgleish, T. & Power, M.J. (2004). The I of the storm — Relations between self and conscious emotion experience: Comments on Lambie and Marcel (2002). *Psychological Review, 111*, 812–819.

De Jong, H.L. (2002). Levels of explanation in biological psychology. *Philosophical Psychology, 15*, 441–462.

De Jong, H.L. (2003). Causal and functional explanations. *Theory & Psychology, 13*, 291–317.

Eysenck, H.J. (1997). Personality and experimental psychology: The unification of psychology and the possibility of a paradigm. *Journal of Personality and Social Psychology, 73*, 1224–1237.

Freud, S. (1923). *The ego and the id*. London: Hogarth.

Funder, D.C. (2001). Personality. *Annual Review of Psychology, 52*, 197–221.

Gergen, K.J. (2001). Psychological science in a postmodern context. *American Psychologist, 56*, 803–813.

Hall, G.C. (2003). The self in context: Implications for psychopathology and psychotherapy. *Journal of Psychotherapy Integration, 13*, 66–82.

Herpertz, S.C. & Sass, H. (2000). Emotional deficiency and psychopathy. *Behavioral Sciences & the Law, 18*, 567–580.

Kuhn, T.S. (1962/1970). *The structure of scientific revolutions*. Chicago: University of Chicago Press.

Lambie, J.A., & Marcel, A.J. (2002). Consciousness and the varieties of emotion experience: A theoretical framework. *Psychological Review, 109*, 219–259.

Machamer, P. (2002). A brief historical introduction to the philosophy of science. In P. Machamer & M. Silberstein (Eds.), *The Blackwell guide to the philosophy of science* (pp. 1–17). Malden, MA: Blackwell Publishers.

Machamer, P., Darden, L. & Craver, C.F. (2000). Thinking about mechanisms. *Philosophy of Science, 67*, 1–25.

Mackay, N. (1996). The place of motivation in psychoanalysis. *Modern Psychoanalysis, 21*, 3–17.

Mackie, J.L. (1974). *The cement of the universe: A study of causation.* Oxford: Clarendon Press.

Markus, H.R. (2004). Culture and personality: Brief for an arranged marriage. *Journal of Research in Personality, 38*, 75–83.

Maze, J.R. (1954). Do intervening variables intervene? *Psychological Review, 61*, 226–234.

Maze, J.R. (1983). *The meaning of behaviour.* London: Allen & Unwin.

McAdams, D.P. (1996). Alternative futures for the study of human individuality. *Journal of Research in Personality, 30*, 374–388.

McAdams, D.P. (2001). The psychology of life stories. *Review of General Psychology, 5*, 100–122.

McMullen, T. (1982). A critique of humanistic psychology. *Australian Journal of Psychology, 34*, 221–229.

Michell, J. (1988). Maze's direct realism & the character of cognition. *Australian Journal of Psychology, 40*, 227–249.

Michell, J. (2000). Normal science, pathological science and psychometrics. *Theory & Psychology, 10*, 639–667.

Passmore, J.A. (1935). The nature of intelligence. *Australasian Journal of Psychology & Philosophy, 13*, 279–289.

Psillos, S. (2002). *Causation and explanation.* Chesham: Acumen Publishing.

Rychlak, J.E. (2000). Agency: An overview. In A.E. Kazdin (Ed.), *Encyclopedia of psychology* (pp. 102–104). Washington, DC: American Psychological Association.

Skinner, B.F. (1953). *Science and human behaviour.* New York: The Free Press.

Sleeth, D.B. (2006). The self and the integral interface: Toward a new understanding of the whole person. *The Humanistic Psychologist, 34*, 243–261.

Chapter

3

Construct Validity of Components of the Type A Behaviour Pattern

John O'Gorman

The chapter reports a program of studies concerned with the construct validity of Achievement Striving (AS) and Impatience Irritability (II), components of the Type A behaviour pattern isolated by Janet Spence and colleagues. The studies examined correlates of the scales in performance and self reported behaviour and emotion, the location of the scales in the personality factor space, and their association with measures of cardiovascular reactivity. AS and II were both found to have replicable correlations with measures of performance and emotion and to relate to major defining factors of personality (AS to Conscientiousness and II to Neuroticism and Agreeableness), but to show only marginal incremental validity against measures of these higher order dimensions. There was no evidence of replicable associations with the measures of cardiovascular reactivity employed. The conclusion drawn is that the scales have little unique value as correlates of behaviour or in elaborating the Type A construct.

The Type A behaviour pattern originated with the observations of Friedman and Rosenman (1959) that patients with a cluster of characteristics (extremes of aggressiveness, easily aroused hostility, a sense of time urgency, and competitive achievement striving) were more likely to suffer coronary heart disease (CHD) than those not demonstrating these characteristics. Initial epidemiological studies supported the observations, with incidence of CHD as much as twice as high for individuals classified as Type A (Rosenman et al., 1975). A second wave of research, however, failed to replicate the early findings (Booth-Kewley & Friedman, 1987), raising considerable doubts about the value of the Type A construct.

One hypothesis advanced to account for the failure to replicate was that the Type A construct is multidimensional, that only some of its components are in fact 'toxic', and that the relationship with negative health outcomes depends on which of the components are captured in any particular operational definition of Type A. The research findings of Spence, Helmreich, and Pred (1987) and Spence, Pred, and Helmreich (1989) supported this hypothesis. Spence et al. (1987) factor analysed a version of the Jenkins Activity Survey (Jenkins, 1979), a widely employed questionnaire in the earlier studies, and found two major dimensions, Achievement Striving (AS) and Impatience Irritability (II), which were relatively independent of each other and showed acceptable internal consistency. Interestingly, the AS dimension related to measures of performance (grade point average, GPA) but not to reported symptoms of ill-health (quality of sleep, problems of digestion and elimination, headaches, and respiratory problems), whereas items making up the II dimension showed the reverse pattern of relationships: no significant correlation with GPA but a significant correlation with health complaints.

The program of studies briefly reported in this chapter was prompted by the reports of Spence and colleagues. The program sought (a) to replicate and extend the reported correlates of AS and II, (b) examine the position of AS and II in the traditional personality space defined by major self-report tests of personality, (c) determine the incremental validity of AS and II in relation to these personality tests, and (d) investigate what, if any, relationships there are between AS and II and indices of cardiac function.

Correlates of AS and II

The early studies in the program sought to replicate the central findings of Spence et al. (1987). In *Study 1* in the program ($N = 270$), AS correlated .24 ($p < .05$) with GPA and −.07 ($p > .05$) with reported symptoms, whereas II correlated −.08 ($p > .05$) with GPA and .15 ($p < .05$) with symptom reports. In *Study 3* ($N = 202$), the corresponding coefficients were .41 and .07 for AS, and .01 and .40 for II. Thus the basic findings of Spence et al. (1987) were replicated. In a later study (*Study 5, N = 130*), AS again correlated with GPA (.39) and, in this study, with marks in a statistics examination (.28, $p < .05$) that all students in the sample had to complete. II showed no significant correlation with GPA (.00) or statistics mark (.09). A similar pattern of correlations has been reported by Barling and Charbonneau (1992) and Conte, Mathieu, and Landy (1998).

In *Study 5*, items from Paunonen's (2003) behaviour checklist were included and two significant correlations with AS emerged. Individuals with high scores on AS were less likely than those with low scores to describe themselves as drinkers ($-.25$, $p < .05$) and were less likely to report they donated to charity ($-.35$, $p < .05$). II showed no significant correlations with any of the Paunonen items employed.

Two health related indices were included in *Study 5*. One involved whether the individual was being treated for one or more of a number of common illnesses and the other the number of visits to a medical practitioner over the preceding six months. As expected, neither correlated with AS, but importantly nor did they correlate with II. An index of practitioner visits had been included in *Study 1* and here the correlation with II had also been nonsignificant ($r = .05$, $p > .05$).

Two other measures included in *Study 5* were a five-item measure of satisfaction with university studies and a four-item measure of partner satisfaction. The former related to AS ($r = .49$, $p > .05$) but the latter did not ($r = .28$, $p > .05$). Neither related to II at a level significantly greater than zero. Significant correlations between AS and work satisfaction have been reported by Bluen, Barling, and Burns (1990) and by Jex, Adams, Elacqua, and Bachrach (2002), although not by Spector and O'Connell (1994). A relationship with partner satisfaction has not been previously reported, but the measure was included in the present program to test for the specificity of the relationship between satisfaction with work and AS.

AS has thus shown itself across a number of studies in this program and elsewhere to be a robust correlate of academic performance and satisfaction but not to relate to indices of health. II has been found to relate to some but not all indices of health, with symptom checklists being the most likely to show statistically significant associations. In later studies in the program, II but not AS was found to correlate significantly with the subscales of the Speilberger (1988) State Trait Anger Scale (STAI). In *Study 7* ($N = 60$) II correlated positively with the subscales of anger expression and negatively with the subscales of anger control. In *Study 8* ($N = 127$), this pattern was replicated.

Relationships With Established Personality Measures

The AS and II scales share a good deal of meaning at the conceptual level with existing personality constructs, including achievement motivation, hostility, and neuroticism and it was therefore of interest to explore the potential overlap between the AS and II scales and established measures of similar constructs. In *Study 1*, the short forms of a number of the

Jackson (1967) PRF scales were included. As expected, AS correlated with the Achievement Motivation scale of the PRF ($r = .65$, $p > .05$) and II with the Aggression scale ($r = .56$, $p < .05$). What was less expected was that both scales correlated with the Impulsivity scale (–.28 and .30 for AS and II respectively, $p < .05$). The latter finding prompted *Study 2* ($N = 125$) in which the sample completed the EPQ (Eysenck & Eysenck, 1975) and the Eysenck and Eysenck (1977) Impulsivity scale, as well as the AS and II scales. II but not AS was found to correlate with EPQ N (.32) and P (.27) scales (both $p < .05$) and with all subscales of Impulsivity. AS correlated with Narrow Impulsivity (–.21) and Non-Planning (–.48) subscales but not with the Risk Taking or Liveliness subscales of Impulsivity.

Study 3 ($N = 124$) examined the relationship between AS and II and three of the subscales of the Costa and McCrae (1992) NEO-FFI: Conscientiousness (C), Neuroticism (N), and Agreeableness (A). AS correlated with C (.61) and II correlated with N (.48) and A (–.36) (all $p < .05$). II correlated .05 with C, and AS correlated –.12 with N and –.11 with A (all $p > .05$). The study employed a multitrait multimethod (MTMM) approach, with the self-report measures supplemented by peer reports of the participants' standing on the several traits. Inspection of the matrix (not reported here) indicated that, in terms of the classic tests applied by Campbell and Fiske (1959) to establish convergent and discriminant validity, II passed all of them, and AS passed all but one: the correlation for AS in the validity diagonal (.59) was slightly lower than that for the self-report measures of AS and C (.61). Thus AS and II are related to the NEO-FFI measures in the ways to be expected but show reasonable discriminant validity as well.

As the short form of the NEO had been used in *Study 4* it had not been possible to examine the relationship between AS and the facets of C. In a later study (*Study 6*, $N = 92$) the long form was employed and here it was found that AS correlated significantly with all of the facets of C, although the correlation with the Achievement Striving facet (.63) was almost as high as the correlation with total score on C across all facets (.67).

The final study in this part of the program involved an exploratory factor analysis using items from the NEO-FFI, the Zuckerman Kuhlman Personality Questionnaire III (ZKPQ; Zuckerman, Kuhlman, Teta, Joireman, & Kraft, 1993), and the AS and II scales. (See Tan, 2000 for details.) The ZKPQ III was included because of the findings with impulsivity in Studies 1 and 2 and the representation of this dimension in the Alternative Five model of trait structure proposed by Zuckerman and colleagues. The NEO-FFI and the ZKPQ III were factor analysed separately

(Multiple Factor Analysis with oblimin rotation) to confirm their factor structures in the sample ($N = 302$) and then six items defining each of the factors were selected in terms of their high loadings and minimal cross loadings and these were factor analysed with the AS and II items. Seven, six, and five factor solutions were tested. The five factor solution accounted for 37% of the variance, which was only slightly less than for the six and seven factor solutions. The first factor was defined by the items from the NEO and ZKPQ Neuroticism scales, the second factor by items from the NEO Conscientious and ZKPQ Activity scales, the third factor by items from the NEO Extraversion and ZKPQ Sociability scales, the fourth by items from the NEO Openness and ZKPQ Impulsive Sensation Seeking scales, and the fifth by items from the NEO Agreeableness and ZKPQ Aggression Hostility scales. Essentially, the Big Five and the Alternative Five collapsed onto each other. Within this factor space, the AS items loaded the Conscientiousness-Activity factor and the II items loaded the Agreeableness–Aggression Hostility factor.

This part of the program indicated that AS and II pass most tests for convergent and discriminant validity but are by no means unique factors. They lie within the established factor space for self-report measures of personality, which at a widely recognised level of aggregation is represented by Conscientious and Agreeableness.

Incremental Validity

In several of the studies in the program it was possible to answer the question of the predictive value of AS and II over more traditional measures of personality using standard multiple/partial correlation techniques. In Studies 1 and 3, AS added statistically significant but small amounts (2% to 9%) to the variance in GPA after the PRF Achievement Motivation or C scales were entered into the predictive equations. The same was true for II when added to the prediction of symptom reports after the PRF Aggression or N and A scales were entered.

In *Study 5*, short forms of the Big Five measures (5 items) and of the EPI (7 items) were included to help answer the question: how do the AS and II scales compare with scales of established personality dimensions when those scales are approximately the same length as the AS and II scales. Test length enhances test reliability that in turn should assist in predicting relevant criterion measures. Comparing the AS and II scales with measures of conventional length is therefore an unfair comparison. AS outperformed the short form C in predicting GPA (.39 versus .19) and Statistics Mark (.28 versus .13), but II was clearly bettered by short form measures of N (.15 versus .25 for number of conditions and .13 versus .30 for doctor visits) in predicting health outcomes.

Cardiovascular Activity

The AS and II measures originated in concerns about CHD and its possible relationship with a style of behaviour and emotional expression termed Type A. The research of Spence and colleagues broadened the reach of components of the Type A pattern to health more generally and, while their work is of undoubted importance, it is reasonable to ask what, if any, relation AS and II have to the concerns originally of central interest to the Type A concept.

One hypothesis advanced for individual differences in susceptibility to coronary disease is that, because of genetic or lifestyle factors, some individuals have a chronic vagal inhibitory deficit causing an overload of the cardiac system that in time results in disease (Thayer & Lane, 2007). *Study 6 (N = 92)* investigated correlations between AS and II and indices of cardiovascular activity (heart rate, systolic and diastolic blood pressure). Meta-analysis of the literature linking Type A with cardiac functioning indicates significant effects for the cardiovascular measures reported on here, but points to these being larger where participants are challenged either interpersonally or cognitively (Lyness, 1993). With this in mind, *Study 6* was designed to present participants with two challenges (in counterbalanced order) following a baseline recording period. One was a letter checking task in which speed and accuracy were emphasised and the other was a video game in which participants maintained a vehicle on a track by manipulating a track ball.

Both tasks induced statistically significant changes in all three cardiovascular indices, but few correlations between the cardiovascular indices and the AS and II scales were statistically significant. There was little variation in this pattern of correlation when a number of control variables, from body mass index to medication history to family history, were added.

Study 7 (N = 60) assessed the same cardiovascular indices at rest and under challenge but in this case used mental arithmetic as the task and sought to manipulate difficulty of the problems presented. There were significant changes in cardiovascular indices induced by the challenge conditions and these were larger in the case of the more difficult set of problems. Again, however, few correlations were statistically significant (none with II) and those that were showed no consistency with those in *Study 6*.

If there is a relationship between the AS and II scales and cardiovascular functioning, at least during routine episodic challenge, one might have expected the relationship to emerge in studies such as those reported here. Other cardiovascular measures may prove more sensitive, older participants may be better candidates to study the association, or more demanding challenges may be necessary to show effects.

Conclusion

The concept of the coronary prone personality has changed considerably over time and the scales isolated by Spence and colleagues have more to do with the earlier conception of it as an impatient, competitive, and driven personality which succumbs in time to coronary disease. The scales can still be of value of course, even though the original concept has changed, and there are several indications in the studies reported here that they have significant correlates in social behaviour. It is also clear from the program that the scales are located in the traditional personality factor space and add little unique variance in prediction to established self-report measures. Indeed, measures of N performed better than II in predicting health outcomes, although AS did show somewhat better predictive validity against GPA than C when a short form of that construct was employed. There are, however, few practical situations in which this advantage becomes important, and measurement at the facet level of the Big Five is likely to provide equivalent predictive value to that obtained with AS. The failure to find correlations between the scales and indices of cardiovascular activity under a number of conditions further limits any particular value they might have. The result in this regard with AS is not surprising given the changed concept of coronary proneness but the failure of II is of more concern, because hostility is still thought to be a relevant predisposing factor in heart disease. The conclusion must therefore be that, notwithstanding their reasonably good psychometrics, AS and II have little unique value in identifying a coronary prone personality and their capacity to predict socially significant criteria such as GPA and health complaints mimics that of established measures of N, C, and A in the Big Five model of personality.

Author Note

The author acknowledges the contribution to the research reported by Adrian Cookson, Amber Dean, Michelle Tan, and Joanna Wyganowska and the university students who participated in the several studies.

The author is now with Griffith University.

References

Barling, J., & Charbonneau, D. (1992). Disentangling the relationship between the achievement striving and impatience-irritability dimensions of Type A behavior, performance and health. *Journal of Organizational Behavior, 13,* 369–377.

Bluen, S., Barling, J., & Burns, W. (1990). Predicting sales performance, job satisfaction, and depression by using the achievement strivings and impatience-irritability dimensions of Type A behavior. *Journal of Applied Psychology, 75,* 212–216.

Booth-Kewley, S., & Friedman, H. (1987). Psychological predictors of heart disease: A quantitative review. *Psychological Bulletin, 101,* 343–362.

Campbell, D., & Fiske, D. (1959). Convergent and discriminant validation by the multitrait-multimethod matrix. *Psychological Bulletin, 56,* 81–105.

Conte, J.M., Mathieu, J.E., & Landy, F.J. (1998). The nomological and predictive validity of time urgency. *Journal of Organizational Behavior, 19,* 1–13.

Costa, P.T. Jr. & McCrae, R.R. (1992). *NEO Personality Inventory (NEO P1-R) and NEO Five-Factor (NEO –FF1) professional manual.* Odessa, FL: Psychological Assessment Resources.

Eysenck, H.J., & Eysenck, S.B.G. (1975). *Manual of the Eysenck Personality Questionnaire (Junior & Adult).* London: Hodder & Stroughton.

Eysenck, H.J., & Eysenck, S.B.G. (1977). The place of impulsiveness in a dimensional system of personality description. *British Journal of Social and Clinical Psychology, 16,* 57–68.

Friedman, M., & Rosenman, R.H. (1959). Association of specific overt behavior pattern with blood and cardiovascular findings. *Journal of the American Medical Association, 169,* 1286–1296.

Jackson, D.N. (1967). *Personality Research Form manual.* Port Huron, MH: Research Psychologists Press.

Jenkins, C.D. (1979). *Jenkins Activity Survey.* New York: The Psychological Corporation.

Jex, S.M., Adams, G.A., Elacqua, T.C., & Bachrach, D.G. (2002). Type A as a moderator of stressors and job complexity: A comparison of achievement strivings and impatience-irritability. *Journal of Applied Social Psychology, 32,* 977–996.

Lyness, S.A. (1993). Predictors of differences between Type A and B individuals in heart rate and blood pressure reactivity. *Psychological Bulletin, 114,* 266–295.

Paunonen, S.V. (2003). Big Five factors and replicated predictions of behavior. *Journal of Personality and Social Psychology, 84,* 411–424.

Rosenman, R.H., Brand, R.J., Jenkins, C.D., Friedman, M., Straus, R., & Wurm, M. (1975). Coronary heart disease in the western Collaborative Group study: final follow-up experience of 81/2 years. *Journal of the American Medical Association, 233,* 872–877.

Spector, P., & O'Connell, B. (1994). Personality and health: Advantages and limitations of the five-factor model. *Journal of Personality, 60,* 395–423.

Speilberger, C.D. (1988). *State-Trait Anger Expression Inventory*. Orlando, FL: Psychological Assessment Resources.

Spence, J.T., Helmreich, R.L., & Pred, R.S. (1987). Impatience versus achievement strivings in the Type A pattern: Differential effects on students' health and academic achievement. *Journal of Applied Psychology, 72*, 522–528.

Spence, J.T., Pred, R.S., & Helmreich, R.L. (1989). Achievement strivings, scholastic aptitude, and academic performance: A follow-up to 'impatience Versus Achievement Strivings in the Type A Pattern'. *Journal of Applied Psychology, 74*, 176–178.

Tan, M. (2000). Location of achievement strivings and impatience irritability in the personality space defined by the big five and the alternative five. Unpublished master's thesis, Griffith University, Australia.

Thayer, J.F., & Lane, R.D. (2007). The role of vagal function in the risk of cardiovascular disease and mortality. *Biological Psychology, 74*, 224–242.

Zuckerman, M., Kuhlman, D.M., Teta, R., Joireman, J., & Kraft, M. (1993). A comparison of three structural models of personality: The big three, the big five, and the alternative five. *Journal of Personality and Social Psychology, 65*, 757–768.

Personality and Birthdate: Taurus, Year of the Ox, or Complete Bull?

Mary E. Rogers and A. Ian Glendon

Despite widespread cynicism, many people believe in astrology — that a person's Sun sign influences individual temperament or personality. The scientific literature on personality and astrological Sun sign published over the last four decades shows varied results. This study explored the validity of such beliefs using a balanced design incorporating age and astrological belief as covariates. One thousand, nine hundred and sixty-seven Australians aged between 28 and 51 completed a web-based survey. Personality was assessed using a 50-item version of the International Personality Item Pool (IPIP). While previous findings on age and belief in astrology were confirmed, no significant effects for the influence of either astrological Sun sign or Oriental year of birth were found.

Astrological principles, laid down around 4,000 years ago in Babylon, relate to how the sun, moon, planets and stars connect with life on earth. Some people believe that the 12 zodiac signs are associated with aspects of a person's temperament. While most astrologers include place and time as well as date of birth to draw up a birth chart, typical media horoscopes are based only on aggregated birthdate ('Star' or 'Sun' sign), or year of birth (Oriental). Oriental astrology is based on 12-month, 12-yearly cycles, with people born in the year of a particular animal thought to reflect its qualities. Although most scientists consider it to be false (Culver & Ianna, 1988) or mystical nonsense (Pellegrini, 1973), astrology is a widespread belief system in contemporary society.

The scientific literature on personality and astrological Sun sign published over the last four decades shows varied results. While some researchers have found a relationship between extraversion and Sun sign (Gauquelin, Gauquelin, & Eysenck, 1979, 1981; Jackson, 1979; Mayo, White, & Eysenck, 1978; Smithers & Cooper, 1978; Van Rooij, 1994; Van Rooij, Brak, & Commandeur, 1988), others found no association between astrologically derived personality profiles and scores on psychometric personality measures (Carlson, 1985; Clarke, Gabriels, & Barnes, 1996; Hartmann, Reuter, & Nyborg, 2006; Hentschel & Kiessling, 1985; Hume & Goldstein, 1977; Jackson & Fiebert, 1980; Mayes & Klugh, 1978; Russell & Wagstaff, 1983; Saklofske, Kelly, & McKerracher, 1982; Silverman & Whitner, 1974; Startup, 1985; Tyson, 1977; Veno & Pamment, 1979). Positive associations have been found between belief in astrology and high extraversion (Eliseo & Urbano, 2006; Shaughnessy, Neely, Manz, & Nystul, 1990), and with being female (Eliseo & Urbano, 2006). Searches of the scientific literature of relationships between personality characteristics and Oriental year of birth revealed one study (Dalhstrom, Hopkins, Dalhstrom, Jackson, & Cumella, 1996) that found no evidence to support any association.

Inconsistencies in results from previous studies may be explained by methodological differences (e.g., personality instruments used, sample sizes, participant age, gender and belief systems and analytical techniques). To overcome limitations of past studies, for example, small and unequal sample sizes, poor statistical control of key variables such as age and self-attribution bias and in some instances lack of multivariate analysis, this study explored the relationship between personality, astrological Sun sign and Oriental calendar year of birth using a large sample size and balanced design incorporating age, gender and astrological belief as covariates.

Considering Dalhstrom et al.'s (1996) recommendation, the five-factor model (FFM) of personality was selected as a widely accepted model of personality structure (Goldberg, 1993), which has been claimed to be the best account of personality ratings (Costa & McCrae, 1992b). The model uses the five dimensions of neuroticism (e.g., comprising: anxiety, anger, depression), extraversion (social, active, dominant), openness (imaginative, curious, sensitive, need for variety), agreeableness (trust, altruism, co-operation, sympathy), and conscientiousness (organised, persistent, achievement oriented). FFM dimensions have been found in many different cultures, suggesting a biological foundation for these traits (Costa & McCrae, 1992a). Gender differences in personality are constant cross-nationally, with females scoring higher than males on neuroticism, openness to experience and on agreeableness (Costa & McCrae, 1992a; Feingold, 1994; Marusic & Bratko, 1998).

While some of the variability in personality has been found to be due to developmental effects (Roberts, Robins, Trzesniewski, & Caspi, 2003; Srivastava, John, Gosling, & Potter, 2003), the genetic foundation for personality suggests that traits are relatively enduring dispositions. The genetic influence on neuroticism has been estimated at 41%, extraversion at 53%, openness to experience at 61%, agreeableness at 41% and conscientiousness at 44% (Jang, Livesley, & Vernon, 1996). A longitudinal study revealed stability coefficients of .67 for Neuroticism, .81 for Extraversion, .84 for Openness to Experience, .63 for Agreeableness and .78 for Conscientiousness (Costa & McCrae, 1992a).

The present study examines the nature of any possible relationship between personality, astrological Sun sign and Oriental calendar year of birth. The main aims were to determine whether significant personality differences exist between respondent groups that:

- share an astrological Sun sign
- were born in the 'same' Oriental year.

In both cases, the null hypothesis was that there will be no differences between groups.

Further hypotheses based on the scientific literature were that:

- extraversion is associated with belief in astrology
- females are more likely than males to report a belief in astrology.

Method

Design

Inconsistent results in the literature prompted a number of design features for this study. While some researchers suggest that in general the five personality factors remain relatively stable in adults (Cervone & Mischel, 2002), others suggest an association between age and neuroticism (Gow, Whiteman, Pattie, & Deary, 2005) and most of the 'Big Five' (Srivastava et al., 2003). A restricted sample covering two complete 12-year cycles of the Oriental calendar was selected to minimise the possible impact of age upon personality. The respondent target age range was set at 28 to 51 years. This period of a person's life generally shows the least change across the Big Five personality variables and the most consistent linear relationship (Srivastava et al., 2003). Because gender is also known to be related to some of the Big Five personality factors (Costa & McCrae, 1992a), a sample with equal numbers of male and female respondents from each astrological Sun sign and from each of the 24 Oriental years was selected.

On the basis of previous studies, effect sizes were predicted to be small or negligible, requiring a sample size large enough to detect such an effect with power at least .8.

Participants

Participants were 1,967 Australian adults (979 males, 988 females) aged 28 to 51 years (born 1954 to 1977), recruited through online methods such as a newsletter, email, and the media. Participation was voluntary and anonymous. Nearly 62% of respondents were born in the first 12-year Oriental cycle, with numbers ranging between 88 and 144 for any one year, while numbers in the second 12-year Oriental cycle ranged between 57 and 67. Mean respondent age was 38.0 years (*SD* 6.8 years). Ages of male (mean 38.1, *SD* 6.8) and female (mean 38.0, *SD* 6.8) subsamples were practically identical.

Materials

Demographic questions asked for respondent's date of birth, gender, country of birth and current country of residence. The International Personality Item Pool (IPIP) developed by Goldberg (1999; 2006), assessed the Big Five personality variables: Neuroticism (N), Extraversion (E), Openness to experience (O), Agreeableness (A), and Conscientiousness (C). The current study used the 50-item version, consisting of 10 items for each of the Big-Five personality factors. To make each item easier to read, the word 'I' was added to the beginning of each statement, for example, 'I have a vivid imagination' and 'I am the life of the party'. Responses were to a 5-point scale ranging from 1 (*Very inaccurate*) to 5 (*Very accurate*). Comparable with those cited in Buchanan, Johnson, and Goldberg (2005) and in Gow et al. (2005), Cronbach reliability coefficients of the five scales for this sample were: N .75, E .83, O .70, A .74 and C .79. Because of possible self-attribution bias in respect of people who believe in an astrological basis for personality (Fichten & Sunerton, 1983; Gauquelin et al., 1979, 1981; Hamilton, 1995, 2001; Synder, 1974; Van Rooij, 1994), respondents rated their belief in astrology on a 5-point Likert-type scale with responses ranging from 1 (*Not at all)* to 5 (*Very much).*

Procedure

Statistical Package for the Social Sciences (SPSS) data entry builder was used to create the web-based questionnaire, which included scale button matrices and drop down lists as appropriate. Mandatory data entry ensured that all respondents returning questionnaires answered all questions. While this method may be considered to be problematic in respect of forcing responses to all items, on balance it was considered preferable to subsequently addressing missing data problems.

While pattern and duplicate responses, outliers and respondents located outside Australia were excluded from the analysis; those born on the cusp of their Sun sign were not excluded. Appropriate adjustments were made to accommodate annual variations in the Oriental calendar year.

Participants were categorised into the 12 Sun signs and 12 Oriental years according to their date of birth. To meet MANOVA assumptions and to ensure robustness of analysis (Tabachnick & Fidell, 2001), multivariate outliers were removed and cell sizes were adjusted using a random number table to ensure a gender balance for all cells in the analysis.

Results

Belief in astrology was normally distributed (mean 2.87, SD 1.19) and there was a highly significant difference between males (mean 2.44, SD 1.11) and females (mean 3.31, SD 1.09), $t(1963.62) = 17.49$, $p < .001$. Females scored significantly higher than males did on all five personality variables, as shown in Table 4.1.

There were significant correlations between all five personality variables and between the five personality variables and belief in astrology. Agreeableness, conscientiousness and neuroticism were significantly correlated with age (see Table 4.2).

In the basic MANOVA design the 12 Sun signs (between-subjects) and 12 Oriental years (between-subjects) were the independent variables and the scores on the five IPIP scales were the dependent variables. Because both age and belief in astrology were correlated with at least some of the personality variables, and were uncorrelated with each other, they were entered as covariates in the MANCOVA analyses. To minimise the likelihood of Type I errors, alpha was set at .01 for the multivariate analyses.

Table 4.1

Gender Differences on Five Personality Dimensions (Independent Samples t tests)

Personality factor	Male mean (SD)	Female mean (SD)	t^1
Extraversion	32.43 (6.70)	33.83 (6.99)	−4.54
Agreeableness	34.99 (5.49)	36.96 (5.58)	−7.88
Conscientiousness	34.27 (5.95)	36.16 (6.04)	−6.97
Neuroticism	26.02 (6.79)	27.74 (7.43)	−5.35
Openness	33.79 (5.06)	34.64 (4.72)	−3.88

Note: [1] All t values are significant at $p < .001$

Table 4.2

Correlations between Five Personality Variables, Belief in Astrology and Age (N = 1967)

Variable	Age	Belief	E	A	C	N
Belief in astrology	−.00					
Extraversion E	−.03	.17**				
Agreeableness A	.11**	.08**	.18**			
Conscientiousness C	.10**	.10**	.27**	.38**		
Neuroticism N	−.07**	.10**	−.38**	−.45**	−.39**	
Openness	−.04	.12**	.35**	.24**	.17**	−.15**

Note: ** = p < .01

Consistent with findings from the correlation analyses, both age and belief contributed significantly to the model. Main effects showed that greater age predicted higher self-reported agreeableness, $F(1) = 23.82$, $p < .001$, partial η^2 .13, higher conscientiousness, $F(1) = 17.93$, $p < .001$, partial η^2 .01, and lower neuroticism, $F(1) = 15.17$, $p < .001$, partial η^2 .01. All power values exceeded .9.

Main effects showed that belief in astrology was predicted by higher extraversion, $F(1) = 52.63$, $p < .001$, partial η^2 .03, greater agreeableness, $F(1) = 13.19$, $p < .001$, partial η^2 .01, higher conscientiousness, $F(1) = 17.04$, $p < .001$, partial η^2 .01, higher levels of neuroticism, $F(1) = 20.57$, $p < .001$, partial η^2 .01, and greater openness, $F(1) = 29.86$, $p < .001$, partial η^2 .02. All power values exceeded .9.

There were no multivariate main effects for Sun sign on any of the personality dimensions: extraversion, $F(11) = 1.73$, $p = .06$, partial η^2 .01, agreeableness, $F(11) = 1.19$, $p = .28$, partial η^2 .01, conscientiousness, $F(11) = 1.52$, $p = .12$, partial η^2 .01, neuroticism, $F(11) = 1.39$, $p = .17$, partial η^2 .01, or openness, $F(11) = 1.13$, $p = .33$, partial η^2 .01. There were no multivariate main effects for Oriental year of birth on any of the personality dimensions: extraversion, $F(11) = 0.90$, $p = .54$, partial η^2 .01, agreeableness, $F(11) = 1.12$, $p = .34$, partial η^2 .01, conscientiousness, $F(11) = 0.96$, $p = .48$, partial η^2 .01, neuroticism, $F(11) = 1.35$, $p = .19$, partial η^2 .01, or openness, $F(11) = 0.55$, $p = .87$, partial η^2 .00. Power values for these analyses ranged between .31 and .86.

Discussion

The results revealed no personality differences between groups who shared an astrological Sun sign or who were born in the same Oriental year. While this may be the first occasion that measures of the Big Five personality factors have been used in a study on this topic, findings are consistent with those from studies that have found no relationship between birthdate and personality (e.g., Carlson, 1985; Hentschel & Kiessling, 1985; Jackson & Fiebert, 1980; Saklofske et al., 1982; Startup, 1985). Given our attempt to minimise design weaknesses, (i.e., the large sample size balanced for gender and age effects, the widely accepted FFM of personality, and multivariate analysis) any effect that existed in these data should have been found using the controlled methodology employed in this study.

Our study is consistent with Shaughnessy et al.'s (1990) and Eliseo and Urbano's (2006) findings that higher extraversion scores are associated with belief in astrology. The finding that females reported significantly higher scores than males on belief in astrology also supports Eliseo and Urbano's findings.

Study Limitations

As data were collected via the Web, it was not possible to control who responded to the study. Given the confirmed association between extraversion and belief in astrology, it is possible that extravert believers, particularly females, were attracted to complete the online survey. Although the belief in astrology variable was normally distributed for this self-selected sample, the distribution in the general population — from which samples for other studies could be drawn — is unknown. To overcome such a possible confounding factor, personality and birthdate data would need to have been collected without revealing the true purpose of the survey.

Conclusion

A large percentage of the population know their zodiac sign and read their star signs regularly (Weinman, 1982). A connection between an individual's personality and their astrological Sun sign or Oriental year of birth could be construed as an example of implicit representation of personality (Asendorpf, 2007). Implicit representation of personality involves such psychological processes as self-attribution and selective self-observation (Furnham, 1991), in this case leading people to see themselves in the personality description of their 'sign'. One test of this theory revealed that 93% of respondents who were shown a personality assessment identical to that of a mass murderer saw themselves in this description (Gauquelin et al., 1979).

Given the strong genetic component of personality dimensions, it will require robust theoretical positions to account for further variability in personality dimensions. One such theoretical stance is that provided by culture (Robins, 2005; Terracciano et al., 2005). A theoretical rationale for birthdate influencing personality might invoke climatic or other variations in different parts of the world influencing critical aspects of early development. Chotai, Seretti, Lattuada, Lorenzi, and Lilli (2003) suggested a possible neurological basis for certain personality differences, based upon season of birth. This might represent a more fruitful avenue of research than using astrological sign or Oriental birth year as a benchmark for determining group membership.

Acknowledgments

We appreciate helpful comments from our colleagues Graham Bradley and Peter Creed.

References

Asendorpf, J.B. (2007). Implicit representations and personality. *International Journal of Psychology, 42*, 145–148.

Buchanan, T., Johnson, J.A., & Goldberg, L.R. (2005). Implementing a five-factor personality inventory for use on the internet. *European Journal of Psychological Assessment, 21*, 115–127.

Carlson, S. (1985). A double-blind test of astrology. *Nature, 318*, 419–425.

Cervone, D., & Mischel, W. (2002). Personality science. In D. Cervone, & W. Mischel (Eds.), *Advances in personality science* (pp. 1–26). New York: Guilford.

Chotai, J., Seretti, A., Lattuada, E., Lorenzi, C., & Lilli, R. (2003). Gene–environment interaction in psychiatric disorders as indicated by season of birth variations in tryptophan hydroxylase (TPH), serotonin transporter (5-HTTLPR) and dopamine receptor (DRD4) gene polymorphisms. *Psychiatry Research, 119*, 99–111.

Clarke, D., Gabriels, T., & Barnes, J. (1996). Astrological signs as determinants of extroversion and emotionality: An empirical study. *The Journal of Psychology, 130*, 131–140.

Costa, P.T., & McCrae, R.R. (1992a). Four ways five factors are basic. *Personality and Individual Differences, 13*, 653–665.

Costa, P.T., & McCrae, R.R. (1992b). Revised NEO Personality Inventory (NEO PR-R) and NEO Five-Factor Inventory (NEO-FFI) professional manual. Odessa: Psychological Assessment Resources.

Culver, R.B., & Ianna, P.A. (1988). *Astrology: True or false? A scientific evaluation.* New York: Prometheus Books.

Dalhstrom, W.G., Hopkins, D., Dalhstrom, L., Jackson, E., & Cumella, E. (1996). MMPI findings on astrological and other folklore concepts of personality. *Psychological Reports, 78*, 1059–1070.

Eliseo, C., & Urbano, L.S. (2006). Belief in astrology inventory: Development and validation. *Psychological Reports, 99,* 851–863.

Feingold, A. (1994). Gender differences in personality. *Psychological Bulletin, 116,* 429–456.

Fichten, C.S., & Sunerton, B. (1983). Popular horoscopes and the 'Barnum effect'. *The Journal of Psychology, 114,* 123–134.

Furnham, A. (1991). Hooked on horoscopes. *New Scientist, 129,* 33–36.

Gauquelin, M., Gauquelin, F., & Eysenck, S.B. (1979). Personality and position of the planets at birth: An empirical study. *British Journal of Social and Clinical Psychology, 18,* 71–75.

Gauquelin, M., Gauquelin, F., & Eysenck, S.B. (1981). Eysenck's personality analysis and position of the planets at birth: A replication on American subjects. *Personality and Individual Differences, 2,* 346–350.

Goldberg, L.R. (1993). The structure of phenotypic personality traits. *American Psychologist, 48,* 26–34.

Goldberg, L.R. (1999). A broad-bandwidth, public domain, personality inventory measuring the lower-level facets of several five-factor models. In I. Mervielde, I. Deary, F.D. Fruyt, & F. Ostendorf (Eds.), *Personality psychology in Europe* (Vol. 7, pp. 7–28). The Netherlands: Tilburg University Press.

Goldberg, L.R., Johnson, J.A., Eber, H.W., Hogan, R., Ashton, M.C., Cloninger, C.R., Gough, H.G (2006). The international personality item pool and the future of public-domain personality measures. *Journal of Research in Personality, 40,* 84–96.

Gow, A.J., Whiteman, M.C., Pattie, A., & Deary, I.J. (2005). Goldberg's 'IPIP' Big-Five factor markers: Internal consistency and concurrent validation in Scotland. *Personality and Individual Differences, 39,* 317–329.

Hamilton, M.M. (1995). Incorporation of astrology-based personality information into long-term self-concept. *Journal of Social Behavior and Personality, 10,* 707–718.

Hamilton, M.M. (2001). Who believes in astrology? Effect of favorableness of astrologically derived personality descriptions on acceptance of astrology. *Personality and Individual Differences, 31,* 895–902.

Hartmann, P., Reuter, M., & Nyborg, H. (2006). The relationship between date of birth and individual differences in personality and general intelligence: A large-scale study. *Personality and Individual Differences, 40,* 1349–1362.

Hentschel, U., & Kiessling, M. (1985). Season of birth and personality: Another instance of noncorrespondence. *The Journal of Social Psychology, 125,* 577–585.

Hume, N., & Goldstein, G. (1977). Is there an association between astrological data and personality? *Journal of Clinical Psychology, 33,* 711–713.

Jackson, M. (1979). Extraversion, neuroticism, and date of birth: A southern hemisphere study. *The Journal of Psychology, 101,* 197–198.

Jackson, M., & Fiebert, M. (1980). Introversion–extraversion and astrology. *The Journal of Psychology, 105*, 155–156.

Jang, K.L., Livesley, W.J., & Vernon, P.A. (1996). Heritability of the Big Five personality dimensions and their facets: A twin study. *Journal of Personality, 64*, 577–591.

Marusic, I., & Bratko, D. (1998). Relations of masculinity and femininity with personality dimensions of the five-factor model. *Sex Roles, 38*, 29–44.

Mayes, B., & Klugh, H.E. (1978). Birthdate psychology: A look at some new data. *The Journal of Psychology, 99*, 27–30.

Mayo, J., White, O., & Eysenck, H.J. (1978). An empirical study of the relation between astrological factors and personality. *The Journal of Social Psychology, 105*, 229–236.

Pellegrini, R.J. (1973). The astrological 'theory' of personality: An unbiased test by a biased observer. *The Journal of Psychology, 85*, 21–28.

Roberts, B.W., Robins, R.W., Trzesniewski, K.H., & Caspi, A. (2003). Personality trait development in adulthood. In J.L. Mortimer & M. Shanaham (Eds.), *Handbook of the life course* (pp. 579–595). New York: Plenum.

Robins, R.W. (2005). The nature of personality: Genes, culture, and national character. *Science, 310*, 62–63.

Russell, J., & Wagstaff, G.F. (1983). Extraversion, neuroticism, and time of birth. *British Journal of Social Psychology, 22*, 27–31.

Saklofske, D.H., Kelly, I.W., & McKerracher, D.W. (1982). An empirical study of personality and astrological factors. *The Journal of Psychology, 110*, 275–280.

Shaughnessy, M.F., Neely, R., Manz, A., & Nystul, M. (1990). Effects of birth order, sex, and astrological sign on personality. *Psychological Reports, 66*, 272–274.

Silverman, B.I., & Whitner, M. (1974). Astrological indicators of personality. *The Journal of Psychology, 87*, 89–95.

Smithers, A.G., & Cooper, H.J. (1978). Personality and season of birth. *The Journal of Social Psychology, 105*, 237–241.

Srivastava, S., John, O.P., Gosling, S.D., & Potter, J. (2003). Development of personality in early and middle adulthood: Set like plaster or persistent change? *Journal of Personality and Social Psychology, 84*, 1041–1053.

Startup, M. (1985). The astrological doctrine of 'aspects'. A failure to validate with personality. *British Journal of Social Psychology, 24*, 307–315.

Synder, C.R. (1974). Why horoscopes are true: The effects of specificity on acceptance of astrological interpretations. *Journal of Clinical Psychology, 30*, 577–580.

Tabachnick, B.G., & Fidell, L.S. (2001). *Using multivariate statistics* (4th ed.). Needham Heights, MA: Allyn & Bacon.

Terracciano, A., Abdel-Khalek, A.M., Ádám, N., Adamovová, L., Ahn, C.-K., Ahn, H.-N. et al. (2005). National character does not reflect mean personality trait levels in 49 cultures. *Science, 310*, 96–100.

Tyson, G.A. (1977). Astrology or season of birth: A split-sphere test. *The Journal of Psychology, 95,* 285–287.

Van Rooij, J.J. (1994). Self-concept in terms of astrological Sun-sign traits. *Psychological Reports, 84,* 541–546.

Van Rooij, J.J., Brak, M.A., & Commandeur, J.J. (1988). Introversion–extraversion and sun-sign. *The Journal of Psychology, 122,* 275–278.

Veno, A., & Pamment, P. (1979). Astrological factors and personality: A southern hemisphere replication. *The Journal of Psychology, 101,* 73–77.

Weinman, G. (1982). The prophecy that never fails. *Sociological Inquiry, 52,* 275–287.

Chapter

5

Personality and Season of Birth: Evidence From Oceania and Northern Hemisphere Samples

Mary E. Rogers and A. Ian Glendon

Associations between season of birth and personality traits have been studied in nonclinical populations with mixed results. The present study explored the relationship between season of birth and personality traits separately for an Oceania-born sample ($N = 2808$) and for a Northern Hemisphere-born sample ($N = 482$). Personality was assessed using a 50-item web-based version of the International Personality Item Pool (IPIP). No significant relationships between personality and season of birth were found in either sample. Researchers who have found personality differences between samples of individuals born in different seasons have attributed these to a variety of factors, including effects of temperature variability on certain neurotransmitters known to influence personality, or sociological and other environmental factors. Our findings challenge the basis for these attributions and suggest that a more robust theoretical framework is required to explain possible season of birth influences upon personality in adult populations.

The sun's position dictates seasonally varying differences in the time of year that a person is born. Changes in the amount of sunlight are known to affect hibernation cycles in animals and dormancy in plants. The time of year of an individual's birth is claimed to be associated with personality traits, health and mental illness. This chapter explores the nature of any association between season of birth and personality within nonclinical samples using a widely accepted personality measure.

Season of birth literature dates back to 1929 when Tramer found that winter-born children had a higher incidence of mental disorders. Other links have been found between individuals born in winter months and psychiatric conditions such as schizophrenia (Chotai, Seretti, Lattuada, Lorenzi, & Lilli, 2003; Takei, Sham, O'Callaghan, Glover, & Murray, 1995), affective psychosis (Hare, 1978), anorexia nervosa (Waller et al., 2002), and suicidal behaviour (Chotai & Renberg, 2002; Chotai, Renberg, & Jacobsson, 1999, 2002; Joiner, Pfaff, Acres, & Johnson, 2002; Pfaff et al., 2006; Rock, Greenberg, & Hallmayer, 2006).

Associations between season of birth and personality traits have been studied in nonclinical populations. Findings revealed that adults who believe they are lucky (Chotai & Wiseman, 2005), who are high on novelty seeking (Chotai, Forsgren, Nilsson, & Adolfsson, 2001), sensational seeking (Joinson & Nettle, 2005), neuroticism, impulsiveness and venturesomeness (Gupta, 1992), and low on morningness (Natale & Adam, 1999; Natale, Adam, & Chotai, 2002) were born during the summer months, while those low on agreeableness were born during winter (Tochigi et al., 2004). Adolescent females born in spring had the highest health status due to low levels of tension, anxiety and stress, while those born in winter had the lowest health status and the highest levels of anxiety (Chichilenko & Barbarash, 2001). Relationships between date of birth and intelligence have also been reported (e.g., Kanekar & Makerjee, 1972). Possible reasons for seasonal differences among individuals include dopamine–melatonin turnover (Chotai & Adolfsson, 2002) and low serotonin turnover (Chotai & Ashberg, 1999), both of which have been shown to influence personality traits such as novelty seeking and reward dependence through genes that modulate neurotransmitters for mood. However, in contrast to these findings, some researchers have found no relationship between season of birth and personality (Hentschel & Kiessling, 1985; Jackson, 1979; Tonetti, Fabbri, & Natale, 2009; Tyson, 1977), season of birth and intelligence (Berglund, 1967; Farley, 1968; Kanekar & Makerjee, 1972; Mascie-Taylor, 1980), and the opposite association between season of birth and the personality trait of novelty seeking among adolescents (e.g., Chotai, Lundberg, & Adolfsson, 2003). Variations in results might be a function of different methodologies. For example, some studies were limited by small sample size (e.g., Gupta, 1992), a restricted sample that included only one sex (e.g., Caci & Boyer, 2004), an unbalanced sample that included a high percentage of females (e.g., Joinson & Nettle, 2005), or used an unvalidated measure of personality (e.g., Chotai & Wiseman, 2005). While two studies have used the Big Five personality traits to measure the association between personality and season of birth (Tochigi et al., 2004; Tonetti et al., 2009), no studies have used standard personality measures for both Northern and Southern hemisphere samples. To our knowledge Jackson (1979) is the only other study that has used a nonclinical Southern Hemisphere-born sample.

Season of birth patterning of mental health problems, inconsistencies in results and a resurgence of interest in the relationship between birth date and personality (Motluk, 2007) prompted this investigation of the relationship between season of birth and personality in both an Oceania-born sample and a Northern Hemisphere-born sample. Based on significant findings from prior studies that used Northern Hemisphere samples and employed a robust methodological approach, it was expected that the present study would confirm a relationship between season of birth and one or more of the big five personality traits. The null hypothesis was that there would be no personality differences between seasons of birth for either sample.

Method

Participants

Participants were 2,808 Oceania-born adults (e.g., Australian, New Zealand; 1,140 males, 1668 females) and 482 European-, North American- and Canadian-born adults (217 males, 265 females) aged 28 to 51 years. Of the Oceania-born participants, 726 were born in spring, 657 in summer, 730 in autumn and 695 in winter (mean age 37.9 years, SD 6.7). Of the European-, American- and Canadian-born participants, 122 were born in spring, 126 in summer, 122 in autumn and 112 in winter (mean age 39.1 years, SD 6.8).

Materials

Participants were asked to indicate their date of birth, sex and country of birth. Personality was assessed using the International Personality Item Pool (IPIP; Goldberg, 1999; Goldberg et al., 2006) a five-factor model and representation of the NEO Personality Inventory (Costa & McCrae, 1989). The IPIP measures the Big Five personality characteristics of Agreeableness (A), Conscientiousness (C), Extraversion (E), Openness to experience (O) and Neuroticism (N). The present study used the 50-item version, which includes five 10-item subscales using a 5-point scale ranging from 1 (*Very inaccurate*) to 5 (*Very accurate*). Sample items include, 'I have a vivid imagination' and, 'I am the life of the party'. Comparable with those cited in Buchanan, Goldberg, and Johnson (2005) and in Gow, Whiteman, Pattie, and Deary (2005) internal reliability coefficients for the five scales for the present sample were N .75, E .83, O .70, A .74 and C .79. Concurrent validity evidence for the IPIP has been demonstrated by associations in the expected direction with the NEO-FFI and the EPQ-R Short Form personality measures (Gow et al., 2005).

Procedure

The IPIP was administered using a web-based survey designed to assess the relationship between personality and birth date. Participants were recruited to participate in the study via online methods such as newsletter, email and the media, explaining the purpose of the study and how to access the online survey. Respondents volunteered anonymously. The Statistical Package for Social Sciences (SPSS) data builder was used to create the web-based survey. Participants were categorised into the four seasons according to their date of birth and hemisphere of birth. Ethical approval was granted by the authors' organisation's human ethics committee.

Results

Intercorrelational data among the five personality factors for both the Oceania-born and Northern Hemisphere-born samples suggested that the sub-scales were related in ways that could be anticipated but were distinct. For example, as seen in Table 5.1, Extraversion was negatively correlated with Neuroticism (–.38, –.41), positively correlated with Openness (.35, .36), but weakly correlated with Conscientiousness (.24, .22) and Agreeableness (.19, .26). Agreeableness was negatively correlated with Neuroticism (–.44, –.42) positively correlated with Conscientiousness (.37, .31) but weakly correlated with Openness (.23, .28). Conscientiousness was negatively correlated with Neuroticism (–.40, –.36) and weakly correlated with Openness (.14, .16). Neuroticism had a weak negative correlation with Openness (–.14, –.16). Table 5.2 shows the means and standard deviations for the personality sub-scales by season of birth and hemisphere.

A MANCOVA was performed on the five dependent variables and the independent variables season of birth with age as a covariate for both the Oceania-born and the Northern Hemisphere-born subsamples. Contrary to the hypotheses, there were no multivariate main effects for season of birth on any of the personality dimensions for the Oceania-born subsample: extraversion, $F(3) = 0.38$, $p = .77$, partial η^2 .00, agreeableness, $F(3) = 1.66$, $p = .17$, partial η^2 .00, conscientiousness, $F(3) = 0.61$, $p = .61$, partial η^2 .00, neuroticism, $F(3) = 1.86$, $p = .13$, partial η^2 .00, or openness, $F(3) = 3.71$, $p = .01$, partial η^2 .00. There were no multivariate main effects for season of birth on any of the personality dimensions for the Northern Hemisphere-born subsample: extraversion, $F(3) = 0.22$, $p = .88$, partial η^2 .00, agreeableness, $F(3) = 0.70$, $p = .56$, partial η^2 .00, conscientiousness, $F(3) = 0.21$, $p = .88$, partial

η^2 .00, neuroticism, $F(3) = 0.37$, $p = .77$, partial η^2 .00, or openness, $F(3) = 0.55$, $p = .65$, partial η^2 .00. Power values for these analyses ranged between .13 and .81 for the Oceania-born sample and .09 and .20 for the Northern Hemisphere-born sample.

Discussion

Our findings are consistent with other research that has found no relationship between season of birth and personality (Hentschel & Kiessling, 1985; Jackson, 1979; Tonetti et al., 2009; Tyson, 1977). The present study overcomes limitations of some past studies (Caci & Boyer, 2004; Chotai & Wiseman, 2005; Gupta, 1992; Joinson & Nettle, 2005) by using a balanced sample that included males and females from both Northern and Southern hemispheres, and a well validated measure of the five factor model of personality. While the Southern Hemisphere sample size was large enough to detect a significant effect, the moderate sized Northern Hemisphere sample together with the small power values indicated that further research is needed to replicate these findings.

Limited temperature variability in some parts of the Oceania region (in particular, Queensland and the Northern Territory) might partly account for the null results for the Oceania-born sample. However, this explanation cannot be used to account for the null results in the Northern Hemisphere-born sample. Researchers who have found personality differences between groups of individuals born in different seasons have attributed these to a variety of factors, including effects of temperature

Table 5.1

Correlations Between Five Personality Variables for Oceania-Born and Northern Hemisphere (NH) Born Samples

| Variables | Oceania-born[1] sample | | | | |
	Extraversion	Agreeableness	Conscientiousness	Neuroticism	Openness
NH born sample[2]					
Extraversion	—	.19**	.24**	−.38**	.35**
Agreeableness	.26**	—	.37**	−.44**	.23**
Conscientiousness	.22**	.31**	—	−.40**	.14**
Neuroticism	−.41**	−.42**	−.36**	—	−.14**
Openness	.36**	.28**	.16**	−.16**	—

Note: [1] Oceania-born sample N = 2,808.
      [2] Northern Hemisphere (NH) born sample N = 482.
      ** = $p < .01$

Table 5.2

Summary Data for Personality Subscales by Season of Birth

Variable	Spring		Summer		Autumn		Winter		Total	
	M	SD	M	SD	M	SD	M	SD	M	SD
Extraversion										
Oceania born[1]	33.09	7.15	33.04	6.85	32.80	7.19	33.23	7.23	33.04	7.11
NH born[2]	33.69	7.46	33.78	6.63	33.29	7.46	33.18	7.20	33.48	7.19
Agreeableness										
Oceania born[1]	35.99	5.78	35.87	5.50	35.82	5.73	35.05	5.98	36.01	5.70
NH born[2]	36.62	5.91	35.58	6.16	36.24	5.81	36.44	5.79	36.23	5.91
Conscientiousness										
Oceania born[1]	35.36	6.24	35.05	5.98	34.94	6.50	35.04	6.38	35.10	6.28
NH born[2]	35.76	6.26	35.26	6.68	35.84	6.93	35.82	7.21	35.68	6.77
Neuroticism										
Oceania born[1]	27.19	7.35	27.14	7.11	27.90	7.52	27.24	7.32	27.38	7.34
NH born[2]	25.98	7.04	26.57	7.66	26.94	7.37	26.28	7.63	26.44	7.41
Openness										
Oceania born[1]	33.37	6.04	34.17	4.76	33.69	4.90	34.53	6.06	34.18	4.95
NH born[2]	35.30	5.56	34.59	5.18	34.59	4.73	34.63	5.13	34.78	5.15

Note: [1] Oceania-born sample N = 2808.
[2] Northern Hemisphere (NH) born sample N = 482.

variability on certain neurotransmitters known to influence personality, or sociological and other environmental factors. Our findings challenge the basis for these attributions and suggest that a more robust theoretical framework is required to explain possible season of birth influences upon personality in adult populations.

References

Berglund, G.W. (1967). A note on intelligence and season of birth. *British Journal of Psychology, 58*, 147–151.

Caci, H., & Boyer, R.P. (2004). Novelty seekers and impulsive subjects are low in morningness. *European Psychiatry, 19*, 79–84.

Chichilenko, M.V., & Barbarash, N.A. (2001). Effect of the season of birth on personality, health, and emotional stress in adolescents. *Human Physiology, 27*, 507–509.

Chotai, J., & Adolfsson, R. (2002). Converging evidence suggests that monoamine neurotransmitter turnover in human adults is associated with their season of birth. *European Archives of Psychiatry and Clinical Neuroscience, 252*, 130–134.

Chotai, J., & Ashberg, M. (1999). Variations in CSF monoamine metabolites according to the season of birth. *Neuropsychobiology, 39*, 57–62.

Chotai, J., Forsgren, T., Nilsson, L., & Adolfsson, R. (2001). Season of birth variations in the temperament and character inventory of personality in a general population. *Neuropsychobiology, 44,* 19–26.

Chotai, J., Lundberg, M., & Adolfsson, R. (2003). Variations in personality traits among adolescents and adults according to their season of birth in the general population: Further evidence. *Personality and Individual Differences, 35,* 897–908.

Chotai, J., & Renberg, E.S. (2002). Season of birth variations in suicide methods in relation to any history of psychiatric contacts support an independent suicidality trait. *Journal of Affective Disorders, 69,* 69–81.

Chotai, J., Renberg, E.S., & Jacobsson, L. (1999). Season of birth associated with the age and method of suicide. *Archives of Suicide Research, 5,* 245–254.

Chotai, J., Renberg, E.S., & Jacobsson, L. (2002). Method of suicide in relation to some sociodemographic variables in Northern Sweden. *Archives of Suicide Research, 6,* 111–122.

Chotai, J., Seretti, A., Lattuada, E., Lorenzi, C., & Lilli, R. (2003). Gene-environment interaction in psychiatric disorders as indicated by season of birth variations in tryptophan hydroxylase (TPH), serotonin transporter (5-HTTLPR) and dopamine receptor (DRD4) gene polymorphisms. *Psychiatry Research, 119,* 99–111.

Chotai, J., & Wiseman, R. (2005). Born lucky? The relationship between feeling lucky and month of birth. *Personality and Individual Differences, 39,* 1451–1460.

Costa, P.T., & McCrae, R.R. (1989). The NEO-PI/NEO-FFI manual supplement. Odessa, FL: *Psychological Assessment Resources.*

Farley, F.H. (1968). Season of birth, intelligence, and personality. *British Journal of Psychology, 59,* 281–283.

Goldberg, L.R. (1999). A broad-bandwidth, public domain, personality inventory measuring the lower-level facets of several five-factor models. In I. Mervielde, I. Deary, F.D. Fruyt, & F. Ostendorf (Eds.), *Personality psychology in Europe* (Vol. 7, pp. 7–28). The Netherlands: Tilburg University Press.

Goldberg, L.R., Johnson, J.A., Eber, H.W., Hogan, R., Ashton, M.C., Cloninger, C.R., & Gough, H.G. (2006). The International Personality Item Pool and the future of public-domain personality measures. *Journal of Research in Personality, 40,* 84–96.

Gow, A.J., Whiteman, M.C., Pattie, A., & Deary, I.J. (2005). Goldberg's 'IPIP' Big-Five factor markers: Internal consistency and concurrent validation in Scotland. *Personality and Individual Differences, 39,* 317–329.

Gupta, S. (1992). Season of birth in relation to personality and blood groups. *Personality and Individual Differences, 13,* 631–633.

Hare, E.H. (1978). Variations in the seasonal distribution of births of psychotic patients in England and Wales. *British Journal of Psychiatry, 132,* 155–158.

Hentschel, U., & Kiessling, M. (1985). Season of birth and personality: Another instance of noncorrespondence. *Journal of Social Psychology, 125*, 577–585.

Jackson, M. (1979). Extraversion, neuroticism, and date of birth: A southern hemisphere study. *The Journal of Psychology, 101*, 197–198.

Joiner, T.E., Pfaff, J.J., Acres, J.G., & Johnson, F. (2002). Birth month and suicidal and depressive symptoms in Australians born in the Southern vs. the Northern hemisphere. *Psychiatry Research, 112*, 89–92.

Joinson, C., & Nettle, D. (2005). Season of birth variation in sensation seeking in an adult population. *Personality and Individual Differences, 38*, 859–870.

Kanekar, S., & Makerjee, S. (1972). Intelligence, extraversion, and neuroticism in relation to season of birth. *Journal of Social Psychology, 86*, 309–310.

Mascie-Taylor, C.G. (1980). Season of birth, IQ components, and personality traits. *Journal of Genetic Psychology, 137*, 151–152.

Motluk, A. (2007). Born under a bad sign: Your date of birth has a bigger influence on your life than you might realise. *New Scientist, 193*, 40-43.

Natale, V., & Adam, A. (1999). Season of birth modulates morningness-eveningness preference in humans. *Neuroscience Letters, 274*, 139–141.

Natale, V., Adam, A., & Chotai, J. (2002). Further results on the association between morningness-eveningness preference and the season of birth in human adults. *Neuropsychobiology, 46*, 209–214.

Pfaff, J.J., Bernert, R.A., Hollar, D.L., Witte, T.K., Merrill, K.A., Pettit, J.W. et al. (2006). Birth month and depressive and suicidal symptoms in an elderly Australian sample born in the Southern or Northern Hemisphere. *Psychiatry Research, 144*, 217–219.

Rock, D., Greenberg, D., & Hallmayer, J. (2006). Season-of-birth as a risk factor for the seasonality of suicidal behaviour. *European Archives of Psychiatry and Clinical Neuroscience, 256*, 98–105.

Takei, N., Sham, P.C., O'Callaghan, E., Glover, G., & Murray, R.M. (1995). Early risk factors in schizophrenia: Place and season of birth. *European Psychiatry, 10*, 165–170.

Tochigi, M., Marumo, K., Hibino, H., Otowa, T., Kato, C., & Marui, T., (2004). Season of birth effect on personality in a general population. *Neuroscience Letters, 365*, 120–123.

Tonetti, L., Fabbri, M., & Natale, V. (2009). Season of birth and personality in healthy young adults. *Neuroscience Letters, 452*, 185–188.

Tramer, M. (1929). The biological significance of the birth month, with special reference to psychosis. *Schweizer Archiv für Neurologie und Psychiatrie, 24*, 17–24.

Tyson, G.A. (1977). Astrology or season of birth: A split-sphere test. *The Journal of Psychology, 95*, 285–287.

Waller, G., Watkins, B., Potterton, C., Niederman, M., Sellings, J., Willoughby, K. et al. (2002). Pattern of birth in adults with anorexia nervosa. *Journal of Nervous and Mental Disease, 190*, 752–756.

Chapter

6

Functional and Dysfunctional Learning

Chris J. Jackson

This chapter suggests that a hybrid model of learning in personality (Jackson, 2005; 2008) can both describe and explain personality processes that lead to functional and effective performance compared to dysfunctional and poor performance. A case for the model is made in which Sensation Seeking is seen as a distal and biologically based drive which must be re-expressed in terms of sociocognitively based skills (comprising Goal Oriented Achiever, Conscientious Achiever, Emotionally Intelligent Achiever and Deep Learning Achiever) to achieve functional learning. Dysfunctional learning results from the failure to re-express Sensation Seeking. Recent evidence in favour of the model is discussed in terms of the prediction of workplace and educational performance and the model is contrasted with other recent models of learning and personality.

A popular saying argues that the most important asset of any organisation is its people. What people do within an organisation can lead to productivity, customer satisfaction, and organisational profit. Yet, despite the positive impact that employees have on organisational outcomes, the opposite is also true. Some employees commit negative behaviours, which are counterproductive and contrary to the legitimate interests of the organisation. The same is also true in education or in the community, such that some people make a tremendous positive impact, whereas others may have a negative impact.

Traditionally, personality tests have been used to predict performance, integrity tests have been used to measure counterproductive behaviour, and learning tests have been used to measure learning. Jackson (2005; 2008) designed a 'hybrid model of learning in personality' that argues for a common basis to these three distinct areas, such that the model has the potential to measure functional and dysfunctional learning within the workplace and general community. This could be a very interesting applied measurement tool as it brings together the measurement of positive and negative behaviours, as well as the possibility of intervention based on training and development.

The hybrid model of learning in personality goes beyond the well-known Eysenckian and Big Five models of personality, which are both based in exploratory factor analysis. Unfortunately, exploratory factor analysis has many well-known weaknesses that prevent proper model development (Block, 1995). A major problem of exploratory factor analysis is that it provides a descriptive model of personality as opposed to one that is explanatory and focuses on the underlying processes. It was for these reasons that Eysenck (1967) went on to develop a biological model of personality to justify his proposed factor analytical solution.

The idea of developing a theoretical model after collection of empirical data seems a little strange, but this reflects the order in which the Big Five and Giant Three models were developed. However, attempts to develop theoretical models of personality prior to the development of measurement systems have also been problematic. A good example of this is Gray's Reinforcement Sensitivity Theory and the revised version (Gray & McNaughton, 2000) in which measurement remains a major problem. To overcome this issue, Jackson's hybrid model of learning has a basis in both theory and measurement.

The Jackson Hybrid Model of Learning in Personality

The hybrid model of learning in personality is based in the neuropsychological theory of approach and avoidance pathways that provide a common link to personality, motivation and learning. This general new way of thinking has big implications for the measurement of personality in organisational psychology (Furnham & Jackson, 2008). Jackson (2005; 2008) specifically argues that Sensation Seeking (which is high approach and low avoidance) represents an instinctive biological urge to explore the environment. Contrary to the work of Zuckerman who focuses on the negative side of Sensation Seeking, Jackson's Sensation Seeking is designed to be neither positive nor negative but simply a strong approach orientation.

The cognitive skills which re-express, harness, direct and delay Sensation Seeking towards achieving positive outcomes are split into the following:

- Goal Oriented Achiever — a mastery goal orientation such that cognitive resources are allocated towards the achievement of long-term, difficult goals
- Conscientious Achiever — reflecting responsibility and perseverance in completing desired outcomes
- Deep Learning Achiever — reflecting the need to understand and know more about issues
- Emotionally Intelligent Achiever — reflecting rational and emotionally independent thoughts such that a logical perspective is maintained.

The reason why these cognitive strategies are chosen is that they are derived from the literature as being important cognitions associated with success and therefore likely to be implicated in functional learning. The Goal Oriented Achiever scale draws its basis from the goal orientation (Dweck & Leggett, 1988; VandeWalle & Cummings, 1997), goal setting (Locke & Latham, 1990) and self-efficacy literature (e.g. Bandura, 1999). The Conscientious Achiever scale is inspired by the empirical evidence, which argues that conscientiousness is probably the most predictive of the Big Five personality traits (Byrne et al., 2005; Hogan & Holland, 2003; Liao & Chuang, 2004). The Emotionally Intelligent Achiever has a basis in the personality basis of emotional intelligence (e.g. Petrides & Furnham, 2000) although it does need to be emphasised that the Emotional Intelligence in the hybrid model of learning in personality is defined in terms of emotional independence, whereas Emotional Intelligence is generally defined in terms of intelligent use of emotions. Deep Learning Achiever is inspired by the experiential learning literature (e.g. Kolb, 1984), which argues that deep processing of material produces more effective learning than shallow learning. Moreover, the hybrid model of learning in personality is defined to provide a better measure of learning style than experiential measures such as, for example, Honey and Mumford's Learning Styles Questionnaire (LSQ), which has recently received much criticism (Duff & Duffy, 2002; Swailes & Senior, 1999).

The hybrid model of learning in personality argues that these cognitive strategies control and direct our Sensation Seeking to achieve positive outcomes across a wide range of situations. For example, a high Sensation Seeker without cognitive control might think how nice it would be to be rich and proceed to achieve wealth by means of a simple cognitive strategy such as a 'smash and grab' crime. Such dysfunctional learners have not learnt to re-express their Sensation Seeking through their cognitive skills. However, a high Sensation Seeker with the cognitive skills to re-express their instinctive drive might think how nice it would be to be rich and proceed to achieve this aim by complex and socially acceptable cognitive strategies such as setting up a company, achieving more sales, getting bonuses, getting an education etc. Such functional learners have re-expressed their Sensation Seeking through their cognitive skills to achieve positive outcomes. The hybrid model of learning in personality argues that the complex strategies for success found in entrepreneurs for example are likely to contrast with the deficient strategies present in delinquents. The model argues that both will be high Sensation Seekers, but entrepreneurs are cognitively equipped for success, whereas delinquents are not.

The Functional, Productive Learner

If a person has the cognitive skills to redirect, control, or delay their Sensation Seeking, then the model of learning argues that the person will be a functional learner and a productive employee, student or trainer. If a person lacks the cognitive skills to control and re-express their Sensation Seeking, then the model argues that the person will be a dysfunctional learner who is potentially counter-productive. People who express their low Sensation Seeking as high cognitive skills are competent workers (who are simply not so very interested in self-development). People who express low Sensation Seeking as low cognitive skills are likely to be relatively low in productivity but not dysfunctional (see Figure 6.1).

Jackson's *Learning Styles Profiler* (LSP; Jackson, 2005) provides the measurement of the hybrid model of learning in personality and is used to differentiate between those likely to have functional and dysfunctional learning outcomes. The manual (Jackson, 2005) contains a full description of theory and very thorough psychometric analysis exploratory factor analysis and reliability and validity coefficients.

Jackson, Hobman, Jimmieson, and Martin (2008) showed that the hybrid model of learning in personality is more predictive of workplace

High Sensation Seeking re-expressed as	High cognitive skills =	Functional learner
High Sensation Seeking re-expressed as	Low cognitive skills =	Dysfunctional learner
Low Sensation Seeking re-expressed as	High cognitive skills =	Competent worker
Low Sensation Seeking re-expressed as	Low cognitive skills =	'Standard' worker

Figure 6.1
The four outcomes of Jackson's Model of Functional and Dysfunctional Workplace Learning.

and educational performance than other modern models of personality (e.g., the Big Five, Giant Three, Zuckerman's). Some models of learning such as Honey and Mumford's Learning Styles Questionnaire were not predictive of performance at all. Moreover, Jackson et al. (2008) demonstrated how the indirect pathway from Sensation Seeking through Goal Oriented Achiever predicted functional outcomes such as work performance and academic success, whereas the direct pathway predicted dysfunctional behaviour.

O'Connor and Jackson (2008) provided a deeper analysis of the indirect pathway from Sensation Seeking through Goal Oriented Achiever to performance in the prediction of school student success, success in a laboratory task and success at work.

In the prediction of academic performance, Jackson, Baguma and Furnham (2009) have found that the hybrid model of learning in personality predicts GPA in both Ugandan and Australian students. This paper continues the process initiated by Jackson (2008) of identifying further indirect pathways from Sensation Seeking through the cognitive skills scales to performance. In this case, Emotional Intelligent Achiever was argued to be the most proximal of the cognitive scales in the prediction of GPA.

Further Applications and Studies

Further papers are planned to show the difference between the hybrid model of learning in personality and traditional models of learning styles in which it will be demonstrated that the hybrid model of learning in personality predicts student performance, whereas the best of the learning styles models predict student engagement. These papers will argue that there is an important difference between the training of students to achieve better performance through the development of their cognitive skills is different from the encouragement of student engagement through matching the learning environment to student learning styles.

The model may also be seen as being useful in corrections and the community since it argues that the development of cognitive skills to re-express Sensation Seeking is more likely to be effective in the promotion of functional learning than trying to change Sensation Seeking. The hybrid model learning in personality might be seen as a useful and optimistic model for helping people to develop their learning and for providing hope that change for the better is possible. The usefulness of the hybrid model of learning in personality in fostering the development of functional learning contrasts with models of personality such as the Big

Five (Costa & McCrae, 1992) and the Giant Three (Eysenck, 1967), which have little to say about how interventions are possible. I want to emphasise, however, that evidence in favour of the application of the hybrid model of learning in personality in corrections and the community has yet to be collected.

Some initial work as to how the hybrid model of learning in personality might work in the training of functional learning has recently been reported. Siadaty and Taghiyareh (2007) report that training based on Conscientious Achievement increases performance but that training based on Sensation Seeking does not. These results strongly support Jackson's model since the model proposes that Conscientious Achievement will respond to intervention, whereas Sensation Seeking (with its proposed biological basis) will not. Much more research into how these cognitive skills can be developed and trained as a way of successfully re-expressing Sensation Seeking needs to be undertaken. Siadaty and Taghiyareh's work suggests that the hybrid model of learning may provide a basis for training interventions in the workplace that will lead to improved work performance outcomes. It might for example be used as a model to improve the performance of job candidates who might otherwise be rejected and to develop training programs focused on increasing performance in both the workplace and education. Table 6.1 provides

Table 6.1

Summary of Evidence in Favour of Jackson's Hybrid Model of Learning in Personality

	SS	GOA	CA	EIA	DLA	Source
Work performance (self-report)	✓	✓	✓			Jackson et al. (2008)
Work performance (supervisor rated)		✓		✓		Jackson et al. (2008)
University work performance (self-report)	✓	✓	✓	✓	✓	Jackson et al. (2008)
Schoolwork performance (self-report)	✓	✓	✓	✓	✓	O'Connor & Jackson (2008)
Grade point average in Year 1, university		✓	✓	✓		Jackson, Makere & Furnham (Submitted)
Leadership (e.g., charisma)	✓	✓	✓	✓	✓	Jackson et al. (2008)
Maze performance	✓	✓				O'Connor & Jackson (2008)
Psychopathy (Psychopathy Personality Inventory [PPI])	✓	✓	✓	✓	✓	Jackson et al. (2008)
Sexual proclivity	✓			✓	✓	Jackson et al. (2008)
Workplace deviance				✓		Jackson et al. (2008)
General delinquency	✓		✓	✓	✓	Jackson et al. (2008)

a summary of the results in favour of the hybrid model of learning in personality. Results indicate that the model has general predictive validity.

In summary, Jackson's (2005; 2008) hybrid model of learning in personality represents a new way of thinking about functional and dysfunctional learning and provides a model that not only describes but also explains processes underlying both high performance and anti-social performance. Moreover, it also provides a way of uniting the different perspectives of the biological theorists of personality (such as Eysenck, 1967; Gray & McNaughton, 2000) with the sociocognitive theorists (e.g., Dweck & Leggett, 1988; VandeWalle & Cummings, 1997) and the experiential learning theorists (e.g., Kolb, 1984).

References

Bandura, A. (1999). Social cognitive theory of personality. In A. Pervin & O.P. John (Eds.), *Handbook of personality: Theory and research* (2nd ed., pp. 154–196). New York: Guilford Press.

Block, J. (1995). A contrarian view of the five-factor approach to personality description. *Psychological Bulletin, 117,* 187–215.

Byrne, Z.S., Stoner, J., Thompson, K., & Hochwarter, W. (2005). The interactive effects of conscientiousness, work effort, and psychological climate on job performance. *Journal of Vocational Behavior, 66,* 326–338.

Costa, P.T., Jr., & McCrae, R.R. (1992). *Revised NEO Personality R (NEO PI-R) and NEO Five-Factor Inventory (NEO FFI) professional manual.* Odessa, FL: Psychological Assessment Resources.

Eysenck, H. (1967). *The biological basis of personality.* Springfield, IL: Charles C. Thomas.

Duff, A., & Duffy, T. (2002). Psychometric qualities of Honey & Mumford's Learning Styles Questionnaire. *Personality and Individual Differences, 33,* 147–164.

Dweck, C.S., & Leggett, E.L. (1988). A social-cognitive approach to motivation and personality. *Psychological Review, 95,* 256–273.

Furnham, A., & Jackson, C.J. (2008). Reinforcement Sensitivity Theory in the work-place. In P. Corr, *Theory and application of Reinforcement Sensitivity Theory.* Cambridge University Press.

Gray, J.A., & McNaughton, N. (2000). *The neuropsychology of anxiety.* Oxford: Oxford University Press.

Hogan, J., & Holland, B. (2004). Using theory to evaluate personality and job performance relations: A socioanalytic perspective. *Journal of Applied Psychology, 88,* 100–112.

Jackson, C.J. (2005). *An applied neuropsychological model of functional and dysfunctional learning: Applications for business, education, training and clinical psychology.* Brisbane, Australia: Cymeon.

Jackson, C.J. (2008). Measurement issues concerning a personality model spanning temperament, character, and experience. In G. Boyle, G. Matthews, & D.H. Saklofske, *Handbook of personality and testing*. Los Angeles: Sage.

Jackson, C.J., Baguma, P., & Furnham, A. (2009). Predicting grade point average from the hybrid model of learning in personality: Consistent findings from Ugandan and Australian Students. *Educational Psychology, 29,* 747–761.

Jackson, C.J., Hobman, E., Jimmieson, N., & Martin, R. (2008). Comparing different approach and avoidance models of learning and personality in the prediction of work, university and leadership outcomes. *British Journal of Psychology,* 1–30. Advance online publication. Doi: 10.1348/000712608X322900

Kolb, D. (1984). *Experiential learning*. Englewood Cliffs, NJ: Prentice Hall.

Liao, H., & Chuang, A. (2004). A multilevel investigation of factors influencing employee service performance and customer outcomes. *Academy of Management Journal, 47,* 41–58.

Locke, E.A., & Latham, G.P. (1990). *A theory of goal setting and task performance*. Englewood Cliffs, NJ: Prentice Hall.

O'Connor, P.C., & Jackson, C.J. (2008). Learning to be saints or sinners: The indirect pathway from sensation seeking to behavior through mastery orientation. *Journal of Personality, 76,* 1–20.

Petrides, K.V., & Furnham, A. (2000). On the dimensional structure of emotional intelligence. *Personality and Individual Differences, 29,* 313–320.

Siadaty, M., & Taghiyareh, F. (2007). *PALS2: Pedagogically adaptive learning system based on learning styles*. Paper presented at the Seventh IEEE International Conference on Advanced Learning Technologies, Niigata, Japan.

Swailes, S., & Senior, B. (1999) The dimensionality of Honey and Mumford's Learning Styles Questionnaire, *International Journal of Selection and Assessment, 7,* 1–11.

VandeWalle, D., & Cummings, L.L. (1997). A test of the influence of goal orientation on the feedback-seeking process. *Journal of Applied Psychology, 82,* 390–400.

Education, personality and emotional intelligence

Emotional Intelligence, Coping, and School Performance

Natalie Games, Gerard J. Fogarty, Carolyn MacCann, and Richard D. Roberts

The aim of the present study was to determine the contribution of emotional intelligence (EI), in conjunction with different facets of coping, to academic performance. To this end, middle school students were recruited from five cities across the United States to participate in an ongoing research project being conducted by the Educational Testing Service. The student sample consisted of 383 middle school students (187 female) who were halfway through the eighth grade. Participants' ages ranged from 12 to 15 years. Results indicated that a performance-based measure of EI predicted school performance but that its contribution was largely subsumed by a measure of problem-focused coping. Other types of coping were weakly related to academic performance. These findings have implications for interventions directed at improving school adjustment, with coping skills perhaps a more realistic target than the more esoteric construct of EI.

The nature of today's workplace dictates that completion of the final years of secondary school education is more crucial than ever, as employers require higher levels of education (Steering Committee for the Review of Government Service Provision [SCRGSP], 2007; Weale, 2007). The growing emphasis on educational attainments has triggered a renewed interest in the predictors of academic success, especially constructs that have emerged in recent times and whose definitions suggest that they may contribute to school performance. Emotional intelligence (EI) is one such construct. The initial focus of studies in this area was to establish whether a relationship exists between EI and academic achievement. An equally important question is whether EI adds to the prediction of academic achievement when variables such as ability and personality have been taken into consideration. The aim of the present study was to test for evidence of incremental validity in educational settings using an ability-based measure of EI as the independent variable, a range of school subjects as the dependent variables, and measures of different forms of coping as control variables.

Popularised by Goleman (1995) and boosted by his claim that it may turn out to be more important than intelligence quotient (IQ), EI was promoted in some quarters as a key predictor of a range of behaviours, including work performance and academic success. The enthusiasm was tempered by subsequent publications pointing out the methodological and definitional problems surrounding the construct of EI (e.g., Matthews, Roberts, & Zeidner, 2003). Taking the definitional problems first, EI has been described as 'the ability to perceive emotions, to access and generate emotions so as to assist thought, to understand emotions and emotional knowledge and to reflectively regulate emotions so as to promote emotional and intellectual growth' (Mayer & Salovey, 1997, p. 10). Defined in this way, EI is clearly a complicated construct with some aspects of EI (e.g., perception of emotions) likely to be more modifiable than others (e.g., regulation of emotions). A further complication arises when one considers that EI involves the awareness and regulation of one's own emotions as well as the awareness and regulation of other's emotions (Cherniss, Extein, Goleman, & Weissberg, 2006).

These definitional problems can be handled by specifying the aspects of EI to be investigated in a particular study, but the methodological problems extend well beyond these considerations. A popular approach to the measurement of EI has been via self-report measures, such as the Emotional Quotient Inventory (EQ-i:YV; Bar-On & Parker, 2000). There is now considerable evidence that, in terms of domain coverage, self-report measures of EI such as the EQ-i:YV overlap substantially with traditional personality tests (Davies, Stankov, Roberts, 1998; MacCann, Matthews, Zeidner, & Roberts, 2004). In view of these problems, Mayer and colleagues advocated the development of objective, performance-based ability indicators of EI, such as their own Mayer-Salovey-Caruso Emotional Intelligence Test (MSCEIT; Mayer, Salovey, & Caruso, 2000). These two fundamentally different ways of assessing EI led Petrides and Furnham (2001) to propose a conceptual distinction between trait EI and ability EI. In other words, to treat the two as different constructs, the former more closely aligned with personality, the latter with intelligence. Our expectations of the relations between EI and academic achievement and the extent to which EI demonstrates incremental validity in the presence of other ability and personality measures may therefore be shaped by the way in which EI is measured.

Research Linking EI with Academic Success

Despite the problems mentioned in the preceding paragraphs, there is now a reasonable body of research linking EI with performance outcomes, including academic performance. In one of the most comprehensive studies of the incremental validity of EI in academic settings, Barchard (2003) used 31 EI measures, including both trait- and ability-based, along with 12 measures of cognitive ability and 23 personality scales to predict grade point average (GPA) for 154 university students. Barchard found that a selection of the EI measures was able to predict approximately 8% of the variance in academic success. However, EI did not improve predictions of academic success when cognitive abilities and personality characteristics were controlled. Bastian, Burns, and Nettlebeck (2005) also used both self-report and ability-based measures of EI in their study involving 246 university students. They found that neither self-report nor ability EI was related to academic success but that self-report EI was related to life skills, problem solving, and coping.

Petrides, Frederickson, and Furnham (2004) observed that studies of trait EI and academic performance typically fail to find a relationship because trait EI is a personality trait rather than a cognitive ability. They argued that a relationship is more likely to emerge in situations where an individual's emotion-related self-perceptions (trait EI) interact with cognitive ability to influence academic outcomes. In their study of 901 British secondary school students, Petrides et al. found that a trait-based measure of EI acted as a moderator of the relationship between IQ and academic achievement. Specifically, trait EI predicted success in English (not Maths and Science) for less able students but not for the more capable ones. They conjectured that EI may help less able students to cope with the psychological demands of the course.

Parker, Summerfeldt, Hogan, and Majeski (2004) also used a trait-based measure of EI to predict academic performance in a group of high school students moving into university study. They found that the high-performing university students were more likely to have scored highly on the EI dimensions of interpersonal abilities, adaptability, and stress management. In a follow-up study with high school students, Parker and colleagues again reported a relationship between social and emotional competency and academic success (Parker et al., 2004). In noting the limitations of their study, they commented on the need for replication with students from a more diverse range of ethnic backgrounds and across a broader range of school subjects. Both studies alluded to the importance of adaptability and stress management skills, which were captured by the trait EI measure used in their study (EQ-i:YV; Bar-On & Parker, 2000). Neither of these studies looked at the issue of incremental validity.

A recently published study investigating 209 Australian high school students found a positive association between trait EI and academic success (Downey, Mountstephen, Lloyd, Hansen, & Stough, 2008). The trait-based measure of EI used in this study, the Adolescent Swinburne University Emotional Intelligence Test (SUEIT; Luebbers, Downey & Stough, 2007), contained subscales for Emotional Recognition and Expression, Understanding Emotions, Emotions Direct Cognition, and Emotional Management and Control. They found that the Understanding Emotions subscale was associated with the subjects of Art ($r = .34$, $p < .01$) and Geography ($r = .28$, $p < .01$), whereas the Emotional Management and Control subscale was associated with Maths ($r = .24$, $p < .01$) and Science ($r = .15$, $p < .05$). A measure of Total EI was associated with grade point average ($r = .15$, $p < .05$).

Summarising what has been found in the literature to date, it appears that trait EI can predict reliable variance in academic achievement but that the relationship is more likely to emerge in groups where low EI is confounded with poor stress management and coping skills. Ability EI can also predict academic success but is unlikely to demonstrate incremental validity when intelligence is controlled. It is also possible that the relationship between EI and academic success may vary across school subjects, although the findings here are inconsistent. There are few studies of ability EI and academic performance and there are even fewer that have examined the issue of incremental validity.

The current study builds upon this earlier work by examining the relationship between an ability-based measure of EI developed specifically for a school population and by considering the strength of the relationship across different school subjects. Following suggestions by Parker and colleagues that for school students the relationship between EI and academic success may be due to the better coping skills of high EI students, we included measures of problem-focused, avoidant-focused, and emotion-focused coping. Again, these measures were developed to suit the educational context. Our aims were first to assess the strength of the relationship among EI, coping, and academic success measures, and second, to determine whether EI contributed to the prediction of academic success when coping was controlled.

Method

Participants

Participants (383 eighth grade students, 49% female) were recruited from five sites across the United States: Atlanta (Georgia), Chicago (Illinois), Denver (Colorado), Fort Lee (New Jersey), and Los Angeles (California). Participants were aged from 12 years to 15 years with a mean of 13.23 years.

Materials and Measures

1. Emotional Intelligence: The Situational Test of Emotion Management for Children (STEM-C). The STEM-C is a performance-based test of emotional intelligence, involving a downward extension of an adult form of the STEM (MacCann & Roberts, 2008) that is suitable for young adolescents. It employs a 4-option multiple-choice response format wherein respondents indicate their preferred response to 16 different scenarios that describe familiar, but challenging, situations in school life. For example, they may be asked to indicate how they would respond to a classmate cheating in a class assignment. Responses from a panel of 18 experts with a background in psychology and education were used to assign weightings to each of the options in the STEM items. The experts were instructed to rate each of the response options from 1 to 5. The score for each student on this test was the average expert rating their 16 responses attracted. A student who scored highly on the STEM-C therefore selected many options that were also chosen by the panel of experts. The Cronbach alpha internal consistency reliability estimate for this measure of emotional intelligence in the present study was .69.

2. Coping with School Life. This 32-item scale was developed for the purposes of the current project. Students were asked whether they would be likely to use particular coping strategies in response to one of three situations. The three situations dealt with homework (14 items), extracurricula activities (9 items), or preparing for and taking class tests (9 items). The situation was described in some detail, and then the coping strategies were presented below. For example, the homework situation was 'You are feeling stressed about the amount of homework that you have been given by your teacher(s). Below are some ways that you might think, feel, or act in this situation, right at the time that you feel stressed-out. Rate how often you do each activity when you feel stressed'. Coping strategies represented one of three types: (a) emotion-focused coping (12 items), (b) problem-focused coping (9 items), and (c) avoidant-focused coping (11 items). Ratings were given on a 4-point frequency-based scale, from (1) Never or rarely to (4) Usually or always. High subscale scores indicated extensive use of these coping strategies. Cronbach alpha coefficients for these three scales in the present study were .83 (emotion-focused), .88 (problem-focused), and .90 (avoidant-focused).

3. School Grades. Students reported their grades in Language Arts, Mathematics, Science, Social Studies, Art and Music subjects over the previous semester. The grades ranged from A+ to F, which were converted to a numerical rating (A+ = 12 to F = 0) for analysis. As a validation check, the accompanying parent was also asked to record the student's grade. Where parents and students rated their grades differently, the average of their scores was used.

Procedure

The project was approved by human research ethics committees at both the University of Southern Queensland (Australia) and the Educational Testing Service (United States). Parents also completed parts of the test protocol (not relevant to this study) and completed parent-report grades for their child in six subjects for the previous semester. Students were taken to a separate testing room to complete a self-paced, proctored computerised test battery that included self-report grades, and the tests listed above, plus other tests that are not relevant to the aims of this study. The test battery took about 90 minutes to complete.

Results

Pearson product moment correlations were calculated among the EI, coping, and six performance scores. In all cases, the relationship was significant ($p < .05$): Language ($r = .18$), Maths ($r = .22$), Science ($r = .17$), Social Studies ($r = .23$), Art ($r = .16$), and Music ($r = .23$). The lack of evidence for differential relations across subject areas led us to continue the analyses with a single measure of academic performance. An overall grade variable was created by taking the first principal component of both parent and student self-report grades in Language, Maths, Science, and Social Studies, which were the four subjects completed by all students. Correlations among the variables are shown in Table 7.1.

From Table 7.1, it can be seen that EI was related to school performance. EI was also related to all three coping measures, most strongly with problem-focused coping. To determine whether EI made any contribution to the prediction of academic performance when coping measures were controlled, a hierarchical regression analysis was conducted with the three coping measures entered at Step 1 and EI at Step 2. The results indicated that the coping measures predicted 21.4% of the variance in school performance at Step 1, $F(3, 379) = 33.63$, $p < .05$. The addition of EI at Step 2 resulted in an increase in R^2 of 1.2%, which represented a marginally significant increment, $F\Delta$ (1, 378) = 5.78, $p < .05$. On its own, EI accounted for 7.3% of the variance in academic performance.

Discussion

These results demonstrate that there is a relationship between ability EI and school performance across all school subject areas. The short, adolescent-specific STEM-C used in the present study captured an equivalent amount of variance to the 8% reported by Barchard for a weighted combination of six EI measures (including the MSCEIT). Our results also demonstrate that an ability EI measure is related to coping, especially problem-focused coping. The relationship between trait EI and coping is well known (e.g., Petrides et al., 2004). It is interesting to see that the relationship also holds with context-specific measures of ability EI.

Other researchers have noted that the contribution of ability EI to academic performance disappears when cognitive ability is controlled (e.g., Barchard, 2003) and it is certainly known that the contribution of trait EI to academic performance can vanish when personality and coping skills are controlled, but this is the first indication that measures of coping resources can also absorb most of the variance in academic performance contributed by ability EI. This is an interesting finding that adds to the mounting evidence linking EI with coping as an explanatory variable for observed improvements in performance. A strong argument can therefore

Table 7.1

Correlations Among EI, Coping, and School Performance Variables*

Variables	(1)	(2)	(3)	(4)
1. EI				
2. Emotion-coping	–.15			
3. Problem-coping	.33	.08		
4. Avoid-coping	–.11	.36	.15	
5. School performance	.27	–.08	.40	–.16

Note: *N = 383; correlations in bold are significant at .05 level.

be made that individuals with high EI employ more adaptive coping strategies in stressful or challenging situations resulting in success in school performance. The finding also suggests that trait EI and ability EI may not be as conceptually distinct as some researchers (Petrides & Furnham, 2001) have suggested, in that they are both clearly linked with problem-focused coping.

Limitations

Although the current study sought to minimise problems associated with self-report measures, a number of possible limitations to the study must be acknowledged. Participants were asked to recall their grades in all subjects. Although possible fake-scoring by students was addressed by also asking for parents to provide grades for their child, it was not possible to check reports against school records. A second limitation concerns the universal problem of developing a scoring key for the situational judgement test that formed the basis of the ability EI measure in this study. We used a panel of 18 experts but some of these experts commented on the difficulty of rating the appropriateness of response options to some of the written scenarios without actually being in the situation. The modest internal consistency reliability coefficient (.69) for the EI measure perhaps reflects this difficulty.

In conclusion, educators and professionals working in the field of education could certainly benefit from further research aimed at assessing the nature of the relationship between EI and constructs such as coping skills. Whether EI interacts with coping skills to influence school performance, as suggested by Petrides et al. (2004), or whether they contribute both common and unique elements to academic performance needs to be ascertained. If coping skills are more important immediate performance shaping factors, as suggested by the present research, the pathway to better academic performance is perhaps a little clearer in that we have more experience teaching coping skills than we do at improving EI.

Author Note

The views expressed are those of the authors and do not represent the views of any of the authors' institutional affiliations.

References

Australian Bureau of Statistics, (2008). *Australian social trends, 2008.* Retrieved December 11, 2008 from http://www.abs.gov.au/AUSSTATS/abs@.nsf/Lookup/4102.0Chapter6002008

Barchard, K.A. (2003). Does emotional intelligence assist in the prediction of academic success? *Educational and Psychological Measurement, 63,* 840-858.

Bar-On, R., & Parker, J.D.A. (2000). *The Bar-On EQ-i:YV: Technical manual.* Toronto, Canada: Multi-Health Systems.

Bastian, V.A., Burns, N.R., & Nettelbeck, T. (2005). Emotional intelligence predicts life skills, but not as well as personality and cognitive abilities. *Personality and Individual Differences, 39,* 1135–1145.

Cherniss, C., Extein, M., Goleman, D., & Weissberg, R.P. (2006). Emotional intelligence: What does the research really indicate? *Educational Psychologist, 41,* 239–245.

Davies, M., Stankov, L., & Roberts, R.D. (1998). Emotional intelligence: In search of an elusive construct. *Journal of Personality and Social Psychology, 75,* 989–1015.

Downey, L.A., Mountstephen, J., Lloyd, J., Hansen, K., & Stough, C. (2008). Emotional intelligence and scholastic achievement in Australian adolescents. *Australian Journal of Psychology, 60,* 10–17.

Goleman, D. (1995). *Emotional intelligence: Why it can matter more than IQ.* London: Bloomsbury Publishing.

Hunt, E. (1995). *Will we be smart enough? A cognitive analysis of the coming workforce.* New York: Russell Sage Foundation.

Luebbers, S., Downey, L.A., & Stough, C. (2007). The development of an adolescent measure of EI. *Personality and Individual Differences, 42,* 999 – 1009.

MacCann, C., Matthews, G., Zeidner, M., & Roberts, R.D. (2003). Psychological assessment of emotional intelligence: A review of self-report and performance-based testing. *The International Journal of Organisational Analysis, 11,* 247–274.

MacCann, C., & Roberts, R.D. (2008). New paradigms for assessing emotional intelligence: Theory and data. *Emotion, 8,* 540–551.

Matthews, G., Roberts, R.D., & Zeidner, M. (2003). Development of emotional intelligence: A skeptical — but not dismissive — perspective. *Human Development, 46,* 109–114.

Mayer, J.D., & Salovey, P. (1997). What is emotional intelligence? In P. Salovey & D. Sluyter (Eds.). *Emotional development and emotional intelligence: Implication for educators* (pp. 3–31). New York: Basic Books.

Mayer, J.D., Salovey, P., & Caruso, D.R. (2000). *Mayer-Salovey-Caruso Emotional Intelligence Test (MSCEIT) user's manual.* Toronto, Canada: Multi-Health Systems Publishers.

Parker, J.D.A., Creque Sr, R.E., Barnhart, D.L., Irons Harris, J., Majeski, S.A., Wood, L.M. et al. (2004). Academic achievement in high school: Does emotional intelligence matter? *Personality and Individual Differences, 37,* 1321–1330.

Parker, J.D.A., Summerfeldt, L.J., Hogan, M.J., & Majeski, S. (2004). Emotional intelligence and academic success: Examining the transition from high school to university. *Personality and Individual Differences, 36,* 163–172.

Petrides, K.V., & Furnham, A. (2001). Trait emotional intelligence: psychometric investigation with reference to established trait taxonomies. *European Journal of Personality, 15,* 425–448.

Petrides, K.V., Fredereickson, N., & Furnham, A. (2004). The role of trait emotional intelligence in academic performance and deviant behavior at school. *Personality and Individual Differences, 36,* 277–293.

Steering Committee for the Review of Government Service Provision (SCRGSP). (2007). *Report on Government Services, Productivity Commission.* Canberra, Australia: Author.

Weale, M. (2007). Following the Atkinson Review: The quality of public sector output. *Economic and Labour Market Review, 1*(7), 22–26.

Zeidner, M., Matthews, G., & Roberts, R.D. (2006). Emotional intelligence, adaptation, and coping. In J.F.J. Ciarrochi & J.D. Mayer (Ed.), *Emotional intelligence in everyday life: A scientific inquiry* (2nd ed.). Philadelphia, PA: Psychology Press.

Zeidner, M., Roberts, R.D., & Matthews, G. (2002). Can emotional intelligence be schooled? A critical review. *Educational Psychologist, 37,* 215–231.

Do Time Management, Grit, and Self-Control Relate to Academic Achievement Independently of Conscientiousness?

Carolyn MacCann and Richard D. Roberts

Recent meta-analyses suggest Conscientiousness is a ubiquitous predictor of academic achievement. This study (N = 291 high school students) tests three new 'academic readiness' constructs (Time Management, Grit, and Self-Control) against a comprehensive model of Conscientiousness. Correlational analyses suggest that these measures could feasibly be considered subcomponents of Conscientiousness. Thus, relationships of Time Management, Grit, and Self-Control to students' grades, teacher ratings, examination percentiles, and gaining a place on the honor roll were entirely mediated by Conscientiousness. However, the Time Management component of Meeting Deadlines related to student absenteeism and disciplinary infractions independently of Conscientiousness. Similarly, Self-Control independently predicted student wellbeing measures of life satisfaction, depression, anxiety, and stress after accounting for Conscientiousness. Results are discussed in term of the potential integration of academic readiness constructs into personality models.

The single best predictor of school grades and other academic outcomes is clearly students' cognitive ability (e.g., Neisser et al., 1996). However, noncognitive constructs such as Conscientiousness, Time Management, Grit, and Self-Control have demonstrated relationships with academic achievement (e.g., Duckworth & Seligman, 2006; Liu, Rijmen, MacCann, & Roberts, 2009; Poropat, 2009; Tangney, Baumeister & Boone, 2004). Of these four noncognitive constructs, the most comprehensively studied is Conscientiousness. A recent meta-analysis reported that Conscientiousness correlates at .23 with college grades, and .21 with high school grades, with these relationships holding after accounting for cognitive ability (Poropat, 2009).

Definitions of Conscientiousness commonly include tendencies to be attentive, hard-working, detail-minded, reliable, and obedient, although different personality models focus on different aspects of the construct. MacCann, Duckworth, and Roberts (2009) developed an 8-facet model of Conscientiousness by empirically integrating results from 12 different models of personality. Briefly, these facets are: *Industriousness* (good work ethic, being effortful, working hard); *Perfectionism* (being competitive, seeking perfection in one's work); *Tidiness* (organisation of one's possessions); *Proactivity* (tendency to begin work straight away, rather than procrastinate); *Control* (control of impulses and rash behaviors); *Cautiousness* (careful consideration and deliberativeness); *Task Planning* (organisation of time, tasks, and workflow); and *Perseverance* (tendency to keep going in spite of obstacles). The present study considers this 8-facet model of Conscientiousness, as well as an overall global measure of Conscientiousness, derived from the Big Five Inventory (BFI; Benet-Martínez & John, 1998).

The three academic readiness constructs of Time Management, Grit, and Self-Control show strong theoretical overlap with Conscientiousness, and particularly some of the underlying facets of Conscientiousness. For instance, Time Management is defined as an awareness of time and deadlines, the tendency to use organisational aids such as lists and electronic reminders to manage time, the propensity to organise time and tasks, and to plan tasks within a timeframe (Liu et al., 2009). As such, Time Management seems conceptually related to Conscientiousness facets representing organisation of possessions and tasks (Tidiness and Task Planning). Similarly, Grit represents attitudes towards long-term goals, including the consistency of goals over time and the degree of perseverance in pursuing these goals (Duckworth & Seligman, 2006). As such, grit seems conceptually related to the Perseverance facet of Conscientiousness. Finally, Self-Control is the intentional inhibition of normal, typical, or desired behavior to delay gratification and to maximise long-term benefits (Tangney et al., 2004). As such, Self-Control would seem to relate to the Control facet of Conscientiousness. Each of these postulated relationships will be empirically tested in the current study.

If these three constructs are found to show a strong degree of relationship to Conscientiousness, a corollary is that any associations of

Time Management, Grit, or Self-Control with academic achievement may be due to Conscientiousness. To test this idea, the relationship of Time Management, Grit, and Self-Control to academic outcomes will be calculated both before and after controlling for the eight facets of Conscientiousness. The criterion space for academic outcomes is conceptualised as more than grades or test scores, in line with recent suggestions that both cognitive and noncognitive components play a key role in school, workplace, and life success (Camara, 2005; Kyllonen, Lipnevich, Burrus, & Roberts, 2009). Although grades and test scores are obviously important, we additionally consider students' wellbeing (life satisfaction, and levels of state anxiety, depression, and stress), teacher ratings of students' classroom behaviours, as well as behavioral indexes of academic outcomes (absenteeism, breaking rules, and the attainment of high academic honours).

Hypotheses

There are three hypotheses in this study. First, Time Management, Grit, and Self-Control will show substantial overlap with the facets of Conscientiousness. Second, Time Management, Grit, and Self-Control will significantly relate to academic outcomes such as school grades, teacher ratings, examination percentiles, disciplinary infractions, and absenteeism before controlling for Conscientiousness. After Conscientiousness is controlled, these relationships will no longer be significant. Third, Time Management, Grit, and Self-Control will significantly relate to life satisfaction, depression, anxiety, and stress before controlling for Conscientiousness. After Conscientiousness is controlled, these relationships will no longer be significant.

Method

Sample

Participants (N = 291, 58% female) were in Grades 9 (n = 52), 10 (n = 82), 11 (n = 75) and 12 (n = 82) in a large private high school on the east coast of the United States. Age ranged from 13 to 19 years (M = 16.35, SD = 1.23).

Test Battery

1. *Conscientiousness* (MacCann et al., 2009). This 8-factor scale has 68 items, drawn from the IPIP, and rated on a 5-point scale from *Not at all like me* (1) to *Very much like me* (5).

2. *The Big Five Inventory* (BFI; Benet-Martínez & John, 1998). Each of the big five personality factors (Extraversion, Agreeableness, Conscientiousness, Neuroticism, and Openness to Experience) were assessed with 8 to 10 items, where test-takers rated their agreement with 44 items on a 5-point scale from *Disagree strongly* (1) to *Agree strongly* (5).

3. *Students' Life Satisfaction Scale* (Huebner, 1991). Students responded to 7 items indicating their satisfaction with life on a 6-point scale from *Strongly disagree* (1) to *Strongly agree* (6).

4. *Depression Anxiety Stress Scale* (DASS-21; Lovibond & Lovibond, 1995). Students responded to 21 items asking for the frequency of clinical symptoms of depression (7 items), anxiety (7 items) and stress (7 items) over the last 2-week period. Items were rated on a 0–3 scale from *Did not apply to me at all* (0) to *Applied to me very much or most of the time* (3).

5. *Grit* (Duckworth et al., 2007). Students responded to 12 items on a 5-point scale, from *Not at all like me* (1) to *Very much like me* (5). Six items assessed consistency of interests, and 6 items assessed perseverance of effort.

6. *Time Management* (e.g., Schulze, Roberts, Krause et al., 2009). In this 37-item assessment, students rate the frequency with which they engage in time management behaviors on a 5-point scale, from *Never* (1) to *Almost always* (5). The four subscales are Meeting Deadlines (9 items), Using Organisational Aids (9 items), Organisation (10 items), and Planning (9 items)

7. *Brief Self-Control Scale* (Tangney et al., 2004). Students responded to 13 items rating their self-control on a 5-point scale, bounded by *Not at all like me* (1) to *Exactly true* (4).

8. Teacher ratings of students' social behaviors. For each student, one teacher rated 13 items assessing the student's positive classroom behaviours (e.g., 'Communicates well', 'Behaves in an open and friendly manner') on the following five-point scale: *Below average* (1), *Average* (2), *Above average* (3), *Outstanding* (4), and *Truly exceptional* (5).

Procedure

Students were emailed a link to a computerised assessment battery, which they accessed in their own time. Students' Secondary School Admission Test percentiles (SSATs), grade point average (GPA), status as 'high honors' students, absences from class, and recorded disciplinary infractions were obtained from school records. A teacher of each student test-taker completed a brief 13-item other-report survey on the student (each teacher rated from 1 to 7 students). All tests and protocols were approved under the Educational Testing Service human subjects review committee and fairness review process.

Results
Reliability and Descriptive Statistic for Conscientiousness Scales and Criterion Variables

Reliability and descriptive statistics for all continuous variables are shown in Table 8.1. Reliability was acceptable for all scales, ranging from .74 (Anxiety) to .95 (teacher-ratings). SSAT percentiles averaged 85, compared to a national median of 50, indicating that this sample is well above average for academic achievement.

Table 8.1
Reliability and Descriptive Statistics

Measure	N	α	Mean	SD
Conscientiousness: Industriousness	291	.91	3.87	0.76
Conscientiousness: Perfectionism	291	.85	3.53	0.73
Conscientiousness: Tidiness	291	.88	3.39	0.84
Conscientiousness: Proactivity	291	.81	2.95	0.82
Conscientiousness: Control	291	.80	3.30	0.71
Conscientiousness: Cautiousness	291	.80	3.71	0.64
Conscientiousness: Task planning	291	.89	3.37	0.76
Conscientiousness: Perseverance	291	.83	3.74	0.65
BFI Conscientiousness	277	.84	3.56	.67
Teacher ratings	175	.95	4.03	.78
GPA	275		3.19	.53
SSAT percentiles	273		85.74	14.03
Life satisfaction	272	.90	4.49	1.06
DASS depression	272	.90	0.68	0.70
DASS anxiety	272	.74	0.55	0.50
DASS stress	272	.82	0.89	0.57
Time management (Meets deadlines)	276	.83	4.26	0.59
Time management (Uses aids)	276	.84	3.29	0.84
Time management (Organisation)	276	.90	3.38	0.82
Time management (Planning)	276	.81	3.45	0.64
Grit (Consistency)	271	.81	3.18	0.71
Grit (Perseverance)	271	.80	4.32	0.81
Self-control	274	.87	2.67	0.72

Relationships of Time Management, Grit, and Self-Control
to Conscientiousness Facets

Correlations of academic readiness scales with Conscientiousness facets are given in Table 8.2. All academic readiness scales correlate significantly with broad Conscientiousness. Correlations with broad Conscientiousness were particularly high for Grit-Perseverance and for Self-Control ($r = .85$ and $.81$ after correcting for reliability). Some academic readiness scales also correlated very highly with the Conscientiousness facets, with correlations approaching unity after correction for attenuation; for example: Time Management–Organisation and Conscientiousness–Tidiness ($r = .99$); Self-Control and Conscientiousness Control ($r = .85$); Time Management–Planning and Conscientiousness–Task Planning ($r = .80$); and Grit-Perseverance with both Conscientiousness–Industriousness and Conscientiousness–Perseverance ($r = .81$ and $.74$).

Relationship of Time Management, Grit, and Self-Control to Academic Outcomes

Table 8.3 shows the correlations of Time Management, Grit, and Self-Control with the continuous academic outcomes (teacher ratings, grade point average, SSAT percentiles, life satisfaction, depression, anxiety, and stress). All academic readiness scales but Time–Management–Organisation related significantly to life satisfaction and depression, and none related significantly to SSAT percentiles. Although Self-Control and

Table 8.2

Correlations of Time Management, Grit, and Self-Control with Conscientiousness Facets and BFI Conscientiousness

	Time management				Grit		Self-control
	Deadlines	Uses aids	Organise	Plan	Consistency	Perseverance	
BFI C	.52**	.31**	.57**	.54**	.46**	.70**	.69**
Industriousness	.46**	.33**	.37**	.47**	.30**	.66**	.58**
Perfectionism	.23**	.19**	.20**	.37**	.05	.46**	.21**
Tidiness	.27**	.44**	.86**	.42**	.10	.27**	.34**
Proactivity	.48**	.18**	.42**	.40**	.47**	.59**	.71**
Control	.38**	.12*	.32**	.29**	.33**	.29**	.52**
Cautiousness	.30**	.32**	.33**	.51**	.19**	.49**	.45**
Task planning	.41**	.51**	.53**	.68**	.25**	.59**	.46**
Perseverance	.44**	.08	.31**	.35**	.58**	.63**	.58**

Note: *$p < .05$, **$p < .01$.

Table 8.3

Correlations Between Academic Readiness Constructs and Academic Outcomes

| | Zero-order correlations | | | | | | | Partial correlations (Controlling Conscientiousness facets) | | | | | | |
| | Time management | | | | Grit | | Self-control | Time management | | | | Grit | | Self-control |
	MD	Aids	Org	Plan	Cons	Pers	Self-control	MD	Aids	Org	Plan	Cons	Pers	Self-control
TRate	.22**	.15	.19*	.17*	.16	.23**	.32**	.04	.04	-.01	.01	.05	.03	.09
GPA	.15	.07	.17*	.22**	.12	.15	.26**	.00	-.09	-.02	.13	.09	.00	.15
SSAT	.10	-.06	-.07	-.01	.00	.10	.03	.10	.02	.06	-.02	-.04	.00	-.05
LSat	.18*	.17*	.13	.24**	.19*	.48**	.39**	-.04	.06	.03	.08	-.08	.28**	.23**
Depression	-.18*	-.18*	-.14	-.21*	-.19*	-.34**	-.43**	.04	-.09	.06	-.03	.03	-.12	-.27**
Anxiety	-.05	.03	.02	-.01	-.24*	-.16	-.32**	.12	-.02	.03	.02	.00	.00	-.23**
Stress	.00	.05	.02	.09	-.27**	-.13	-.28**	.11	-.01	.05	.10	-.08	-.12	-.28**

Note: Partial correlations controlling for the facets of conscientiousness are shown in parentheses.
TRate = Teacher ratings, LSat = Life Satisfaction, MD = Meeting Deadlines, Aids = Uses Organisational Aids, Org = Organisation, Plan = Planning,
Cons = Consistency, Pers = Perseverance
*p < .05, **p < .01

two dimensions of Time Management related significantly to GPA, these relationships were not significant after Conscientiousness-facets were controlled (not surprisingly, given the strong relationships between some of the Conscientiousness-facets and academic readiness scales). The only scales to show incremental validity were Grit–Perseverance (which related to life satisfaction) and Self-Control (which related significantly to life satisfaction, depression, anxiety, and stress). These significant correlations were recalculated after additionally controlling for the five BFI dimensions, to account for the role of Neuroticism, Openness, Extraversion, and Agreeableness. All but the relationship with Self-Control and life satisfaction remained significant.

The mean difference on Time Management, Grit, and Self-Control scores was calculated for students who had recorded absences, disciplinary infractions, or a place on the honour role compared to students who did not (using an ANOVA procedure to evaluate the significance of these differences). Marginal means controlling for the eight facets of Conscientiousness were also calculated using an ANCOVA procedure. Effect sizes and significance levels for these analyses are shown in Table 8.4. All scales except for the Uses Organisation Aids component of Time Management were significantly related to Absences. Grit-Perseverance and Self-Control were significantly related to obtaining a place on the honour roll, and Meeting Deadlines, Using Organisational Aids, Grit–Perseverance, and Self-Control were significantly related to disciplinary infractions. However, after controlling for the eight facets of Conscientiousness, only Time Management showed any relationship to the three outcomes: Meeting Deadlines related significantly to absences and disciplinary infractions, and Organisation related significantly to absences. After additionally controlling for the BFI dimensions, the relationship of Meeting Deadlines with absenteeism and discipline remained significant, but the relationship between Organisation and absenteeism was no longer significant.

Discussion

There was clearly a large degree of overlap between the academic readiness variables and the facets of Conscientiousness, particularly for Grit and for the Organisation and Planning components of Time Management. This degree of overlap suggests that such academic readiness dimensions might be conceptualised as underlying facets of Conscientiousness (indeed, the Time–Management–Organisation is clearly equivalent to the Conscientiousness–facet of Tidiness). However,

Table 8.4

Effect Size of Mean Differences in Academic Readiness Constructs for Students with or without Recorded Absences, Academic Honours, and Disciplinary Infractions[a]

	Mean difference (d0)			Marginal mean difference (dC) (Controlling conscientiousness facets)		
	Absences	Honour roll	Disciplinary infractions	Absences	Honour roll	Disciplinary infractions
	($n1 = 80$, $n2 = 196$)	($n1 = 119$, $n2 = 157$)	($n1 = 68$, $n2 = 208$)	($n1 = 80$, $n2 = 196$)	($n1 = 119$, $n2 = 157$)	($n1 = 68$, $n2 = 208$)
Time management						
Deadlines	−0.93**	0.16	−0.60**	−0.58**	−0.11	−0.34**
Use aids	−0.10	0.05	−0.32*	0.11	−0.11	−0.18
Organise	−0.35**	0.08	−0.23	−0.15*	−0.04	−0.03
Plan	−0.35*	0.16	−0.17	−0.00	−0.12	0.07
Grit						
Consistency	−0.57**	0.17	−0.18	−0.18	−0.08	0.05
Perseverance	−0.85**	0.58**	−0.37*	−0.10	0.06	−0.02
Self-control						
Self-control	−0.66**	0.36**	−0.43**	−0.10	0.03	−0.05

Note: [a] $d = (M1–M2)/SD$
*$p < .05$, **$p < .01$

Time Management's 'Meeting Deadlines', Self-Control, and Grit's 'Perseverance' related to some of the outcomes independently of personality, suggesting that these constructs' utility is not wholly derived from their overlap with Conscientiousness or other personality traits.

None of the academic readiness measures were incrementally related to traditional measures of scholastic achievement (i.e., grades, test performance, teacher-ratings, making the 'honor roll'). However, the Time Management's 'Meeting Deadlines' incrementally predicted deviant behavior (i.e., unexplained absences, breaking school rules), both Grit–Perseverance and Self-Control incrementally predicted life satisfaction, and Self-Control also incrementally predicted students' anxiety and stress. Given that wellbeing and absenteeism relate to college attrition, college exam performance, job turn-over and other important consequences, understanding the correlates of these variables is important for both identification of 'at risk' students and the development of remediation programs (e.g., Marburger, 2001; Mitra, Jenkins, & Gupta, 1992).

The nature of Meeting Deadlines, Grit–Perseverance, and Self-Control may inform intervention development for programs aimed at lowering truancy, behavior problems, or student wellbeing. For instance, Meeting Deadlines relates to an awareness of time and deadlines, including an instrumental attitudinal component (considering that completing tasks to time is important). As such, attitude change regarding awareness of deadlines may be a key component for intervention programs targeting truancy and behavioral problems. The relative independence of Meeting Deadlines from personality further implies that Meeting Deadlines may be changeable, since individual differences in personality are conceptualised as stable or fixed over time (McCrae et al., 2000). Similarly, Grit–Perseverance is conceptualised as an attitude towards goal attainment, such that attitude change procedures could conceivable be used as the basis for intervention development. Self-Control in conceptualised as an intentional behavior, and since attitudes are a strong causal factor in the development of behavioral intentions (Ajzen, 2002; Armitage & Conner, 2001) attitude change procedures may also prove useful in this instance.

Limitations and Future Directions

An important future direction for this study would be to replicate results on diverse samples. The current sample was likely to be range-restricted on ability (as implied by the well-above-average SSAT scores), which may have attenuated correlations with achievement. In addition, cognitive ability was not controlled for in the current study, such that incremental validity estimates for the Conscientiousness facets were not available. One further concern was that participants were administered the Conscientiousness items for facet scales as a block (rather than inter-mixed with items of other personality dimensions). Conceivably, this may have affected results through context effects.

Findings illustrate the importance of considering personality at the facet level rather than as broad over-arching dimensions, of considering the criterion space for desirable behaviors and outcomes beyond grade-point-average, and of integrating research paradigms from educational psychology and positive psychology into the personality domain. The nature of Meeting Deadlines, Grit–Perseverance, and Self-Control (the components showing evidence of incremental validity) suggest that attitude change programs may be a useful avenue for interventions targeting truancy, behavior problems, and student wellbeing.

References

Ajzen, I. (2002). Perceived behavioral control, self-efficacy, locus of control, and the theory of planned behavior. *Journal of Applied Social Psychology, 32*, 665–683.

Armitage, C., & Conner, M. (2001). Efficacy of the theory of planned behaviour: A meta-analytic review. *British Journal of Social Psychology, 40*, 471–499.

Benet-Martínez, V., & John, O.P. (1998). Los Cinco Grandes across cultures and ethnic groups: Multitrait multimethod analyses of the Big Five in Spanish and English. *Journal of Personality and Social Psychology, 75*, 729–750.

Camara, W.J. (2005). Broadening criteria of college success and the impact of cognitive predictors. In W.J. Camara & E.W. Kimmel (Eds.), *Choosing students: Higher education admissions tools for the 21st Century* (pp. 53–80). Mahwah, NJ: Lawrence Erlbaum.

Duckworth, A.L., & Seligman, M.E.P. (2006). Self-discipline gives girls the edge: Gender in self-discipline, grades, and achievement test scores. *Journal of Educational Psychology, 98*, 198–208

Huebner, E.S. (1991). Initial development of the Student's Life Satisfaction Scale. *School Psychology International, 12*, 231–240.

Kyllonen, P.C., Lipnevich, A.A., Burrus, J., & Roberts, R.D. (2009). *Personality, motivation, and college readiness: A prospectus for assessment and development* (Educational Testing Service Research Report No: RR-09-xx). Princeton, NJ: Educational Testing Service.

Liu, O.L., Rijmen, F., MacCann, C., & Roberts, R.D. (2009). The assessment of time management in middle school students. *Personality and Individual Differences, 47*, 174–179.

Lovibond, P.F., & Lovibond, S.H. (1995). The structure of negative emotional states: Comparison of the Depression Anxiety Stress Scales (DASS) with the Beck Depression and Anxiety Inventories. *Behaviour Research and Therapy, 33*, 335–343.

MacCann, C., Duckworth, A.L., & Roberts, R.D. (2009). Empirical identification of the major facets of Conscientiousness. *Learning and Individual Differences, 19*, 451–458.

Marburger, D.R. 2001. Absenteeism and undergraduate exam performance. *Journal of Economic Education, 32*, 99–109.

McCrae, R.R., Costa, P.T., Hrebíčková, M., Ostendorf, F., Angleitner, A., Avia, M.D. et al. (2000). Nature over nurture: Temperament, personality, and life span development, *Journal of Personality and Social Psychology, 78*, 173–186.

Mitra, A., Jenkins, G.D., & Gupta, N. (1992) A meta-analytic examination of the relationship between absence and turnover. *Journal of Applied Psychology, 77*, 879–889.

Neisser, U., Boodoo, G., Bouchard, T.J., Boykin, A.W., Brody, N., Ceci, S.J. et al. (1996). Intelligence: Knowns and unknowns. *American Psychologist, 51*, 77–101.

Noftle, E.E., & Robins, R.W. (2007). Personality predictors of academic outcomes: Big Five correlates of GPA and SAT scores. *Journal of Personality and Social Psychology, 93,* 116–130.

Poropat, A. (2009). A meta-analysis of the five-factor model of personality and academic performance. *Psychological Bulletin, 125,* 322–338.

Schulze, R., Roberts, R.D., Krause, H., Lee, S-K., Covic, T., Pallier, G. et al. (Manuscript in preparation). *On the dimensional structure and psychological correlates of time management.*

Soto, C.J., John, O.P., Gosling, S.D., & Potter, J. (2008). The developmental psycho-metrics of big five self-reports: Acquiescence, factor structure, coherence, and differentiation from ages 10 to 20. *Journal of Personality and Social Psychology, 94,* 718–737.

Tangney, J.P., Baumeister, R.F., & Boone, A.L. (2004). High self-control predicts good adjustment, less pathology, better grades, and interpersonal success. *Journal of Personality, 72,* 271–322.

Zins, J.E., & Elias, M.E. (2006). Social and emotional learning. In G.G. Bear & K.M. Minke (Eds.), *Children's needs III* (pp. 1–13). National Association of School Psychologists.

Is Low Emotional Intelligence a Primary Causal Factor in Drug and Alcohol Addiction?

Elise Brown, Edmond Chiu, Lloyd Neill, Juliet Tobin, and John Reid

This study was conducted with the cooperation of 103 residents in a residential drug and alcohol rehabilitation program to confirm Goleman's (1995) assertion that low emotional intelligence (EI) was a major causal factor in drug and alcohol addiction. A range of measures including EI, level of psychological distress, and the Big Five factors of personality were administered to the participants and compared against the criterion of an individual's recovery. The study also used a repeated measures design where the participants were surveyed again 1 month later. It was found that participants improved significantly in EI scores and experienced a significant reduction in psychological distress during the additional month in the rehabilitation program. It was also found that EI scores were significantly related to addiction levels, but this was fully mediated by the psychological distress variable.

Emotional intelligence (EI) has been proposed as the basis for success in life because it underpins a wide range of adaptive behaviour in humans. Low EI on the other hand is said to be associated with personal and social problems at home and at work (Goleman, 1995). Individuals with low EI have difficulty managing their emotions and delaying gratification and are thus believed to be vulnerable to alcohol and substance abuse (Goleman, 1995; Riley & Schutte, 2003). But is EI the root causal factor behind addictive behaviour? If low EI is the root cause of addiction it has been suggested that EI coaching interventions could potentially remove the reliance on alcohol and other substances, thus improving the quality of life of the individual and society overall (Goleman, 1995).

Many individuals suffering from addiction will incur serious lifelong health consequences and a substandard quality of life as they attempt to self-medicate using alcohol and other substances to obtain respite from their problems (Hser, Hoffman, Grella, & Anglin, 2001). Unfortunately, hospitalisation and detoxification is only partially successful, with only 3% of admissions successfully abstaining for a full year after treatment. Further, less than 40% of alcohol and heroin addicts report a stable pattern of abstinence 12 years after treatment (Vaillant, 1988). Addiction problems are costly for society as they lead to health problems, personal relationship breakdown, criminal behaviour, incarceration, unemployment, and high mortality rates (Hser et al., 2001). In the light of the serious personal costs and cost to society overall it is worthwhile to investigate Goleman's (1995) claim that EI may be the key to alleviating much of the suffering and cost to society.

The present study investigated the personality and EI characteristics of over 100 individuals in a live-in, residential program for drug and alcohol addiction rehabilitation. The study investigated the relationship between measures of recovery in the program and a range of psychological constructs.

Emotional Intelligence and Addiction

The connection that Goleman (1995) described between addiction and EI was compelling, but based mainly upon anecdotal evidence rather than peer-reviewed research. However, EI research conducted since 1995 has produced findings that support Goleman's assertion. Schutte et al. (1998) found that addicts had significantly lower EI scores than a sample of psychotherapists. EI was also found to be inversely related to alcohol and tobacco use (Austin, Saklofske, & Egan, 2005; Brackett & Mayer, 2003), indicating that low EI scores were associated with excessive alcohol consumption and drug use.

These studies suggest that low EI may be at the root of substance abuse problems (Austin et al., 2005; Riley & Schutte, 2003). However, most of these studies, with the exception of Bracket and Mayer (2003), did not control for other variables such as psychological distress and personality. To clearly demonstrate the causal relationship between level of addiction and EI requires investigating beyond the univariate relationships between these measures (Riley & Schutte, 2003).

The Self-Medication Hypothesis

One of the current theories regarding addiction is the use of substances to self-medicate or soothe negative feelings such as anger, loneliness and depression (Goleman, 1995). Sometime during their formative years, addicts find that certain drugs or chemicals relieved their anxiety and depression, thus leading to a lifelong habit of self-medication. The Self-Medication Hypothesis (SMH) proposes that addiction is more than a simple pleasure seeking activity, but a way of reducing aversive emotional states through the use of drugs and alcohol (Khantzian, 1997). The SMH hypothesis is supported by a considerable body of research (e.g., Aharonovich, Nguyen, & Nunes, 2001; Harris & Edlund, 2005) and thus provides a suitable theoretical grounding for this study.

Emotional Intelligence and Self-Medication

The SMH proposes that self-medication is used by individuals to reduce psychological distress arising from an inability to regulate and positively direct emotions (Khantzian, 1997). The ability to perceive, understand and manage emotions is the basis of the emotional intelligence (EI) theories (Bar-On, 2005; Petrides & Furnham, 2001). Thus, deficits in EI may lead to psychological distress, which finally manifest as addictive behaviour. High EI is generally associated with adaptive coping and positive mood (Schutte, Malouff, Simunek, McKenley, & Hollander, 2002) thus it is useful to explore whether high EI precedes psychological distress, and in turn, addictive behaviour.

Studies into the antecedents of addictive behaviour have found that negative emotional states often lead to relapse, while a lack of emotional coping skills have also been shown to precede addictive behaviour (Connors, Longabaugh, & Miller, 1996). Thus, this study will explore the hypothesis that low EI leads to psychological distress, and thus to addictive behaviour.

Study Overview

This study will first determine whether EI is lower, and psychological distress scores are higher in participants in a drug rehabilitation program when compared with the general population. This study will also test the hypothesis that low EI is the primary cause of addictive behaviour and also explore the relationship with psychological distress. Finally, the study will use repeated measures to examine whether EI and psychological distress scores changed significantly after 4 weeks in the rehabilitation program.

Hypotheses

Hypothesis 1. Participants in an addictions rehabilitation program will score lower on a measure of EI than members of the general population.

Hypothesis 2. Participants in an addictions rehabilitation program will score higher on a measure of Psychological Distress than members of the general population.

Hypothesis 3. EI will be significantly related to the behavioural measure of recovery (staff rating) even after controlling for psychological distress.

Hypothesis 4. Participants of an addictions rehabilitation program will score higher on a measure of EI and lower on a measure of psychological distress after four weeks of rehabilitation.

Method

Participants

The sample of 103 participants from a residential rehabilitation program consisted of 90 males and 13 females with ages ranging from 19 to 73 years ($M = 34.03$, $SD = 10.62$). The primary drugs of addiction were reported as alcohol (48%), amphetamines (23%), cannabis (11%), heroin (10%), with cocaine and 'other' making up the balance. The participants were offered a $10 shopping voucher as an incentive to complete the survey.

Biographical details. The participants' date of birth, gender, week in program, and primary addiction were collected.

Trait Emotional Intelligence Questionnaire. The Trait Emotional Intelligence Questionnaire — Short Form (TEIQue-SF) was used to measure EI (Petrides & Furnham, 2003).

Psychological Distress Scale. The Kessler-10 (K10) is a short, 10-question, self-report scale that measures psychological distress over the previous 4-weeks (Kessler et al., 2002).

Personality Questionnaire. Saucier's mini markers (1994) is a brief, 40-item version of Goldberg's (1992) Big-Five Factor (BFF) questionnaire (1992).

Staff Questionnaire. Staff rated each participant on their 'level of recovery' from addiction. Staff responses were made on a 10-point Likert scale. The low end of the scale was labelled *Low level of recovery* and the high end of the scale was labelled *High level of recovery*.

Results

Descriptive statistics are presented in Tables 9.1 and 9.2 alongside norms from a larger reference sample. Due to the small number of female participants ($N = 13$) no comparative statistics were calculated for gender. A correlation matrix for all test variables is presented in Table 9.3.

Partial Correlation

When the correlation between TEIQue score and the Staff rating (recovery score) is calculated while controlling for K10 (psychological distress) the correlation drops from $r(102) = 0.22$, $p < .05$, to an insignificant value $r(102) = 0.04$, $p = .68$. The path diagram in Figure 1, produced by AMOS, graphically depicts the mediating effect of the K10 psychological distress measure on EI and the Staff rating.

Hypothesis Testing

Hypothesis 1. Participants in the rehabilitation program had significantly lower EI scores than the reference sample ($t = 11.25$, $p < .0001$). Thus, Hypothesis 1 is confirmed; on average, individuals with addictions have lower EI scores than the general population.

Table 9.1

Descriptive Statistics for Rehabilitation Participants in Phase 1 of the Study Together With Normative Data for Comparison Purposes

Variable	Rehabilitation sample			Normative sample (note 1)		Difference statistic	
	Mean	SD	α	Mean	SD	t value	p value
Rehabilitation measures							
Age	34.03	10.62	—	—	—	—	—
Week in program	13.52	10.42	—	—	—	—	—
Staff rating	6.15	1.42	—	—	—	—	—
K10	23.29	8.04	.91	14.20	—	12.68	< .0001
EI							
TEIQue	4.16	.86	.87	5.08	0.73	11.25	< .0001
Personality							
O	29.76	5.36	.78	29.36	4.92	0.029	.98
C	27.72	5.91	.79	30.76	4.8	6.28	< .0001
E	24.57	5.89	.77	27.69	5.27	6.08	< .0001
A	30.13	5.96	.83	32.40	4.34	4.67	< .0001
N	21.28	5.69	.80	18.49	4.86	6.36	< .0001

Note: [1] The normative sample consisted of 330 participants made up of 110 first year university students and an organisational sample of 220 clerical staff (Reid, 2007).

Table 9.2

Descriptive Statistics for Rehabilitation Participants From Phase 2 of the Study Including Difference Statistic From Phase 1 Testing

	Variable rehabilitation sample 4 weeks later (Phase 2)			Difference statistic from Phase 1	
	Mean	SD	α	t value	p value
Rehabilitation measures					
Staff rating	6.73	1.44	—	1.19	.049
K10	20.17	7.08	.92	4.94	< .0001
EI					
TEIQue	4.53	0.88	.88	5.22	< .0001
Personality					
O	30.40	4.73	.72	1.13	.26
C	29.14	5.49	.78	3.37	.001
E	25.54	5.61	.76	3.00	.003
A	30.85	5.54	.81	0.94	.35
N	20.24	5.20	.79	2.13	.035

Table 9.3

Correlation Matrix Showing the Test Variables in the Phase 1 Study

	1	2	3	4	5	6	7	8	9
1. Age	1								
2. Staff rating	.23*	1							
3. Week no.	−.22	.62**	1						
4. K10	−.19*	−.37**	−.49**	1					
5. TEIQue	.14	.22*	.23	−.59**	1				
6. O	.07	.18	.19	−.34**	.43**	1			
7. C	.29**	.22*	.04	−.41**	.49**	.43**	1		
8. E	.06	.04	.11	−.18*	.39**	.29**	.23**	1	
9. A	.19*	.02	−.10	−.22*	.40**	.42**	.46**	.12	1
10. N	−.23**	−.19*	−.15	.27**	−.45**	−.19*	−.43**	−.15	−.39**

Note: * designates that correlation is significant at the 0.05 level, while ** indicates that correlation is significant at the 0.01 level (2-tailed).

Hypothesis 2. Participants in the rehabilitation program scored significantly higher on the K10 measure of psychological distress than the general population norm (see Table 9.1, $t = 12.68$, $p < 0.0001$). Thus, Hypothesis 2 is accepted and confirmed.

Hypothesis 3. It was proposed that the EI score would be a significant predictor of addiction recovery status (staff rating) in the rehabilitation program, even after controlling for psychological distress (K10). This hypothesis was tested following the Kenny mediation steps (2008); Step 1: the initial variable, the TEIQue is significantly correlated with the outcome variable, the Recovery score, $r(117) = 0.22$, $p < .05$; Step 2: the TEIQue is significantly correlated with the mediator, K10, $r(117) = -0.58$, $p < .01$); Step 3: the mediator (K10) affects the outcome, $r(117) = -0.37$, $p < .01$; Step 4: the mediator (K10) completely mediates the relationship between the TEIQue and the outcome and the correlation drops to virtually zero, $r(113) = 0.04$, $p = .68$. Thus, Hypothesis 3 is rejected; the effect of EI on the outcome variable, the Recovery score, is fully mediated by the psychological distress variable, the K10.

Hypothesis 4. It was proposed that participants in the program would score higher in EI and lower in psychological distress in Phase 2, that is, after an additional month of participation in the rehabilitation program. The EI scores (TEIQue) were significantly higher and the psychological distress scores were significantly lower in Phase 2 (see Table 9.2). Thus, Hypothesis 4 is confirmed and accepted.

Discussion

Previous research had indicated that participants with addictions would score lower on EI than the general population (e.g., Austin et al., 2005; Brackett & Mayer, 2003; Riley & Schutte, 2003). This was confirmed in the current sample with the average rehabilitation participants' score one *SD* below the general population (Hypothesis 1). This represents a large effect size approaching one. Thus, initial results appeared to bear out Goleman's proposition (1995) that the main indicator of drug addiction was an inability to soothe and manage negative feelings due to low EI.

The next step, addressed by Hypothesis 2, was to determine whether psychological distress was also directly related to addictive behaviour. The SMH suggests that an inability to tolerate psychological distress can lead to substance abuse (Khantzian, 1997). It was expected that rehabilitation participants would therefore score higher on a measure of psychological distress (K10) than members of the general population. This hypothesis was confirmed, once again demonstrating a large effect size ($d = 1$), and a highly significant correlation with the recovery level criterion ($r = -0.37$, $p < .0001$). High psychological distress in people with addictions does not in itself provide evidence for a causal relationship, but is an important finding when combined with research that psychological distress generally predates addiction (Abraham & Fava, 1999; Deykin, Levy & Wells, 1987; Gilman & Abraham, 2001).

With both EI and psychological distress (K10) significantly related to the level of recovery from addiction (see correlation matrix Table 9.3) the question arises as to which variable precedes the other, and which is the primary variable of the two that directly relates to drug addiction recovery status.

If Goleman (1995) was correct and addictive behaviour was primarily due to low levels of EI as a causal precedent, then a participant's EI score should still be able to significantly predict the level of addictive behaviour while controlling for other variables. However, hypothesis 3 was disconfirmed; the relationship between EI and the behavioural measure of recovery (staff rating) reduced to virtually zero when psychological distress (K10) was controlled for. Thus, the psychological distress measure was shown to be more directly related to the recovery score than EI was to the recovery score. In other words, the effect of EI on the recovery score is fully mediated by the psychological distress score. While Goleman's assertion was correct inasmuch as EI had a significant positive relationship with level of recovery in the individual, self-reported psychological distress turned out to be the primary causal factor of addictive behaviour.

The final step in this study was to determine if the participants improved their EI scores and reduced their level of psychological distress during the course of the rehabilitation program. A re-testing of the participants one month later found that EI scores had significantly improved and psychological distress scores had significantly decreased, thus confirming hypothesis 4. The ability to improve ones EI score was confirmed by this study, and since no specific EI training had been given to participants, the improvement appears to arise from general relationship building and emotional coping exercises included in the rehabilitation program.

Conclusion

The significant improvement in EI scores and the reduction of psychological distress over a 1-month period were key findings for this study. Clearly, the statistically significant reduction in psychological distress after one month was a major benefit for the participants in the program. The improvement in EI scores, however compelling, appear to be a by-product of the general interpersonal and emotional coping skills taught in the program, since no specific EI training was provided. EI was not found to be the primary causal factor relating to addiction, but simply another indicator of 'general wellness' fully mediated by the level of psychological distress being experienced by the individual.

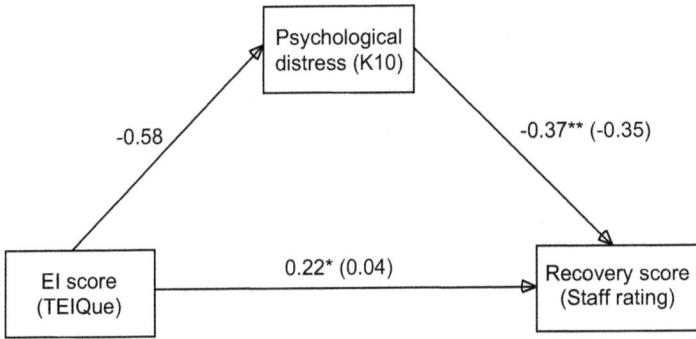

Figure 9.1
Path diagram produced by AMOS showing relationships between EI, psychological distress and individual recovery scores as determined by the staff rating. This indicates how the significant relationship between the EI score and recovery from addiction scores ($r = 0.22*$) reduces to an insignificant value ($r = 0.04$) through complete mediation by the psychological distress variable (K10).

Thus, it appears to be more effective to teach persons suffering from addictive behaviour techniques for reducing psychological distress, rather than using an EI skills intervention. The finding that the primary causal factor of addictive behaviour was psychological distress supports the SMH model that proposes that individuals use substances to self medicate to reduce psychological distress. Teaching alternative methods of reducing psychological distress thus appears to be the most promising direction for rehabilitation programs to take in the future.

In conclusion, the EI scores in this application only appear to provide a very general measure of personal and interpersonal levels of emotional functioning. As has been demonstrated by the path analysis in Hypothesis 3 (Figure 9.1), low EI, contrary to Goleman's assertion, was not the root cause of addictive behaviour. Psychological distress was found to be the primary causal factor leading to addictive behaviour and thus, interventions aimed at teaching participants how to manage psychological distress would appear to most effective in future drug rehabilitation programs.

References

Abraham, H.D., & Fava, M. (1999). Order of onset of substance abuse and depression in a sample of depressed outpatients. *Comprehensive Psychiatry, 40*(1), 44–50.

Aharonovich, E., Nguyen, H.T., & Nunes, E.V. (2001). anger and depressive states among treatment-seeking drug abusers: testing the psychopharmalogical specificity hypothesis. *The American Journal on Addictions, 10*, 327–334.

Austin, E.J., Saklofske, D.H., & Egan, V. (2005). Personality, well-being and health correlates of trait emotional intelligence. *Personality and Individual Differences*, 38(3), 547–558.

Bar-On, R. (2005). The Bar-On model of emotional-social intelligence. In P. Fernández-Berrocal & N. Extremera (Eds.), Special Issue on Emotional Intelligence, *Psicothema*, 17.

Brackett, M.A., & Mayer, J.D. (2003). Convergent, discriminant, and incremental validity of competing measures of emotional intelligence. *Personality and Social Psychology Bulletin*, 29(9), 1147–1158.

Connors, G.J., Longabaugh, R., & Miller, W.R. (1996). Looking forward and back to relapse: implications for research and practice. *Addiction*, 91(suppl.), S191–S196.

Deykin, E.Y., Levy, J.C., & Wells, V. (1987). Adolescent depression, alcohol and drug abuse. *American Journal of Public Health*, 77(2), 178–182

Gilman, S.E., & Abraham, H.D. (2001). A longitudinal study of the order of onset of alcohol dependence and major depression. *Drug and Alcohol Dependence*, 63, 277–286.

Goldberg, L.R. (1992). The development of markers for the Big-Five factor structure. *Psychological Assessment*, 4(1), 26–42.

Goleman, D. (1995). *Emotional intelligence: Why it can matter more than IQ*. London: Bloomsbury Publishing Plc.

Harris, K.M. & Edlund, M.J. (2005). Self-medication of mental health problems: New evidence from a national survey. *Health Services Research*, 40(1), 117–134.

Hser, Y., Hoffman, V., Grella, C.E., & Anglin, M.D. (2001). A 33-year follow-up of narcotics addicts. *Archives of General Psychiatry*, 58, 503–508.

Kenny, D.A. (2008, February 8). *Mediation*. Author. Retrieved from http://davidakenny.net/cm/mediate.htm

Kessler, R.C., Andrews, G., Colpe, L.J., Hiripi, E., Mroczek, D.K., Normand, S.-L.T. et al. (2002). Short screening scales to monitor populations prevalences and trends in non-specific psychological distress. *Psychological Medicine*, 32, 959–976.

Khantzian, E.J. (1997). The self-medication hypothesis of substance use disorders: A reconsideration and recent applications. *Harvard Review of Psychiatry*, 4(5), 231–244.

McCrae, R.R., & John, O.P. (1992). An Introduction to the Five-Factor Model and its applications. *Journal of Personality*, 60, 175–215.

Petrides, K.V., & Furnham, A. (2001). Trait emotional intelligence: Psychometric investigation with reference to established trait taxonomies. *European Journal of Personality*, 15, 425–448.

Petrides, K.V., & Furnham, A. (2003). Trait emotional intelligence: Behavioural validation in two studies of emotion recognition and reactivity to mood induction. *European Journal of Personality, 17*, 39–57.

Petrides, K.V., & Furnham, A. (2006). The role of trait emotional intelligence in a gender-specific model of organisational variables. *Journal of Applied Social Psychology, 36*(2), 552–569.

Reid, J.R., (2007). *Establishing the predictive validity of emotional intelligence using real-world criteria* (Doctoral thesis). Department of Psychology, Macquarie University, Sydney, Australia.

Riley, H., & Schutte, N. (2003). Low emotional intelligence as a predictor of substance-use problems. *Journal of Drug Education, 33*(4), 391–398.

Saucier, G. (1994). Mini-markers: A brief version of Goldberg's Unipolar Big-Five markers. *Journal of Personality Assessment, 63*(3), 506–516.

Schutte, N.S., Malouff, J.M., Hall, L.E., Haggerty, D.J., Cooper, J.T., Golden, C.J. et al. (1998). Development and validation of a measure of emotional intelligence. *Personality and Individual Differences, 25*, 167–177.

Schutte, N.S., Malouff, J.M., Simunek, M., McKenley, J., & Hollander, S. (2002). Characteristic emotional intelligence and emotional well-being. *Cognition and Emotion, 16*(6), 769–785.

Vaillant, G.E. (1998). What can long-term follow-up teach us about relapse and prevention of relapse in addiction? *British Journal of Addiction, 83*, 1147–1157.

Moral, social and individual aspects
in personality psychology

The Role of Emotional Intelligence and Personality in Moral Reasoning

V.S. Athota, Peter J. O'Connor and Chris J. Jackson

In this study we investigated the potential role of emotional intelligence (EI) in moral reasoning (MR). A sample of 131 undergraduate students completed a battery of psychological tests, which included measures of EI, MR and the Big Five dimensions of personality. Results revealed support for a proposed model of the relationship between emotional intelligence, personality and moral reasoning. Specifically, emotional intelligence was found to be a significant predictor of four of the Big Five personality dimensions (extraversion, openness, neuroticism, agreeableness), which in turn were significant predictors of moral reasoning. These results have important implications in regards to our current understanding of the relationships between EI, moral reasoning and personality. We emphasise the need to incorporate the constructs of EI and moral reasoning into a broader, explanatory personality framework.

The aim of this chapter was to investigate the relationships between emotional intelligence (EI), personality, and moral reasoning (MR). In the following literature review, we outline relevant existing research focusing on these constructs, and also highlight conceptual links between them. Emotional intelligence can be defined as 'the ability to perceive emotions, to access and generate emotions so as to assist thought, to understand emotions and emotion knowledge, and to reflectively regulate emotions so as to promote emotional and intellectual growth' (Salovey & Mayer, 1995, p. 5). Thus, in this research we conceptualise EI as an ability as opposed to a dispositional trait.

Substantial research has been conducted on the various relationships between personality traits and EI. All of the Big Five personality traits (i.e., agreeableness, openness, extraversion, neuroticism, and conscientiousness) have been found to correlate at least moderately with EI (McCrae, 2000). In particular, EI measures have generally been found to have at least moderate significant correlations with extraversion (positive direction) and neuroticism (negative direction), and smaller significant positive correlations with openness, agreeableness and conscientiousness (Matthews et al., 2006). Conceptually, such relationships make sense as both personality and EI are comprised of both cognitive and emotional components (see Mayer & Salovey, 1995; also see Shulman & Hemenover 2006). Indeed, it can be argued that EI, which is conceptualised as ability, influences the development of personality. Regardless of the direction however, it is clear that a relationship exists between EI and personality.

There have been different views expressed about the moral dimension of EI in the work of influential EI researchers. Specifically, Goleman (1995) suggests that there is a moral dimension to EI, whereas Mayer and Cobb (2000) argue that there is not. Consistent with Goleman, (1995), we argue that there is considerable conceptual overlap between the two constructs. As mentioned previously, EI involves the *ability* to perceive and regulate emotions. Similarly, moral reasoning is defined as the *ability* to 'frame socio-moral problems using one's standards and values in order to judge the proper course of action' (Rest, 1979; p.198). Thus, while EI involves using one's understanding of emotions (both of self and other) to guide decision making, moral reasoning involves using one's standards and values to guide decision making. Theoretically, it follows that one's 'standards and values' will depend largely on one's ability to accurately perceive both one's own and others' emotion, and regulate one's own emotions effectively. Overall, however, there has been little empirical research investigating how EI affects moral reasoning.

One difference between EI and moral reasoning is their levels of specificity. Emotional intelligence tends to refer to a generalised ability to regulate one's emotions, which theoretically influences most of our behaviours at some level. In this way, EI is best thought of as a generalised *distal* ability. Moral reasoning on the other hand, is only relevant to specific situations (e.g., moral dilemmas) and is best regarded as a specific *proximal* ability. We therefore argue that EI has a distal influence on moral reasoning.

Some research has also focused on the relationship between personality and moral reasoning For example, Curtis, Billingslea, and Wilson (1998) found significant associations between moral maturity and the traits of empathy (similar to agreeableness) and socialisation (extraversion). Conceptually, this relationship makes sense: the Big Five personality dimensions — which represent the primary behavioural and cognitive dimensions upon which people differ — should predict the specific behavioural and cognitive strategies people engage in when faced with moral dilemmas. There is, however, a lack of informative research in this area.

As noted above, the relationship between EI and personality is well established, and there has also been some research on the relationship between personality and moral reasoning. There has been little research, however, on the relationship between EI, personality and moral reasoning. The purpose of this study was to test the relationship between EI and moral reasoning, with the potential mediating role of personality also being taken in consideration. Within this model, a number of specific hypotheses were examined. First, consistent with previous research on personality and EI, it was hypothesised that self-reported EI and the Big Five personality factors would positively correlate with each other — specifically, since EI is modelled as a precursor to personality factors as it represents an *ability*; (Salovey & Mayer, 1995) which is different from personality, but likely influences personality development. Second, it was hypothesised that the Big Five personality dimensions would significantly predict moral reasoning. Third, it was hypothesised that EI would significantly predict moral reasoning, via its effect on personality.

Method

Participants

The participants were 131 psychology students from the University of Wollongong who volunteered to take part in the study. Fifty-four participants (41.22%) were male and 77 (58.79%) were female (2 people did not indicate their gender). Participants' ages ranged from 17 to 73, with mean age 22.63 years and *SD* = 7.86 years.

Measures

The International Personality Item Pool (IPIP; Goldberg et al., 2006). Participants completed the IPIP, a 50-item scale targeting the Big Five personality factors. The scale has 10 items assessing each of the dimensions of Neuroticism (N), Extraversion (E), Openness (O), Agreeableness (A), and Conscientiousness (C). The items are based on one's behaviours and reactions answered on a 5-point scale, ranging from 1 = *Very accurate* to 5 = *Very inaccurate*. Sixteen items are reverse-scored. Goldberg (1999) points out that there has been only one comparative validity study conducted on the psychometric properties of the IPIP scale. Goldberg (2006; cited on the IPIP website) reported the following alpha reliability for the IPIP scale: Extraversion, .87; Agreeableness, .82; Conscientiousness, .79;

Neuroticism, .86; and Openness to Experience, .84. According to Goldberg (1999) the scores on these scales have relatively high reliability and also have convergent validity with other measures of personality.

Self-Report Emotional Intelligence Test (SREIT; Schutte, et al., 1998). The SREIT is based on Salovey and Mayer's (1990) early model of EI. It is a self-report measure of EI scored on a 6-point scale (1 = *Strongly disagree*, 6 = *Strongly disagree*). This 33-item scale was developed to assess participants' ability to perceive, understand, regulate and express emotions. According to Bracket and Mayer (2003) the SREIT has good internal consistency and test–retest reliability.

Machiavellian IV Scale (Mach IV; Christie & Geis, 1970). The Mach IV scale is made up of three categories: interpersonal tactics, cynical view of human nature, and disregard for conventional morality. In this study, people who score high on Mach IV were regarded as having high levels of moral reasoning. The Mach IV is made up of 20 items, 10 indicating high moral reasoning and 10 indicating the opposite (low moral reasoning). The items reflect ways of thinking and opinions about people and things. Participants were requested to rate the extent to which they agreed or disagreed with the statements on a 5-point scale. In the Mach IV, 'tactics' are defined as the nature of an individual's interpersonal tactics; 'views' are defined as the views of human nature; and 'morality' is regarded as abstract or generalised morality. Subscales were summed to give a total score of 'moral reasoning' in this study.

Procedure

The scales containing the IPIP, the SREIT, and the Mach IV scale were administered to participants. The participants were tested individually. The participants were asked to read the instructions carefully before proceeding with the survey. Participants were given about 30 minutes to complete the survey. Demographic data were also collected from the participants at the beginning of the session. Participants were thanked for their participation and given a debriefing.

Results

Table 10.1 presents the descriptive statistics along with the alpha reliabilities for the moral reasoning scale, emotional intelligence scale, and the five factors of personality. Table 10.2 shows the correlations between intelligence, moral reasoning, personality and moral judgement variables.

The model illustrated in Figure 10.1 was tested using path analysis (AMOS version 17). Standardised estimates for the hypothesised relation-

Table 10.1

Means, Standard Deviations and Alpha for Emotional Intelligence, Moral Reasoning, Personality and Moral Judgment Variables†

	Mean	SD	Alpha	EI	E	A	C	N	O
Emotional intelligence (EI)	133.29	12.44	0.89						
Extraversion (E)	32.94	7.13	0.88	0.35**					
Agreeableness (A)	40.83	5.41	0.81	0.42**	0.30**				
Conscientiousness (C)	34.56	5.83	0.76	0.01	−0.05	0.01			
Neuroticism	30.00	8.05	0.89	0.47**	0.41**	0.07	0.05		
Openness (O)	36.38	5.44	0.79	0.33**	0.26**	0.22*	0.15	0.20*	
Moral reasoning (MR)	56.7	8.65	0.75	0.23**	0.28**	0.41**	−0.11	0.21*	−0.08

Note: †N = 131
  *Indicates significance at the p < .05 level
  **Indicates significance at the p < .01 level.

ships between EI, personality and moral reasoning are presented in Table 10.2. As can be seen, support was obtained for Hypotheses 1 and 3. Specifically, EI was found to significantly predict four of the Big Five personality traits (i.e., Extraversion, Agreeableness, Neuroticism, and Openness). Additionally, agreeableness, neuroticism and openness were found to significantly and uniquely predict moral reasoning. Parametric bootstrapping was used to test the hypothesis that EI would indirectly predict moral reasoning via personality (see Kline, 1998, for a discussion on indirect effects). Consistent with this hypothesis, the indirect effect of EI on Moral reasoning was significant ($\beta = 0.23$, $p = .002$). This finding indicates that individuals with high levels of EI tend to have high levels of moral reasoning.

Table 10.2

Parameter Estimates and Levels of Significance for the Proposed Relationships Between Emotional Intelligence, Personality and Moral Reasoning*

	To				
From reasoning	Extraversion	A	N	O	Moral
Emotional intelligence (EI)	0.35*	0.42*	0.47*	0.32*	
Agreeableness (A)					0.40*
Neuroticism (N)					0.17**
Openness (O)					0.23*

Note: †Only significant coefficients are reported
  *Indicates significance at the p < .01 level
  **Indicates significance at the p < .05 level.

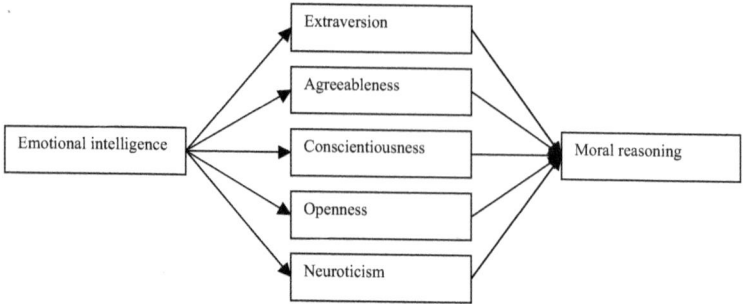

Figure 10.1

A model of the relationships between emotional intelligence, personality and moral reasoning.

Discussion

The aim of the current study was to test and explain the various relationships between EI, the Big Five dimensions of personality, and moral reasoning. A model of the relationship between these variables was tested; specifically, it was hypothesised that EI would indirectly predict moral reasoning, via its relationship with personality traits.

Consistent with McCrae (2000) and Matthews (2006) we found a significant relationship between personality and EI. In contrast to such researchers however, we do not interpret this relationship to indicate that EI is simply an aspect of personality, or even synonymous with personality (Shulman & Hemenover 2006). Instead we argue that since EI represents an ability, rather than a disposition, it influences the development of adult personality, and can therefore be modelled as a distal precursor to personality. This line of reasoning is consistent with those explanatory models of personality, which view surface dimensions of personality as having a distal basis in emotional control (e.g., Cloninger, Svrakic, & Przybeck, 1993).

Only limited research has explored the relationship between moral reasoning and personality, and so one aim of this study was to add to this research. In this study, we found that several dimensions of personality were significant, direct predictors of moral reasoning. Specifically, Agreeableness, Neuroticism and Openness were found to be positive, unique predictors of moral reasoning. Agreeableness was the strongest predictor of moral reasoning. This relationship makes conceptual sense since those with high levels of empathy and concern for others are expected to be more likely to approach with care situations where moral reasoning is required.

As discussed earlier, the literature provides conflicting views about the relationship between EI and moral reasoning. For example, Goleman's (1995) beliefs regarding the moral reasoning–EI relationship differs from that of Mayer and Pizarro's (2000). Mayer and Pizarro's (2000). Consistent with Goleman (1995), we propose that there is a relationship between EI and moral reasoning. Specifically, we argue that personality traits (in combination) mediate the relationship between EI and moral reasoning. The results of the current study are consistent with this proposition.

It is very timely to expand the scholarship in relation to EI and moral reasoning. Based on the established importance of the connection between EI and moral reasoning, further investigation can be conducted in the areas of stem cell research, healthcare settings, the leadership arena, and cross-cultural and academic settings. The apparent failures in some corporate organisations, academic institutions and other organisational settings, challenge us to do more research about why this occurs and whether interventions can make a difference. Research is needed involving interventions aimed at improving moral reasoning and EI among business leaders, students, and in cross-cultural settings and other related fields.

A limitation of this study is that, having tested our proposition among university students, the results of this study may not generalise to other subject groups. A further limitation of this research is the cross-sectional nature of the design. Future research should attempt to replicate our findings using a longitudinal design.

References

Brackett, M.A., & Mayer, D.J. (2003). Convergent, discriminant, and incremental validity of competing measures of emotional intelligence. *Personality and Social Psychology Bulletin, 29*(9), 1147–1158.

Burger, J.M. (1990). *Personality* (2nd ed). Belmont, CA: Wadsworth Publishing.

Christie, R., & Geis, F. (1970) *Studies in Machiavellianism*. New York: Academic Press.

Cloninger, C.R., Svrakic, D.M., & Przybeck, T.R. (1993). A psychobiological model of temperament and character. *Archives of General Psychiatry, 50,* 975–990.

Curtis, J., Billingslea, R., & Wilson, J. (1988). Personality correlates of moral reasoning and attitudes toward authority. *Psychological Reports, 63*(3), 947–954.

Goldberg, L.R. (1999). A broad-bandwidth, public-domain, personality inventory measuring the lower-level facets of several five-factor models. In I. Mervielde, I. Deary, F. De Fruyt, & F. Ostendorf (Eds.), *Personality psychology in Europe* (Vol. 7, pp. 1–28). Tilburg, the Netherlands: Tilburg University Press.

Goldberg, L.R., Johnson, J.A., Eber, H.W., Hogan, R., Ashton, M.C., Cloninger, C. R., Gough, H.G. (2006). The international personality item pool and the future of public-domain personality measures. *Journal of Research in Personality, 40,* 84–96.

Goleman, D. (1995). *Emotional intelligence: Why it can matter more than IQ.* London: Bloomsbury Publishing.

Hoffman, M.K. (2000). *Empathy and moral development: Implications for caring and justice.* Cambridge, UK: Cambridge University Press.

Kyte, R. (1996). Moral reasoning as perception: A reading of Carol Gilligan, *Academic Research Library, 11*(3), 97.

Lind, G. (2008). The meaning and measurement of moral judgment competence revisited: A dual-aspect model. In D. Fasko & W. Willis (Eds.), *Contemporary philosophical and psychological perspectives on moral development and education* (pp. 185–220). Cresskill, NJ: Hampton Press.

Matthews, G., Emo, A.K., Funke, G., Zeidner, M., Roberts, R.D., Costa, Jr, P.T. Schulze, R. (2006). Emotional intelligence, personality and task-induced stress. *Journal of Experimental Psychology: Applied, 12*(2), 96–107.

Mayer, J.D., & Cobb, C.D. (2000). Educational policy on emotional intelligence: Does it make sense? *Education Policy Review, 12,* 163–183.

McCrae, R., (2000). Emotional intelligence from the perspective of the Five-Factor Model. In R. Bar-On & J.D.A. Parker (Eds.), *Handbook of emotional intelligence* (pp. 263–276). San Francisco: Jossey-Bass.

Mudrack, P. (2006, June). Moral reasoning and personality traits. *Psychological Reports, 98*(3), 689–698.

Pizarro, D.A., & Salovey, P.(2002). Being and becoming a good person: The role of emotional intelligence in moral development and behavior. In J. Aronson (Ed.), *Improving academic achievement: Impact of psychological factors on education* (pp. 263–276). New York: Academic Press.

Raine, A., & Yang, Y. (2006). Neural foundations to moral reasoning and antisocial behavior. *Social, Cognitive, and Affective Neuroscience, 1,* 203–213.

Rest, J. (1979). *Development in judging moral issues.* Minneapolis, MN: University of Minnesota Press.

Salovey, P., & Mayer, J.D. (1990). Emotional intelligence. *Imagination, Cognition, & Personality, 9,* 185–211.

Schutte, N.S., Malouff, J.M., Hall, L.E., Haggerty, D.J., Cooper, J.T., Golden, C.J., & Dornheim, L. (1998). Development and validation of a measure of emotional intelligence. *Personality and Individual Differences, 25,* 167–177.

Shulman, E.T., & Hemenover, S. H. (2006). Is dispositional emotional intelligence synonymous with personality? *Self and Identity, 5,* 147–171.

Social Identity and Moral Judgement: The Impact of Political Affiliation on the Evaluation of Government Policy

Lisa Abel and Matthew Hornsey

This chapter explores issues of social identity and moral judgement. Of specific interest was the extent to which participants' political identity would influence their moral judgement of government policy. Participants with strong political affiliation were selected and policy scenarios presented including policies identified as associated with the affiliated party. The results suggest individuals' political affiliation does make a partial contribution to the way in which they evaluate reference group information in terms of its moral soundness. However, factors above and beyond social group affiliation also appear to inform and direct the moral evaluations individual group members make, even when those evaluations are directly concerned with the behaviour of one's social group.

According to the Social Intuitionist Model (Haidt, 2001; Haidt & Bjorklund, 2007), moral judgements are directly shaped by two factors. First, the model specifies that it is our immediate affective reactions (i.e., our intuitions) to events that are the overriding cause of moral judgement. Second, the model also specifies that emergent group norms directly shape the moral judgements we make. In relation to this social component of moral judgement, Haidt posits that the moral judgements of friends, allies and acquaintances have a direct bearing on the moral judgements one makes, even those judgements that one privately holds.

To date, it has been the intuition aspect of Haidt's model that has received the majority of attention (e.g., Haidt & Graham, 2007; Haidt &

Hersh, 2001; Haidt & Joseph, 2007; Hauser, 2006; Saltzstein & Kasachkoff, 2004; Sunstein, 2005). However, little (if any) empirical assessment has examined the model's second but equally important component; the social aspect of moral judgement. Given the readily testable hypotheses regarding the direct influence of emergent group norms on moral judgement, it was the effect of social identity on moral judgement that was the subject of empirical investigation in this study. Specifically, using the methods and meta-theoretical framework provided by the social identity approach (Tajfel, 1972; Tajfel & Turner, 1979, 1986; Turner, 1982) to group processes, the influence of social identity on people's moral evaluations was assessed.

In the research literature only limited attention has been paid to the impact of social identity salience and group member behaviour on moral judgement. For example Ryan, David, and Reynolds (2004) employed self-categorisation theory to address the effect of gender and context on the self and moral orientation. When participants were asked to respond to scenarios that either involved ingroup or outgroup members, it was found that social category salience resulted in participants invoking a more care-based orientation during the moral reasoning process when reasoning about ingroup members than when reasoning about outgroup members. Furthermore, Ryan and colleagues found that gender differences in moral orientation arose when participants' gender was made salient. When their gender was made salient to them, females evoked more care-based reasoning while males evoked more justice-based reasoning. In drawing conclusions from their research findings, the researchers proposed that the individual's moral orientation is not bound by gender but rather is fluid across social and relationship contexts.

Also focusing on the effects of social identification on participants' evaluations of social dilemmas is the research of Begue (2001). Under investigation in this study was the impact of participants' religious identification on their judgement of a target's decision to have an abortion. Overall, high identifiers judged the target more negatively than low identifiers. High identifiers also judged the target more negatively when her religious affiliation was known (i.e., when she was a Catholic) than when her religious affiliation was unspecified. On the basis of these results, Begue concluded that both social identity and the extent to which an individual identifies with their social group play a part in directing the individual's attitudes, at least in relation to the issue of abortion.

Finally, Turiel and colleagues (Turiel, Hildebrandt, & Wainryb, 1991; Study 2) assessed the impact of religious affiliation on individuals' social reasoning. The aim of their research was to compare Catholics' judgements about moral issues (e.g., killing, rape, theft) with their judgements about nonprototypical acts (e.g., homosexuality, abortion, incest) so as to assess the extent to which the doctrine of their religious order influenced their thinking. All but one of the participants agreed with the church's position regarding the moral issues. However, for the nonprototypical acts, only 31% participants agreed with the church's stance. A further 30% stated that they disagreed with the church's stance, while 39% of the sample stated their judgement of the nonprototypical acts depended upon the context in which the acts occurred.

Likewise, the results of participants' interview responses also revealed a mutual and bidirectional relationship between their judgements and the position of the church. Although participants judged the moral acts to be noncontingent on the position of the church, they viewed the engagement of such acts as violation of the standards of what it means to be a good Catholic. In this way, good standing in the group is seen to be dependent upon group member adherence to moral standards (Turiel et al., 1991). In summarising their findings, Turiel and colleagues concluded that individuals' reasoning about the group includes both dependence and independence. There is group dependence insofar as the moral standards held by the group appear to dictate group members' behaviour (i.e., what it means to be a good Catholic) as well as their standing within the group (i.e., whether one is seen as being good a Catholic). However, individuals' judgements about particular acts are not always and solely contingent upon the stance of the group. That is, participation in a group holding a strong position on a set of issues is not the sole determinant of group members' reasoning.

In sum, social identity appears to play a role in the moral judgement process. However, given that the main focus of these studies was on moral reasoning, and given that the results of these studies appear to contradict one another, it remains unclear the extent to which social identity influences moral judgement. More specifically, the impact of social identity on the evaluation component of moral judgement remains unknown. With this in mind, the aim of the current study was to investigate the impact of social identity on moral evaluation. Specifically, the impact of social group affiliation on the moral evaluation of reference group information was investigated.

This study was inspired by the program of research conducted by Cohen (2003), which focused on the impact of political identification on participants' evaluation of social welfare. In this research, participants were recruited on the basis of their political affiliation and attitude toward social welfare. Participants evaluated a generous welfare policy or a stringent welfare policy that had either been proposed by Democrats or Republicans. In all studies, the main dependent variable was participants' expressed level of support for the (bogus) social welfare policy.

The research hypotheses were based on the premise that, because social groups serve as a primary source of personal values, individual group members come to expect that other group members share the same values. Furthermore, when individuals evaluate issues that represent different moral commitments (e.g., abortion), they tend to appeal to the set of commitments that justifies the attitude they wish to hold, which is typically the attitude held by their ingroup. It was expected that when reference group information was available, this information would override the influence of participant ideology and policy content. That is, participants' policy evaluations would be shaped directly by the stance taken by their political reference group. As anticipated, across all studies the position of the reference group was found to direct participant responding. Both Republican supporters and the Democrat supporters were found to endorse the social welfare policy of their political reference group regardless of how generous or stringent the policy was. It was also found that participants were blind to the impact of group influence, with many stating that it was the details of the policy proposal and their own philosophy of government that contributed to their attitude rather than the beliefs of other Republicans or Democrats.

The results of these studies clearly demonstrate the impact of group influence on attitude change. However, the studies did not directly ask participants to record their moral evaluation of the policies, and so it remains to be seen whether reference group information affects moral evaluations. This is the goal of the current study. For this study, participants were recruited on the basis and strength of their political affiliation. Of specific interest was the extent to which participants' political identity would influence their moral judgement of government policy. From a social identity perspective, it was predicted that participants' political identification would significantly influence their moral evaluations of the presented government policies. Specifically, it was anticipated that when participants were led to believe that the government policies had been proposed by the political party for whom they expressed support, they would view the policies as being more morally sound than when they had been led to believe that the policies had been proposed by the opposing political party. Additionally, in line with the findings of Cohen (2003)

regarding participants' self-perceived bases of their attitude, it was anticipated that participants would state that their opinion of the proposed
policies were driven by the specific details of the policy rather than by
their political affiliation.

Method

Participants

Sixty-eight students took part in the study. Participants were recruited from
a selection of heterogeneous undergraduate courses (social policy, music,
and veterinary science) at a Brisbane university. The mean age of the participants was 21.78 years ($SD = 3.54$). Twenty-eight participants (41%) identified themselves as being supporters and/or voters of the Australian Liberal
Party, and 40 (59%) participants in the sample identified themselves as
being supporters and/or voters of the Australian Labor Party.

Design

This study implemented a 2 (political affiliation) × 2 (party policy)
between-subjects design. Participants were recruited on the basis of their
political affiliation, with only Labor or Liberal Party supporters selected for
participation. The Labor Party and Liberal Party are the dominant political
groups in Australian state and federal politics. The Australian Liberal Party
is traditionally the more conservative of the two, while the Australian Labor
Party's political orientation is more moderate and left-of-centre. The
manipulated independent variable was party policy (Labor or Liberal [i.e.,
conservative]). The dependent variable was moral evaluation.

Materials and Procedure

Recruitment. Participants were recruited on the basis of their political
affiliation, and their responses to the item 'To what extent do you feel
your political beliefs are important to who you are?' (1 = *Not at all important*, 7 = *Very important*). Only Labor and Liberal supporters who rated
the importance of their political beliefs on or above the mid-point of the
scale were contacted for participation.

Policy Evaluation Questionnaire. Prior to completing the main sections
of the questionnaire participants were first presented with an information
summary describing the purpose of the study. Participants were told that
the policies presented to them were either proposed by the Australian
Liberal Party, or were proposed by the Australian Labor Party. In reality,
all participants received the same policies. Participants were told that the
presented policies were currently up for discussion and approval by that

respective political party and that, if approved, the policies would become part of that party's policy portfolio. Participants were then presented with each of the proposed policies in turn (voluntary euthanasia policy; the Aboriginal welfare policy; the stem cell research policy). Presented on its own page, each policy summary provided participants with a reason for the policy's proposal, an outline of the specific details of the policy, and the criticisms levelled at it by the political opposition.

Dependent measures. Participants' moral evaluation of each of the policies was assessed. Participants used a 9-point scale to rate how moral they considered the proposed policy to be; how ethical they considered the proposed policy to be; how fair they considered the proposed policy to be; and finally, how responsible they considered the proposed policy to be. All items were measured on a 9-point scale (1 = *Very immoral/unethical/unfair/irresponsible*, 9 = *Very moral/ethical/fair/responsible*). Items were combined to create moral evaluation scores for each policy. The internal consistency for each composite moral evaluation measure was high (alphas ranging from .95 to .97). Finally, participants were asked to rate the extent to which various factors contributed to their opinion of each policy. These factors were: the specific details of the proposal and their own political allegiance and were adapted from the work of Cohen (2003). Both items were measured on a 9-point scale (1 = *Not at all*; 9 = *Contributes a great deal*).

Main Analyses

Moral evaluation. On moral evaluation of the voluntary euthanasia policy, there were no significant main effects of party policy, $F(1, 64) = 0.45$, $p = .51$, $\eta^2 = .01$, or voting preference on participants' evaluation, $F(1, 64) = 0.74$, $p = .39$, $\eta^2 = .01$. However, a significant party policy by voting preference interaction was found, $F(1, 64) = 10.98$, $p = .002$, $\eta^2 = .15$. Follow-up simple effects revealed that Liberal Party supporters evaluated the proposed euthanasia policy as more morally acceptable when they had been led to believe it had been proposed by the Liberal Party than when they had been led to believe it had been proposed by the Labor Party, $F(1, 64) = 6.79$, $p = .01$. In contrast, Labor Party supporters evaluated the proposed euthanasia policy as more morally acceptable when they had been led to believe it had been proposed by the Labor Party than when they had been led to believe it had been proposed by the Liberal Party, $F(1, 64) = 4.20$, $p = .045$ (see Table 11.1).

On moral evaluation of the Aboriginal welfare policy, there was no significant main effect of party policy, $F(1, 64) = 1.35$, $p = .25$, $\eta^2 = .02$, or voting preference, $F(1, 64) = 1.28$, $p = .26$, $\eta^2 = .02$. Finally, no significant party policy by voting preference interaction was found, $F(1, 64) = 1.95$, $p = .17$, $\eta^2 = .03$ (see Table 11.1).

On moral evaluation of the stem cell research policy, there was no significant main effect of party policy, $F(1, 64) = 0.71$, $p = .40$, $\eta^2 = .01$. There was also no significant main effect of voting preference, $F(1, 64) = 0.29$, $p = .59$, $\eta^2 = .00$. However, a significant party policy by voting preference interaction was found, $F(1, 64) = 6.95$, $p = .01$, $\eta^2 = .10$. Follow-up simple effects revealed that Liberal Party supporters evaluated the proposed stem cell research policy as more morally acceptable when they had been led to believe it had been proposed by the Liberal Party than when they had been led to believe it had been proposed by the Labor Party, $F(1, 64) = 5.19$, $p = .03$. No such significant difference was found in the moral evaluation by Labor Party supporters of the proposed stem cell research policy, though the trend in the data was in the expected direction, $F(1, 64) = 1.93$, $p = .17$ (see Table 11.1).

Assessment of influencing factors. Three repeated measures t tests tested whether there were significant differences in participants' ratings of the factors that influenced their opinion of the policies. For each policy, participants' responses on the 'specific details of the policy' item were compared against their responses on the 'own political allegiance' item. The results of the analyses revealed that for all three policies participants rated the specific details of the policy as being more important for determining their opinion than their own political allegiance (Voluntary Euthanasia: $t(67) = 6.44$, $p < .001$; Aboriginal Welfare: $t(67) = 7.63$, $p < .001$; and Stem Cell Research: $t(67) = 8.86$, $p < .001$). As can be seen in Table 11.2, partici-

Table 11.1

Means and Standard Deviations (in parentheses) of Moral Evaluations

Policy	Liberal Party proposed policy	Labor Party proposed policy
Voluntary euthanasia		
Liberal Party supporters	6.53_a (2.56)	4.52_b (1.83)
Labor Party supporters	5.29_a (2.17)	6.63_b (1.63)
Aboriginal welfare		
Liberal Party supporters	4.83 (2.03)	4.71 (1.90)
Labor Party supporters	3.51 (2.32)	4.85 (2.09)
Stem cell research		
Liberal Party supporters	6.20_a (2.86)	4.07_b (1.95)
Labor Party supporters	4.26 (2.59)	5.36 (2.33)

Note: Different subscripts across rows indicate that means are significantly different ($p < .05$).

Table 11.2

Mean Participant Ratings of Influencing Factors*

Influencing Factors	Voluntary euthanasia	Aboriginal welfare	Stem cell research
Specific details of policy	6.12a (1.81)	6.63a (1.95)	6.74a (2.16)
Own political allegiance	3.75b (2.52)	3.44b (2.58)	3.40b (2.63)

Note: *Standard deviations reported in parentheses. Different subscripts within columns denote a significant difference in mean scores ($p < .05$).

pants' scores on the 'own political allegiance' item were below the mid-point on the scale.

Discussion

In sum, it appears that participants' political affiliation contributed to their moral evaluation of the presented government policies. That is, for two of the policies, participants' moral evaluations were found to vary as a function of the interaction between party policy and voting preference. The results of this study correspond at least in part with those of Cohen (2003), and also of Begue (2001). Specifically, it was found that participants' social identity served to inform the evaluations they made, indicating that social identity does play a role in directing the evaluation component of the moral judgement process.

Like the results of Turiel et al. (1991) however, the results of the current study showed that participants' political affiliation did not fully direct their moral evaluations of the presented policies and nor did participants' responses uniformly vary as function of both the type of policy they received and their political affiliation. That is, it was not always the case that both Liberal Party and Labor Party supporters evaluated the policies of their own party more favourably than they evaluated the policies of the political opposition.

In summarising their findings, Turiel et al. (1991) concluded that while the moral standards held by the group dictate group member behaviour and standing within the group, individuals' judgements about particular acts are not always and solely contingent upon the stance of the group. In keeping with this, when the results of Turiel and colleagues and the findings of this study are considered in unison, it does not seem unreasonable to conclude that in particular relation to moral judgement, membership in a group that holds a strong position on a set of issues does not appear to be the sole determinant of the stance taken by every individual group member.

In drawing conclusions about the impact of social identity on moral judgement, the results of the current study highlight the complexity of its effect. The results suggest individuals' political affiliation does make a partial contribution to the way in which they evaluate reference group information in terms of its moral soundness. However, because the expected pattern of responding did not hold across all policies, this indicates that other information (e.g., policy content) or within-person factors (e.g., prior beliefs and knowledge; one's own personal moral perspective) also serve to inform individuals' moral evaluations. In this way, factors above and beyond social group affiliation appear to inform and direct the moral evaluations individual group members make, even when those evaluations are directly concerned with the behaviour of one's social group.

References

Begue, L. (2001). Social judgement of abortion: A black-sheep effect in a catholic sheepfold. *Journal of Social Psychology, 141*, 640–649.

Cohen, G.L. (2003). Party over policy: The dominating impact of group influence on political beliefs. *Journal of Personality and Social Psychology, 85*, 808–822.

Haidt, J. (2001). The emotional dog and its rational tail: A social intuitionist model of moral judgement. *Psychological Review, 108*, 814–834.

Haidt, J., & Bjorklund, F. (2007). Social Intuitionists answer six questions about moral psychology. In W. Sinnott-Armstrong (Ed.), *Moral psychology: Vol 2. The cognitive science of morality* (pp. 181–217). Cambridge, MA: MIT Press.

Haidt, J., & Graham, J. (2007). When morality opposes justice: Conservatives have moral intuitions that liberals do not recognise. *Social Justice Research, 20*, 98–116.

Haidt, J., & Hersh, M. A. (2001). Sexual morality: The cultures and emotions of conservatives and liberals. *Journal of Applied Social Psychology, 31*, 191–221.

Haidt, J., & Joseph, J. (2007). The moral mind: How 5 sets of innate moral intuitions guide the development of many culture-specific virtues, and perhaps even modules. In P. Carruthers, S. Laurence, & S. Stich (Eds.), *The innate mind: Vol. 3* (pp. 367–391). New York: Oxford.

Hauser, M.D. (2006). *Moral minds: How nature designed our universal sense of right and wrong.* London: Abacus.

Ryan, M.K., David, B., & Reynolds, K.J. (2004). Who cares? The effect of gender and context on the self and moral reasoning, *Psychology of Women Quarterly, 28*, 246–255.

Saltzstein, H.D., & Kasachkoff, T. (2004). Haidt's moral intuitionist theory: A psychological and philosophical critique. *Review of General Psychology, 8*, 273–282.

Sunstein, C.R. (2005). Moral heuristics. *Behavioral and Brain Sciences, 28*, 531–542.

Tajfel, H. (1972). Experiments in a vacuum. In J. Israel & H. Tajfel (Eds.), *The context of social psychology* (pp. 69–119). London: Academic Press.

Tajfel, H., & Turner, J.C. (1979). An integrative theory of intergroup conflict. In W.G. Austin, & S. Worchel (Eds.), *The social psychology of intergroup relations* (pp. 33–47). Monterey, CA: Brooks/Cole.

Turiel, E., Hildebrandt, C., & Wainryb, C. (1991). Judging social issues: Difficulties, inconsistencies, and consistencies. *Monographs of the Society for Research in Child Development, 56,* 1–103.

Turner, J.C. (1982). Towards a cognitive redefinition of the social group. In H. Tajfel (Ed.), *Social identity and intergroup relations* (pp. 15–40). Cambridge, UK: Cambridge University Press.

Chapter

12

Applying Evolutionary Theory to Individual Differences: Insights From Moral Psychology

Timothy Marsh and Simon Boag

Evolutionary theory and adaptation-based explanations in psychology have become increasingly common within the last 20 to 30 years, and researchers are beginning to utilise the evolutionary paradigm in the study of personality and individual differences. This chapter examines several evolutionarily oriented personality trait studies to highlight apparent tendencies towards simple genetic determinism, and contrasts this method with the more developmentally sensitive approach pursued in some recent works in moral psychology. Salient theoretical concerns addressed include the direct inheritance of behavioural predispositions, and the environmental and developmental calibration of universally inherited potentials. The implications of these issues are discussed.

Psychology can be conceptualised as the behavioural and cognitive arm of biological science (Burghardt, 2009). In the neurosciences and psychology, explanations of the configurations and functions of tissue structures require an understanding of the conditions under which these contemporary structures developed (cf., Symons, 1990). For this reason, the theory of evolution by natural selection is regarded as an explanatory cornerstone of biological science. In taking the 'adaptationist' approach to a biological system, one supplements the particularly challenging and detailed historical question of 'How did this develop?' with the more functional concern of 'Why did this develop?' It is an approach wherein one views mechanisms as adaptations (cf., Gigerenzer, 2002; Tooby & Cosmides, 2005).

While this approach has proven instrumental to the development of informative explanatory theories, the effectively speculative nature of the method raises a number of theoretical and empirical concerns. One relates to thoughts about a remote prehistory where the environmental and contextual details of interest are at best educated guesses. Subsequently there are problems in formulating testable and falsifiable hypotheses based on a well-supported explanatory theory rather than 'storytelling' (Symons, 1990).

The goal of this chapter is to examine evolutionary psychology in relation to the domain of personality and individual differences. This paper therefore discusses the broad application of evolutionary theory in psychology, and then gives examples of how the evolutionary paradigm has been recently applied to the study of personality traits. These methods will be compared to recent evolutionary work in the field of moral psychology.

Evolution in Psychology

Evolution by natural selection — the fitness-based nonrandom selection of individual differences — is a theoretical framework that attempts to organise and explain the morphological and functional features observed in all biological systems. The theory postulates that organisms naturally diversify developing phenotypic properties that permit heightened success in the given environment, becoming 'better adapted' to the specific environmental challenges faced (cf., Gigerenzer, 2002).

The growth of evolution-dependant theories in psychology has been evident over the past two decades in particular. The evolutionary paradigm was proposed to consist primarily of the identification of modular, adaptive psychological mechanisms in humans, evolving from our distant hominid and pre-hominid ancestors. This modularity theory meshed well with empirical findings in human cognition, and provided fresh explanatory insights into many of areas in psychology (cf., Buss, 1999; Figueredo et al., 2005). Examples concern (1) seeing emotions as circumstance-specific motivational states (Turner, 1996; e.g., anger and jealousy are theorised to play an important role in social and reproductive success — Buss, Larsen, Westen, & Semmelroth, 1992; Cosmides, 1989); (2) mating preferences and intuitive mating strategies (cf., Buss & Dedden, 1990); and (3) the perception of attraction and aggression in facial expressions and structures (cf., Langois & Roggman, 1990).

Overall, humans display an innate talent for processing concerns of reciprocal social exchange, social hierarchies, and cheat-detection in social circumstances (Kyl-Heku, 1990). They also seem to possess in-born language acquisition talents, evidence for which appears extensive, so much so that competing nonevolutionary theories, such as domain-general social-learning models, only hold a fraction of the explanatory power (cf., Pinker, 2002). Today evolutionary psychology plays pivotal theoretical roles in cognitive neuroscience (Krill, Platek, Goetz, & Shackelford, 2007), learning (Jiménez-Díaz, Sancho-Bielsa, Gruart, López-García, & Delgado-García, 2006), and notably developmental psychology generally (e.g., Carroll, 2008; Moore, 2008; Whittle, Allen, Lubman, & Yucel, 2006).

Variation in adaptive mechanisms is best understood as differential levels of efficacy or totality, though developing research methods to examine the complexity of the adaptive variations in the environmental contexts is not easy and is a central challenge of researchers seeking to apply the power of the evolutionary paradigm to personality and individual differences.

Personality and Adaptation

Critics such as de Jong and van der Steen (1998) have suggested that there is a fundamental incongruity between explanations relying on evolutionary theory, and the study of personality and individual differences in psychology, primarily because evolved mechanisms are generally regarded as species-wide solutions to age-old problems, and interpersonal variation appears to be neither ubiquitous nor genetically contingent enough to be anything more than residual 'noise' to an evolutionary study. Such concerns mirror similar objections originating within the social sciences, where the concept of an inherited 'human nature' conflicts with popular theories that rely exclusively on social-learning (Pinker, 2002).

Despite this, in recent decades, research into personality and individual differences within an evolutionary paradigm has been expanding (Nettle, 2008). The majority of research in this area has focused on traits, partly since trait-theory is one of the most extensively studied and applied domains in personality psychology, and also because traits are argued to be among the most stable of personality factors (Digman, 1990). Furthermore, trait levels are correlated with a number of key life outcomes, such as life expectancy and marital stability, and thus are expected to have a reasonable impact on selective fitness (cf., Friedman et al., 1995).

In the early 1990s, Buss (1991) articulated a set of guiding principles for how one may conceptualise the evolutionary origins of common personality variation. He outlined a number of theoretically plausible

Darwinistic origins for the kind of variance observed in personality research including: (1) competing strategies based on inherited genetic predispositions; (2) environmental or developmental calibration of a standardised set of inherited potential strategies; and (3) nonadapted variance in personality constituting selectively neutral 'noise'. Buss and Grieling (1999) later refined this further, offering methodological advice focussing primarily on the identification of genetic influences in the absence of environmental factors during development.

Recent evolutionary personality psychology studies have attempted to discover the direct heritability of genetic predispositions in personality. Bouchard (1994), and MacDonald (1995) indicated strong biological determination implying adaptive strategies characterised by varying levels on the Five Factor dimensions (cf., Canli, 2004; Plomin & Nesselroade, 1990). Bouchard and Loehlin (2001) also suggested a high heritability of personality traits, though they also note that determining nonshared environmental influences is an ongoing challenge in genetic personality research. Building off MacDonald's work, Nettle (2008) has formulated a detailed theoretic framework to explain the apparent equilibrium of presumably highly heritable personality traits.

While offering many valuable insights, particularly into transmission of personality traits within families, an issue with these studies is their high reliance on what appear to be simplistic assumptions of high genetic determinism. Since there is ample evidence to suggest that there are strong continuities in personality traits through one's lifetime, it is possible this has been interpreted as evidence that personality traits are a biological 'fixture', and thus are likely to have directly genetic causes. These elements need to be examined in more detail in current research.

The Impact of Evolution in Moral Psychology

Another field of individual differences that has recently received extensive insights from evolution theory is moral psychology, particularly its most well researched domain, moral judgment. The work that arguably founded the empirical field of moral judgment was that of Kohlberg (1969), which was influenced heavily by the earlier developmental work of Piaget and the moral philosophy of John Rawls.

In his works, Kohlberg developed a model comprising of six ordinal steps intended to hierarchically represent both the progression most people go through as they morally develop from childhood, and also account for the differences in sophistication in adult moral reasoning. Kohlberg's work founded a tradition of cognitive-developmental focus in the moral judgment literature that is now referred to as the Neo-Kohlbergian paradigm (see Rest, Narvaez, Thoma, & Bebeau, 2000). This paradigm retains the core components of focusing on cognitive deliberation, personal 'upward' development, and the vital distinctions between rule and norm-based 'conventional' reasoning, and principle and consideration-based 'post-conventional' reasoning.

There are, however, numerous weaknesses to this approach to moral judgment, with its focus on conscious deliberation being continually challenged by empirical findings, such as Reber's (1993) work on the centrality of implicit, rapid decision making. During this same time there was a rise in biologically-based research concerning how emotional reactions guide moral reactions and judgments. The works of Haidt (e.g., Haidt, 2001, 2004; Haidt, Koller, & Dias, 1993) provided evidence for the primary role of affective and intuitive responses in determining the majority of moral judgments, including a number of studies that specifically demonstrated the failure of post hoc cognitive justifications to explain initial reactions to taboo yet harmless scenario stimuli (cf., work by Narvaez & Vaydich, 2008; O'Neill & Petrinovich, 1998; Pizarro & Bloom, 2003). This affective–intuitive paradigm based on evolutionary accounts of the formation of prosocial, antitaboo intuitions challenges the cognitive–developmental paradigm (see Krebs & Denton, 2006; Krebs & Hemingway, 2008).

This movement in moral psychology towards biologically-integrated theories guided heavily by evolution has yielded strong insights into the function of the underlying mechanisms of moral judgment (cf., Hauser, 2006). For instance, using neuro-imaging methodology Anderson, Bechara, Damasio, Tranel, and Damasio (1999) confirmed the theorised functional links between moral judgment and moral action. Further neuro-imaging work has extensively mapped the regions of the brain associated with as diverse components of moral functioning as judgment, interpreted context, altruism and punishment cues, and the perception of transgressions (Borg, Lieberman, & Kiehl, 2008; Harbaugh, Mayr, & Burghardt, 2007; Moll, de Oliveir-Souza, Krueger, & Graftman, 2002; Moll, Eslinger, & de Oliveir-Souza, 2001; Moll, Zahn, de Oliveir-Souza, Krueger, & Graftman, 2005). Evolutionary theories of modular specialisation in moral functioning have also been supported by research into disgust and moral judgment (Danovitch & Bloom, 2009; Gutierrez & Giner-Sorolla, 2007; Jones & Fitness, 2008; Schnall, Haidt, Clore, & Alexander, 2008).

While initially adversarial, the cognitive-developmental and affective-intuitive paradigms of moral psychology are now moving towards a synthesis; for example, see Narvaez's (2008) Triune Ethics Theory. The result of this detailed synthesis is a model that maximises the explanatory power of inputs from the cognitive-developmental and the affective-intuitive approaches, to produce the individual differences observed in moral functioning. More research is needed using appropriate investigative techniques (cf., Caldwell & Millen, 2008), but the successful theoretic synthesis of prior social-learning and childhood development-based findings into a biologically robust evolutionary account of underlying mechanisms serves as an example to other fields of psychology, such as personality.

Beyond 'Selecting For'

Several conceptual approaches can be adopted when investigating evolutionary accounts of personality and individual differences. The trait-based evolutionary personality psychology investigations (e.g., MacDonald, 1995; Nettle, 2008) provide bases for a more comprehensive understanding of the evolution of personality. The assessment of heritability of personality traits is complicated, however, since one's theoretic interpretation of the causal path between genetic inheritance and manifested trait behaviour makes it possible to prematurely commit to a model of high direct heritability.

Both Gottlieb (e.g., 2004) and Finlay (2007) note that among many researchers employing the evolutionary psychology paradigm, there is a common functional assumption of high genetic determinism. Under such a conception, genetic inheritance is seen as the primary cause of the manifest behaviours described by personality traits, and, based on the situational benefits and liabilities of the given traits, the related genes are differentially 'selected for'.

Finlay (2007) argued that if psychologists are going to integrate the theories and frameworks of Darwinism into their analyses, especially in the assessment of individual differences, then great care in theory building will be needed. This is because there is a lack of species-wide standardisation of observable phenotypes, sharply increasing the number of theoretic 'stories' that can be speculated to explain them. Making the key explanatory distinction between developmental-configuration and directly inherited predispositions is confounded further still when it is likely that both mechanisms are likely true to different degrees.

First, research to clarify the contributions of genetic and developmental influences is hampered because minor genetic changes can influence the phenotypic, behavioural manifestations (Nettle, 2008; Rowe & Houle, 1996). But shared environmental (e.g., family) influences could also give the illusion of higher genetic influence than is truly present and careful research is needed to unravel the respective (nature-nurture) contributions (cf., Gerhard & Kirschner, 1997).

Second, when considering the calibration of psychological mechanisms by ontogenic, developmental and culturally inherited factors, it is important to keep in mind that one of the most potent selective pressures applied to organisms in highly dynamic environments is selection in favour of intragenerational adaptation (Narvaez, 2008; Tooby & Cosmides, 1992, 2005). This poses further challenges to tracing the reliability of genetic determinants of behaviour, since even casually shared kin environments may elicit the development of very similar calibrated strategies (Lickliter, 2008).

Third and last, while the proposition that the differential value of (say) the inherited Five Factor personality traits, can generate testable predictions (cf., Canli, 2004), the statistical analyses can potentially be confounded by other sources of equilibrium-maintenance in a gene-pool. Livnat, Papadimitriou, Dushoff, and Feldman (2008) argued that pairing many genes and their alleles in the selection process into complex combinations over many generations, leads to an overall selective pressure to produce genes that work well in multiple genomic contexts. The subsequent selective pressure towards genes and gene complexes that work well in multiple contexts is likely to obscure the effects of a simple system of moderate-selection due to benefits and trade-offs, and is made more confounding under circumstances where genetically ubiquitous sets of strategies are being ontogenically calibrated by developmental and environmental factors (Schwartz & Begley, 2003).

Consequently, as seen in these three aspects, the theoretical challenges and sheer number of practical considerations facing an evolutionary psychologist are magnified when studying personality and individual differences.

Final words

This chapter has reviewed several recent endeavours to conceptualise and study major areas in personality and individual differences through the lens of evolutionary science. In comparing and contrasting examples from both personality and moral psychology, the goal has been to demonstrate the theoretic differences between developmental calibration-based and genetic determinism-based accounts of individual differences, and in doing so to clarify how a highly sophisticated understanding of the nuances of evolutionary biology is necessary to experimentally and conceptually distinguish between the two. Far from seeking to discourage research into directly heritable predispositions in personality variance, the present chapter seeks to suggest essential considerations that can elevate the quality of generated hypotheses in all domains of evolutionarily focused individual differences research. It is also essential to the success of further research in this field that more evolutionarily guided structural and neuro-imaging research is done into the potential, functionally distinct psychological mechanisms of personality differentiation. In this way it may be possible to fulfil the aspirations of researchers such as Buss, Toobey, and Cosmides, in integrating a well-supported developmental and evolutionary framework, as the functional core of personality psychology.

References

Anderson, S.W., Bechara, A., Damasio, H., Tranel, D., & Damasio, A.R. (1999). Impairment of social and moral behavior related to early damage in human prefrontal cortex. *Nature Neuroscience, 2*(11), 1032–1037.

Borg, J.S., Lieberman, D., & Kiehl, K.A. (2008). Infection, incest, and iniquity: Investigating the neural correlates of disgust and morality. *Journal of Cognitive Neuroscience, 20*(9), 1529–1546.

Bouchard, T. (1994). Genes, environment, and personality. *Science, 264,* 1700–1701.

Bouchard, T.J., & Loehlin, J.C. (2001). Genes, evolution and personality. *Behavior Genetics, 31,* 243–273.

Burghardt, G.M. (2009). Darwin's legacy to comparative psychology and ethology. *American Psychologist, 64*(2), 102–110.

Buss, D.M. (1989). Sex differences in human mate preferences: Evolutionary hypothesis testing in 37 cultures. *Behavioral and Brain Sciences, 12,* 1–49.

Buss, D.M. (1991). Evolutionary personality psychology. *Annual Review of Psychology, 42,* 459–491.

Buss, D.M. (1999). *Evolutionary psychology: The new science of the mind.* Boston, MA: Allyn & Bacon.

Buss, D.M., & Dedden, L. (1990). Derogation of competitors. *Journal of Cross Cultural Psychology, 21,* 5–47.

Buss, D.M., & Greiling, H. (1999). Adaptive individual differences. *Journal of Personality, 67,* 209–243.

Buss, D.M., Larsen, R., Westen, D., & Semmelroth, J. (1992). Sex differences in jealousy: Evolution, physiology and psychology. *Psychological Science, 3,* 251–255.

Caldwell, C.A., & Millen, A.E. (2008). Experimental models for testing hypotheses about cumulative cultural evolution. *Evolution and Human Behavior, 29,* 165–171.

Canli, T. (2004). Functional brain mapping of extraversion and neuroticism: Learning from individual differences in emotion processing. *Journal of Personality, 72,* 1105–1131.

Carroll, S.B. (2008). Evo-devo and an expanding evolutionary synthesis: A genetic theory of morphological evolution. *Cell, 134*(1), 25–36.

Cosmides, L. (1989). The logic of social exchange: Has natural selection shaped how humans reason? *Cognition, 31,* 187–276.

Danovitch, J. & Bloom, P. (2009). Children's extension of disgust to physical and moral events. *Emotion, 9*(1), 107–112.

de Jong, H.L., & van der Steen, W.J. (1998) Biological thinking in evolutionary psychology: Rockbottom or quicksand? *Philosophical Psychology, 11*(2), 183–205.

Digman, J. (1990). Five factor model. *Annual Review of Psychology, 41,* 417–440.

Friedman, H.S., Tucker, J.S., Schwartz, J.E., Martin, L.R., Tomlinson-Keasey, C., Wingard, D.L. et al. (1995). Psychosocial and behavioural predictors of longevity: The aging and death of the 'termites'. *American Psychologist, 50,* 69–78.

Figueredo, A.J., Sefcek, J.A., Vasquez, G., Brumbach, B.H., King, J.E., & Jacobs, W.J. (2005). Evolutionary personality psychology. In D.M. Buss (Ed.), *Handbook of evolutionary psychology* (pp. 851–877). Hoboken, NJ: John Wiley & Sons, Inc.

Finlay, B.L. (2007). Endless minds most beautiful. *Developmental Science, 10*(1), 30–34.

Gerhart, J., & Kirschner, M. (1997). *Cells, embryos and evolution.* Malden, MA: Blackwell Science.

Gigerenzer, G. (2002). *Adaptive thinking: rationality in the real world.* Oxford, England: Oxford University Press.

Gottlieb, G. (2004). Normally occurring environmental and behavioral influences on gene activity: From central dogma to probabilistic epigenesis. In C.G. Coll, E.L. Bearer, & R.M. Lerner (Eds.), *Nature and nurture: The complex interplay of genetic and environmental influences on human behavior and development* (pp. 85–106). Mahwah, NJ: Lawrence Erlbaum Associates Publishers.

Gutierrez, R., & Giner-Sorolla, R. (2007). Anger, disgust, and presumption of harm as reactions to taboo-breaking behaviors. *Emotion, 7*(4), 853–868.

Haidt, J., Koller, S., & Dias, M. (1993). Affect, culture, and morality, or is it wrong to eat your dog? *Journal of Personality and Social Psychology, 65,* 613–628.

Haidt, J. (2001). The emotional dog and its rational tail: A social intuitionist approach to moral judgment. *Psychological Review, 108*(4), 814–834.

Haidt, J. (2004). The emotional dog gets mistaken for a possum. *Review of General Psychology, 8*(4), 283–290.

Harbaugh, W.T., Mayr, U., & Burghart, D.R. (2007). Neural responses to taxation and voluntary giving reveal motives for charitable donations. *Science, 316*(5831), 1622–1625.

Hauser, M. (2006). *Moral minds: how nature designed our universal sense of right and wrong.* New York: Harper Collins.

Hoffman, M.L. (2000). Empathy and moral development: implications for caring and justice. New York: Cambridge University Press.

Jiménez-Díaz, L., Sancho-Bielsa, F.J., Gruart, A., López-García, C., & Delgado-García, J. (2006). Evolution of cerebral cortex involvement in the acquisition of associative learning. *Behavioral Neuroscience, 120,* 1043–1056.

Jones, A., & Fitness, J. (2008). Moral hypervigilance: The influence of disgust sensitivity in the moral domain. *Emotion, 8*(5), 613–627.

Kohlberg, L. (1969). Stage and sequence: The cognitive developmental approach to socialization. In D.A. Goslin (Ed.), *Handbook of socialization theory* (pp. 347–480). Chicago: Rand.

Krebs, D.L., & Denton, K. (2006). Explanatory limitations of cognitive-developmental approaches to morality. *Psychological Review, 113*(3), 672–675.

Krebs, D.L., & Hemingway, A. (2008). The explanatory power of evolutionary approaches to human behavior: The case of morality. *Psychological Inquiry, 19*(1), 35–38.

Krill, A.L., Platek, S.M., Goetz, A.T., & Shackelford, T.K. (2007). Where evolutionary psychology meets cognitive neuroscience: A précis to evolutionary cognitive neuroscience. *Evolutionary Psychology, 5,* 232–256.

Kyl-Heku, L. (1990). Effects of context and sex on hierarchy negotiation (Unpublished doctoral dissertation). University of Michigan.

Langois, J.H., & Roggman, L.A. (1990). Attractive faces are only average. *Psychological Science, 1,* 115–121.

Lickliter, R. (2008). The growth of developmental thought: Implications for a new evolutionary psychology. *New Ideas in Psychology, 26,* 353–369.

Livnat, A., Papadimitriou, C., Dushoff, J., & Feldman, M.W. (2008). A mixability theory for the role of sex in evolution. *Proceedings of the National Academy of Sciences, 105,* 19803–19808.

MacDonald, K. (1995). Evolution, the 5-factor model, and levels of personality. *Journal of Personality, 63,* 525–567.

Moll, J., de Oliveira-Souza, R., Bramati, I.E., & Grafman, J. (2002). Functional networks in emotional moral and nonmoral social judgments. *NeuroImage, 16*(3), 696–703.

Moll, J., Eslinger, P.J., & de Oliveir-Souza, R. (2001) Frontopolar and anterior temporal cortex activation in a moral judgment task. *Arquivos de Neuro-Psiquiatria, 59*(3-B), 657–664.

Moll, J., Zahn, R., de Oliveira-Souza, R., Krueger, F., & Grafman, J. (2005). Opinion: The neural basis of human moral cognition. *Nature Reviews Neuroscience, 6*(10), 799–809.

Moore, D.S. (2008). Integrating development and evolution in psychology: Looking back, moving forward. *New Ideas in Psychology, 26*(3), 327–331.

Narvaez, D. (2008). Triune ethics: The neurobiological roots of our multiple moralities. *New Ideas in Psychology, 26,* 95–119.

Narvaez, D., & Vaydich, J.L. (2008). Moral development and behaviour under the spotlight of the neurobiological sciences. *Journal of Moral Education, 37*(3), 289–312.

Nettle, D. (2008). Putting ethology (back) into human personality psychology. *European Journal of Personality, 22*(5), 464–465.

O'Neill, P., & Petrinovich, L. (1998). A preliminary cross-cultural study of moral intuitions. *Evolution and Human Behavior, 19,* 349–367.

Pinker, S. (2002). *The blank slate.* New York: Viking Press.

Pizarro, D.A., & Bloom, P. (2003). The intelligence of the moral intuitions: A reply to Haidt (2001). *Psychological Review, 110,* 193–198.

Plomin, R., & Nesselroade, J.R. (1990). Behavioral genetics and personality change. *Journal of Personality, 58,* 191–220.

Reber, A.S. (1993). Implicit learning and tacit knowledge. New York: Oxford University Press.

Rest, J.R., Narvaez, D., Thoma, S.J., & Bebeau, M.J. (2000). A neo-Kohlbergian approach to morality research. *Journal of Moral Education, 29*(4), 381–395.

Rowe, L., & Houle, D. (1996). The lek paradox and the capture of genetic variance by condition dependent traits. *Proceedings of the Royal Society of London, Series B: Biological Sciences, 263,* 1415–1421.

Schnall, S., Haidt, J., Clore, G.L., & Alexander, J. (2008). Disgust as embodied moral judgment. *Personality and Social Psychology Bulletin, 34*(8), 1096–1109.

Schwartz, J., & Begley, S. (2003). *The mind and the brain: Neuroplasticity and power of mental force.* New York: Harper Perennials.

Symons, D. (1990). On the use and misuse of Darwinism in the study of human behaviour. In J. Barkow, L. Cosmides, & J. Tooby (Eds.), *The adapted mind: Evolutionary psychology and the generation of culture* (pp. 137–159). New York: Oxford University Press.

Tooby, J., & Cosmides, L. (1992). The psychological foundations of culture. In J.H. Barkow, L. Cosmides, & J. Tooby (Eds.), *The adapted mind: Evolutionary psychology and the generation of culture.* New York: Oxford University Press.

Tooby, J., & Cosmides, L. (2005). Conceptual foundations of evolutionary psychology. In D.M. Buss (Ed.), *The handbook of evolutionary psychology* (pp. 5–67). Hoboken, NJ: John Wiley & Sons, Inc.

Turner, J.H. (1996). The evolution of emotions in humans: A Darwinian–Durkheimian analysis. *Journal for the Theory of Social Behaviour, 26*(1), 1–33.

Whittle, S., Allen, N.B., Lubman, D.I., & Yucel, M. (2006). The neurobiological basis of temperament: Towards a better understanding of psychopathology. *Neuroscience and Biobehavioral Reviews, 30,* 511–525.

The Rejection Alarm: Person and Situation Moderators of Rejection Effects

Jonathan P. Gerber and Wayne Warburton

Recent research on social rejection has emphasised the power of its effects. Some accounts argue that such rejection causes evolutionary-based pain signals in the brain that override individual differences and situational constraints. This chapter reviews emerging evidence and recent data suggesting that both individual differences and situational variables *do* moderate the impact of social rejection, and in some cases can even eradicate its effects. The factors explored are rejection sensitivity, social anxiety, degree of situational control, level of social scrutiny, self-construal style, and the severity of the rejection.

Rejection can be a distressing experience that causes considerable emotional pain (MacDonald & Leary, 2005). A recent program of research (see Williams, 2008, for a review) has argued that the pain of one form of rejection, ostracism, is not moderated by either situation or person variables. Evidence for this comes from a series of papers demonstrating that the distress caused by ostracism is not eliminated by factors that, a priori, might be reasonably thought to moderate such effects. For example, even when people are rejected online by Ku Klux Klan members, they still feel some distress (Gonsalkorale & Williams, 2007).

But is it always the case that the effects of social rejection cannot be moderated? This chapter will draw together emerging evidence that some situation and person variables moderate the pain of rejection.[1] We will argue that, whereas some situational factors may moderate but not eliminate adverse reactions to social rejection, some personality variables may both moderate and eliminate such adverse reactions.

Some theorists believe that rejection and physical pain are phenomenologically close (e.g., MacDonald & Leary, 2005), and like physical pain, rejection seems to act like a warning. Although the complete neurological circuitry has not been specified clearly enough (Corr, 2005), it appears that when people are socially rejected, a warning is activated, their mood is lowered, self-esteem drops and they may become physically and emotionally aroused (Gerber & Wheeler, 2009a). These processes, in turn, prepare the person for actions that seem principally to involve restoring a sense of personal control and a sense of belonging to one's social group(s).

For the purposes of this chapter we will liken this warning to an alarm. In general, past research suggests that when rejection activates an automatic threat response in the brain, it sets off an alarm (Eisenberger, Lieberman & Williams, 2003). People respond to this alarm by taking steps to reduce the negative impacts of the rejection experience. Using this analogy, we will address three questions:

1. Are there factors that moderate the impact of rejection? In alarm terms, does rejection always cause the alarm to ring at the same volume, or are there factors that cause the alarm to go off less strongly? Of relevance to this question is evidence regarding people's initial response to rejection. It is clear that various *deliberate* responses to rejection can help an individual's rejection alarm to ring less loudly or turn off altogether. For example, thinking of a loved one can help a person to recover following a rejection episode (Gardner, Pickett, & Knowles, 2005). However, the *automatic* response to rejection is often antisocial in nature. Some researchers argue that this is always the case (e.g., Twenge, Baumeister, Tice & Stucke, 2001), while others present evidence that such responses can be modified (Warburton & Williams, 2005; Warburton et al., 2006; Williams & Warburton, 2003).

2. Do any factors allow us to perceive that we have been rejected and yet not feel hurt by it? That is, does rejection always make our alarm ring?

3. The last question we wish to address is how, given the situation and personality variables that exist, might we buffer ourselves from the automatic pain of rejection?

We suggest six different variables that might moderate the impact of rejection: restoration of control, level of social scrutiny, rejection 'schedule', trait anxiety level, self-construal style and level of trait rejection sensitivity. The former three represent situational variables while the latter reflect individual differences.

Situation Moderators of Rejection

Restoration of Control

Warburton et al. (2006) report a 2 × 2 study where experimental participants were initially included in a game of ball-toss with two confederates while waiting for a study to begin. These confederates either continued to include the participant in the game or excluded the participant after several throws. Participants were then assigned to a restored control condition (in which they controlled the self-administration of a very aversive noise) or a yoked condition (in which participants listened to the same aversive noise without having any control over it). All participants then completed a behavioural measure of aggression (the hot sauce paradigm: Lieberman, Solomon, Greenberg & McGregor, 1999). The results showed that an intervening manipulation of restoring control can reduce aggression following rejection and that further control loss can provoke aggression. Interestingly, the groups did not differ in terms of the degree to which their mood was lowered, and changes to affective state were not correlated with the level of aggressive responding to rejection.

Warburton, McIlwain, Cairns, and Taylor (2006) have shown that some people have a 'control-aggression schema', which is centred around a deeply-rooted belief that aggressive behaviour will restore a sense of personal control. They showed that when such people experience a control loss, this schema is automatically activated, and impels the person to behave aggressively, usually in the absence of any awareness as to what is motivating their aggressiveness. Warburton, McIlwain et al. have theorised that in people who hold this schema, social rejection will produce an aggressive response to the extent that the person experiences a loss of control. If the person experiences rejection but does not experience a reduction in control, the schema will not be activated and the aggressive response will not be forthcoming. Such an explanation is certainly consistent with data so far. It seems likely, then, that a restoration of perceived control may stop the rejection alarm ringing.

Level of Social Scrutiny

Numerous studies in the literature show both pro- and antisocial responses to rejection (pro-social: Baumeister & Tice, 1990; Gardner, Picket & Brewer, 2000; Williams, Cheung & Choi, 2000; Williams & Sommer, 1997; anti-social: Twenge et al., 2001; Warburton et al., 2006). Although a recent meta-analysis suggests the differences may come from attempts to restore control (Gerber & Wheeler, 2009a; 2009b), another possibility is that pro-social responses come at times where people are under social scrutiny and have an explicit motivation to be included and/or positively evaluated by others. Conversely, at times when there is little social scrutiny, and thus fewer consequences for antisocial behaviour, rejection may elicit aggressive behaviour that is a response to an implicit motivation to restore a sense of control (Warburton & Williams, 2005). Again this explanation fits with current experimental findings — aggressive responding to social rejection is always shown in the absence of social scrutiny.

Although this suggests some moderation of actions following rejection, it is hard to determine from such studies whether or not the immediate reaction to rejection is always some form of distress. So we are still left looking for something that clearly keeps the alarm from ringing.

The Amount of Ostracism

Chen and Williams (2007) used Cyberball, a computerised program (Williams & Jarvis, 2006), to either fully ostracise or to partially ostracise individuals. They found that complete ostracism was much more painful than partial ostracism and that reducing the amount of ostracism reduced the effect of ostracism. Chen and Williams dub this 'the velvet hammer'. Unfortunately, even partial ostracism resulted in pain.

In summary, several situation variables seem to moderate the effects of social rejection, but it is not clear whether they will completely eliminate the associated pain. At the group level, rejection seems to make the alarm ring, although if perceived control is restored or if the rejection is only partial, the alarm may ring a lot less strongly. As such, we must turn to individual differences in our search for factors that may eliminate entirely the pain of rejection.

Individual Difference Moderators of Rejection Effects
Trait Anxiety

In an as-yet-unpublished doctoral dissertation, Amy Waldrip (2007) tested whether trait levels of anxiety moderated reactions to rejection. One hundred and forty-five participants were included or excluded via the Cyberball paradigm and then distress was measured via a common needs measure used in social rejection research. The results suggested that individuals with high trait anxiety had an exacerbated distress reaction to rejection. Low anxiety individuals were also distressed, albeit at a lower level, by the rejection manipulation. This suggests that levels of trait anxiety may affect the strength of the ring of the rejection alarm but that even low levels of trait anxiety will not stop the alarm from sounding in the face of rejection. Averil Cook, a student of (Gerber) the first author in this chapter, is following up these results in her clinical doctorate.

Self-Construal

Self-construal is the way in which various group and social identities (e.g., race, gender) are spontaneously included in definitions of the self. Whereas an independent self-construal style is primarily focused on the individual, an interdependent construal style has a fundamental relationship focus. The research of Knowles and Gardner (2008, Study 1) suggests that one's self-construal style may moderate the effect of social rejection. Participants wrote about either a time they were included or a time they were excluded and then their state self-esteem was measured. Participants with interdependent self-construals (+1 SD above the mean) had self-esteem indistinguishable from included participants. However, participants with independent self-construals (−1 SD below the mean) reported lowered self-esteem when rejected.

It is possible that individual rejection of an interdependent individual may be a partial rejection only, as it does not involve rejection of the larger groups and social identities that are part of the interdependent self. This may explain, in part, the findings of Knowles and Gardner (2008). Nevertheless, the buffering effect of interdependent self-construals is the first evidence for any possible elimination of the distress of social rejection.

Rejection Sensitivity

Rejection sensitivity is the tendency to readily perceive and overreact to ambiguous social situations as if they are instances of rejection (Downey & Feldman, 1996). By definition, the relationship between rejection sensitivity and *actual* social rejection experiences is unclear, as rejection sensitivity is about responses to ambiguous social situations. Despite this, Cook (2006) used rejection sensitivity as a covariate within the Cyberball paradigm. She found that all participants accurately perceived whether they had been rejected or not. However, the level of distress that followed rejection was moderated by rejection sensitivity. As rejection sensitivity increased, so did the level of distress felt in the face of rejection. More importantly, Cook found that some participants who were low in rejection sensitivity reported being aware that they had been rejected during Cyberball but did not feel distressed by the experience.[2] It seems that low rejection sensitivity can stop the rejection alarm from ringing altogether.

The Un-Rejectable Individual

To close, we wish to speculate on how these six variables can be used to protect the individual from the distress of rejection. The three situational variables covered suggest several ways to minimise the distress of being socially rejected. First, it is important not to experience further decrements in control immediately following rejection. Indeed, to gain control over something salient during this period may have a beneficial effect. In addition, people should respond publicly to rejection, as this may have a restraining effect on antisocial or aggressive tendencies. Finally, it would be optimal to avoid situations of complete rejection, although such an outcome seems somewhat difficult to achieve.

Overall, these situational factors can minimise the distress of being rejected, but they cannot eliminate it fully. The alarm can be turned down but not off.

Individual differences offer a more promising avenue for minimising the pain of rejection. Being less anxious can lead to less distress (although it will not eliminate the effect). However, having low rejection sensitivity and construing oneself in an interdependent manner can, in some cases, eliminate the pain of rejection entirely.

Having said this, the causes of interdependent self-construal and low rejection sensitivity are very likely to be prior acceptance experiences. In essence, those people who haven't been rejected much in the past and who generally feel included by those around them in the present may not be hurt by brief experiences of rejection. In this way, a history of social acceptance may be protecting the individual from the effects of temporary rejection (see Gardner, Pickett & Knowles, 2005, for an account of social shielding that accords with this position). We do not believe that it is easy to eradicate the distress of rejection, but neither do we find support for the position that social rejection/ostracism is always painful. For some people, those high in interdependent construal or low in rejection sensitivity, rejection may be recognised but not cause pain.

Author Note

The authors would like to thank Gerard Fogarty for comments on the presentation on which this chapter is based.

Endnotes

1. To date, the only paper addressing individual differences as rejection-effect moderators was by Kelly (2001), who speculated about such effects but provided no empirical data.

2. These results go beyond the original rejection sensitivity model in showing that the effects of rejection sensitivity are not limited to the highly rejection sensitive.

References

Baumeister, R.F., & Tice, D.M. (1990). Anxiety and social exclusion. *Journal of Social and Clinical Psychology, 9,* 165–195.

Chen, Z., & Williams, K.D. (2007, May). *Partial ostracism as a means of discovering moderators.* Paper presented at the 2007 annual meeting for the Midwestern Psychological Association, Chicago.

Cook, A. (2006) Rejection sensitivity: A potential moderator of ostracism. *Australian Journal of Psychology, 58*(Suppl. 1), 125.

Corr, P.J. (2005). Social exclusion and the hierarchical defense system: Comment on MacDonald and Leary (2005). *Psychological Bulletin. 131,* 231–236.

Downey, G., & Feldman, S. (1996). Implications of rejection sensitivity for intimate relationships. *Journal of Personality and Social Psychology, 70,* 1327–1343.

Eisenberger, N.I., Lieberman, M.D., & Williams, K.D. (2003). Does rejection hurt? An fMRI Study of Social Exclusion. *Science, 302,* 290–292.

Gardner, W.L., Pickett, C.L., & Brewer, M.B. (2000). Social exclusion and selective memory: How the need to belong influences memory for social events. *Personality and Social Psychology Bulletin, 26,* 486–496.

Gardner, W.L., Pickett, C.L., & Knowles, M. (2005). Social snacking and shielding: Using social symbols, selves and surrogates in the service of belonging needs. In K.D. Williams, J.P. Forgas, & W. von Hippel (Eds.), *The social outcast: Ostracism, social exclusion, rejection, and bullying* (pp. 227–242). Hove, NY: Psychology Press

Gerber, J.P., & Wheeler, L. (2009a). On being rejected: A meta-analysis of experimental rejection research. *Perspectives on Psychological Science, 4,* 468–488.

Gerber, J.P., & Wheeler, L. (2009b). Rejoinder to Baumeister, DeWall & Vohs (2009). *Perspectives on Psychological Science, 4,* 494–495.

Gonsalkorale, K., & Williams, K.D. (2007). The KKK won't let me play: Ostracism even by a despised outgroup hurts. *European Journal of Social Psychology, 37,* 1176–1186.

Knowles, M.L., & Gardner, W.L. (2008). Benefits of membership: The activation and amplification of group identities in response to social rejection. *Personality and Social Psychology Bulletin, 34,* 1200–1213.

Lieberman, J.D., Solomon, S., Greenberg, J., & McGregor, H.A. (1999). A hot new way to measure aggression: Hot sauce allocation. *Aggressive Behavior, 25,* 331–348.

MacDonald, G., & Leary, M.R. (2005). Why does social exclusion hurt? The relationship Between social and physical pain. *Psychological Bulletin, 131,* 202–223.

Twenge, J.M., Baumeister, R.F., Tice, D.M., & Stucke, T.S. (2001). If you can't join them, beat them: Effects of social exclusion on aggressive behavior. *Journal of Personality and Social Psychology, 81*, 1058–1069.

Waldrip, A. (2007). The power of ostracism: Can personality influence reactions to social exclusion? *Dissertation Abstracts International, 68, 3-B*, 1969. (UMI No. 2007-99018-206).

Warburton, W.A., McIlwain, D.J.F., Cairns, D.R., & Taylor, A.J. (2006, July). *Restoring perceived control with aggression: Why, how, and who?* Paper presented at the 17th Meeting of the International Society for Research on Aggression, Minneapolis, MN.

Warburton, W.A., & Williams, K.D. (2005). Ostracism: When social motives collide. In J.P. Forgas, K.D. Williams, & W. von Hippel (Eds.), *Social motivation: Conscious and unconscious processes* (pp. 294–313). London: Cambridge University Press.

Warburton, W.A., Williams, K.D., & Cairns, D.R. (2006). When ostracism leads to aggression: The moderating effects of control deprivation. *Journal of Experimental Social Psychology, 42*, 213–220.

Williams, K.D. (2008). Ostracism: The kiss of social death. *Social and Personality Psychology Compass, 1*, 236–247.

Williams, K.D., Cheung, C.K.T., & Choi, W. (2000). Cyberostracism: Effects of being ignored over the internet. *Journal of Personality and Social Psychology, 79*, 748–762.

Williams, K.D., & Jarvis, B. (2006). Cyberball: A program for use in research on interpersonal ostracism and acceptance. *Behavior Research Methods, 38*, 174–180.

Williams, K.D., & Sommer, K.L. (1997). Social ostracism by one's coworkers: Does rejection lead to social loafing or compensation? *Personality and Social Psychology Bulletin, 23*, 693–706.

Williams, K.D., & Warburton, W.A. (2003). Ostracism: A form of indirect aggression that can result in aggression. *International Review of Social Psychology, 16*, 101–126.

Creativity and Individual Differences Among People With Different Sexual Orientation

Sarang Kim and Wendy Wan

Gay men are believed to be artistically creative and gifted in various forms of arts. It was argued that being sexual minorities and being marginalised from society may motivate homosexuals to be creative. However, limited previous research has shown that homosexuals scored lower on creativity tasks than heterosexuals. The current project investigated creativity and individual differences among people with different sexual orientation. Homosexuals' levels of creativity (measured with the Torrance Tests of Creative Thinking and play-doh making task) were compared with the levels of creativity of heterosexuals. In addition, the current study examined whether self-perception related variables (self-esteem, isolation, alienation, and marginalisation) contribute to the level of creativity. Sixty-two adults (31 heterosexuals, 31 gay men and women) participated in the study through face-to-face interviews. Gay men were significantly more creative than heterosexuals in play-doh making task. No significant relation was found between self-perception and creativity.

There has been a popular belief that gay men are highly creative and unusually gifted in different forms of arts (Demb, 1992). Performance fields seem to be especially populated with a large number of homosexual or bisexual males, in particular, dance, film, and theatre (Rothenberg, 1990). Moreover, popularisation of media, especially television, in recent years has supported this lay belief by showing homosexual males as hairdressers or fashion and interior designers; those who are sensitive to fashion and are generally creative. The most popular example could be *Queer Eye for the Straight Guy*, which was the American reality television series aired from 2003 to 2007.

The program had five gay men, each were talented in cooking, fashion, culture, hair, and interior design helping people in 'fashion crisis' who were almost all straight men and giving them makeovers. A television program such as this may have led people to believe gay men are more creative than heterosexual men, or may have made the existing belief stronger. However, the connection between being gay and being creative has not yet been scientifically supported (Rothenberg).

Only two empirical studies have been conducted (Ellis, 1959; Domino, 1977) on this subject, which showed homosexuals scored lower on creativity tasks than heterosexual counterparts. Ellis was the first researcher who studied the relationship between homosexuality and creativity with 66 homosexual and 150 heterosexual patients in his therapy. His finding showed that the exceptionally heterosexual participants (those who attracted to opposite sex mostly) were significantly more often rated as highly or moderately creative and less often rated as non-creative than the exceptionally homosexual participants.

Domino (1977) conducted a similar study on creativity and homosexuality two decades after the Ellis's study. The participants were administered with nine tests, including the measures of divergent thinking and creative achievement. In his finding, homosexuals scored lower than heterosexuals, suggesting homosexuals were less creative than heterosexuals, which did not support the lay belief but was consistent with the results drawn from Ellis's (1959) study.

However, criticisms towards these two studies should be considered. All of Ellis's subjects were in his own therapy and, therefore, he was both the therapist and the rater for the experiment, which could have led him to be biased either consciously or unconsciously. Moreover, subjects being patients in the therapy made them unrepresentative of the general population. The other criticism was with the way he measured the level of creativity. Ellis judged the participants on the basis of his personal psychotherapeutic experience with the participants, as to whether they were highly creative, moderately creative, or noncreative, which made his findings highly questionable (Domino, 1977). The validity of nine different instruments used to measure the creativity in Domino's study was also low and different results could have drawn if the instruments were more reliable and had a higher validity. Furthermore, these two studies were conducted three and five decades ago and there have been changes in the perceptions towards homosexuals throughout the years (from a mental disorder to an alternative lifestyle), thus further and more recent studies were needed.

Homosexuality was considered a crime, unnatural and a mental illness when Ellis' study was conducted, which might have influenced the findings of the study. By the time Domino's study was conducted, society's perception towards homosexuality was changing. However, it was only a couple of years after the change in pathological view towards homosexuality; homosexuality was removed from the Diagnostic and Statistical Manual of Mental Disorders (DSM; American Psychiatric Association, 1973). Therefore, homosexuals in 1970s might still have felt isolated, alienated and less confident in themselves in comparison to homosexuals nowadays who have more rights and face less discrimination.

Gay men and women were and still are members of a minority group in heterosexual centred society and, therefore, they are being marginalised from the society they are living in (Rothenberg, 1990). Rothenberg argued that this marginalisation might motivate homosexuals to be creative, which was also supported by Chung and Katayama (1996) stating that as male homosexuals are still subject to social disapproval, they often find acceptance in and are attracted to publicly visible artistic fields. Additionally, the way they see themselves in the society, such as their level of self-esteem, feeling of isolation and alienation were also suggested to be the elements that contribute to their creativity. Thus, it was examined whether there are any differences in the levels of creativity for gay men and lesbians and heterosexuals since gay men and women now face less marginalisation, isolation, and alienation.

The current study was therefore designed to explore whether there is a relationship between sexual orientation and creativity and to test what other social factors may contribute in influencing people's level of creativity. The following hypotheses were drawn in this study:

Hypothesis 1: Gay men would be significantly more creative than heterosexual men.

Hypothesis 2: There would be no significant difference in creative level for gay women and heterosexual women since the myth only seem to apply for homosexual men.

Hypothesis 3: Marginalisation, isolation, alienation, and self-esteem would be significantly related to creativity.

Hypothesis 4: There would be no significant relationships between self-perception related variables (marginalisation, isolation, alienation and self-esteem) and sexual orientation. Homosexuals would perceive themselves in the same way as heterosexuals.

Method

Participants

Sixty-two adult participants (31 heterosexuals and 31 gay men and women) from the Gold Coast and Brisbane were recruited through advertisements in local newspapers, around universities, and from social groups and clubs. The majority of participants (68%) were students from universities in Queensland with the mean age of 24 (*SD* = 5.485, range 18–40). Sixty-three per cent (*n* = 39) were male and the remaining 37% (*n* = 23) were female.

Materials

The materials consisted of an explanatory letter, a questionnaire, Torrance Test of Creative Thinking (TTCT; Torrance, 1974) and play-doh making task. The first part of questionnaire contained basic demographic information such as participants' age, gender, education and occupation. The rest of questions aimed at deriving the participants' sexual orientation (using parts of Klein sexual orientation grid (KSOG; dimensions of sexual attraction and emotional preference; Klein, Sepekoff, & Wolf, 1985), isolation (Dean's social isolation scale; Dean, 1961), marginalisation (modification of Barry's [2001] East Asian Acculturation Measure [EAAM]), alienation (Jessor & Jessor's alienation scale; Jessor & Jessor, 1977) and self-esteem (Rosenberg self-esteem scale; Rosenberg, 1965).

Procedures

Potential participants showed their interest through a phone call or an e-mail in response to the advertisements. All subjects were tested individually or in small groups of less than six people.

The experiment started by participants filling out questionnaire. After the completion of the questionnaire, participants were given the creativity tasks. First creativity task was the figure form of TTCT, which was the picture completion task. Participants were given five minutes to complete incomplete figure activity and ten minutes to complete the line activity. Participants were then asked to create model(s) with play-doh in any ways or forms they wanted while trying to make something unique and interesting for the second creativity task. Participants were free to use as much or as little play-doh and plastic parts as they wish in a given time (15 minutes). To measure whether the participant engaged in divergent or convergent thinking, seven play-doh reference models were shown to the participant that were selected because of their involvement of plastic parts. After the completion of the creation, the photos were taken with a digital camera for later scoring.

A master student in psychology who was trained to rate the TTCT and who was also unaware of the nature of the project and of the subjects' identities scored the TTCT task. For the scoring of the play-doh making task, one doctoral student in film study and a graduate student in industrial design, who were also unaware of the purpose of study and the identity of subjects, were asked to score the play-doh products.

Results

Overall Creativity Index on TTCT and Sexual Orientation
Based on the TTCT manual (1974), Fluency, Originality, Abstractness of Titles, Elaboration, Resistance to Premature Closure, and 12 creative strengths of emotional expressiveness, storytelling articulateness, movement or action, expressiveness of titles, synthesis of figures, synthesis of lines, unusual visualisation, internal visualisation, humour, richness of imagery, colourfulness of imagery, and fantasy, were measured by a trained examiner. These scores were then summed up to make an overall creativity index. Independent t tests indicated that there was no significant difference in the mean of TTCT for heterosexuals ($M = 52.48$, $SD = 10.95$) and gay men and women ($M = 55.00$, $SD = 11.84$), $t (60) = -.87$, $p = .39$ (two-tailed).

Overall Creativity Index on Play-doh Making and Sexual Orientation
Two examiners rated the digital pictures of the play-doh products independently, which were then added together to make a total score for play-doh making task. The independent samples t test revealed that homosexuals ($M = 16.03$, $SD = 4.04$) were significantly more creative than heterosexuals ($M = 13.39$, $SD = 3.88$) in the play-doh making task, $t (59) = -2.62$, $p < .05$. The magnitude of the difference in the means (mean difference = -2.65, 95% CI: -4.68 to $-.62$) was moderate ($\eta^2 = .10$).

When participants were divided into two gender groups of males and females and examined separately, it was shown that there was a significant difference found between gay men ($M = 16.93$, $SD = 3.95$) and heterosexual men ($M = 13.11$, SD = 3.31; $t (37) = -3.24$, $p < .01$, η^2 of .22 [very large]), but not between lesbians and heterosexual women. Therefore, the play-doh making task supported the first two hypotheses that gay men were more creative than heterosexual men, and that there would not be significant differences between lesbians and heterosexual women in their level of creativity.

Self-Perceptions and Creativity

Correlation analysis was performed to test the Hypothesis 3, regarding the relationship between self-perception and creativity. The results showed that there were no significant relationships between self-perception (marginalisation, isolation, alienation, and self-esteem) and creativity (play-doh making and TTCT). Therefore, the prediction that self-perception would be related to the level of creativity was not supported with this sample.

Self-Perception and Sexual Orientation

The independent samples *t* test was used to test the fourth hypothesis that there would not be any differences between two sexual orientation groups (homosexuals and heterosexuals) in their self-perception. The results revealed that there were no significant differences in scores for self-perception related variables between homosexual and heterosexual samples.

Subjects were then divided into two groups according to their gender and independent samples *t* tests were conducted to test whether there were any differences between heterosexual and homosexuals in their self-perception when examined separately by gender. There was no difference between gay men and straight men in their self-perception but there were two significant differences between gay women and straight women, which were in their levels of self-esteem and satisfaction with life (lesbians scored higher on these two variables than heterosexual women). Thus, the prediction that both heterosexuals and homosexuals would perceive themselves in the same manner was supported with the male sample but not fully supported with the female sample.

Discussion

The current study was conducted to test a popular myth that gay men are more creative than heterosexuals, examining a relationship between sexual orientation and creativity. It was also aimed to test whether self-perception (feeling of being marginalised, feeling of isolation, alienation and self-esteem) affects people's level of creativity and whether these self-perceptions are related to sexual orientation.

The results showed that homosexual men were significantly more creative than heterosexual men in play-doh making task but not in TTCT, which could have been due to the low reliability of TTCT ($\alpha = .413$). This finding did not support Ellis's (1959) and Domino's (1977) studies, which found that homosexuals were less creative than heterosexuals. The opposite result could be due to changes in the way society perceives homosexuality and it could also be suggested that when the self-perception of heterosexuals and gay men are similar, gay men may show higher creativity level than heterosexuals.

The results also indicated that marginalisation, isolation, alienation, and self-esteem were not significantly related to creativity for this sample. In addition, homosexuals did not feel marginalised, isolated, and alienated any more than heterosexuals did, which also could be explained with the changes in the society's perception toward homosexuality: The discrimination against homosexuals has decreased as society now accept or tolerate rather than resist their differences.

Limitations and Suggestions for Future Research
This study has some limitations and one of the limitations was that the sample size used in the study was small. Small sample size made the generalisation of the results difficult. Thus, the similar studies are needed with larger sample size to have clearer correlations of sexual orientation with creativity and other social factors. Moreover, future studies should also examine broader range of ages, areas of living, and socioeconomic status. In this study, participants came from metropolitan areas in Queensland, either in Brisbane or on the Gold Coast. Thus, future research should study homosexuals living in rural areas for the comparison since people in rural areas may be less accepting towards homosexuality.

The participants who responded to the advertisements were also relatively open and comfortable about their sexual orientation for both homosexual and heterosexual groups. Thus, the participants gathered in this study may not have been representative of general population. Moreover, majority of participants were students who were either enrolled in undergraduate or postgraduate courses. Thus, results may have been a representative of tertiary students rather than the general population.

Yet another limitation of this study was that both TTCT and the play-doh making task measured the visual creativity rather than the creativity in writing, science or music. Other forms of creativity should be studied in the future studies.

It is also important to know whether or not homosexuals really feel that they get more acceptance nowadays as society's view towards homosexuality has changed and is still changing. Surveys measuring how gay men and women feel about society's perception should be suggested to see if changes in society's perception towards homosexuality have any impact on them.

References

American Psychiatric Association. (1973). *Diagnostic and statistical manual of mental disorders* (2nd ed.). Washington, DC: Author.

Barry, D.T. (2001). Development of a new scale for measuring acculturation: The East Asian Acculturation Measure (EAAM). *Journal of Immigrant Health, 3,* 193–197.

Chung, Y.B., & Katayama, M. (1996). Assessment of sexual orientation in lesbian/gay/bisexual studies. *Journal of Homosexuality, 30,* 49–62.

Dean, D. (1961). Alienation: Its meaning and measurement. *American Sociological Review, 26,* 753–758.

Demb, J. (1992). Are gay men artistic? A review of the literature. *Journal of Homosexuality, 23,* 83–92.

Domino, G. (1977). Homosexuality and creativity. *Journal of Homosexuality, 2,* 261–267.

Ellis, A. (1959). Homosexuality and creativity. *Journal of Clinical Psychology, 15,* 376–379.

Jessor, R., & Jessor, S. (1977). *Problem behavior and psychosocial development.* New York: Academic Press.

Klein, F., Sepekoff, B., & Wolf, T. (1985). Sexual orientation: A multi-variable dynamic process. *Journal of Homosexuality, 1,* 35–49.

Rosenberg, M. (1965). *Society and the adolescent self-image.* Princeton, NJ: Princeton University Press.

Rothenberg, A. (1990). *Homosexuality and creativity: Creativity and madness. New findings and old stereotypes* (pp. 103–113). Baltimore: The Johns Hopkins University Press.

Torrance, E.P. (1974). *Torrance test of creative thinking.* Lexington, MA: Personnel Press.

Performance aspects
and personality influences

The Significance of Different Viewpoints in Self-Regulation Studies: Similarities and Differences Between Mastery and Performance Approach Orientations

Zahra Izadikhah and Chris J. Jackson

Despite much research, the literature regarding goal orientation is surrounded by controversy. Some researchers believe that mastery and performance approach orientations are both typically positive predictors of performance, since they both represent approach forms of regulation. We, therefore, investigated the moderated effect of rewarding climate on these two approach forms of goal orientation in predicting self-ratings (258 employees) and supervisors' ratings of job performance (for 120 employees). Results of hierarchical moderated regression suggested significant interactions between mastery and performance approach orientations and rewarding climate in predicting job performance with both self and supervisors' ratings. However, when the interactions were plotted, supervisors' ratings showed different patterns of the relationship for the two types of goal orientations. These results suggest differences between performance approach and mastery approach orientations.

Goal orientation is defined as competence relevant conceptualisations of motivation. They consist of general reasons and purposes for the behaviour and the standards or criteria, which are used to evaluate performance (Dweck & Leggett, 1988; Pintrich, 2000). The most useful framework in the literature of goal orientation includes mastery approach orientation, performance approach orientation and performance avoidance orientation (Elliot, McGregor, & Gable, 1999). Mastery approach orientation is focused on understanding and learning new tasks and increasing or developing competence. Performance approach orientation is focused on demonstrating competence, gaining favourable judgements from others and being concerned with normative based standards of improvement (Dweck, 1996). Performance avoidance orientation is focused on avoiding looking stupid and incompetent or being negatively judged by others (Elliot & Harackiewicz, 1996).

The focus of the current research is on mastery approach and performance approach orientations. While a rather clear pattern has emerged for mastery approach orientation, the pattern of findings for performance approach orientation is complicated and inconsistent (Grant & Dweck, 2003). Mastery approach orientation is widely accepted as a positive predictor of performance (see Grant & Dweck; Elliot et al., 1999). Performance approach orientation has been associated with positive outcomes such as higher course grades and better exam performance (e.g., Elliot & Harackiewicz, 1996). However, other research has shown that performance approach orientation was also associated with negative processes and outcomes such as test anxiety and an unwillingness to seek help with schoolwork (Elliot et al.). Students who adopt performance approach orientations have shown less interest in the task, less positive affect, and more negative affect (Pintrich, 2000).

Nevertheless, some researchers believe that the similarities between mastery and performance approach orientations outweigh their differences (Urdan, 2004; Wolters, 2004). They argue that since performance approach orientation is an approach motivation, then self-regulation according to a performance approach orientation also involves trying to move toward a desirable end state and consequently a positive outcome. It has been argued that performance approach orientation is also grounded in the need for achievement and focuses on positive possibilities. Therefore, mastery and performance approach orientations are thought to be typically positive predictors of performance since they both represent approach forms of regulation (Wolters; Urdan).

The Current Research

We argue that a moderator effect may exist in the relationship between the two approach orientations and outcome performance and may help to better understand the similarities and differences between the two constructs. One factor likely to interact with the approach tendencies of these two constructs is the nature of the environment; for example, a rewarding environment. Therefore, we investigate the moderated effect of rewarding climate on the relationship between mastery approach and performance approach orientations and job performance. In addition, we argued that one of the limitations of previous research in this area was focusing only on self-ratings data. We therefore investigated the above interaction in predicting both self and supervisor's ratings of job performance.

Study 1

Predicting self-ratings of job performance from mastery approach and performance approach orientations

In the first study we investigated the interaction between mastery approach orientation and rewarding climate with self-ratings of job performance in a sample of part-time and full time job employees. The same process was used to study performance approach orientation.

Method

Participants

Participants were 258 part-time workers (103 full time and 155 part time) from a multitude of different organisations (67.4% female). Part-time workers were also in tertiary education (12% in production; 36% in service, 19% in education, 17% in administration and 16% others). In terms of hours of work, 5% worked between 20–24 hours, 78% worked between 16–20 hours, 11% worked between 12–18 hours, and there were some unspecified cases. Full-time workers were contacted through their organisations (a hospital and two schools). The average age of all participants was 28.78 years (range 17 to 48, $SD = 3.76$).

Procedure

During each session, participants completed a number of electronically administered questionnaires under the direct supervision of a researcher.

Measures

All the measurements used in this study utilised 5-point Likert-type response scale ranging from 5 (*strongly agree*) to 1 (*strongly disagree*).

Performance Approach and Mastery Approach Orientation

The Jackson Goal Orientation Questionnaire (JGOQ) was developed in light of recent research in the goal orientation literature and to overcome the limitations of the existing measurements of goal orientation (see Elliot & Thrash, 2002; Grant & Dweck, 2003). Internal consistency of subscales in the JGOQ were .87 for performance approach orientation (6 items), .88 for mastery approach orientation (7 items), and .79 for performance avoidance orientation (5 items). An example item of mastery approach orientations is 'I like to be challenged'. An example item for performance approach orientation is 'Outperforming my peers motivates me'. An example item for performance avoidance orientation is 'I am afraid to look foolish in front of my peers'.

Exploratory and confirmatory factor analysis of JGOQ was conducted by Izadikhah (2009) using two samples (total size 847 participants of which 28% were university students and the remaining were recruited from the general community). A subsample ($n = 412$) of this group, which was used for exploratory factor analysis (EFA), also completed the VandeWalle (1997) goal orientation questionnaire. EFA and confirmatory factor analysis (CFA) showed that the JGOQ adequately represented the conceptual domain that it was designed to cover and provided evidence of content validity for this measurement (see Kaplan & Saccuzzo, 2005). Additionally, high correlation between the JGOQ and VaneWalle's (1997) goal orientation questionnaire (an established measurement tool) provided evidence of concurrent validity. In addition, the JGOQ is closely related to Jackson's Goal Oriented Achiever Scale from the Learning Styles Profiler (Jackson, 2008; O'Connor & Jackson, 2008).

Rewarding Climate

The Occupational Climate Questionnaire (OCQ; Furnham & Gunter, 1993). The reward scale in the OCQ includes 10 items in which the employee assesses the degree to which their organisation is rewarding. Construct validity and reliability of this measure was established by Levine and Jackson (2002). An example item for rewarding climate is: 'In my organisation I receive appropriate salary'.

Job Performance

Overall Job Performance Questionnaire (Johnson, 1998). This questionnaire contains six items, with higher scores indicating greater job performance. This scale has shown high internal consistency at .75; and has been utilised as a measure of job performance in different research (e.g., see Izadikhah, 2009; O'Connor & Jackson, 2008). An example of a questionnaire item is: 'I work hard and do my job to the best of my abilities'.

Data Analysis

In both studies, to test for moderated effect of rewarding climate on both mastery approach and performance approach orientations, hierarchical moderated multiple regression analyses were conducted. Mean centred variables were used to reduce possible multicollinearity between predictors and the interaction term. All data were screened prior to the analyses, for violations of the assumptions of normality, missing data and outliers; two cases were removed from the analysis due to completely missing data and one outlier was detected. Investigation into the skewness and kurtosis of the data using statistical tests in combination with visual screening of the histogram and stem-and-leaf diagram indicated no skewness and kurtosis. To control for potential confounding effects of gender and age, which preliminary analyses revealed exerted significant effects on all three contexts of job performance, these variables were entered into the regression equations at Step 1. In Step 2, the two predictors that are performance approach orientation and rewarding climate were entered. In Step 3, mastery approach orientation × rewarding climate interaction term was entered. The same process was conducted for performance approach orientation × rewarding climate.

Results

Mean, standard deviation, apha coefficients, and correlations between variables are shown in Table 15.1. Using the hierarchical moderated multiple regression models described above, was not found a significant main effect of age and gender in predicting job performance. However, there were both a significant main effect of performance approach orientation ($\beta = .111$, $t = 1.72$, $p = .03$), and rewarding climate ($\beta = .121$, $t = 1.86$, $p = .02$). There was a significant performance approach orientation × rewarding climate interaction ($\beta = -.137$, $t(248) = -2.14$, $p = .03$; $R^2 = .077$, R^2 change $= .014$), which is shown in Figure 15.1a. Simple slopes analysis shows that both at low rewarding climate ($\beta = .27$, $t = 3.10$, $p = .001$), and at high rewarding

Table 15.1

Mean, Standard Deviation, Cronbach's Alpha and the Correlations Between Variables in Study 1

	Mean	*SD*	Alpha	1	2	3
1. Performance approach orientation	22.63	3.48	.83			
2. Mastery approach orientation	28.68	3.56	.86	.43**		
3. Reward climate	27.18	5.18	.89	.24**	.19 **	
4. Job performance	32.54	5.37	.82	.26**	.33**	.38**

Note: *$p < .05$, **$p < .01$, ***$p < .001$.

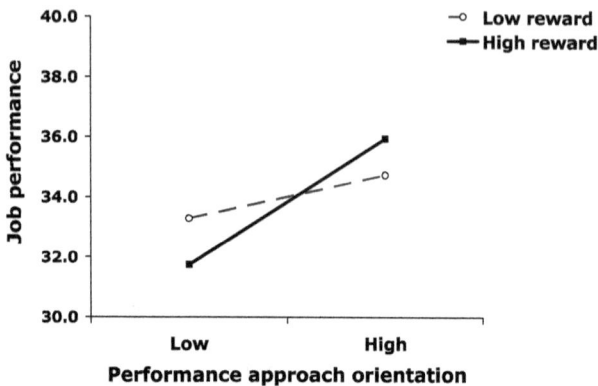

Figure 15.1a

Predicting job performance from the interaction between performance approach orientation and rewarding climate in Study 1.

climate ($\beta = .49$, $t = 5.11$, $p < .00$; Figure 15.1a), performance approach orientation is a significant positive predictor of job performance.

There was no main effect of age and gender in predicting job performance from the interaction between mastery approach orientation and rewarding climate. In predicting job performance from the proposed moderated multiple regression model, results show significant effects of mastery orientation in predicting job performance ($\beta = .362$, $t = 5.74$, $p \leq .001$). Additionally, analysis showed a significant effect of rewarding climate in predicting job performance ($\beta = .243$, $t = 4.75$, $p \leq .001$). There was significant mastery orientation × rewarding climate interaction in predicting job performance ($\beta = .141$, $t[248] = 2.16$, $p = .01$; $R^2 = .149$, R^2 change $= .017$). Simple slopes analysis shows that both at low ($\beta = .23$, $t = 2.41$, $p = .02$), and high rewarding climate ($\beta = .48$, $t = 5.67$, $p < .001$; Figure 15.1b), mastery orientation is a positive predictor of job performance.

Study 2

Predicting supervisors' ratings of job performance from mastery approach and performance approach orientations.

The aim was to investigate how supervisors evaluate mastery approach and performance approach oriented employees in low and high rewarding climates.

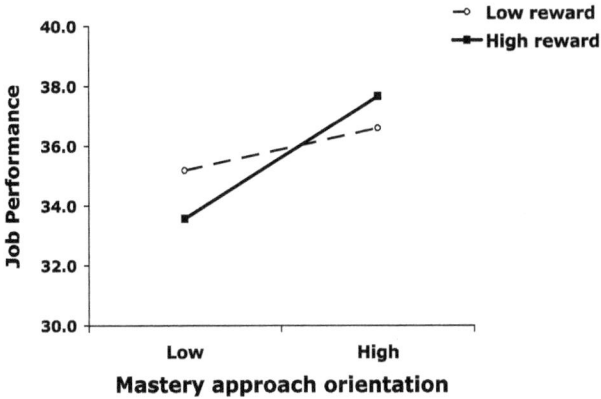

Figure 15.1b

Predicting job performance from the interaction between mastery approach orientation and rewarding climate in Study 1.

Method

Participants and Procedure

A total of 117 participants (63% female) participated in this study. The average age was 29.23 years ($SD = 4.58$; range 17 to 46 years). A total of 34% of participants had full-time jobs and the remaining 66% had part-time jobs. Part-time workers were also in tertiary education; so job characteristics in terms of types of jobs and number of hours of work were similar to the Study 1. Full-time workers were recruited from an architecture company, a hospital (nurses and staff) and a university (staff). All participants completed the same questionnaires as Study 1, except for the self-report measures of work performance, which were not completed. Questionnaires were electronically completed under the direct supervision of a research assistant. Once the questionnaire was completed, the immediate work supervisor of the participant was emailed and asked to complete a supervisor evaluation of the participant's job performance used in first study except adapted for use by supervisors. Supervisors' names and details were not saved during this process and supervisor and participant questionnaires were matched by a numerical code generated by the computer.

Measures

Participants completed the same questionnaires as in Study 1 with the exception of self-reported measures of job performance. Instead, the job performance rating scale was adapted for use by supervisors (which were sent to supervisors). An example of supervisors' ratings of job performance is, '... (i.e., John) works hard and does his job to the best of his abilities'.

Data Analysis

As in Study 1, hierarchical multiple moderated regression was used to test for moderation effects between mastery approach/performance approach orientation and rewarding climate on the supervisor job performance rating scale. Similar to Study 1 the assumptions for regression analysis were checked and there was no violation of the assumption. To control for potential confounding effects of gender and age, these were entered into the regression equations at Step 1.

Results

Two univariate outliers in job performance were deleted. Mean, standard deviation, alpha coefficients, and correlations between variables are shown in Table 15.2. There are also significant positive correlations between mastery approach orientation and the measures of rewarding climate and job performance. In addition, rewarding climate also has significant positive correlations with job performance.

Using hierarchical moderated multiple regression in predicting job performance, neither gender nor age effects were significant. In predicting job performance, performance approach orientation as a main effect was significant ($\beta = -.2418$, $t = -2.28$, $p = .02$), but not rewarding climate ($\beta = .059$, $t = .68$, ns). There was a significant performance approach orientation × rewarding climate interaction ($\beta = .259$, $t[115] = 2.36$, $p = .01$; $R^2 = .085$, R^2 change $= .034$). The interaction is shown in Figure 15.2a. Simple slopes analysis shows that at low rewarding climate, performance approach orientation is a significant negative predictor of job performance ($\beta = -.523$, $t = -2.17$, $p = .02$), but not at high rewarding climate ($\beta = .011$, $t = 0.06$, ns).

Table 15.2

Mean, Standard Deviation, Cronbach's Alpha and the Correlations Between Variables in Study 2

	Mean	SD	Alpha	1	2	3
1. Performance approach orientation	20.15	4.76	.83			
2. Mastery approach orientation	28.16	3.27	.84	.38**		
3. Reward climate	21.38	4.23	.85	.12	.18*	
4. Job performance	31.36	5.21	.79	.13	.17*	.29**

Note: *$p < .05$, **$p < .01$, ***$p < .001$

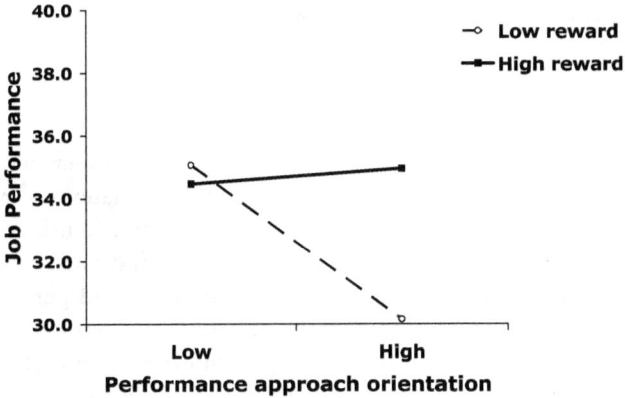

Figure 15.2a
Predicting supervisors' ratings of job performance from the interaction between performance approach orientation and rewarding climate in Study 2.

There were no support of main effects of mastery orientation and rewarding climate in predicting supervisors' ratings of job performance. There was a significant mastery orientation × rewarding climate interaction in predicting supervisors' ratings of job performance ($\beta = .234$, $t(115) = 2.24$, $p = .02$; $R^2 = .103$, R^2 change $= .028$). Simple slopes analysis shows that at high rewarding climate mastery orientation is a positive predictor of job performance ($\beta = .52$, $t = 2.54$, $p = .004$); but there was

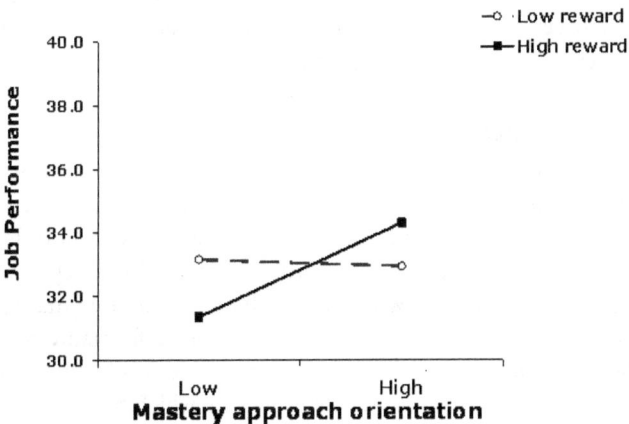

Figure 15.2b
Predicting supervisors' ratings of job performance from the interaction between mastery approach orientation and rewarding climate in Study 2.

no significant relationship at low rewarding climate ($\beta = -.01$, $t = -.10$, ns; Figure 15.2b).

Discussion

The current research investigated the interaction between rewarding climate and mastery and performance approach orientations in predicting self and supervisors' ratings of job performance. Considering the moderating effect of rewarding climate helped to understand the similarities and differences between mastery approach and performance approach orientation in predicting job performance. Consistent interactions were found between mastery approach orientation/performance approach orientation and rewarding climate in predicting job performance across both self and supervisors' ratings.

Mastery Approach Orientation

According to self-ratings, mastery approach orientation positively predicts job performance both at low and high rewarding climates. In contrast, the use of supervisors' ratings suggests that mastery approach orientation was a positive predictor of job performance only at high rewarding climate but not at low rewarding climate. As such, the results with self-ratings confirm the positive potential of mastery approach orientation as it is widely accepted in the literature of goal orientation (e.g., see Grant & Dweck, 2003). However, supervisors' ratings challenge this perspective and suggest that mastery approach orientation positively predict job performance only in high rewarding climate conditions, but not low rewarding climate conditions.

Performance Approach Orientation

Self-ratings indicated that performance approach orientation positively predicts job performance both in low and high rewarding climates. From supervisors' perspectives, performance approach orientation does not predict job performance at high rewarding climate; and it negatively predicts job performance at low rewarding climate. It appears that supervisors do not see positive potential in adopting performance approach orientation in predicting job performance. These results from supervisors' ratings are similar to some other research, which has questioned the benefit of a performance approach orientation (e.g., Elliot et al., 1999; Printrich, 2000). For example, it seems that external reference standards of evaluation limit the extent to which performance approach orientation produces positive outcomes (Printrich, 2000). It was argued that concentrating on comparison, outperforming others and being concerned with negative judgements from others would bring about distractions and negative outcomes.

Therefore, the findings with self-ratings may lend support to the idea that similarities between mastery and performance approaches outweigh their differences. However, supervisors' ratings clearly show differences between the two goal orientations and imply that mastery and performance approach orientations function differently both in high and in low rewarding climates. Supervisors' ratings suggest that mastery approach orientation positively predicts job performance when the climate is highly rewarding, but does not predict job performance in low rewarding climates. Additionally, the performance approach orientation does not predict job performance in high rewarding climates and negatively predicts job performance in low rewarding climates. Therefore, according to supervisors' ratings, mastery and performance approach orientations do not have many similarities (as also indicated in some earlier research; see Urdan, 2004; Wolters, 2004).

In sum, considering the moderating effect of a rewarding climate helps to understand how consistent or inconsistent the results are with self and supervisors' ratings. In addition, it elaborates the similarities and differences between mastery and performance approach orientations. In view of the fact that throughout the literature most discussions on goal orientation are based on self-rating studies, the current research lends support to the need for self *and alternative ratings* of performance to gain a full understanding of goal orientation. Researchers should be wary of making general conclusions based solely on self-report work performance data.

References

Dweck, C.S. (1996). Social motivation: Goals and social-cognitive processes. A comment. In J. Juvonen & K.R. Wentzel (Eds.), *Social motivation: Understanding children's school adjustment.* Cambridge studies in social and emotional development. New York: Cambridge University Press.

Dweck, C.S., & Leggett, E.L. (1988). A social-cognitive approach to motivation and personality. *Psychological Review, 95*(2), 256–273.

Elliot, A.J., & Harackiewicz, J.M. (1996). Approach and avoidance achievement goals and intrinsic motivation: A mediational analysis. *Journal of Personality and Social Psychology, 70*(3), 461–475.

Elliot, A.J., McGregor, H.A., & Gable, S. (1999). Achievement goals, study strategies, and exam performance: A mediational analysis. *Journal of Educational Psychology, 91*(3), 549–563.

Elliot, A.J., & McGregor, H.A. (1999). Test anxiety and the hierarchical model of approach and avoidance achievement motivation. *Journal of Personality and Social Psychology, 76*(4), 628–644.

Elliot, A.J., & Thrash, T.M. (2002). Approach-avoidance motivation in personality: Approach and avoidance temperaments and goals. *Journal of Personality and Social Psychology, 82*(5), 804–818.

Furnham, A., & Gunter, B. (1993). *Corporate assessment: Auditing a company's personality.* London: Routledge.

Jackson, C.J. (2008). When avoidance leads to approach: How ear preference interacts with neuroticism to predict disinhibited approach. *Laterality: Asymmetries of Body, Brain and Cognition, 13*(4), 333–373.

Griffin, M.A., Neal, A., & Parker, S.K. (2007). A new model of work role performance: Positive behaviour in uncertain and interdependent contexts. *Academy of Management Journal, 50*(2), 327–347.

Grant, H., & Dweck, C.S. (2003). Clarifying achievement goals and their impact. *Journal of Personality and Social Psychology, 85*(3), 541–553.

Johnson, D.E. (1998). *Applied multivariate methods for data analysts.* Pacific Grove, CA: Duxbury Press.

Izadikhah, Z. (2009). Personality processes underlying the approach construct in the prediction of every day life outcomes. Doctoral dissertation, The University of Queensland, Australia.

Kaplan, A., & Middleton, M.J. (2002). Should childhood be a journey of a race? Response to Harackiewicz et al. (2002). *Journal of Educational Psychology, 94*(3), 646–648.

Levine, S.Z., & Jackson, C.J. (2002). Aggregated personality, climate and demographic factors as predictors of departmental shrinkage. *Journal of Business and Psychology, 17*(2), 287–297.

O'Connor, P.J., & Jackson, C. (2008). Learning to be saints or sinners: The indirect pathway from sensation seeking to behavior through mastery orientation. *Journal of Personality, 76*(4), 733–752.

Pintrich, P.R. (2000). An achievement goal theory perspective on issues in motivation terminology, theory, and research. *Contemporary Educational Psychology, 25*(1), 92–104.

Urdan, T. (2004). using multiple methods to assess students' perceptions of classroom goal structures. *European Psychologist, 9*(4), 222–231.

VandeWalle, D. (1997). Development and validation of a work domain goal orientation instrument. *Educational and Psychological Measurement, 57*(6), 995–1015.

Wolters, C.A. (2004). Advancing achievement goal theory: Using goal structures and goal orientations to predict students' motivation, cognition, and achievement. *Journal of Educational Psychology, 96*(2), 236–250.

Personality and Task Performance

Trishita Mathew and Richard E. Hicks

While the positive effects of goal setting and self-efficacy on performance are well established (Bandura, 1997; Locke & Latham, 1990) and it is known that task anxiety can lead to detriments in performance (Locke & Latham, 1990); it is not known which variable affects task performance the most. The present study aimed to identify the strongest predictor of task performance among self-efficacy, goal setting and task anxiety. The study was conducted with a total of 80 participants who were students from an Australian university. It was hypothesised that self-efficacy, goal setting and task anxiety would be significant predictors of task performance with self-efficacy being the most important predictor, followed by goal setting, followed by task anxiety. The hypothesis was partially supported as self-efficacy was found to be a significant, and the most important, predictor, but goal setting and task anxiety were not found to be significant predictors of task performance. Implications of the results are discussed.

The last 35 years have seen well-established positive effects of goal setting on performance, such as increases in employee productivity that are related to goal setting (e.g., Latham & Kinne, 1974; Latham & Yukl, 1975; Locke & Latham, 2002). Goal setting directs expenditure of effort, while self-efficacy determines how much effort people will expend and how long they will persist in the face of obstacles and aversive experiences (Locke & Latham, 2002). The stronger the perceived self-efficacy, the more effort expended (Bandura, 1977). However, previous research has also demonstrated that as tasks become more complex, the effects of goals on performance may become detrimental (e.g., Earley, Connolly, & Eakergen, 1989; Huber, 1985). While it is evident that self-efficacy, task anxiety and goals influence performance, it is not clear which one is the strongest predictor of performance. Therefore, the present study aimed to identify the most important predictor of task performance among goal setting, task anxiety and self-efficacy. Goal setting and task anxiety are addressed first followed by self-efficacy.

Locke and Latham's (1990) goal-setting theory states that a goal refers to attaining a specified standard of competence on a given task, usually within a specified time limit, thereby directing an individual's attention and effort expenditure in a specific direction. It is further stated that difficult and specific goals lead to higher task performance than easy or ambiguous goals such as 'do your best' goals. Difficult goals require higher expenditure of effort and attention compared to easy goals. Ambiguous goals such as 'do your best' can have subjective interpretations of the standard of competence required and, therefore, may not lead to higher task performance (Locke & Latham, 1990). Locke and Latham further add that sometimes when people have to deal with a complex task asking them to do their best leads to better task strategies than setting a specific, difficult performance goal. A possible explanation is that a performance goal can make people anxious to succeed, leading them to formulate unsystematic and ineffective task strategies, thereby leading to lower performance. Previous goal setting studies have found positive performance effects on a range of tasks of varying complexity, ranging from simple brainstorming tasks, to college course work to complex scientific work (Wood, Mento & Locke, 1987). Wood (1986) proposed that task complexity involves three aspects: component complexity, which is the number of actions to be performed and the number of information cues provided; coordinative complexity, which is the type and number of relationships among actions; and information cues and dynamic complexity, which is changes in actions and information cues and the relationships among them. In a meta-analytic study, Wood et al.(1987) using Wood's outline for task complexity rated a range of tasks used in goal setting studies. Tasks such as reaction time and brainstorming were classified as less complex tasks, school or college coursework was classified as moderately complex and scientific and engineering work were classified as complex tasks. The researchers found that that goal-setting effects were strongest for easy tasks ($d = .76$) and weakest for more complex tasks ($d = .42$).

Bandura (1997) defines perceived self-efficacy as people's beliefs in their own capabilities to attain certain outcomes. However, Bandura cautions that self-efficacy needs to be evaluated at domain specific levels as people differ in their areas of efficacy and the levels of efficacy developed. For example, a student may have high academic efficacy but low social efficacy. Therefore, in the present study self-efficacy refers to domain specific efficacy and not global self-efficacy. In relation to goals, there is a high correlation between self-set goals and self-efficacy as those with high self-efficacy set higher goals and use better task strategies to attain the goals than those with lower self-efficacy (Heslin & Latham, 2004; Latham, Winters & Locke, 1994; Locke & Latham, 2002; Wood & Bandura, 1989). On the other hand, when people are assigned goals, self-efficacy is raised, as it is an implicit indication that the person assigning the goal has confidence that the assignee can obtain the goal (Locke & Latham, 2002). In relation to task anxiety, Meece, Wigfied and Eccles (1990) found that efficacy beliefs had an independent effect on performance; whereas, level of anxiety bore little or no relationship to performances on stressful academic tasks. However, in a meta-analytic study on the contribution of self-efficacy to performance, it was found that self-efficacy predicted performance for task, but not job performance (Judge, Jackson, Shaw, Scott, & Rich, 2007).

In summary, it has been found that goal setting and self-efficacy positively influence performance (Bandura, 1997; Locke & Latham, 1990), while task anxiety may or may not influence performance (Locke & Latham, 1990; Meece et al., 1990). It has also been found that the effects of goal setting on performance are strongest for simple tasks (Wood et al., 1987). As the task utilised in the present study was similar to school and college course work, it was classified as moderately complex. It was hypothesised that self-efficacy, goal setting and task anxiety would be significant predictors of task performance with self-efficacy being the strongest predictor of task performance, followed by goal setting, followed by task anxiety.

Method
Participants
A sample of 80, university level, psychology students from an Australian university was recruited for the present study. The participants' ages ranged from 18 to 60 years ($M = 28.16$, $SD = 11.21$). Among the participants, there were 20 males and 60 females, in which 49 were undergraduates and 31 were postgraduates.

Materials
Task Evaluation Questionnaire (Intrinsic Motivation Inventory [IMI]; Ryan 1982). The IMI is a multidimensional instrument intended to assess participants' subjective experience related to a target activity in laboratory experiments. There are four versions of the IMI; for the present study the

Task Evaluation Questionnaire (TEQ) version of the IMI was utilised. Responses to items are indicated on a 7-point Likert scale ranging from *Not at all true* to *Very true*. For the present study responses were indicated on a 4-point Likert scale ranging from *Strongly disagree* to *Strongly agree*.

Subscale 'Perceived competence' is theorised to be a positive predictor of both self-reported and behavioural measure of intrinsic motivation. There were no negatively worded items in the subscale. Subscale 'Pressure-Tension' is theorised to be a negative predictor of intrinsic motivation and consisted of items such as 'I did not feel at all nervous about doing the task' and 'I felt tense while doing the task'. There were two negatively worded items in the scale (Ryan, 1982).

Scores for each subscale were calculated by taking the average of the constituent items. Higher scores indicate more of the concept described by each subscale. In the present study the subscales of Pressure-Tension and Perceived Competence were utilised as indicators of task anxiety and task specific efficacy respectively. The IMI was found to have adequate reliability and validity (McAuley, Duncan, &Tammen, 1989). In the present study the internal consistencies of both the subscales were adequate as measured by Chronbach's alpha (Perceived Competence α = .80 and Pressure-Tension α = .87).

Manipulation Check Question

To check the validity of the goal-setting manipulation, participants were asked what their goals for the task were. Participants responded by circling one of three options: 'I had no goal', 'Goal as set by the researcher' and 'To do my best'.

Task

In previous goal-setting studies the positive effects of goal setting on performance has been found using a wide range of tasks. However, in a meta-analytic study Wood et al. (1987) found that the positive effects of goal setting on performance were the strongest for simple tasks. The task utilised in the present study was designed to be similar to a general cognitive ability test and comprised of 24 questions with multiple-choice answers. The questions fell into four broad categories of general knowledge (e.g., how many cents in one Australia dollar?), mathematics (e.g., what does 95 minus 46 equal?), vocabulary (e.g., another word for a dictionary would be?), and logical reasoning (e.g., sculpture is to sculptor as architecture is to?). Depending on the condition participants were assigned to, the task questions were either presented in three sets of 8 questions each or all 24 questions together. The first 8 questions were simple questions and it was expected that participants would be able to answer all 8 questions. The next 8 questions were designed to be slightly more difficult than the first 8 questions and it was expected that most participants would be able to answer at least 7 out of 8 questions correctly. The last 8 questions were designed to be more difficult than the first 16 questions and it was expected that most participants would get at least 4 out of 8 questions correct. Since each correctly answered question got a score of 1, the total scores could range from a minimum of 0 to a maximum of 24. The level of difficulty of all three sets of questions was evaluated by two independent raters (an undergraduate student and a university professor) with adequate inter-rater reliability ($r = .90$). In addition, a pilot study was conducted to test the suitability of the task questions.

Design

Since the aim of the study was to identify the strongest predictor of task performance among self-efficacy, goal setting and task anxiety, a hierarchical multiple regression was deemed to be the most suitable statistical analysis tool. Self-efficacy, goal setting and task anxiety were the predictor variables and performance operationalised as total scores on the task was the criterion variable. Self-efficacy and task anxiety were continuous variables, whereas goal setting was a dichotomous variable coded 1 for presence of goal setting and 0 for absence of goal setting. As it was hypothesised that self-efficacy would be the strongest predictor of performance, followed by goal setting, followed by task anxiety, the predictors were entered into the model in 3 steps, with task anxiety entered first, followed by goal setting, followed by self-efficacy.

Procedure

The study was carried out in a quiet room. Participants were randomly allocated to one of two experimental conditions based on their entry into the testing venue. The first participant was allocated to the 'goal setting' condition, the second participant to 'no goal setting' condition, and so on. In the goal setting condition the participants had to achieve a score of at least 4 out of 8 to move onto the second set of questions. Each question in the first set was displayed for 15 seconds. Unanswered questions were considered incorrect and participants could not reattempt a missed question. For the second set of questions, participants needed to get a score of at least 5 out of 8 to move onto the third set of questions. Each question in the second set was displayed for 12 seconds. Questions in the third set were displayed for 10 seconds each only. There were no minimum scores to achieve for the participants in the no goal setting condition to move onto the next set of questions. They were asked to do their best and all questions were displayed for 15 seconds each. All participants were given a practice task before commencing on the actual task. After performing the task, participants were asked to complete the self-report measures and provide demographic information.

Results

Data Diagnostics

Prior to data analyses, all data were screened for accuracy of data entry, coding errors and missing values. All assumptions of statistical tests utilised were examined and deemed satisfactory. All tests were considered significant at $\alpha = .05$, and exact probabilities are reported to three decimal places. All analyses were conducted using SPSS for Windows 15.0.

Manipulation Check

Validity of goal setting manipulation. Participants in the goal setting condition were assigned specific quantitative goals by the researcher, which was assumed to be accepted by the participants, but participants in the no goal setting conditions were told to do their best on the task with no specific goals to achieve. In the 'no goal setting' condition, 15% of the participants stated that they had 'no goal', 5% said 'goal as set by the researcher', and 80% stated their goal was 'to do my best'. The majority of the participants in the 'no goal setting' condition did not have a specific goal for the task.

Data Analysis

A hierarchical multiple regression was conducted to determine the strongest predictor of performance. In Step 1, task anxiety was entered into the model and the overall model was found to be significant with $F(1, 78) = 5.98$, $p = .017$. In Step 2, presence or absence of goal setting was entered into the model, which explained an additional 5% of variance as indicated by R^2 change (.05). This additional variance accounted for was significant as indicated by F change $(1, 77) = 4.42$, $p = .039$. The overall model in Step 2 was also significant as indicated by $F(2, 77) = 5.33$, $p = .007$. In Step 3, self-efficacy was entered, which explained an additional 8.3% of variance as indicated by R^2 change (.083). This additional variance accounted for was significant as indicated by F change $(1, 76) = 7.91$,

$p = .006$. The overall model at step 3 was also significant as indicated by $F(3, 76) = 6.51$, $p = .001$. On examination of the standardised coefficients (β) it was found that self-efficacy was the strongest predictor of task performance as hypothesised. Presence or absence of goal setting and task anxiety were not found to be significant predictors of task performance. Overall, the predictors accounted for 17.3% of variance in the criterion variable as indicated by Adjusted R^2 (.173). Table 16.1 summarises the range, means and standard deviations of task performance scores, self-efficacy and task anxiety, correlations among predictors and the standardised and unstandardised coefficients.

As can be seen in Table 16.1, judging by the standardised coefficients the strongest predictor of task performance in the present study was self-efficacy, followed by goal setting, followed by task anxiety as hypothesised. However, goal setting and task anxiety were not significant predictors of task performance, contrary to the hypothesis.

Discussion

Based on previous research findings, it was hypothesised that self-efficacy, goal setting and task anxiety would be significant predictors of task performance and it was also hypothesised that self-efficacy would be the most important predictor of task performance followed by goal setting, followed by task anxiety. The hypotheses were partially supported as although self-efficacy was the most important predictor of task perform-

Table 16.1

Range, Means (*M*), Standard Deviations (*SD*) of Predictor and Criterion Variables, Correlations Among Predictor Variables and Standardised (B) and Unstandardised (β) Coefficients

Parameter	Score	Self-efficacy	Task anxiety	B	β
Minimum	6.00	1.60	1.60		
Maximum	23.00	4.00	3.20		
M	15.79	2.59	2.45		
SD	3.71	2.80	.37		
Correlations					
Score		.38**	−.26*		
Self-efficacy			−.27*	2.52*	.30
Task anxiety				−1.60	−.15
Goal setting				−1.36	−.18

Note: * $p < .05$, two-tailed
      ** $p < .01$, two-tailed

ance in the present study, goal setting and task anxiety were not found to be significant predictors.

Congruent with the findings of Meece et al. (1990), self-efficacy was found to have a significant effect on task performance, whereas task anxiety did not have a significant impact on task performance. Therefore, in the present study participants' efficacious beliefs were more influential than the anxiety they might have felt while performing a moderately complex task. Contrary to previous research findings on goal setting (e.g., Latham & Kinne, 1974; Locke & Latham, 2002), goal setting was not found to be a significant predictor of task performance in the present study. However, in their meta-analytic study Wood et al. (1987) found that the effects of goals on performance are the strongest on simple tasks. As the task utilised in the present study was a moderately complex one, the effects of goal setting on performance may have been moderated. The results of the present study imply that as tasks get complex, performance can be improved by enhancing people's self-efficacy.

As the present study was a laboratory study conducted with a student sample, the generalisability of the findings is limited. Future studies should investigate other self-evaluative variables that affect performance of complex tasks, as findings from such studies will be beneficial to both academic institutions and organisations.

References

Bandura, A. (1977). Self-efficacy: Toward a unifying theory of behavioral change. *Psychological Review, 84*, 191–215.

Bandura, A. (1997). *Self-efficacy: The exercise of control.* New York: W.H. Freeman and Company.

Earley, P.C., Connolly, T., & Ekegren. (1989). Goals, strategy development, and task performance: Some limits on the efficacy of goal setting. *Journal of Applied Psychology, 74*, 24–33.

Heslin, P.A., & Latham, G.P. (2004). The effect of upward feedback on managerial behavior. *Applied Psychology: An International Review, 53*, 23–37.

Huber, V.L. (1985). Effects of task difficulty, goal setting, and strategy on performance of a heuristic task. *Journal of Applied Psychology, 70*, 492–502.

Judge, T.A., Jackson, C.L., Shaw, J.C., Scott, B.A., & Rich, B.L. (2007). Self-efficacy and work-related performance: The integral role of individual differences. *Journal of Applied Psychology, 92*, 107–127.

Latham, G.P., & Kinne III, S.B. (1974). Improving job performance through training in goal setting. *Journal of Applied Psychology, 59*, 187–191.

Latham, G.P., Winters, D., & Locke, E.A. (1994). Cognitive and motivational effects of participation: A mediator study. *Journal of Organizational Behaviour, 15*, 49–63.

Latham, G.P., & Yukl, G.A. (1975). A review of research on the application of goal setting in organizations. *Academy of Management Journal, 18*, 824–845.

Locke, E.A., & Latham, G.P. (1990). *A theory of goal setting and task performance.* Englewood Cliffs, NJ: Prentice Hall.

Locke, E.A., & Latham, G.P. (2002). Building a practically useful theory of goal setting and task motivation. *American Psychologist, 57*, 705–717.

Meece, J.L., Wigfield, A., & Eccles, J.S. (1990). Predictors of math anxiety and its influence on young adolescents' course enrollment intentions and performance in mathematics. *Journal of Educational Psychology, 82*, 60-70.

McAuley, E., Duncan, T., & Tammen, V.V. (1989). Psychometric properties of the Intrinsic Motivation Inventory in a competitive sport setting: A confirmatory factor analysis. *Research Quarterly for Exercise and Sport, 60*, 48–58.

Ryan, R.M. (1982). Control and information in the intrapersonal sphere: An extension of cognitive evaluation theory. *Journal of Personality and Social Psychology, 43*, 450-461.

Wood, R.E. (1986). Task complexity: Definition of the construct. *Organizational Behavior and Human Decision Processes, 37*, 60-82.

Wood, R., & Bandura, A. (1989). Social-cognitive theory of organizational management. *Academy of Management Review, 14*, 361–384.

Wood, R.E., Mento, A.J., & Locke, E.A. (1987). Task complexity as a moderator of goal effects: A meta-analysis. *Journal of Applied Psychology, 72*, 416–425.

Chapter
17

Taking a Break Increases Visual Creativity More Than Verbal Creativity

Gerry Pallier and Niko Tiliopoulos

Scientific and anecdotal accounts indicate that taking a break facilitates the production of creative ideas. Most accounts concern verbal or mathematical insight, but does visual creativity follow that pattern? We found that breaks engendered a distinct advantage to visual creativity. Commonly, a burst of new ideas follows a break, but never previously has an *increase* between before and after sessions been reported. Participants' visual creativity *did* increase after a break. There appears to be a bias towards visual over verbal creativity in nonconscious processing. This necessitates some revision to conventional accounts of break benefits.

Numerous past accounts, both anecdotal and scientific, have indicated that taking a break (Dijksterhuis, Bos, Nordgren & van Barren, 2006; Einstein, 1949a; Fulgosi & Guilford, 1968; Gregory, 2004; Hadamard, 1949; Mazzarello, 2000; Poincare, 1913; Snyder, Mitchell, Ellwood, Yates & Pallier, 2004) — or literally 'sleeping on it' (Cohen, Pascual-Leone, Press & Robertson, 2005; Fenn, Nusbaum & Margoliash, 2003; Stickgold, Malia, Maguire, Roddenberry & O'Connor, 2000; Wagner, Gais, Haider, Vergler & Born, 2004) — can enhance idea production. Commonly, a burst of new ideas follows a break, but never has the number of ideas produced in the post-break session been greater than in the pre-break period. Recently, there has been an upsurge of interest in the, apparently nonconscious, phenomenon of additional solutions appearing after a break from problem solving (see, e.g., Dijksterhuis, et al., 2006; Snyder, Mitchell, Ellwood et al., 2004). While most reports have considered verbal or mathematical problems, the research we report here concentrates on comparing verbal and visual (artistic?) creativity. We wondered whether a break would differentially advantage creative idea production in the visual over the verbal domain.

An early account by Wallas (1926) singled out incubation as essential to the creative process and to problem solving, stating that the benefit of breaks results from nonconscious production of ideas. Whilst this has some empirical support, others have sought to explain the value of a break in more prosaic terms, contending that the benefit lies in enabling recovery from neural fatigue, or relief from functional fixedness (Posner, 1973).

The study reported here investigates the incubation effect from the perspective of nonconscious idea generation. Many readers will have experienced the phenomenon of a solution suddenly springing to mind when one has given up working on a problem, and the occurrence of the 'Aha!' or 'Eureka!' phenomenon is, as already noted, well documented in the creativity literature. Notably, no previous accounts have compared an advantage of verbal versus visual creativity following a break. Here we do so.

Our experimental paradigm differs from others. Most investigations have utilised convergent tasks, with a single correct solution (e.g., Dijksterhuis et al., 2006; Fenn et al., 2003; Hadamard, 1949). However, we contend that convergent problem solving is not necessarily equivalent to creativity. For this reason, our method uses tasks with multiple solutions in the verbal and visual domains, which we believe to be superior markers of creativity. In summary, our approach is unique in utilising tasks that require multiple responses, and by the inclusion of a break for both verbal and visual creativity.

To set the stage, it is worthwhile here to give an overview of the procedure, although a more thorough description is provided in the Method section. We first presented participants with two creativity tests: (1) a verbal task that asked them to generate as many uses as they could for a piece of paper (paper was chosen as it is presumably equally familiar to all and thus required no specialist knowledge, a factor that may account for differences in performance), and (2) a visual (artistic) task that required them to construct as many varied drawings as they could from a series of pairs of parallel lines, adapted from the Torrance Tests of Creative Thinking (Torrance, 1990; see Figure 17.1).

After participants had failed to respond for 30 seconds on each of those two tasks they were told that the test had finished and to move on to the next task. Based on previous protocols that included a short distracting break (see, e.g., Snyder, Mitchell, Ellwood et al., 2004), we considered this time delay in responding to be indicative of people having exhausted their current capacity to rapidly produce creative ideas.

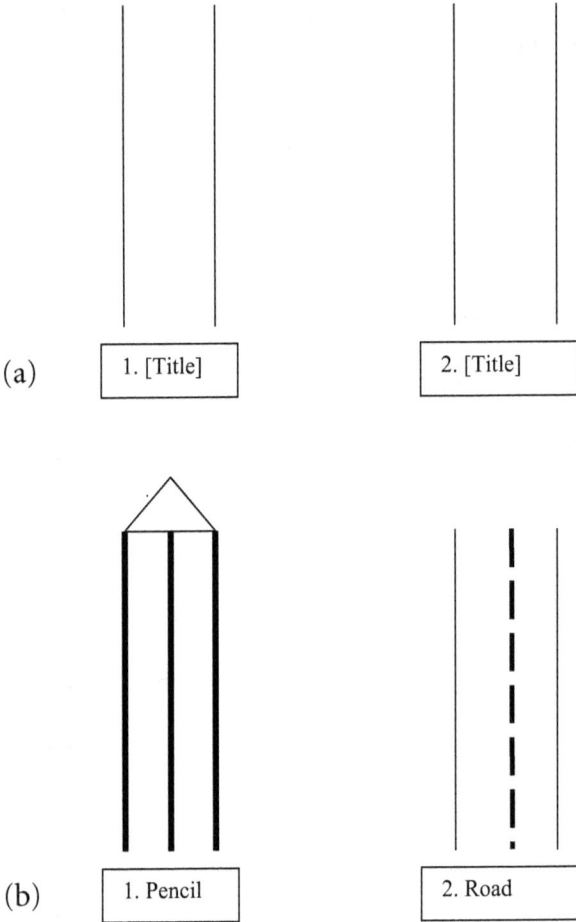

Figure 17.1

(a) Example of the blank Visual Creativity Task and (b) two solutions.

Participants were then given six tests of intelligence, which included an equivalent number of visual and verbal tasks. This was because relief from neural fatigue has been suggested as an alternative to nonconscious idea production (Posner, 1973). Having participants complete verbal and visual intelligence tests during the break maximised the possibility of detecting a genuine incubation effect, rather than a beneficial relief from neural fatigue in either modality. When the intelligence tests were completed, and to their surprise, the participants were asked to think of more uses for a piece of paper, and then to generate as many more drawings as they could, until they once again ran out of ideas.

Method

Participants

Students from the University of Sydney (N = 107, 32 (27%) males and 75 (64%) females), with an average age of 19.79 years (range 18–49, SD 4.02), participated in the study. The study was conducted in strict compliance with the University's Human Research Ethics Committee (HREC) requirements.

Task Descriptions

Apart from the Verbal Creativity Test (Snyder, Mitchell, Ellwood et al., 2004), and the Visual Creativity Test (Pallier, 2005), there were standardised psychometric tests, (derived from within the Cattell-Horn-Carroll framework), of fluid intelligence (Gf), crystallised intelligence (Gc) and visualisation ability (Gv). All tests are described in detail below.

1. *Pre-break Verbal Creativity Test* — this task is based on Cattell's Uses Test (French, Ekstrom & Price, 1963), and required participants to list as many possible different uses for a piece of paper, an item that is familiar to all. The Test was administered on computer and ceased automatically when no response was provided for 30 seconds, after which participants were told (by the computer) that the task was over.

2. *Pre-break Visual Creativity Test* — the experimenter instructed participants to construct as many varied drawings as they could utilising a series of parallel lines, presented in paper-and-pencil format, adapted from Torrance's (Torrance, 1966) test battery. When a participant had ceased producing drawings for 30 seconds, the experimenter announced that the Test had ended and to begin the computerised cognitive ability tasks.

3. *Matrices (Gf)* — in this Test (Stankov & Roberts, 2001), participants were presented with a series of 3 × 3 matrices, with all but the bottom right-hand block containing patterns made up of o's, +'s, and blanks. Participants were required to identify the logical series, and to fill in the empty square with the appropriate selection of o's, +'s, or blanks that logically completed the matrix pattern. The task involved two practice and ten test items.

4. *Letter Swaps (Gf)* — this Test (Stankov & Crawford, 1993) presented participants with three letters (J, K and L) in various orders, and

required them to carry out (mentally) a number of letter swaps (e.g. 'Swap the 1st and 3rd letters') and identify the resulting order of letters. There were two practice and eight test items, employing either 2, 3, 4, or 5 'Swaps' operations (i.e., two presentations of each difficulty level).

5. *Vocabulary (Gc)* — in this Test (Stankov, 1997), participants were asked to select the most appropriate definition (from four alternatives) for a series of words. The Test comprised two practice and ten test items.

6. *Paper Folding Test (Gv)* — this Test measured the primary mental ability of visualisation (French et al., 1963). It consisted of two rows of figures. The top row represented a square piece of paper being folded, with the final figure indicating where holes had been punched into the paper. The bottom row presented five alternative representations of how the paper would look when unfolded. The task was to pick the correct solution. There were two practice and ten test items.

7. *Proverb Matching (Gc)* — this Test was developed by Stankov and Roberts (2001). Each item showed a typical proverb and a selection of five alternative 'proverbs', one of which had a very similar meaning to the test item. The requirement was to identify that 'proverb'. There were two examples and ten test items.

8. **Hidden Figures (Gv)** — another task developed by Stankov and Roberts (2001), this Test measures the ability to identify a simple figure hidden amongst a complex pattern. Participants were presented with a set of five alternative shapes and a complex set of intersecting lines within a rectangle. The task requirement was to identify which of the alternatives was 'hidden' within the rectangle. There was one example and six test items.

9. *Post-break Verbal Creativity Test* — this task was identical to Test 1.

10. *Post-break Visual Creativity Test* — this task was identical to Test 2.

Procedure

The experiment was conducted with small groups of up to three people to ensure that the supervisor could efficiently monitor the artistic creativity task. Participants were first welcomed, informed of their rights, as governed by the HREC, and informed consent was obtained. They were then given an overview of the testing session, but not of the repetition of the creativity tasks, which minimised the possibility of participants consciously seeking extra solutions. They were asked to complete forms requesting basic demographic information and at the same time were given a unique numerical identification for the experiment. They were then introduced to the computer equipment and shown how to initiate the testing session. When they failed to respond to Test 1 for 30 seconds, the computer instructed them to call for the experimenter who gave them the visual test form (paper-and-pencil) to complete. The experimenter timed the visual creativity task to adjudge when a new drawing was not started for 30 seconds, at which point the experimenter instructed the participant to commence the computerised cognitive ability tasks. When those tests were all completed the computer again presented the verbal creativity Test. Participants were then handed another sheet of parallel lines and instructed 'to produce as many original drawings as possible'. The previous protocol was followed, after which the volunteers were debriefed on the true nature of the experiment, apologised to for the mild deception (i.e., the repetition of the creativity tasks), and thanked for taking part. The entire experimental session lasted about an hour and a half, but varied slightly as the tasks were self-paced.

Results

Table 17.1 presents the mean and standard deviation for the various tasks. To further examine the relationship between the creativity and cognitive ability test scores, an exploratory factor analysis was conducted. Although the 'Eignevalue-over-1' rule allowed the extraction of four factors, a more parsimonious three factor solution was preferred. The results, using the data in Table 17.2, are presented in Tables 17.3 and 17.4 below.

Table 17.1

Means and Standard Deviations for the Tasks

Task assessments	Mean (total score)	Standard deviation
1. Pre-break verbal fluency	13.10	5.82
2. Pre-break visual fluency	4.20	2.38
	Mean (% score)	
3. Matrices	59.72	24.70
4. Letter swaps	73.01	24.83
5. Vocabulary	93.18	9.99
6. Paper folding	71.31	22.28
7. Proverbs	61.12	17.06
8. Hidden figures	44.08	34.13
	Mean (total score)	
9. Post-break verbal fluency	7.26	4.84
10. Post-break visual fluency	4.69	2.33

Table 17.2

Correlations Between the Scores on the Tasks

Task assessments	1	2	3	4	5	6	7	8	9	10
1. Pre-verbal	—									
2. Pre-visual	.009	—								
3. Matrices	−.201	.025	—							
4. Letter swaps	−.081	.017	.449	—						
5. Vocabulary	.076	−.043	.293	.173	—					
6. Paper folding	−.041	−.044	.506	.354	.197	—				
7. Proverbs	.044	−.001	.200	.298	.171	.078	—			
8. Hidden figures	−.055	−.020	.274	.348	.085	.366	.033	—		
9. Post-verbal	.428	.007	−.003	−.049	−.009	.035	.121	−.014	—	
10. Post-visual	.138	.528	.076	.138	.166	−.038	−.029	.163	.038	—

Note: Pre-verbal = Pre-break verbal fluency; Pre visual = Pre-break visual fluency; Post-verbal = Post-break verbal fluency; Post visual = Post-break visual fluency.

Table 17.3

Results of a Principal Axis Factoring Analysis With Promax Rotation of the Variables

	Factor		
Task assessments	1 Intelligence	2 Visual creativity	3 Verbal creativity
Pre-break verbal fluency			.844
Post-break verbal fluency			.521
Pre-break visual fluency		.607	
Post-break visual fluency		.930	
Vocabulary percentage correct	.350		
Proverbs percentage correct	.288		
Matrices percentage correct	.697		
Swap percentage correct	.607		
Paper folding percentage correct	.642		
Hidden figures percentage correct	.449		

Note: For ease of interpretation values below .25 are omitted.

The factors are interpreted as follows:

Factor 1: clearly represents an 'intelligence' or cognitive ability factor.

Factor 2: is defined solely by fluency on the visual creativity task and is interpreted as artistic creativity.

Factor 3: is defined solely by fluency on the verbal creativity task and is interpreted as verbal creativity.

Table 17.4

Intercorrelations Between the Factors in Table 17.3

Factor	1	2	3
1. Intelligence	1		
2. Visual creativity	.195	1	
3. Verbal creativity	−.149	.122	1

Table 17.4 presents intercorrelations between the factors identified in Table 17.3. Inspection of Table 17.4 indicates that there is virtually no relationship between the factors (i.e., they represent quite distinct abilities). This outcome supports the view that creativity is domain dependent.

Creativity tests may be evaluated in several ways (see, e.g., Torrance, 1990; Snyder, Mitchell, Bossomaier & Pallier, 2004; Snyder, Mitchell, Ellwood et al., 2004), the most germane here being the number of ideas produced (technically known as Fluency). The questions of interest were 'After running out of ideas, does a break induce extra solutions?' and 'Does this break benefit differ between verbal and visual tasks?' (Note that 'breaks' in past research have generally been of longer duration, often literally involving a period of sleep; Dijksterhuis et al., 2006; Fenn et al., 2003; Mazzarello, 2005; Wagner et al., 2004.) Table 17.5 presents pre- and post-break fluency scores for visual and verbal creativity.

The scores on the verbal task were as expected from previous studies using that test (e.g., Snyder, Mitchell, Bossomaier, & Pallier, 2004; Snyder, Mitchell, Ellwood et al., 2004) — people can immediately produce some extra solutions, even when they seemed to have run of ideas before the break (see Table 17.5 for pre- and post-break scores). However, the outcome of the visual creativity test was unexpected — not only did people produce extra ideas after the break but, unlike the verbal test, they

Table 17.5

Means and Standard Deviations for Fluency Scores on rhe Creativity Tasks

Task assessments	Mean score	SD
Verbal fluency		
Pre-break	13.10	5.82
Post-break	7.26	4.84
Visual fluency		
Pre-break	4.2	2.38
Post-break	4.69	2.33

produced *more* ideas than in the first session. Overall, scores for intelligence exhibited means and standard deviations similar to those reported elsewhere using the same (or very similar) tests and participant populations (e.g., Danthiir, Roberts, Pallier & Stankov, 2001; Pallier et al., 2002). Thus, the current sample does not appear to be unusual.

Discussion

The difference in break benefit for verbal versus visual creativity cannot, in this case, be easily explained in terms of relief from neural fatigue as the participants worked on cognitively demanding tasks of a similar nature for roughly an hour between creativity sessions. Furthermore, it is unlikely that there is a differential effect of neural fatigue for visual and verbal abilities, particularly since equally demanding tasks were presented in both modalities. Neither is conscious processing of additional solutions a likely explanation because: (1) participants had no reason to believe that they would be asked to produce more ideas at a later time, in fact they were clearly told that the task was over, and (2) people were asked at the end of the session if they had been thinking about the creativity tasks during the intelligence tests, and they reported that they had not. In fact, they were surprised to be asked to produce more responses.

Therefore, we suggest that these results point to nonconscious idea generation taking place in both tasks, but in the visual task this leads to more creative ideas after the break than before it. This is the first time that such a combination of tests has been used in conjunction with the investigation of a break benefit to the creative process. Furthermore, whilst a number of studies have looked at 'sleeping on it' in a literal sense (Cohen et al., 2005; Fenn et al., 2003; Stickgold et al., 2000; Wagner et al., 2004), that is, being retested after an overnight break, our investigation contributes to the relatively sparse knowledge regarding briefer interludes. What essentially differentiates our research from previous studies is the shorter break time employed, alongside our choice of both visual and verbal tasks. We hypothesise that nonconscious processing occurs continuously, independent of the type of break or its duration.

We can only speculate on the cause of our unexpected outcome. Perhaps what we are seeing is a division of thought processes involving the two modalities (visual and verbal), providing further evidence that the Whorfian hypothesis in its extreme form (Whorf, 1956) is overstated. Not all thought appears dependent on language. Anecdotal accounts, perhaps best thought of as case studies, of the differentiation between verbal and visual processing abound. For example, Einstein stated that his thinking processes were mainly visual 'The words or the language, as they are written or spoken, do not seem to play any role in my mechanism of thought ... (the) elements are, in my case, of (the) visual ... type' (1949b, pp. 142–143). Researchers are yet to fully explore possible differences in the neural underpinnings of incubation for artistic versus verbal creativity. Recently, however, neuropsychological investigations into creative insight have indicated the involvement of the right anterior superior temporal gyrus (Bowden, Jung-Beeman, Flech & Kounios, 2005; Jung-Beeman et al., 2004). There is also an increase in alpha-band followed by gamma-band activity accompanying insightful solutions for verbal tasks (without a break; Bowden et al., 2005; Jung-Beeman et al., 2004). A fruitful line of research would be to examine the extent to which these purported neural correlates apply during and after breaks and for both verbal and artistic creativity tasks.

Even though there is a break benefit to creativity in both modalities, the size of the effect appears reliant on whether verbal or visual creativity is involved, strongly favouring the latter. The results reported here suggest that, while meeting deadlines is important, performance could well be enhanced by taking time out during the decision-making processes, particularly for tasks with a visual component.

References

Bowden, E.M., Jung-Beeman, M., Fleck, J., & Kounios, J. (2005). New approaches to demystifying insight. *Trends in Cognitive Science, 9*, 322–328.

Cohen, D.A., Pascual-Leone, A., Press, D.Z., & Robertson, E.M. (2005). *Off-line learning of motor skill memory: A double dissociation of goal and movement.* Proceedings of the National Academy of Science, USA, 102, 18237–18241.

Danthiir, V., Roberts, R.D., Pallier, G., & Stankov, L. (2001). What the nose knows: Olfaction and cognitive abilities. *Intelligence, 29,* 337–361.

Dijksterhuis, A.P., Bos, M.W., Nordgren, L.F., & van Baaren, R.B. (2006). On making the right choice: The deliberation-without-attention effect. *Science, 311*, 1005–1007.

Einstein, A. (1949a). Autobiographical notes. In, *Albert Einstein: Philosopher-scientist* (pp. 1–95). (P.A. Schilpp, Trans.). La Salle, IL: Open Court.

Einstein, A. (1949b). A testimonial from Professor Einstein, in J. Hadamard, (Ed.) *An essay on the psychology of invention in the mathematical field* (pp. 142–143). Princeton, NJ: Princeton University Press.

Fenn, K.M., Nusbaum, H.C., & Margoliash, D. (2003). Consolidation during sleep of perceptual learning of spoken language. *Nature, 425,* 614–616.

French, J.W., Ekstrom, R.B., & Price, L.A. (1963). *Manual for kit of reference tests for cognitive ability.* Princeton, NJ: Educational Testing Service.

Fulgosi, A., & Guilford, J.P. (1968). Short-term incubation in divergent production. *American Journal of Psychology, 81,* 241–248.

Gregory, R.L. (2004). *The Oxford companion to the mind.* Oxford, UK: Oxford University Press.

Hadamard, J. (1949). *An essay on the psychology of invention in the mathematical field.* Princeton, NJ: Princeton University Press.

Jung-Beeman, M., Bowden, E.M., Haberman, J., Frymiare, J.L., Arambel-Liu, S., Greenblat, R. et al. (2004). Neural activity when people solve verbal problems with insight. *Public Library of Science, Biology, 2,* 500–510.

Mazzarello, P. (2000).What dreams may come? The scientific benefits of eating cheese before bedtime. *Nature, 408,* 523.

Pallier, G. (2005). *A Test of Artistic Creativity.* Unpublished test, available from the School of Psychology, The University of Sydney.

Pallier, G., Wilkinson, R., Danthiir, V., Kleitman, S., Knezevic, G., Stankov. L. et al. (2002). The role of individual differences in the realism of confidence judgements. *Journal of General Psychology,129,* 257–299.

Poincare, H. (1913). Mathematical creation. In G.B. Halsted, (Trans.), *The foundations of science* (pp. 383–394). New York: Science Press.

Posner, M.I. (1973). *Cognition.* Glenview, IL: Scott Foresman.

Snyder, A., Mitchell, J., Bossomaier, T., & Pallier, G. (2004). The creativity quotient: An objective scoring of ideational fluency. *Creativity Research Journal, 16,* 415–420.

Snyder, A., Mitchell, J., Ellwood, S., Yates, A., & Pallier, G. (2004). Nonconscious idea generation. *Psychological Reports, 94,* 1325–1330.

Stankov, L., & Crawford, J. (1993). Ingredients of complexity in fluid intelligence. *Learning & Individual Differences, 5,* 73–111.

Stankov, L., & Roberts, R.D. (2001). *Matrices test.* Unpublished cognitive test, available from the School of Psychology, The University of Sydney, Australia.

Stankov, L. (1997). *The Gf/Gc Quickie Battery.* Unpublished test battery, available from the School of Psychology, The University of Sydney, Australia.

Stickgold, R., Malia, A., Maguire, D., Roddenberry, D., & O'Connor, M. (2000). Replaying the game: Hypnagogic images in normals and amnesics. *Science, 290,* 350–353.

Torrance, E.P. (1966).*Thinking creatively with pictures* (Booklet A). Lexington, MA: Personnel Press.

Torrance, E.P. (1990). *Torrance Tests of Creative Thinking Norms — Technical Manual Figural (Streamlined) Forms A and B.* Bensenville, IL: Scholastic Testing Service.

Wagner, U., Gais, S., Haider, H., Verleger, R., & Born, J. (2004). Sleep inspires insight. *Nature, 427,* 352–355.

Wallas, G. (1926). *The art of thought.* New York: Harcourt Brace.

Whorf, B. (1956). *Language, thought, and reality.* Cambridge, MA: MIT Press.

Part 2:

On Professional Context and Applications of Personality Knowledge

Applications in organisational psychology:
Wellbeing and distress, 'role stress'
and reputation at work

Longitudinal Modelling of the Influence of Individual Differences and the Workplace on Wellbeing and Work Engagement

Prudence M.R. Millear and Poppy L. Liossis

A set of non-nested longitudinal models tested the relationships between personal and workplace resources, wellbeing and work engagement. The reciprocal model, trimmed of trivial paths had the best fit and parsimony. The model showed the strong influences of concurrent functioning, stability of variables over time and weaker reciprocal relationships between variables across time. Individuals with greater confidence in themselves and the future experience better work conditions and have greater wellbeing and work engagement. These day-to-day influences are equalled by the long-term strength and stability of Individual Factors, Positive Workplace Factors, and Overall Wellbeing. While the reciprocal paths had only weak to mild effects, there was mutual reinforcement of Individual Factors and Overall Wellbeing, with Positive Workplace Factors and Work Engagement counterbalancing each other, indicating a more complex relationship. Wellbeing, particularly, is anchored in the immediate and distant past and provides a robust stability to functioning into the future.

Personal and environmental resources allow the individual to manage the challenges in their lives, balancing work and family concerns and adapting to changing circumstances.

The Conservation of Resources theory states that individuals have a reservoir of resources and are motivated to obtain, retain and protect their resources, and will feel stressed or burnt out when resources are threatened, lost or not gained after appropriate effort. Resources are valuable alone or as ways to achieve valued ends, such as improving wellbeing and engagement in work (Hobfoll, 2002). In the work environment, work demands have a negative influence on resources, such as work satisfaction, while job social support has a positive effect (de Jonge et al., 2001). Loss of resources, as a 'loss spiral', can be seen among employees when work pressure increased emotional exhaustion (a component of burnout) six weeks later, which in turn further increased the work pressure experienced another six weeks later (Demerouti, Bakker, & Bulters, 2004). However, 'gain spirals' of resources also exist. Positive reciprocal links were found over time between efficacy and engagement and the task resources of students, with efficacy beliefs as central to the process (Llorens, Schaufeli, Bakker, & Salanova, 2007).

Individual differences represent an individual's personal resources, with high levels of self-efficacy and dispositional optimism linked to greater wellbeing and health. By moderating the impact of long work hours and high work overload (Jex & Bliese, 1999) and reducing the perception of job demands (Schaubroeck, Lam, & Xie, 2000), self-efficacy has been shown to be central to how stress is appraised and handled (Karademas & Kalantzi-Azizi, 2004) and to coping with challenging situations (Chesney, Chambers, Taylor, Johnson, & Folkman, 2003).

Optimism for the likely success of behaviours and activities has strong influence on how persistently resources will be directed toward achieving the individual's desired outcomes or goals. Similarly, negative outcomes can be reinterpreted in a more positive way to lessen distress (Armor & Taylor, 1998). Along with self-esteem, high dispositional optimism moderated the influence of time pressures at work, job insecurity and poor organisational climate on the mental distress and emotional exhaustion in Finnish employees (Makikangas & Kinnunen, 2003).

The long-term effects of differences in personal resources can be seen in the results of longitudinal studies. In both the Harvard study (Peterson, Seligman, & Vaillant, 1988) and the Nun study (Danner, Snowdon, & Friesen, 2001), early negative emotional expression was associated with poorer health and earlier mortality. Developmental processes are affected by the accumulated combinations of resources, as aggregated 'resource caravans' (Hobfoll, 2002). The developmental pathways associated with the resource caravans of greater positive emotions, more positive individual differences, and better working conditions favour the development of resources at any time across the lifespan and the stability of these resources (Shmotkin, 2005).

The aim of this research was to model the relationships between the individual's personal and workplace resources and their wellbeing and work engagement. It is hypothesised that resource accumulation, as shown by gain spirals, will be modelled longitudinally and that higher levels of individual differences and workplace variables will be associated with higher levels of wellbeing and work engagement.

Method

Participants

A prospective panel study was conducted, with participants (n = 198, 78.8% women) completing three online surveys, approximately four months apart. Participants ranged in age from 19 to 62 years (M = 38.18 years, SD = 11.14 years), worked similar hours across the three time periods (M = 41.24 hours per week, SD = 12.00 hr), and most had university qualifications (undergraduate (49.7%), postgraduate (23.9%)). Most participants were either married or living with their partner (63.6%) or single (25.3%). Over half of the sample did not have children, whilst most parents (75.5%) had two or three children.

Measures

Scales were rated on Likert scales of 1, *Strongly disagree*, to 5, *Strongly agree*, except for the Coping Self-Efficacy scale, which used 1, *Cannot do at all*, to 7, *I can do this*. Each scale has a range of Cronbach's alphas for the three measurement times.

'Individual Factors' were measured by dispositional optimism and coping self-efficacy. Dispositional optimism was measured by the Life Orientation Test — Revised (Scheier, Carver, & Bridges, 1994), six items, Cronbach's alphas = .831–.859. Coping self-efficacy (Chesney et al., 2003) was measured with 26 items, as confidence in managing in difficult situations, Cronbach's alphas = .964–.969.

'Positive Workplace Factors' were measured as skill discretion and job autonomy. Skill discretion (Schwartz, Pieper, & Karasek, 1988) measures skills or creativity used at work, 6 items, Cronbach's alphas = .853–.875. Job autonomy (Voydanoff, 2004) measures control of work tasks, 4 items, Cronbach's alphas = .847–.885.

'Overall Wellbeing' was measured by life satisfaction and psychological wellbeing, as the Satisfaction with Life Scale (Diener, Emmons, Larsen, & Griffin, 1985), 5 items, Cronbach's alphas = .878–.894, and Ryff's Scales of Psychological Wellbeing (Ryff, 1989), 18 items, Cronbach's alphas = .820–.839, respectively.

'Work engagement' was measured with two subscales of the Utrecht Work Engagement Scale (Schaufeli, Salanova, Gonzalez-Roma, & Bakker, 2002), as Work Dedication, 5 items, Cronbach's alphas = .907–.912 and Work Absorption, 6 items, Cronbach's alphas = .761–.796.

Procedure and Data Analysis

University alumni and hospital administrative staff volunteered for an online study, with participants completing identical surveys three times, four months apart. Of the 461 participants who completed the Time 1 survey, 198 (43.0% retention) provided complete information at each of the three measurement times.

Longitudinal modelling can be problematic where there are many variables and smaller sample sizes (Holmes-Smith, Cunningham, & Coote, 2006). To overcome this, a confirmatory factor analysis (CFA) was conducted in AMOS (Arbuckle, 2006) with the indicator variables at Time 1. The latent variables were defined by the indicator variables as follows: 'Individual Factors' as dispositional optimism and coping self-efficacy; 'Positive Workplace Factors' as skill discretion and job autonomy; 'Overall Wellbeing' as life satisfaction and psychological wellbeing; and 'Work Engagement' as work dedication and absorption. The latent variables were converted to observed variables for the longitudinal models using the factor score weights generated by the CFA. Following previous research (de Jonge et al., 2001; Demerouti et al., 2004), the longitudinal models were compared in AMOS using a set of four nonnested models: the Stability model (synchronous correlations between the variables and auto-lagged paths), the Causality model (Stability model and cross-lagged causality paths), the Reverse Causality model (Stability model and cross-lagged reverse causality paths) and the Reciprocal Model (Stability model and causality and reverse causality paths). A fifth, Trimmed model assessed the fit after removing trivial paths from the Reciprocal model.

Good fit for the CFA and longitudinal models was assessed as the normed chi-squared (X^2/df) < 2.00, the Comparative Fit Index (CFI) > .90, the root mean square error of approximation (RMSEA) < .08, with the RMSEA 90% CI between .00 and .08. The lowest value for Akaike Information Criteria (AIC) indicates most parsimonious model (Byrne, 2001; Holmes-Smith et al., 2006).

Results

The Confirmatory Factor Analysis of the four latent factors had good fit; X^2/df =1.987, CFI = .949, RMSEA =.046 (90%CI = .019–.072), with each indicator variable loading well onto the latent variables, with the loadings ranging from $\beta = .557$ ($p < .001$) for job autonomy to $\beta = .994$ ($p < .001$) for work dedication. Means, standard deviations and correlations between indicator variables are available from the authors. The correlations between the latent factors show that Individual Factors and Overall Wellbeing are closely related ($r = .924$, $p < .001$) and Positive Workplace Factors and Work Wellbeing are closely related ($r = .882$, $p < .001$), with positive correlations also between Individual Factors and Positive Workplace Factors ($r = .490$, $p < .001$) and Work Wellbeing ($r = .463$, $p < .001$), Positive Workplace Factors and Overall Wellbeing ($r = .546$, $p < .001$), and Overall Wellbeing and Work Wellbeing ($r = .460$, $p < .001$). Composite variables for the longitudinal models were constructed from factor score weights generated by the CFA. The means and standard deviations of the composite variables and the correlations between the variables are shown in Table 18.1, with the synchronous correlations shown in italics. The close relationships found between variables, particularly between work dedication and positive workplace factors, in the CFA are reflected in the composition and correlations between the composite variables.

The results of the model testing are shown in Table 18.2. The Stability Model is the least well fitting, with the Causality Model and Reciprocal Model being equivalent in their fit. However, removing the trivial pathways (i.e., $\beta < .10$, $p > .50$) from the Reciprocal Model improved the fit and parsimony and the Trimmed Model is the best fitting and parsimonious of the models, $\chi^2/df = 1.127$, CFI = .999, RMSEA = .025 (90% CI = .000–.062), AIC = 130.68.

The standardised regression weights (β) of the auto-lagged and cross-lagged paths between the variables over time are shown in Table 18.3. Regression weights indicate the strength of the relationships between variables and can be interpreted in a similar manner to effect sizes (Holmes-Smith et al., 2006). From Table 18.3, the strong effects, $\beta > .50$, were the auto-lagged paths between the same variables over time (shown on the leading diagonal), although the direct path from Time 2 to Time 3 for Work Engagement was trivial and removed from the final model. Moderately strong effects, $\beta = .30$ to $.50$, were also found between the remaining auto-lagged paths and the reciprocal cross-lagged paths between Positive Workplace Factors and Work Engagement. The remaining cross-lagged paths have mild, $\beta = .20$ to $.30$, and weak, $\beta < .20$, effects, indicating that any gain in resources is gradual. There is substantial variance explained by the model, as shown in Table 18.3, from 82.5% for Individual Factors at Time 3 to 62.7% of Work Engagement at Time 3.

Table 18.1

Means, Standard Deviations and Correlations Between the Composite Variables Used for the Longitudinal Model Composite

Variables	Mean (SD)	1	2	3	4	5	6	7	8	9	10	11	12
1 IFtm1	19.55 (3.00)	1	.895***	.864***	.582***	.494***	.479***	.982***	.879***	.854***	.515***	.421***	.409***
2 IFtm2	19.49 (3.17)		1	.869***	.569***	.584***	.537***	.833***	.987***	.880***	.494***	.499***	.466***
3 IFtm3	19.69 (3.11)			1	.517***	.493***	.556***	.857***	.888***	.986***	.448***	.410***	.481***
4 PWFtm1	18.71 (3.54)				1	.861***	.817***	.591***	.579***	.528***	.967***	.814***	.768***
5 PWFtm2	18.53 (3.61)					1	.817***	.495***	.587***	.496***	.828***	.968***	.779***
6 PWFtm3	18.44 (3.61)						1	.477***	.546***	.557***	.782***	.767***	.971***
7 OWbtm1	49.98 (7.21)							1	.887***	.867***	.495***	.403***	.387***
8 OWbtm2	49.82 (7.60)								1	.891***	.488***	.479***	.459***
9 OWbtm3	50.17 (7.43)									1	.445***	.400***	.460***
10 WEtm1	18.97 (4.40)										1	.823***	.771***
11 WEtm2	18.87 (4.49)											1	.767***
12 WEtm3	18.67 (4.44)												1

Note: *p < .05, **p < .01, ***p < .001. Synchronous correlations are shown in italics.
IF: Individual Factors; PWF: Positive Workplace Factors, OWB: Overall Well-Being; WE: Work Engagement; tm1=Time 1, tm2=Time 2, tm3=Time 3.

Table 18.2

Results of Comparisons Between the Longitudinal Models

Model	χ^2/df	CFI	RMSEA	(90% CI)	AIC
Stability	2.648	.990	.091	(.069–.114)	179.34
Causality	1.265	.999	.037	(.000–.070)	135.43
Reverse Causality	1.457	.998	.048	(.000–.078)	140.79
Reciprocal	1.202	.999	.032	(.000–.072)	140.03
Trimmed	1.127	.999	.025	(.000–.062)	130.68

Note: Good fit of indices: 1 < χ^2/df < 2; CFI > .950; RMSEA < .050; RMSEA 90% CI, range with lower end including .000 (indicates exact fit) and upper range < .08; AIC: lowest AIC most parsimonious, AIC of Saturated model = 156.00.

Discussion

The present study was designed to model, over time, an individual's resources, as represented by their individual differences, workplace characteristics, and their wellbeing and work engagement. The results of the study show that resources are maintained and can be gained over time, with the strongest relationships in the model between the variables at each particular time and within the same variable over time. The reciprocal paths

Table 18.3

Standardised Regression Weights for Auto-Lagged and Cross-Lagged Paths in the Trimmed Longitudinal Model

'Predictor' variables:	'Criterion' variables: Time 2 and Time 3 variables							
Time 1 and Time 2 variables	IFtm2	IFtm3	PWFtm2	PWFtm3	OWBtm2	OWBtm3	WEtm2	WEtm3
IFtm1	.685***	.304***			.143			
IFtm2		.444***						
PWFtm1	.		.860***	.395***	.077**		.219***	
PWFtm2				.808***				.484***
OWBtm1	.184				.699***	.340***		
OWBtm2		.181***				.589***		
WEtm1	.054*						.611***	.366***
WEtm2		–.340***						
Variance explained	80.2%	82.5%	74.0%	72.1%	79.3%	82.2%	65.5%	62.7%

Note: $p < .10$, *$p < .05$, **$p < .01$, ***$p < .001$.
  Auto-lagged paths: leading diagonal; Causality cross-lagged paths: upper triangle; Reverse Causality cross-lagged paths: lower triangle
  IF: Individual Factors; PWF: Positive Workplace Factors, OWB: Overall Wellbeing; WE: Work Engagement; tm1 = Time 1, tm2 = Time 2, tm3 = Time 3.

between the variables across time, except for Positive Workplace Factors and Work Engagement, are weaker, although still have significant effects.

The importance of concurrent relationships and the closeness of the relationships between Individual Factors and Overall Wellbeing reflect previous research. Rather than indicating redundancy, the results support previous findings that individuals who have more positive personal characteristics have greater wellbeing (Armor & Taylor, 1998; Hobfoll, 2002; Shmotkin, 2005). The surprisingly strong influence of work dedication on workplace conditions would indicate that the intrinsic value of work (as zest and enthusiasm, pride and challenges at work) colours the individual's experiences of autonomy and skill use at work.

The stability of constructs over time would indicate that individuals have a reservoir of resources (Hobfoll, 2002) that are maintained over time. The findings reflect the need to follow variables over time, rather than just focusing on reciprocal influences, although these are still important. As such, much of the variance at later times can be explained by the variance of the variable at an earlier time. Similar continuity over time can be seen in longitudinal modelling (for example, de Jonge et al., 2001; Demerouti et al., 2004; Makikangas & Kinnunen, 2003), where the auto-lagged paths are considerably stronger than the cross-lagged paths. Stability over time also suggests that resource caravans exist, where resources progress together over time, keeping up and reinforcing each other.

The reciprocal paths between Individual Factors and Overall-Wellbeing are evidence of a gain spiral in resources over time. But rather than a surge, this could be better described as a drift because the effect is only weak. As shown by the Harvard and Nun studies (Danner et al., 2001; Peterson et al., 1988), differences between positive and negative functioning can take many years to be seen.

However, the reciprocal relationships between Positive Workplace Factors and Work Engagement are more complex, being counterbalanced rather than additive. The net result is a positive gain in resources, as Positive Workplace Factors has a greater positive cross-lagged effect than the negative cross-lagged effect of Work Engagement. This is surprising, given the close links at each measurement time between the variables and the importance of dedication or intrinsic work rewards to how work conditions are experienced. It could be speculated that the individual who is overly enthusiastic or involved for their work could have a perceived loss in workplace resources, when the effect of high levels of engagement, that is, being overly absorbed and excessively enthusiastic about work, changes the perception of supportive work environments. Work engagement may be problematic for resource gain due to the enthusiasm and absorption in work depleting the individual's energy levels, providing a paradox where too much engagement leads to burnout, as found among nurses (Vinje & Mittelmark, 2007).

Taken together, the longitudinal models present an insight into the way that resources are maintained and gained over time. At each measurement time, there are close links between individual characteristics, their wellbeing and their work conditions and their view of their work. For the individual and their wellbeing, these relationships are straightforward, being carried forward over time, yet with the weak influences of reciprocal relationships gradually moving functioning to a more positive direction in the much longer term. The more complex relationships between work engagement and how work is experienced could indicate the possibility of curvilinear relationships making gains in resources less predictable.

Conclusions and Limitations

Individual functioning is the sum of current influences, how each construct was in the past, along with the milder reciprocal influences. The longitudinal modelling indicated that resource accumulation is a life long process that has significant consequences for wellbeing, health and longevity. The complexity of the relationship between the workplace and work engagement could explain why, when taken to extremes, the positives of work engagement could become problematic. Wellbeing, however, is more straightforward, being anchored in the near and distant past, with gradual increases over time.

The longitudinal modelling indicates that targeting individual factors and the balance with non-work interests could be used to further increase wellbeing and work engagement. Two recent studies investigated this proposition, using a CBT and strengths-based program. By bolstering self-efficacy and reaffirming the importance of relationships, stress and depression were reduced among resource-sector employees (Millear, Liossis, Shochet, Biggs, & Donald, 2008), while work-life balance and work satisfaction were increased and exhaustion was decreased among local government employees (Liossis, Shochet, Millear & Biggs, 2009). Such workplace programs would add to the preventative mental health strategies available to practitioners.

References

Arbuckle, J.L. (2006). *AMOS 7.0.* Spring House, PA: Amos Development Corporation.

Armor, D.A., & Taylor, S.E. (1998). Situated optimism: Specific outcome expectancies and self-regulation. In M.P. Zanna (Ed.), *Advances in experimental social psychology* (Vol. 30, pp. 309–379). San Diego, CA: Academic Press.

Byrne, B.M. (2001). *Structural equation modeling with AMOS: Basic concept, applications and programming.* Mahwah, NJ: Lawrence Erlbaum.

Chesney, M.A., Chambers, D.B., Taylor, J.M., Johnson, L.M., & Folkman, S. (2003). Coping effectiveness training for men living with HIV: Results from a randomized clinical trial testing a group-based intervention. *Psychosomatic Medicine, 65,* 1038–1046.

Danner, D.D., Snowdon, D.A., & Friesen, W.V. (2001). Positive emotions in early life and longevity: Findings from the Nun Study. *Journal of Personality and Social Psychology, 80*(5), 804–813.

de Jonge, J., Dormann, C., Janssen, P.P.M., Dollard, M.F., Landeweerd, J.A., & Nijhuis, F.J.N. (2001). Testing reciprocal relationships between job characteristics and psychological wellbeing: A cross-lagged structural equation model. *Journal of Occupational and Organizational Psychology, 74,* 29–46.

Demerouti, E., Bakker, A.B., & Bulters, A.J. (2004). The loss spiral of work pressure, work-home interference and exhaustion: Reciprocal relations in a three-wave study. *Journal of Vocational Behavior, 64,* 131–149.

Diener, E., Emmons, R.A., Larsen, G., & Griffin, S. (1985). The Satisfaction With Life scale. *Journal of Personality Assessment, 49*(1), 71–75.

Hobfoll, S.E. (2002). Social and psychological resources and adaptation. *Review of General Psychology, 6*(4), 307–324.

Holmes-Smith, P., Cunningham, E., & Coote, L. (2006). *Structural equation modelling: From the fundamentals to advanced topics.* Melbourne: School Research, Evaluation, and Measurement Services.

Jex, S.M., & Bliese, P.D. (1999). Efficacy beliefs as a moderator of the impact of work-related stressors: A multi-level study. *Journal of Applied Psychology, 84*(3), 349–361.

Karademas, E., & Kalantzi-Azizi, A. (2004). The stress process, self-efficacy expectations, and psychological health. *Personality and Individual Differences, 37,* 1033–1043.

Liossis, P., Shochet, I.M., Millear, P.M., & Biggs, H. (2009), The Promoting Adult Resilience (PAR) program: The effectiveness of the second, shorter pilot of a workplace prevention program, *Behaviour Change, 28*(2), 97–112.

Llorens, S., Schaufeli, W.B., Bakker, A.B., & Salanova, M. (2007). Does a positive gain spiral of resources, efficacy beliefs and engagement exist? *Computers in Human Behavior, 23,* 825–841.

Makikangas, A., & Kinnunen, U. (2003). Psychosocial work stressors and wellbeing: Self-esteem and optimism as moderators in a one-year longitudinal sample. *Personality & Individual Differences, 35,* 537–557.

Millear, P.M., Liossis, P., Shochet, I.M., Biggs, H., & Donald, M. (2008) Being on PAR: Outcomes of a pilot trial to improve mental health and wellbeing in the workplace with the Promoting Adult Resilience (PAR) Program. *Behaviour Change, 25*(4), 215–228

Peterson, C., Seligman, M.E.P., & Vaillant, G. (1988). Pessimistic explanatory style is a risk for physical illness: A thirty-five-year longitudinal study. *Journal of Personality and Social Psychology, 55*(1), 23–27.

Ryff, C.D. (1989). Happiness is everything, or is it? Explorations on the meaning of psychological wellbeing. *Journal of Personality and Social Psychology, 57*(6), 1069–1081.

Schaubroeck, J., Lam, S.S.K., & Xie, J.L. (2000). Collective efficacy versus self-efficacy in coping responses to stressors and control: A cross-cultural study. *Journal of Applied Psychology, 85*(4), 512–525.

Schaufeli, W.B., Salanova, M., Gonzalez-Roma, V., & Bakker, A.B. (2002). The measurement of engagement and burnout: A two sample confirmatory factor analytic approach. *Journal of Happiness Studies, 3,* 71–92.

Scheier, M.F., Carver, C.S., & Bridges, M.W. (1994). Distinguishing optimism from neuroticism (and trait anxiety, self-mastery, and self-esteem): A reevaluation of the Life Evaluation Test. *Journal of Personality and Social Psychology, 67*(6), 1063–1078.

Schwartz, J.E., Pieper, C.F., & Karasek, R. (1988). A procedure for linking psychosocial job characteristics data to health surveys. *American Journal of Public Health, 78*(8), 904–909.

Shmotkin, D. (2005). Happiness in the face of adversity: Reformulating the dynamic and modular bases of subjective wellbeing. *Review of General Psychology, 9*(4), 291–325.

Vinje, H.F., & Mittelmark, M.B. (2007). Job engagement's paradoxical role in nurse burnout. *Nursing and Health Sciences, 9,* 107–111.

Voydanoff, P. (2004). Implications of work and community demands and resources for work-to-family conflict and facilitation. *Journal of Occupational Health Psychology, 9*(4), 275–285.

Sad, Bad or Mad: Common Personality Disorders in Firms

David A. Robinson

This chapter examines psychological theory relating to the three clusters of personality disorder and to the normal development of firms, indicating pitfalls that constrain the firm from achieving optimal growth and providing guidelines to ensure organisational wellness through the growth stages of entrepreneurial firms. This chapter relates common personality disorders in individuals to problems encountered in firms (e.g., entrepreneurial firms) as they transition across 6 developmental steps. Mal-alignment of practices, over-reliance on the negative manifestations of each step, and/or an inability to advance up the steps, if unchecked, may become endemic to the firm, and a hindrance to growth.

Just as personality disorders afflict individuals, so too can they apply to firms. This chapter brings together the fields of personality psychology and organisational behaviour to create a road map that depicts the development journey of individuals and firms, with reference to the three clusters of personality disorders. Firms that suffer from such 'personality disorders' have a lower propensity for growth. The chapter defines three clusters of firm disorders, which correspond to the established clusters of individual personality disorders, and also defines guidelines to ensure firm wellness.

Disorders of personality consist of 'configurations of traits considered socially undesirable' (Funder, 2007), and have been defined as 'a class of disorders marked by extreme, inflexible personality traits that cause subjective distress or impaired social and occupational functioning' (Weiten, 2008). Personality disorders in individuals have been grouped by the *Diagnostic and Statistical Manual* (DSM) and may be seen in terms of clusters (Morey, 1988).

Cluster A comprises the so-called mad disorders, characterised by odd, eccentric or dysfunctional patterns of thinking. These include paranoid, schizoid, and schizotypal personality disorders. Paranoid refers to suspiciousness and mistrust of others' motives, while seeing self as blameless. Schizoid includes the lack of desire and inability to form attachments to others, with a preference for being alone, leading to impaired social relationships. Schizotypal includes eccentricity, with reduced capacity for close interpersonal relationships.

Cluster B comprises the so-called bad disorders, characterised by erratic, impulsive or dramatic patterns of behaviour, specifically histrionics, narcissism, antisocial, and borderline personality disorder. Histrionic refers to excessive attention seeking, theatrical, provocative, and seductive behaviour. Narcissistic includes self-promoting, grandiose or self-absorbed behaviour with a corresponding lack of empathy. Antisocial behaviour comprises deceitfulness, shameless manipulation of or disregard for others, the violation of others rights, and is associated with a lack of moral development or conscience. Borderline is characterised by impulsiveness, boredom, instability in interpersonal relationships, affect and self-image, with attempts at self-mutilation or suicide.

Cluster C comprises the so-called sad disorders characterised by dysfunctional, anxious or fearful emotional processes. These include the dependent, avoidant, and obsessive–compulsive personality disorders. Avoidant emotional processes include extreme shyness, social inhibition and hypersensitivity to negative evaluation. Dependent emotional processes include indecisiveness, submissiveness, reluctance to disagree with others for fear of rejection. Obsessive–compulsive emotional processes include exaggerated conscientiousness, overt perfectionism, lack of warmth, and inability to relax. In business these may translate to an over-concern with rules and detail, perfectionism, workaholism, inflexibility, reluctance to delegate, miserliness, and stubborn rigidity (Funder, 2007), resulting in work being done slowly, though thoroughly.

Table 19.1 shows a classification of personality disorders in individuals. This model will be related to organisations that are 'mad', 'bad', or 'sad', after discussing the values journey taken by organisations.

There appears to be general consensus that personality disorders originate in childhood, although full-blown symptoms may only appear in adolescence or early adulthood. This would appear to have parallels with the field of entrepreneurship, in terms of business venture creation/growth/maturity.

Table 19.1

Personality Disorders in Individuals

Cluster	A	B	C
Main affect	Thinking	Behaviour	Emotion
Symptoms	Eccentric	Erratic	Avoidant
	Suspicious	Impulsive	Dependent
	Dysfunctional	Dramatic	Obsessive–compulsive
Abbreviated label	MAD	BAD	SAD

Personality variations occur across five dimensions (The Big Five; according to McRae & Costa, 2003): extraversion ('positive emotionality'), neuroticism ('negative emotionality'), agreeableness, conscientiousness, and openness to experience.

According to the Big Five theory, these characteristics each follow the normal curve with most people being average (in the middle of a range) and a few being at the extremes. In Aristotelian philosophy, the extremes are depicted as one of excess and one of deficiency, which appears a convenient way to categorise some of the common personality disorders. For example, excessive extraversion may be associated with histrionics, while deficient extroversion/excessive introversion may be more akin to avoidant and schizoid disorders.

Table 19.2 shows the relationship between the ten principal personality disorders and the Big Five traits of personality. Blanks in the table indicate that no association has been found to exist between that trait and the disorder.

It can be seen that while most sufferers of personality disorder are high in neuroticism, there are specific variations in the other four traits. Extraversion, for example is low for the 'MAD' cluster but high for the 'BAD' cluster. Even the clusters contain variations. Within the 'SAD' cluster, for instance, dependent disorder scores high on agreeableness, while obsessive–compulsive scores low.

Although this may be too crude a way to classify personality disorders in individuals, it may be helpful in an attempt to explain personality disorders in firms.

The development of firms has been depicted as a values journey (Robinson, 2008) consisting of three phases, each having an expressive and submissive track (see Figure 19.3). The way a firm, as a collection of the individuals comprising it, thinks feels and behaves is referred to as its culture, which it lives out through its day-to-day practices. When firms

Table 19.2

The Ten Principal Personality Disorders in Terms of The Big Five Traits of Personality (Widiger et. al., 1994)

Personality disorder	The Big Five Traits				
	Neuroticism	Extraversion	Agreeable	Conscientious	Open to experience
MAD Schizotypal	High	Low			High
Schizoid		Low			Low
Paranoid	High		Low		
BAD Histrionic	High	High	High		High
Narcissistic	High		Low	High	High
Antisocial	High	High	Low	Low	
Borderline	High		Low	Low	
SAD Dependent	High		High		
Avoidant	High	Low			
Obsessive–compulsive		High	Low	High	Low

employ day-to-day practices that correspond to those commonly associated with their particular phase of development; that is, congruence exists between what is done and what is effective, they may be said to be normal. Firms that fail to consistently apply managerial practices that fall within the normal range, or are incongruent with the requirements for effectiveness in business, however, may be said to be suffering from personality disorders. For example, a firm that over emphasises profits at all cost while ignoring moral conscience and/or neglecting to give sufficient resources to sustainability. The firm's culture could be seen as excessively mercenary, or obsessive-compulsive in a monetary sense. The identification of the organisational disorder is aimed at ensuring that the firm remains 'on track' during its various developmental phases. To that end the Values Journey model (Robinson, 2008) has been developed to explore what might ensue in firms whose critical mass strays from the track or becomes stuck in a value station that is no longer developmentally appropriate.

A typical business lifecycle includes a firm's phases of growth and then decline, namely Infancy (start-up), Childhood, Adolescence (periods of high growth), Prime, Maturity (stability), Ageing (declining performance), and ultimately death. Just as with people, the ailments that accentuate a firm's decline may arguably originate during its growth phases. Some typical disorders that commonly occur in firms are: profits at all cost; erratic styles of management, as evidenced by lack of focus, too many projects, too much change/insecurity, instability; resistance-to-change or arrested development. On a more positive note, organisational wellness (or lack of disorder) is characterised by engaged and empowered staff, timely and open communication, a sustainable work ethic, and continuous improvement.

Various theoretical models explain personal development, and these models have been incorporated into Robinson's (1998) Personal and Corporate Values Journey Chart. The model refers to theories of Beck and Cowan (1995), Crain (1985), Maslow (1954), McCleland (1961), Covey (1990), Egan (1997), Piaget (1965), Alderfer (1969), Rotter (1996). Beck and Cowan developed a continual growth model using value stations (building on Graves's 1970 theory on levels of human existence). Maslow's Hierarchy of Needs model is used in the Robinson model within each of the values stations. Kohlberg's Stages 1 and 2 equate to the submissive and egocentric stations of the Values Journey, in which people have to learn the rules of society to advance; his Stages 3 and 4 equate to duty-compliance in which rules are enforced for long-term stability and safety; and his Stage 5 is equivalent to the success-striving station of the Values Journey. The sixth stage looks at the 'big picture' requiring a substantially more relativistic worldview, thus approximating the harmony-seeking and synergy-seeking stations of Robinson's (1998) values chart. The value stations are sometimes colour-coded for ease of reference. Readers should see the original for more detailed information. Essentially, the Robinson Values Journey Chart applies to individuals, mirroring some of the leading researchers and theorists of the 20th century.

As in people, the development path to a healthy, functionally mature, sustainable firm may be viewed as a step-wise journey, in which each step is intended, alternately, toward greater autonomy or responsibility. Firms can be seen to develop one step at a time (discussed further in the next paragraph) across each of 10 identified dimensions of organisational maturity. The 10 dimensions are the type of people employed; the approach to employee development; how performance is ensured; how recognition and reward are given; how promotion is earned; the style of management; how the work is structured; the way communication occurs within the firm; how problems are solved; and what are viewed as worthwhile opportunities.

A firm ensures employee performance in each of the 10 dimensions via the stepwise journey, through roughly the following path (values in italics in brackets):

Step 1: Close supervision of small groups and a helping hand when needed (safe-bonding).

Step 2: Heavy-handed control of individuals who might otherwise cheat or manipulate things (power-seeking).

Step 3: Implementing the standard company review procedure (duty-compliant).

Step 4: Agreeing on performance goals and expecting achievement (success-striving).

Step 5: Interacting with team members as equals and resolving issues by consensus (peace-loving)

Step 6: Allowing each to use their creative talents to advance the firm (synergy-building).

For a visual map, see the Personal and Corporate Values Journey chart (in Robinson, 1998). However, at the most basic level individuals possess low levels of responsible citizenship and lack autonomy, thus seeking safe-bonding. Naturally, the leadership priorities at this level are survival and care oriented. Power-seeking, Step 2 in maturity development, is typified by egocentric aggression. Residents of this values station enjoy a higher level of autonomy, yet have not advanced in responsibility. The leadership imperative here is to lead by example and show strength of character. Next, social mores begin to emerge. Residents of this value station are duty-compliant and it is common for them to display absolute respect for procedure and authority. Leadership at this level entails formal and cen-tralised control and is thus authoritarian and procedural. The next value station, a step in the direction of increased autonomy, is characterised by the intense drive for success, usually manifesting as materialism and afflu-ence. Residents display a high need for achievement. It demands a corre-sponding leadership style; that is, goal-directed leadership.

More systemic thinking emerges beyond this, where peace and harmony are the ideals sought. Residents display a high need for affiliation and this tends to generate accommodative behaviour in followers. Leaders are there-fore expected to play a facilitative role. It is at this station that Greenleaf's (1977) servant leadership, with its emphasis is on collaboration, trust, empathy, and the ethical use of influence, is best considered. Finally, the sixth and ultimate value station represents interdependency. Here, leadership is about recognising and harnessing individual strengths, at whatever level of development or station, and requires the ability to integrate and synergise.

Figure 19.1 illustrates the six value stations (rows) and the correspon-ding dimensions (columns).

Dominant individual behaviours	Culture type	Typical organisation structure	Typical managerial orientation	Preferred management process	Typical response	Positive manifestations	Negative manifestations	Motivating need	World view
Instinctive self-denial	Submissive	Tribal	Obedience	Parental	Listen	Pride	Blind following	Belonging	Tribalistic
Impulsive self-expression	Aggressive	Mini-empire	Task	Tough paternalistic	Force	Self-reliance	Exploitive	Independence	Egocentric
Sacrificial self-denial	Compliant	Passive hierarchy	Procedural	Authoritarian	Conform	Respect	Rigid	Security	Absolutistic
Rational self-expression	Progressive	Active hierarchy	Results	Entrepreneurial	Initiate	Affluence	Manipulative	Achievement	Materialistic
Accommodative self-denial	Harmonious	Social network	Relationships	Facilitative	Discuss	Peace	Indecisive	Acceptance	Relativistic
Considerate self-expression	Synergistic	Functional access	Solutions	Integrative	Consider	Flexibility	Non-directive	Inter-dependence	Existential

Figure 19.1

Consistency within value stations.

Each row in Figure 19.1 represents a step in the values journey. As can be seen, a firm wishing to create or maintain a progressive-type culture (level 4, success-striving, on the values journey steps) that is results-oriented should seek to encourage entrepreneurial processes within an active hierarchical structure. Typical employees will be self-expressive, rational, achieving and materialistic. The firm should take care to discourage manipulative behaviours.

The notion of a six-step developmental process makes it possible to consider the alignment of the dimensions at each step. If, for example, the firm used Step 4 practices to select the people it employed, but then attempted to reward or manage them according to Step 3 practices, the firm would be 'out of alignment' (or 'incongruent'). Figure 2 can be used as a guide to the degree of alignment. The extent to which a firm gets itself 'out of alignment' is a possible measure of its disorder. A firm that then chooses to remain 'out of alignment' perpetuates erratic behaviours, thereby displaying the symptoms of a personality disorder.

Furthermore, each step is characterised by positive and negative attributes in each of the ten dimensions. For example, a Step 4 firm that adopts the appropriate performance management practice; that is, agree on performance goals and expecting achievement, but forces or manipulates the agreement and measurements relating to goal achievement (to pay less commission, or whatever), would be practising Step 4 in the negative.

In addition, as a firm's culture may be seen as the aggregate of individuals' personalities, every firm tends to adopt an internal way of working that relates to the critical mass of thinking, emotions and behaviours. Table 19.3 shows how the firm's Big Five profile would tend to change as it develops along the values journey.

Table 19.3 shows that the higher level stages in a firm's development are dominated by conscientiousness, openness and agreeableness; neuroticism is associated with low end stages of development; and extraversion aligns only with the three expressive stations.

Implications for Management

There appears to be three origins of personality disorder and lack of organisational health in firms. The first is when the firm exhibits only the negative traits of its value station, rather than the positive. Let us refer to these 'dysfunctional' firms as type A. Another is where the firm advances in most dimensions but remains trapped in, or inappropriately connected to, lower stations in some. The firm is thus inconsistent in its day-to-day practices and thereby creates a confused culture. Let us call these firms

Table 19.3

The Likely Prevalence of the Big Five Personality Traits at Various Stages of Firm Development

The Big Five Traits	The six stages of firm development					
	1. Submissive	2. Aggressive power-seeking	3. Duty-compliant	4. Success-striving	5. Harmonious	6. Integrative
Neuroticism	X	X	X			
Extraversion		X		X		X
Agreeableness	X		X		X	X
Conscientiousness			X	X	X	X
Openness				X	X	X

type B. The third is where the firm suffers from 'arrested development', being incapable of advancing along the values journey, becoming stuck at the low-level value stations. This mainly applies to those unable to develop beyond safe-bonding and power-seeking, and includes an inappropriate over-reliance on duty-compliance too. Because such firms know no better, they do not recognise themselves as being stuck. In a sense they are incapable of seeing beyond their current stage of development. Let us call them type C. Table 19.4 shows this classification of personality disorders in firms, with their corresponding symptoms.

Table 19.1 and Table 19.4 appear to contain direct similarities. Because of these we can apply similar cluster abbreviations for personality disorders in individuals to firms. Thus, a mad firm would be one where the dominant day-to-day practices are experienced as negative manifestations of its stage in the values journey; a bad firm would be one in which the day-to-day practices are inconsistent, leading to erratic behaviour. A sad firm would be one suffering from immature emotional responses. Table 19.5 relates the common personality disorders to the development stages of a firm.

Table 19.4

Personality Disorders in Firms

Type	A	B	C
Cause	Negative traits of value station	Inconsistent practices	Arrested development
Symptoms	Stressed	Erratic	Avoidant
	Dysfunctional	Confused	Dependent
	Self-destructive	Dissonant	Obsessive–compulsive
Abbreviated label	MAD	BAD	SAD

Table 19.5

Common Personality Disorders Related to Firm's Stage of Development

Personality disorder	The six stages of firm development					
	1. Submissive	2. Aggressive power-seeking	3. Duty-compliant	4. Success-striving	5. Harmonious	6. Integrative
MAD						
Schizotypal		X				
Schizoid	X					
Paranoid		X				
BAD						
Histrionic		XX		X		
Narcissistic		X		XX		
Antisocial		X		X		
Borderline		X				
SAD						
Dependent	X		X			
Avoidant	X		X			
Obsessive–compulsive			XX			

Table 19.5 depicts the stages of development at which firms are most likely to be prone to personality disorders should unhealthy workplace practices be allowed to prevail. It can be seen that the 'BAD' cluster mainly afflicts firms in the aggressive 'power-seeking' and progressive 'success-striving' stages, while the 'SAD' cluster is more closely associated with the 'submissive' and 'duty-compliant' stages. The table also depicts an apparent lack of pathologies in the 'harmonious' and 'integrative' mature stages of the firm.

So how may a developing firm avoid becoming sad, bad or mad and advance to a level of optimal effectiveness or organisational wellness?

There is no sharp dividing line between normality and abnormality in individuals (Clark & Watson, 1999; Furr & Funder, 1998; Krueger & Tackett, 2003; O'Connor, 2002), so it appears to be so for the firm. Having a mild degree of one characteristic cannot be taken to imply pathology. Nevertheless, recurring symptoms that constrain the firm's progress or effectiveness demand attention. As prevention is almost always better than cure, the way to ensure organisational wellness (lack of personality disorder in the firm) is to ensure that the firm develops its day-to-day practices with appropriate thinking patterns, behaviours and emotional responses.

To be free from type A disorders, managers must ensure that the firm is managed predominantly in the positive aspects of the appropriate value station. For example, at level 4, rather than manipulate they should negotiate; at level 3, instead of stubbornly imposing a set of policies, they should communicate the logic underlying them, thereby negating mistrust or suspicion.

To be free from type B disorders, managers must ensure that its day-to-day practices are experienced as indicative of the appropriate value station. For example, a firm at level 4 on the values journey, namely duty-compliance, should be careful to manage all ten dimensions of its culture in ways that are seen to correspond with Step 4.

To be free from type C disorders, a firm that has reached the success-striving value station should be free of practices associated with the sub-missive and power-seeking stations, and be skilful in only utilising those from the duty-compliant value station to the extent that they support success-striving. Should the firm persist in carrying inappropriate thinking patterns, behaviours, or emotional responses with it along its journey, it may be said to have formed a type C personality disorder.

Table 19.6 shows some of the dos and don'ts for firms at the duty-compliant, success-striving and synergy-seeking steps in the values journey, respectively.

As it is impractical to mention every aspect of each dimension of culture for each of the six levels, the following guidelines are proposed to ensure that the firm's practices remain in alignment as it embarks on its stepwise journey to maturity:

1. *Development of a corporate vision.* There must be a clearly articulated vision for the overall organisation that is consistent with the appropriate identifiable value station. For example, if the company that includes in its corporate vision statement that it strives to become the market leader, then it is placing itself, aspirationally, at the success-striving station. By so doing it raises the bar, so to speak, for all day-to-day practices to be aligned with success-striving.

Table 19.6

Some Dos and Don'ts to Avoid Personality Disorders in Firms

Duty-Compliant (level 3)		Success-Striving (level 4)		Synergy-Seeking (level 6)	
Do	Don't	Do	Don't	Do	Don't
Reward loyalty	Single out individuals	Encourage career advancement	Treat everyone as equal	Allow staff to use their competencies	Enforce constraints
Standard operator manuals	Expect change initiatives	Negotiate	Cite inflexible policies	Be flexible	Demand compliant behaviour
Pay by seniority	Show favourites	Link reward to results	Expect loyalty	Allow social interaction	Show bias

2. *Assessment of adherence to the vision.* Management needs to take stock of how the firm's practices currently measure up to those implied in the vision. For example, to what extent is the concept of 'market leadership' understood and regarded as a driving force.

3. *Articulation of values.* Appropriate organisational values should be developed to create a sense of holism throughout the organisation. This is best illustrated by the case where sales employees request remuneration based on performance, rather than straight salaries, resulting in a stand-off between policy-wielding financial controllers and results-eager sales directors.

4. *Ongoing development.* Managers across all levels and functional areas may require assistance through education/training in order to adjust their respective thinking paradigm and leadership styles For example, financial controllers might need to be reorientated toward seeing their primary role as the supporters of orderly change that enables the company to be demand hungry and sales-led.

5. *Monitoring.* Expectations and performance measures should be identifiably congruent with the value station that is relevant to that level and function. An important element in all of this is the feedback loop, whereby leaders themselves may assess the effectiveness with which they are achieving congruency. Ultimately, that will enable the custodians of the organisation to continually adjust the degree of emphasis placed on the vision and the values necessary to lead the firm along its developmental journey.

Conclusion

Personality disorders in individuals present as inappropriate thinking patterns, behaviours and emotional responses. The same may be true for firms in which day-to-day practices are mal-aligned and incongruent with their phase of development. A firm's journey to maturity may be seen to entail six steps, each relying on the alignment of 10 dimensions. Personality disorders occur when the firm harbours practices from the first two steps, thereby limiting its effective transition. The way to prevent personality disorder in the firm (organisational wellness) is to have a clearly articulated aspirational vision for the firm's future, and then constantly monitor the firm's practices to ensure adherence to the articulated values and apply corrective measures as and when needed to maintain congruency and consistency.

References

Alderfer, C.P. (1969). An empirical test of a new theory of human needs. *Organizational Behavior and Human Performance*, May, 142–175.

Beck, D.E., & Cowan, C.C. 1996. *Spiral dynamics: Mastering values, leadership, and change*. Oxford: Blackwell Publishers.

Clark, L.A., & Watson, D. (1999). Personality, disorder, and personality disorder: Toward a more rational conceptualization. *Journal of Personality Disorders*, 13, 142–151.

Covey, S.R. (1990). An inside-out approach, *Journal*, 7(10), 3–4.

Egan, K. (1997). *The educated mind: How cognitive tools shape our understanding*. Chicago: University of Chicago Press.

Funder, D.C. (2007). *The personality puzzle*. New York: Norton.

Gable, S.L., & Haidt, J. (2005). What (and why) is positive psychology? *Review of General Psychology*, 9, 103–110.

Furr, R.M., & Funder, D.C. (1998). A multi-modal analysis of personal negativity. *Journal of Personality and Social Psychology*, 74, 1580–1591.

Crain, W.C. (1985). *Theories of development*. New York: Prentice-Hall.

Kohlberg, L. (1973). The claim to moral adequacy of a highest stage of moral judgment. The *Journal of Philosophy*. Retrieved from http://www.vtaide.com/blessing/Kohlberg.htm

Krueger, J.I., & Tackett, J.L. (2003). Personality and psychopathology: Working toward the bigger picture. *Journal of Personality Disorders*, 17, 109–128.

Maslow, A. 1954. *Motivation and personality*. New York: Harper & Row.

McClelland, D.C. (1961). *The achieving society*. New York: Van Nostrand Reinhold.

McCrae, R.R., & Costa, P.T. (2003). *Personality in adulthood: A five factor theory perspective*. New York: Guilford.

Morey, L.C. (1988). Personality disorders in DSM-III and DSM-III-R: Convergence, coverage, and internal consistency. *American Journal of Psychiatry*, 145, 573–577

O'Connor, B.P. (2002). The search for dimensional structure differences between normality and abnormality: A statistical review of published data on personality and psychopathology. *Journal of Personality and Social Psychology*, 83(4), 962–982.

Oldham, J.M., & Morris, L.B. (1995). *The new personality self-portrait*. New York: Bantam.

Piaget, J. (1965), *The moral judgement of the child*. New York: Free Press.

Robinson, D.A. (1998). *The personal and corporate values journey*. Chart. Port Elizabeth: PSI.

Robinson, D.A. (2002). *A phenomenological study of how entrepreneurs experience and deal with ethical dilemmas*. (Doctoral dissertation). Rhodes University, Grahamstown, South Africa.

Robinson, D.A., Goleby, M., & Hosgood, N. (2007). *Entrepreneurship as a values and leadership paradigm.* Conference proceedings, AGSE International Entrepreneurship Research Exchange. Brisbane, Australia: Queenland University of Technology.

Robinson, D.A., & Harvey, M. (2008). Global leadership in a culturally diverse world. *Management Decision, 46*(3), 466–480.

Rotter, J. 1966. Generalized expectancies for internal versus external control of reinforcements. *Psychological Monographs,* Whole No. 609, 80.

Seligman, M.E.P., & Csikszentmihalyi, M. (2000). Positive psychology: An introduction. *American Psychologist, 55,* 5–14.

Weiten, W. (2007). *Psychology themes and varaitions.* Belmont, CA: Thomson Wadsworth.

Widiger, T.A., Trull, T, J., Clarkin, J.F., Sanderson, C., & Costa, P.T. Jr. (1994). A description of the DSM-III-R and DSM-IV personality disorders with the five-factor model of personality. In P.T. Costa, Jr. & T.A. Widiger (Eds.), *Personality disorders and the Five-Factor Model of Personality* (pp. 41–56). Washington, DC: American Psychological Association.

Chapter
20

Stakeholder Perspectives of Organisational Reputation

Mark Bahr, Jeni Warburton, Yolanda van Gellecum, and Margaret Shapiro

Good reputation management is becoming increasingly important as organisations and the social environments in which they function become more complex (Caruana, 2000; Fombrun & van Riel, 2003). Organisations are being evaluated by far more demanding standards than in the past, and are increasingly being held responsible for their environmental, social and ethical decisions as well as their economic decisions. Mishandled social, ethical and environmental issues can have dire consequences for corporate reputation. Well-known and well-documented examples include the Royal Dutch/Shell Brent Spar and Nigeria incidents, in which perceived social violations were detrimental to their reputation (see, e.g., Dickson & McCulloch 1996; Livesey, 2001). In 2009 the loss of 30 containers of ammonium nitrate and tons of oil from the Pacific Venturer and the subsequent impact on the corporate reputation of the mother company Swire, demonstrates the ongoing nature of these concerns. The current study investigated how stakeholder heterogeneity impacts on organisational reputation. A sample of 1208 respondents was drawn from six stakeholder groups. Differences in stakeholder perceptions are compared through structural equation modeling.

Managing corporate reputation has become an essential activity in business today, yet the development of systematic measures of good corporate reputation is at a relatively early stage (Cornelissen & Thorpe, 2002; Davies & Chun, 2002). Business media measures have tended to dominate thinking about reputation (Fombrun, Gardberg, & Sever, 2000). Of these, Fortune Magazine's America's Most Admired Companies (AMAC) is arguably the most well-known measure of corporate reputation (Fombrun et al., 2000). However, the Fortune AMAC is essentially a measure of economic performance, which like other available measures neglects noneconomic attributes of corporate reputation.

The bias towards economic attributes in instruments arises, as these measures are top-down peer review instruments, with reputation assessed from a corporate executive's perspective (Caruana & Chircop, 2000, Fombrun et al., 2000). This focus on business leaders to evaluate reputation neglects consideration of the social context from which reputations emerge, and the recognition of the diversity of stakeholders whose perceptions form the basis of organisational reputation. Companies are embedded within a social community with many diverse stakeholders who actively construct reputations (Rao, 1994). In the instance of the recent Pacific Venturer cargo spill in Queensland, Australia, the immediate and powerful impact of noncorporate stakeholders on reputation was evident in media calls for immediate government action.

The expectations of stakeholders go beyond simple notions of customer satisfaction with products and services (Caruana & Chircop, 2000) to a broad mix of economic and social criteria (Fombrun & van Riel, 2003). These criteria increasingly emphasise the business's relationship with all its communities (Burke, 1999). Social responsibility of business includes themes such as respect for staff, customers, and for the broader community, honesty and ethics, providing help for the community, and contributing to society as a whole (Collins & Poras, 1994). Organisations are expected to be good corporate citizens, and their reputations are increasingly dependent on this (Andriof & McIntosh, 2001).

Fombrun and his colleagues (Fombrun et al., 2000; Gardberg & Fombrun, 2002) have developed a conceptual model of reputation that represents a theory-based, empirical evaluation of reputation. The result has been the development of a reputation instrument the authors call The Reputation Quotient (Fombrun et al., 2000), which includes economic and noneconomic measures of reputation across six domains (refer to Table 2). These six domains can be broadly classified as tapping two higher order dimensions — termed 'rational appeal' and 'emotional appeal'. The first dimension 'rational appeal' encompasses traditional economic attributes including financial performance, products and services, vision and leadership and noneconomic attributes of workplace environment as well as social responsibility. The second dimension 'emotional appeal' includes broader noneconomic measures of reputation, such as respect and trust for the company. It seems likely that different stakeholder groups will differentially value these factors. An investor in a company, shareholder or management may be more concerned with the companies rational appeal as a marker of corporate reputation than say an 'ethical investor', a worker or a potential customer.

This chapter argues that recent instruments such as the Reputation Quotient (Fombrun et al., 2000) are important in addressing the deficit in prior instruments which have predomionantly focused on economic measures. However, there is a need for further empirical refinement of those instruments and in particular, a need to evaluate the impact of stakeholder differences on the assessment of reputation. Stakeholder theorists propose that organisations do not have one reputation but instead a number of reputations, with different groups viewing issues and events in different ways (Cornelissen & Thorpe, 2002; Svenson, 2001). Shenkar and Yuchtman-Yaar (1997) argue that attributes cannot be treated as having equal relevance to reputation, as different facets of performance are likely to matter to different stakeholder groups (Dowling, 2006; Shenkas & Yuchtman-Yaar, 1997). Thus, it is important to include the views of varied stakeholders in developing reputation measurement and to understand the different emphases placed on different components of reputation by stakeholders. The observation that stakeholders vary in their values raises a question as to the utility of a single measure of organisational reputation. The present study addresses the question of stakeholder heterogeneity, and asks whether a single model of organisational reputation holds for all stakeholder groups?

Method

The University of Queensland Reputation Survey was developed with the aim of building on current developments in reputation measurement, while ensuring the appropriateness of the model to the Australian context. In order to comply with these aims, The Reputation Quotient (Fombrun et al., 2000) is used as a basis for survey development. Participants were asked to rate the importance of these attributes to a good corporate reputation with a particular corporation as a reference point. To ensure that the current instrument had adequate domain coverage of both economic and noneconomic aspects of reputation a two-stage study was initiated. In a qualitative first stage (reported elsewhere, Warburton, Shapiro, Buckley, & Van Gellecum, 2004) content domain coverage of Fombrun's model and its applicability to the Australian context was explored. The Queensland Reputation index used in the present chapter reflects the issues relevant to reputation in a diverse sample of Queensland stakeholders. The initial study identified relevant stakeholder groups and structure of the content domains of the instrument used in the current study.

Participants

A sample of 1208 respondents was drawn from six stakeholder groups with interests pertaining to a single very large Australian corporation (see Table 20.1) providing a range of goods and services to clients.

Instrument and Procedure

Stage 1 of the study involved testing the construct validity of the Fombrun et al. (2000) instrument. A review of the literature, and a qualitative interview study suggested that aspects of social responsibility merited further empirical development.

The second general area that merited further investigation was the relationship of an organisation with its communities. If businesses are to be good corporate citizens then they need to adopt a strong and coherent attitude towards the community. Strategic corporate citizenship is about long-term sustainability and building strong relationships among all its communities (Andriof & McIntosh, 2001).

These findings suggested that the six domains utilised in the Reputation Quotient (Fombrun et al., 2000) were recognised as important aspects of reputation. However, further refinement was required. Table 20.2 shows the six domains utilised in the Reputation Quotient (Fombrun et al., 2000) were refined by the findings of Stage 1 investigations. These 6 subdomains are measured by a total of 22 measured variables.

The use of a single organisation as a sampling frame diminished the impact of business type conflating reputation differences between subgroups but prevented comparison across organsations as in Fombrun and colleagues' (2000) study. Respondents were asked to rate statements describing domains of corporate reputation domains shown in Table 20.2 on an 11-point scale. Response values for the items ranged from zero 'no impact', five 'medium impact' to 10 'very high impact'. Second, respondents were asked to directly rate the company's overall reputation using a

Table 20.1

Sampling Frame

Group	N	Description
Urban	303	Urban, low cost users.
Rural	301	Regional high cost users
Staff	100	Managers, professionals and general employees
Commercial	100	Business customers
Suppliers	100	Suppliers of a range of goods and services.
Media/government	100	Diverse high impact nonuser group

Table 20.2

Corporate Reputation Attributes Designed for the Queensland Reputation Instrument

Domains of Corporate Reputation (Fombrun et al. 2000)	The Queensland Reputation Instrument
Financial performance	Making profits
	Being financially sound
Products and services	Having quality services
	Having quality products
	Being competitive
	Understanding customer needs
	Being innovative, that is, ahead of the times
Vision and leadership	Having a well balanced vision for the future
	Having good leadership
Workplace environment	Having quality management
	Having a good workplace environment
	Being able to keep good staff
Social responsibility	Being responsible to the community
	Having good relations with community groups
	Being responsive to rural needs
	Giving to good causes
	Being environmentally responsible
Emotional appeal	Being trustworthy
	Being an organisation that people feel good about
	Taking responsibility when things go wrong
	Being transparent, that is, not trying to hide things
	Having strong ethical practices, that is, doing what is right

scale from 0 to 10, where 0 is a very bad reputation, and 10 is a very good reputation.

Results

Preliminary screening was conducted to assess data quality. The overall pattern of correlations suggested the data was sufficiently structured to permit Structural Equation Modeling. The data distributions did not show serious deviations from normality. Mahalanobis distance was used to detect potential multivariate outliers, 8.6% of cases were potentially multivariate outliers and analyses were conducted with both the full dataset ($n = 1208$) and with a reduced dataset excluding the multivariate outliers ($n = 1108$). No substantive difference in solution was found with outliers excluded from the analysis. One item was dropped from the analysis due to multicolinearity.

Table 20.3 shows the results of CFA of the individual congeneric measurement models for each of the 8 factors. Maximum likelihood estimation suggested adequate fit for 7 of the 8 factors. With the exception of financial performance, the models all have fit indices exceeding .90 on the NFI, CFI, IFI, & AGFI. Table three also shows the χ^2 approximation as a further measure of model fit. Significant values indicate deviation of the data from the model. In this instance model fit was inadequate for the products and services factor, the workplace environment factor, and the financial performance factor.

To further investigate the multidimensional nature of Fombrun et al.'s (2000) model a higher order analysis was conducted including each of the separate factors as a predictor of an independent measure of a specific organisation's reputation. There was a significant departure of the data from the model specification, χ^2 (36, n = 1108) = 2171.54, p < .001.. Moreover, fit indices indicated overall model fit was poor (all indices < .70) and residuals were uniformly high (> .20) and indicated substantial unaccounted for covariation between the sub-domains. It appeared from the analysis and analysis of residuals that separation of the 8 subdomains was not warranted. The relatively high correlation between items suggested that organisational reputation may be unidimensional. Figure 20.1 shows the revised model of organisational reputation which preserves the emotional appeal and rational appeal constructs but which drops Fombrun et al.'s (2000) original six constructs.

Model fit for the revised model using the entire cohort as a single group was significant, χ^2 (186, N = 1208) = 1112.70, p < .001 indicating that there was a significant departure of the data from the model specification. The NFI, CFI, and IFI goodness-of-fit indices indicated acceptable or near adequate fit (NFI = .92, CFI = .93 , and IFI = .93 respectively) and

Table 20.3

Fit Statistics for the Eight Dimensions of Corporate Reputation

Factors	χ^2	df	NFI	CFI	IFI	AGFI
Ethics	0.19	1	1.00	1.00	1.00	.99
Feeling good	.00	2	1.00	1.00	1.00	.80
Products & services	40.65	5	.97	.98	.98	.98
Vision & leadership	.00	1	1.00	1.00	1.00	.74
Workplace environment	16.65	1	.94	.94	.95	.94
Social & environmental	.00	0	1.00	1.00	1.00	1.00
Community responsibilities	.04	1	1.00	1.00	1.00	1.00
Financial performance	59.13	1	.65	.65	.65	.85

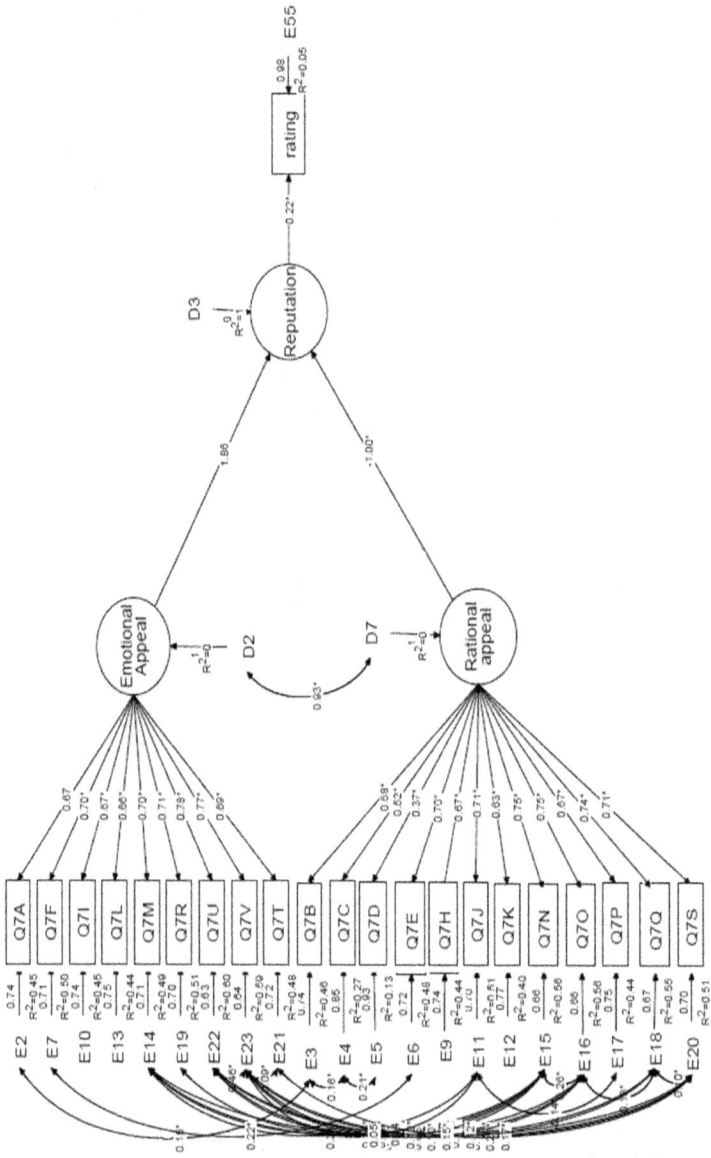

Figure 20.1

Revised overall model.

the AGFI indicated inadequate fit (AGFI = .87). The fit statistics are some-what misleading, however, as the solution obtained was not very stable and small model changes resulted in much less adequate solutions. RMSEA indicated an acceptable residual consistent with the notion that the model adequately fits the data (RMSEA = .07). The result is somewhat equivocal, while there is evidence of consistency between the data and model it is clear that there is room for improvement. To further examine the issue of sample heterogeneity a stakeholder analysis was conducted. The revised model was tested against each of the six stakeholder groups separately.

Table 20.4 shows model fit statistics for the overall model and for each of the six stakeholder groups. There is significant deviation from the theo-rised data structure for each stakeholder group. Poor fits were further sub-stantiated by numerous large residuals (> .20), with clear evidence of unaccounted for covariation of error terms. Moreover, the analysis of $\chi^2(1)$ of differences between groups shown in Table 4 indicates that model fit varies significantly between subgroups ($p < .001$). While it may be true that a general model of reputation can be derived that describes organisational reputation in a large sample, It would seem that the derived model does not fit any particular stakeholder groups particularly well.

Discussion

It is clear from the literature that developments in reliable measures of corporate reputation are at an early stage and lack theoretical robustness (Cornelissen & Thorpe, 2002; Davies & Chun, 2002). In particular, insuf-ficient attention has been given to non-economic attributes of a good reputation (Caruana & Chirop, 2000). The present study aimed to build on current developments in reputation measurement, while ensuring the appropriateness of the model in the Australian context.

Table 20.4

Goodness of Fit Indices for the Overall Model and Individual Stakeholder Groups

Model	χ^2	df	NFI	CFI	IFI	AGFI
Overall model	1190.68	186	.91	.92	.93	.86
Mg1 Group 1 model	841.94***	186	.81	.85	.85	.73
Mg2 Group 2 model	874.57***	186	.77	.81	.81	.71
Mg3 Group 3 model	675.48***	186	.78	.83	.83	.69
Mg4 Group 4 model	458.06***	186	.75	.83	.83	.72
Mg5 Group 5 model	892.35***	186	.64	.69	.70	.51
Mg6 Group 6 model	373.02***	186	.67	.80	.80	.64

This study had two key aims, both of which related to previous critiques of corporate reputation measurement. The first aim was to test and develop an inclusive model of corporate reputation. To this end a new instrument was developed based on the conceptual framework proposed by Fombrun et al. (2000) revised to reflect increasingly important non-economic factors. The resultant instrument was tested with a large sample of stakeholders related to one key Australian business. The intention was to improve construct validity in the local context.

The aim of the study was to investigate the impact of stakeholder heterogeneity on ability to measure organisational reputation. In particular, the model was tested among different stakeholders to determine the extent to which a single model could capture reputation amongst a diverse group of stakeholders. It was anticipated that differences in stakeholder values would complicate assessment of reputation and this may mean that a single instrument would not prove adequate to assess corporate reputation.

In regard to the first of these issues, the instrument tested included the six domains identified in the Reputation Quotient (Fombrun et al., 2000). Findings from structural equation analyses conducted here show that reputation can be construed as a uni-dimensional structure, or in a way which is consistent with Fombrun et al.'s (2000)'s notion of a two dimensional structure to reputation including aspects of emotional appeal and rational appeal (refer to Figure 1). However, the overall fit obtained taking that approach is not all that it should be.

Individual analysis of different stakeholder groups further support the notion that different stakeholders differentially emphasised domains of corporate reputation. To further investigate this notion exploratory Factor analyses were conducted for two stakeholder groups chosen to maximise difference (customers and suppliers). The results of those analyses (not reported here because of space limitations) are consistent with the CFA analyses in as much as a uni-dimensional structure can be found, but the model of best fit for the customer group consisted of three factors quality of service, responsiveness, and commercial responsibility. Whereas for the supplier group five factors emerged; Ethics, Responsiveness, Innovation and quality, Commercial responsibility, Customer needs & Transparency. These results clearly suggest that different stakeholders bring different perspectives to corporate reputation, and that differences between stakeholder groups' views must be taken into account when assessing corporate reputation.

References

Andriof, J., & McIntosh, M. (Eds.). (2001). *Perspectives on corporate citizenship*. Sheffield, United Kingdom: Greenleaf.

Caruana, A., & Chircop, S. (2000). Measuring corporate reputation: A case example, *Corporate Reputation Review*, 3(1), 43–57.

Collins, J.C., & Porras, J. (1994), *Built to last*. New York: Harper Business

Cornelissen, J., & Thorpe, R. (2002) Measuring a business school's reputation: Perspectives, problems and prospects. *European Management Journal*, 20(2), 172–178.

Davies, G. & Chun, R., (2002) Gaps between the internal and external perceptions of the corporate brand. *Corporate Reputation Review*, 5, 144–160.

Dickson, L., & McCulloch, A. (1995) Shell, The Brent Spar and Greenpeace: A doomed tryst? *Environmental Politics*, 5(1), 122–129.

Dowling, G.R. (2006). How good corporate reputation creates corporate value. *Corporate Reputation Review*, 9(2), 134–143.

Fombrun, C.J., Gardberg, N.A., & Sever, J.M. (2000). The Reputation Quotient: A multi-stakeholder measure of corporate reputation. *Journal of Brand Management*, 7(4), 241–55.

Fombrun, C., & van Riel, C. (2003) The reputational landscape. In J. Balmer & S. Greyser, (Eds.), *Revealing the corporation: Perspectives on identity, image, reputation, corporate branding, and corporate-level marketing* (pp. 223–233), Routledge: London, 223–233.

Livesey, S.M. (2001). Eco-identity as discursive struggle: Royal Dutch/Shell, Brent Spar, and Nigeria. *The Journal of Business Communication*, 38, 58–91

Rao, H. (1994). The social construction of reputation: Certification contests, legitimation, and the survival of organizations in the American Automobile Industry: 1890-1912. *Strategic Management Journal*, 15, 29–44.

Shenkar, O., & Yuchtman-Yaar, E. (1997) Reputation, image, prestige and goodwill: An interdisciplinary approach to organizational standing. *Human Relations*, 50(11), 1361–1381.

Warburton, J., Shapiro, M. Buckley, A., & Van Gellecum, Y. (2004) A nice thing to do but is it critical for business? Corporate Responsibility and Australian Business. *Australian Journal of Social Issues*, 39(2), 117–127.

Chapter

21

Coping Strategies Employed by University Students in Handling Their Occupational Role Stress

Tanya Paspaliaris and Richard E. Hicks

Research has reported that high levels of stress exist among university students and that the common coping strategies used by the students add to their stress. Stress associated with student role requirements appears not unlike the stress experienced in occupational roles in the workplace. However, no previous research in Australia had investigated the relationships among combined facets of the work environment (roles and related stresses) of university students, the types of coping strategies used and the relationship to stress and to depression. This study addressed this gap by using a workplace stress inventory, the Occupational Stress Inventory — Revised, the Ways of Coping Questionnaire Revised and the Depression, Anxiety and Stress Scales. The results showed that the more highly stressed university students in the sample used ineffective coping strategies (emotion focused, especially avoidant) and lacked social support. No gender differences in the handling of stress were noted, but females scored higher than males on emotion-focused and specifically avoidant coping and on levels of depression. Implications are drawn for practice.

University students, like other community members, are subject to stress. Stress is experienced when there is an imbalance between the demands being made and the availability of resources needed to cope with those demands (e.g., Lo, 2002; Tully, 2004). University life can be an exciting time for university students; however, it can also be very stressful. This stress is comparable to occupational role stress, which is defined as the outcome people have to extreme pressures or demands placed upon them due to their role (Cotton, Dollard, & de Jonge, 2002; Salanova, Grau, &

Martinez, 2006). The inputs to occupational role stress can be seen in terms of role overload, role ambiguity, role boundary and role conflict demands and role responsibilities (Osipow, 1998). Demands relate to tasks and assignments to be completed, deadlines, availability of choice of tasks or topics, managing social relationships including with staff members (cf., Cotton et al.) and they also relate to such elements as grade competition, study/work time demands, student/staff ratios, future career goals and quality of teaching (cf., Archer & Murphy, 1996; Misra & McKean, 2000; Winefield, et al., 2003).

Research has suggested that the way in which people cope with stressors can reduce or increase the effects of stress on emotional well being (Lazarus & Folkman, 1984; Misra & McKean, 2000). For example, it has been found that specific types of coping strategies such as emotion-focused may contribute to the higher levels of stress and depression experienced by some university students (Arthur, 1998; Carver, Scheier, & Weintraub, 1989; Heiman & Kariv, 2005; Lo, 2002; Tully, 2004). Some inconsistent results have been found, and one possibility for differences has been considered to lie in how the emotion-focused items relate to direct approaches to stress resolution or relate more to avoidance of facing the stress situation. This current study examined whether university students used problem-focused coping, or emotion-focused coping, but divided the emotion-focused coping into approach coping and avoidant coping.

There has been limited research conducted in the area of occupational role stress experienced by university students and few studies found by the researchers where the relationships between stresses experienced, coping strategies used (whether avoidant or approach strategies, or emotion-focused vs. problem-focused), and depression were examined together. This current study was designed to investigate the relationships between these elements.

To understand how university students cope with stress, their perceptions of what constitutes a stressful or demanding situation and their resources to cope, need to be understood. The Ways of Coping Questionnaire Revised (WCQ-R; Lazarus & Folkman, 1988) has been used to evaluate how individuals cope with stressful situations in their life, by assessing their thoughts and actions (Farrelly, Ffrench, Ogeil, & Phillips, 2007; Krpan, Levine, Stuss, & Dawson, 2007). This current study used this instrument for comparison purposes and to examine the use of ineffective and effective coping strategies employed in the sample of university students. Ineffective strategies are defined as those leading to or associated with increased stress and depression scores. The 18 strategies given in the WCQ-R were divided into problem-focused and emotion-focused coping, with the emotion-focused approaches further divided into approach and avoidant coping strategies for purposes of this study.

Aims and Hypotheses

There were three main hypotheses in this study. First, in line with overseas research in the main, it was hypothesised that level and type of coping would predict (1) depression levels and (2) stress levels in the university sample. Second, consistent with occupational and clinical research in general, it was hypothesised that females would score higher on stress, emotion-focused coping and depression compared to males. Last, it was hypothesised that types of coping style, particularly avoidant coping/ emotion-focused coping would be significantly associated with experienced levels of stress and depression. Given the importance of social support in many studies, social support was incorporated also into the prediction of stress and depression (separately) and compared with coping styles as predictors.

Method

Participants and Materials

The sample consisted of 117 Australian university students with ages ranging from 17 to 54 years ($M = 24.60$ years, $SD = 8.03$ years). The participants were recruited through both convenience and snowball sampling.

A general demographic questionnaire and three relevant stress, coping and depression questionnaires were used in this study. The Occupational Stress Inventory Revised (OSI-R; Osipow, 1998) is a 140 item self-report questionnaire, developed to assess occupational stress across three dimensions: roles, strain experienced and resources. The questionnaire has been used in studies linking occupational roles, strain and coping and has been suggested as valuable for cross-occupational studies (cf., Hicks, Fujiwara, & Bahr, 2006). The 21-item Depression Anxiety Stress Scales (DASS-21; Lovibond & Lovibond, 1995) was used to assess the student's emotional state over the past week. The WCQ-R (Lazarus & Folkman, 1988) was used to examine the coping styles individuals used when confronted with stressful encounters also over the past week. Problem-focused and emotion-focused scales are part of the WCQ-R. These two questionnaires have also been used extensively.

As indicated above, the present study also divided the emotion focused coping scale into avoidance coping and approach coping. This was done in a two-step process. The first step involved using six subject matter experts initially to identify whether the items presented were an approach coping strategy or an avoidant coping strategy, and whether they were a distress item (emotional distress) or an item, which measured more direct coping (that is not emotional distress). In the second step, exploratory analysis was conducted as a guide only (given the relatively low *N*) to help confirm whether the items hung together. Principal factor analysis with oblimin rotation helped confirm the two-factor solution of approach and avoidant coping. The results also confirmed that the avoidance coping items were related to distress, whereas the approach coping items measured more direct coping. The use of the subject matter experts and of the exploratory factor analysis confirmed that the developed subscales were acceptable for the current research aimed in part at determining which types of coping strategies were most effective (not linked to increased depression or stress outcomes).

Results

The results of standard multiple regressions indicated that Hypothesis 1 in relation to prediction of depression was supported, as can be seen in Table 21.1. There were differences reflected in the type of emotion focused coping used by university students when experiencing depression; $F(4, 112) = 17.18$, $p < .001$, $R^2 = 38\%$ (adjusted $R^2 = 35.8\%$). Avoidance coping was the strongest predictor of depression, in which 36% of the variance was explained. To a lesser extent Approach-coping (as part of emotion-focused coping) and younger age levels were also associated with depression; however, problem-focused coping was *not* associated with depression. It can be seen in Table 21.1 that problem-focused coping is also related to emotion-focused coping (approach and avoidant), but each aspect of coping is related to depression differently.

The second part of Hypothesis 1 related to prediction of stress is examined as part of Hypothesis 3 below.

Hypothesis 2, that females would score higher on depression, emotion focused coping and occupational stress, was partly supported. A series of one-way ANOVAs indicated a significant effect of gender on avoidance coping (emotion-focused; $F[1, 115] = 4.80$, $p < .05$, $\eta^2 = .04$). Female university students reported a greater use of avoidance coping compared to males. There were, however, no gender differences found in responses to items covering occupational role stress, depression, problem-focused coping and approach coping.

Table 21.1

Standard Multiple Regression and Intercorrelations of Coping Style and Age and Their Prediction of Depression

Variables	Dep[a]	Pfc[b]	Apc[c]	Avc[d]	β	SE	B	$sr^{2\%}$
Pfc[b]	.12				-.10	.06	-.17	
Apc[c]	.22**	.72***			.02	.07	.03	
Avc[d]	.58***	.41***	.50***		.32	.05	.60***	36.0
Age	-.26**	-.12	-.06	-.18*	-1.20	.56	-.16*	2.6

Note: [a]Dep was depression, [b]Pfc was problem-focused coping, [c]Apc was Approach coping and [d]Avc was Avoidance coping.
$*p < .05. **p < .01. ***p < .001$

Hypothesis 3 was the central hypothesis dealing with types of coping strategies used, and outcomes in stress or depression. The results of a series of hierarchical multiple regressions indicated that Hypothesis 3 was supported. There were differences reflected in the type of emotion-focused coping used by university students when experiencing stress and depression. As indicated in Table 21.2, avoidance coping significantly predicted the occupational role stress experienced by students. In addition, social support significantly and negatively predicted occupational role stress. Similar results were found in predicting depression but avoidance coping carried the highest weight at Step 2 (.56) followed by social support (.24).

Table 21.2

Hierarchical Multiple Regression and Inter-Correlations of Coping Styles, Age and Social Support and Their Prediction of Stress

Variable	Stress	Pfc[a]	Avc[b]	Apc[c]	Age	β	SE B	B	sr^2
1 Pfc[a]	.10					.08	.26	.04	
Avc[b]	.29***	.41***				.58	.20	.32**	10.2%
Apc[c]	.09	.72***	.50***			-.22	.30	-.10	
Age	-.06	-.12	-.18*	-.06		-.10	2.39	.00	
2 Sosd	-.38***	.11	-.14	-.02	-.00	-.85	.21	-.36***	13.0%
Age						-.18	2.24	-.01	
Apc[c]						-.32	.29	-.14	
Avc[b]						.46	.19	.25*	6.3%
Pfc[a]						.28	.25	.14	

Note: [a]Pfc was problem-focused coping, [b]Avc was avoidance coping, [c]Apc was approach coping and [d]Sos was social support.
$*p < .05; **p < .01; ***p < .001$

Discussion

This study investigated stress related to the role of students, the types of coping strategies used and depression scores of a sample of Australian university students. Gender and ageing impacts were also considered. The main focus of this study was to discover which types of coping strategies were used by students, and whether these were effective.

Hypothesis 1, that depression levels in particular would be predicted from levels of coping, was supported. In this current sample, emotion-focused coping impacted student distress at a higher level than problem-focused coping. The results of this study are consistent with studies of stress, coping and mental health attributes already reported (e.g., Arthur, 1998; Farrelly et al., 2007; Garnefski et al., 2002; Moskowitz & Folkman, 2004; Salanova et al., 2006).

However, there were differences reflected in the type of emotion-focused coping used by university students when experiencing emotional distress. Results indicated that avoidance coping strategies contributed more than approach coping to greater distress in students. This finding (of a differential between two types of emotion-focused coping) may be useful for further studies of depression — and, of course, stress.

Hypothesis 2, that gender differences would exist in terms of stress, coping styles and depression, was only partially supported. Both male and female university students experienced the same levels of stress. This may indicate that students are faced with similar problems in their academic environment; however, they may be ill equipped to cope with the stressful encounters involved in carrying out their student 'work' roles. The results, suggesting similar high levels of stress and workload across gender, are consistent with several earlier studies.

The second part of Hypothesis 2, that females would score higher on emotion-focused coping, was supported, consistent with most earlier studies (e.g., Heiman & Kariv, 2005; Matud, 2004; Misra & McKean, 2004). The current results indicated that there was no gender difference in the use of problem-focused coping and approach coping. However, there was a significant gender difference in the reported use of emotion-focused coping, with female students reporting a greater use of avoidance coping to males. A possible explanation of these findings is the socialisation hypothesis theory which suggests that males are socialised to use more active problem-focused coping strategies, and females are socialised to use the more expressive emotion-focused coping strategies (Ptacek, Smith, & Dodge, 1994).

The third part of Hypothesis 2, that females would score higher on depression, was not supported in this sample. This is inconsistent with most earlier studies which show females as scoring higher than males on depression. A possible explanation of the finding in the current study is that we are dealing with a small and highly educated group not representative of the general population. However, it is noted that there were gender differences in the use of coping strategies. Although male and female university students report similar levels of stress and depression, they may differ in the ways they express their emotional distress. This is reflected by the higher use of avoidance coping by females, which is found to be a significant predictor of depression.

Hypothesis 3, that types of coping strategies would be associated with levels of experienced stress and depression, was supported. These results suggest that selected coping styles used by some university students may not alleviate stress and depression. The use of ineffective coping strategies, such as emotion-focused coping and in particular avoidance coping, may result in unsatisfactory support, which in turn leads to increased negative outcomes. These results appear consistent with studies linking study or work role demands, and stress (e.g., Blalock & Joiner, 2000; Cotton et al., 2002; Dipboye, Phillips, Macan, & Shahani, 1990; Krpan et al., 2007).

Results indicated that avoidance coping strategies in particular contributed to greater levels of experienced stress and depression. This provides evidence that avoidance coping strategies are confounded with distress. This study also indicated that some students who avoided dealing with their stressful situations did not provide sufficient cues to their social network that they were experiencing stress or depression. This observation is in line also with the fact that younger students face more stress in the university.

Implications for Intervention

The results of the present study suggest that stress and depression are evident among university students and some students are employing ineffective coping strategies, specifically avoidance coping. Although it is unknown why some students use ineffective coping strategies when confronted with stressful situations, universities may need to assume that these students have never been taught problem solving or approach coping techniques. Universities could introduce strategies such as teaching sessions or university preparatory sessions, which educate students to recognise potential stressful situations and what constitutes effective coping strategies versus ineffective coping strategies. These sessions could involve potential mental health issues if ineffective coping strategies are used, and some attention to both the younger and mature age students, given the age related differences in how these students cope with stressful situations.

Conclusion

This study investigated coping strategies, occupational role stress, and depression in a sample of Australian university students. The results of the study suggest that there is a relationship between emotion-focused coping strategies, especially avoidant coping strategies, and depression and stress as outcomes. These avoidant strategies are clearly ineffective in dealing with the role responsibilities and requirements of students and need to be replaced by more effective strategies. Counselling services within universities could provide more support to these selected students, by assessing their coping strategies; and curricula especially in introductory subjects could introduce more specific material aimed at teaching effective rather than ineffective ways of coping in university. This could reduce the amount of stress and depression experienced by university students, and could promote the use of more effective forms of coping, thus helping to enhance student academic and personal success. This current study provided further validation of the Cotton et al. (2002) job design and work stress theory, that university students are comparable to the occupational workforce in their task structuring and in their responses. It has also provided evidence that dividing emotion-focused coping strategies into two factors, one dealing with an approach orientation, the other with an avoidant orientation, can contribute additional understanding of how coping strategies work.

References

Archer, J., & Murphy, M.C. (1996). Stressors on the college campus: A comparison of 1985 and 1993. *Journal of College Student Development, 37,* 20-28

Arthur, N. (1998). The effects of stress, depression and anxiety on postsecondary students' coping strategies. *Journal of College Student Development, 39,* 11–22.

Blalock, J.A., & Joiner, T.E. (2000). Interaction of cognitive avoidance coping and stress in predicting depression/anxiety. *Cognitive Therapy and Research, 24,* 47–65

Carver, C.S., Scheier, M.F., & Weintraub, J.K. (1989). Assessing coping strategies: A theoretical based approach. *Journal of Personality and Social Psychology, 56,* 267–283

Cotton, S.J., Dollard, M.F., & de Jonge, J. (2002). Stress and student job design: Satisfaction, well-being, and performance in university students. *International Journal of Stress Management, 9*, 147–162.

Dipboye, R.L., Phillips, A.P., Macan, T.H., & Shahani, C. (1990). College students' time management: Correlations with academic performance and stress. *Journal of Educational Psychology, 82*, 760–768

Endler, N.S., & Parker, J.D.A. (1990). State and trait anxiety, depression and coping styles. *Australian Journal of Psychology, 42*, 207–220.

Farrelly, S., Ffrench, C., Ogeil, R.P., & Phillips, J.G. (2007). Coping strategies and problem gambling. *Behaviour Change, 24*, 14–24

Garnefski, N., Legerstee, J., Kraaij, V., Van Den Kommer, T., & Teerds, J. (2002). Cognitive coping strategies and symptoms of depression and anxiety: A comparison between adolescents and adults. *Journal of Adolescence, 25*, 603–611.

Heiman, T., & Kariv, D. (2005). Task-oriented versus emotion-oriented coping strategies: The case of college students. *College Student Journal, 39*, 72–84 perceptions

Hicks, R., Fujiwara, D., & Bahr, M. (2006). *Confirmatory factor analysis of the Occupational Stress Inventory-Revised, among Australian teachers.* Published in the Proceedings of the Social Science Methodology Conference, ACSPRI (Australian Consortium for Social and Political Research, Inc.). The University of Sydney, December

Krpan, K.M., Levine, B., Stuss, D.T., & Dawson, D.R. (2007). Executive function and coping at one-year post traumatic brain injury. *Journal of Clinical and Experimental Neuropsychology, 29*, 36–46

Lazarus, R.S. & Folkman, S. (1984). *Stress, appraisal and coping.* New York: Springer.

Lazarus, R.S. & Folkman, S. (1988). *The Ways of Coping Questionnaire.* Palo Alto, CA: Consulting Psychological Press.

Lo, R. (2002). A longitudinal study of perceived level of stress, coping and self-esteem of undergraduate nursing students: An Australian case study. *Journal of Advanced Nursing, 39*, 119–126

Lovibond, S.H., & Lovibond, P.F. (1995). *Manual for the Depression Anxiety Stress Scales.* (2nd ed). Sydney, Australia: Psychology Foundation of Australia.

Matud, M.P. (2004). Gender differences in stress and coping styles. *Personality and Individual Differences, 37*, 1401–1415

Misra, R., & McKean, M. (2000). College student's academic stress and its relationship to their anxiety, time management, and leisure satisfaction. *American Journal of Health Studies, 16*, 41–51

Moskowitz, J.T., & Folkman, S. (2004). Coping: Pitfalls and promise. *Annual Review of Psychology, 55*, 745–774.

Osipow, S.H. (1998). *Occupational Stress Inventory Revised Edition (OSI-R): Professional manual.* Lutz, FL: Psychological Assessment Resources, Inc.

Ptacek, J.T., Smith, R.E., & Dodge, K.L. (1994). Gender differences in coping with stress: When stressor and appraisals do not differ. *Personality and Social Psychology Bulletin, 20,* 421–430

Salanova, M., Grau, R.M., & Martinez, I.M. (2006). Job demands and coping behaviour: The moderating role of professional self-efficacy. *Psychology in Spain, 10,* 1–7

Tully, A. (2004). Stress, sources of stress and ways of coping among psychiatric nursing students. *Journal of Psychiatric and Mental Health Nursing, 11,* 43–47

Winefield, A.H., Gillespie, N., Stough, C., Dua, J., Hapuarachchi, J., & Boyd, C. (2003). Occupational stress in Australian university staff: Results from a national survey. *International Journal of Stress Management, 10,* 51–63.

Applications in clinical and health psychology:
Wellbeing in older adults, depression in
young adults

Physical Decline and Psychological Wellbeing in Older Adults: A Longitudinal Investigation of Several Potential Buffering Factors

Navjot Bhullar, Donald W. Hine, and Bronwen R. Myall

This longitudinal study, involving 233 older Australians (mean age = 61.96 yrs, SD = 8.89; females = 61%), investigated whether decline in physical health was a reliable negative predictor of psychological wellbeing, and whether this relation was moderated by three individual difference variables (sense of coherence, positive life attitudes, and perceived social support). After controlling for psychological wellbeing at Time 1 and several demographic covariates, there was a significant negative association between physical decline and psychological wellbeing 3 years later at Time 2. As predicted by the buffering hypothesis, moderation analysis revealed this association was significantly attenuated for respondents who reported higher levels of social support relative to those with less support. Contrary to our predictions, the magnitude of the relationship between physical decline and psychological wellbeing did not vary as function of sense of coherence and positive life attitudes, suggesting that these factors may not buffer older adults against the possible negative psychological effects of age-related declines in physical health.

Recent increases in life expectancy, stemming from medical advances and lifestyle changes, have resulted in an exponential increase in the number of older adults in developed nations (Reichstadt, Depp, Palinkas, Folsom, & Jeste, 2007). This demographic shift, and the associated increase in age-related health problems (Hays, Steffens, Flint, Bosworth, & George, 2001), represents one of the largest challenges facing the Western world (Westendorp, 2006). Several studies indicated that chronic physical problems in later life are important risk factors for developing depressive symptoms and psychological distress (e.g., van Gool, et al., 2003).

It is important to note that not all older adults who experience decline in physical health become depressed and/or distressed. Existential and humanistic theorists (e.g., Maslow, 1955) have pointed out the benefits of positive existential resources in facilitating successful ageing. Finding meaning and purpose in one's life and experiencing a sense of coherence and control appear to be important factors that help older adults transcend adversity and maintain mental health (Myall, et al., 2008). For example, Nygren, et al. (2005) found Antonovsky's (1987) construct of sense of coherence to be related to inner strength, and psychological well-being. In addition, perceived social support has also been shown to be predictive of positive mental health outcomes in a range of age groups in both sexes (Ranchor, 1994). The potential impact of each of these variables on mental health is summarised in the sections that follow.

Positive Existential Resources
Positive existential life attitudes and beliefs are potentially powerful internal resources that help maintain a sense of meaning, purpose, coherence and control over one's life (Reker, 1992). These psychological variables facilitate a positive view of the world and the ability to successfully cope with potential stressors that may arise during the later stages of life, when older individuals often feel compelled to re-evaluate their lifestyles. We included two measures in the present study to assess these existential concepts: Antonovsky's (1987) Sense of Coherence Scale and Reker's (1992) Life Attitude Balance Index.

According to Antonovsky (1987), sense of coherence is a global orientation based on three core factors (comprehensibility, manageability, and meaningfulness) that underlie successful coping in response to social and environmental stressors (Antonovsky, 1996). *Comprehensibility* is the degree to which individuals perceive information about themselves and the surroundings as ordered, structured, consistent, and understandable. *Manageability* is the degree to which individuals believe that they possess sufficient resources to adequately meet the demands imposed by internal and external stressors. Finally, *meaningfulness* refers to the extent to which individuals feel that certain areas of life are worthy of time and effort, and to their degree of involvement in various life domains.

Gana (2001) reported that sense of coherence can serve as an important buffering factor that limits the negative impact of adverse experiences on psychological wellbeing. A strong sense of coherence predicts better use of available psychological resources, more adaptive coping, and greater resiliency. Previous research has also shown that sense of coherence buffers the impact of situational or illness-related factors on distress. For instance, Johansson, Larsson, and Hamrin (1998) reported that older adults with a stronger sense of coherence coped better after a hip fracture (an adverse and stressful experience). In a more recent study, Gustavsson-Lilius, Julkunen, Keskivarra, and Hietanen (2007) found that a strong sense of coherence predicted significantly lower levels of anxiety and depression at 14-month follow-up in cancer patients, even after controlling for baseline levels of distress.

Reker's (1992) Life Attitude Balance Index assesses the extent to which individuals find their lives meaningful, and their level of motivation to find purpose in life. Reker (2002) suggested that the existential construct of finding meaning and purpose in life facilitates optimal adaptation to life's changing circumstances that accompany the ageing process. Positive attitudes towards life may bolster self-esteem, life satisfaction, and personal growth in the face of disability and losses that accompany advancing age. For example, Fry (2001) found that personal meaning was the key existential predictor of psychological wellbeing for older adults coping with spousal death.

Perceived Social Support

Perceived social support has been found to be a protective factor against a wide variety of life stressors. Stressful life events occurring in the presence of social support may produce less distress than if they occur in its absence (Kornblith, et al., 2001). Dohrenwend, Krasnoff, Askenasy, and Dohrenwend (1982) suggested a pathogenic triad which is a cluster of major negative life events outside a person's control (e.g., physical illness or injury, death of spouse or child) and highly related to poor adjustment. Social support buffers the effects of stressful life events on adjustment by helping individuals redefine a stress so that it is no longer seen as stressful, and/or to supply resources, thus reducing the severity of the stressful event (Kornblith, et al., 2001). For instance, in a cross-sectional study, Hays, Saunders, Flint, Kaplan, and Blazer (1997) reported that the relationship between functional decline and depressive symptoms was attenuated in older adults who had more perceived social support.

In the current study, we employed a longitudinal design to investigate whether physical decline is a reliable negative predictor of psychological wellbeing in a sample of older Australians over a 3-year period. We also examined whether the magnitude of this relationship varies as function of three 'buffering' resources (sense of coherence, positive life attitudes, and perceived social support).

Hypotheses

There were two main hypotheses. First, we predicted that after controlling for pre-existing levels of psychological wellbeing, physical decline would be associated with decreased psychological wellbeing at Time 2 (T2). Second, we predicted that this relationship would be moderated by sense of coherence, positive life attitudes, and perceived social support. That is, we expected that physical decline would be a stronger negative predictor of psychological wellbeing for respondents with lower levels of sense of coherence, positive life attitudes, and social support relative to individuals who possessed more of these buffering resources.

Method

Participants and Procedure

Two hundred and thirty-three volunteers (age range = 50–87; mean age = 61.96; SD = 8.89; females = 61%) from a range of urban and rural Australian communities provided data.

Participants were recruited through advertisements, placed in local newspapers and on public notice boards, inviting them to participate in a study on 'wellbeing in older adults'. Researchers provided contact information in the recruitment letter and phoned those individuals who indicated their interest. Of the 418 questionnaires that were initially distributed, 402 (96%) were returned. All questionnaires with greater than 5% missing data were excluded from the analyses, leaving a total of 391 participants for the initial stage of the longitudinal study. Approximately 3 years later (T2), questionnaires were sent to the 391 participants who provided data at T1. The return rate was 61% (240 participants), out of which seven were excluded due to excessive missing data (> 5%), leaving 233 for subsequent analyses. Remaining missing values at both T1 and T2 (< 5%) were imputed using the Expectation Maximisation algorithm in SPSS Version 16.

We computed t tests to compare the characteristics of those individuals who completed questionnaire at both time points relative to those who participated at T1 only. These analyses revealed that respondents who remained in the study scored significantly higher on physical wellbeing at T1, $t(389) = 2.09$, $p = .04$. No differences were found between these two groups on psychological wellbeing at T1, $t(389) = 1.22$, $p = .22$ or age, $t(387) = -.82$, $p = .41$.

Materials
The following scales were administered:

Perceived Wellbeing Scale-Revised (PWB-R; Reker, 1992). Psychological and physical wellbeing were measured with the 16-item PWB-R. The psychological wellbeing subscale assesses the presence of positive emotions and the absence of negative emotions. The physical wellbeing subscale represents self-rated physical health and the perceived absence of physical discomforts. Cronbach's alpha was .79 for physical wellbeing and .84 for psychological wellbeing in the present study.

Sense of Coherence Scale (SOCS; Antonovsky, 1987). Sense of coherence was measured using the 29-items SOCS. Cronbach's alpha was .90 in the present study.

Life Attitude Profile (LAP; Reker, 1992). This 48-item instrument measures the extent to which individuals find meaning and purpose in their lives. Cronbach's alpha was .86 in the present study.

Social Support. Perceived social support was assessed by averaging two standardised items assessing the extent to which respondents had access to confidantes and social support groups.

Results
Descriptive Statistics
Sixty-six per cent of the sample exhibited decline in physical health, and 59% reported decrements in psychological wellbeing over time. Table 22.1 provides the means and standard deviations for the main variables included in the study.

Main Analyses
Decline in physical health was computed by subtracting respondents' physical health scores at T2 from their T1 scores. Given that we are interested in physical decline (as opposed to change in physical health), all respondents who reported no change or improvement from T1 to T2 were assigned a score of 0, representing no physical decline. Consistent

Table 22.1

Means and Standard Deviations for Physical Wellbeing and Psychological Wellbeing at T1 and three years later at T2

	Theoretical		T1		T2		
Variable	Min.	Max.	M	SD	M	SD	t
Physical wellbeing	1	7	5.09	1.15	4.74	1.06	5.44***
Psychological wellbeing	1	7	6.21	0.82	6.02	0.95	3.95***

Note: $N = 233$, ***$p < .001$

with our hypotheses, multiple regression analysis indicated that physical decline significantly predicted psychological wellbeing at T2 after controlling for age, gender, and psychological wellbeing at T1, $F(4, 228) = 51.88$, $R^2 = .04$, $B = -.26$, $SE = .07$, $p < .001$), a small, but statistically significant, effect.

To determine whether the potential negative effect of physical decline on psychological wellbeing was moderated by sense of coherence, positive life attitudes, and perceived social support, we conducted three regression analyses.[1] For each analysis, age, gender, and psychological wellbeing at T1 were entered as covariates, physical decline and the respective moderator were entered as predictors in block 1, and the interaction of physical decline with the moderator was entered in block 2. Following the recommendations of Cohen, Cohen, West, & Aiken (2003), main effects for the continuous variables were centered at the mean prior to computing the interaction term. Given that all hypotheses were directional, one-tailed significance tests were employed. The results of the analyses were summarised in Table 22.2.

Of the three hypothesised moderation effects, only one involving social support was statistically significant. As predicted, the magnitude of the negative relationship between physical decline and psychological wellbeing at T2 varied substantially as a function of perceived social support. As social support increased, the negative relationship between physical decline and psychological wellbeing became weaker (for low levels of social support, $B = -.26$; for moderate levels of social support, $B = -.13$; for high levels of social support, $B = .00$).

Discussion

The primary aim of this study was to examine whether decline in physical health is associated with reduced psychological wellbeing in older adults.

Table 22.2

Summary of Moderation Analyses Investigating the Relationships between Physical Decline and Psychological Wellbeing at T2

Dependent variable predictors	R2	B	SE	sr^2
Psychological wellbeing at T2	.48**			
Physical decline (A)		−.25**	.07	.03
Sense of coherence (B)		.00	.00	.00
A × B		.00	.00	.00
Psychological wellbeing at T2	.48**			
Physical decline (A)		−.26**	.07	.04
Positive Life Attitude (B)		−.00	.00	.00
A × B		−.00	.00	.00
Psychological wellbeing at T2	.49**			
Physical decline (A)		−.27**	.07	.04
Perceived Social Support (B)		−.04	.07	.00
A × B		−.26*	.15	.01

Note: *$p < .05$, ** $p < .01$.

All main effects in the table are from block 1 of the analyses. Interaction effects from block 2. B = unstandardised beta coefficients, SE = standard error, and sr^2 = squared semi-partial correlations (amount of unique variance in the DV accounted for by a predictor). Covariates (age, gender, and psychological wellbeing at T1) are not reported in the table.

Consistent with the previous findings (Hays et al., 2001), results revealed significant decrements in both physical health and psychological wellbeing over the 3-year period of the study, and physical decline explained 4%, a small but statistically significant amount of variation in psychological wellbeing at T2, after statistically controlling for age, gender, and psychological wellbeing at T1.

Overview of Main Findings

A significant buffering effect was found for perceived social support. That is, the relationship between physical decline and psychological wellbeing at T2 was attenuated in individuals with greater perceived social support. This is consistent with previous research (e.g., Kornblith, et al., 2001) which indicated that individuals who perceive to have social support seem to have better psychological wellbeing in the face of stressful life events.

Contrary to our hypotheses, sense of coherence and positive attitudes toward life did not moderate the relationship between physical decline and psychological wellbeing, suggesting that these two may not help attenuate the potential negative effects of declining physical health on psychological wellbeing. Our finding is inconsistent with Gana (2001) and Reker (2002) who found that a strong sense of coherence and positive existential attitudes act as a buffer against adversity and life stressors. It may be possible that decrements in physical health in the elderly undermine sense of coherence as well as positive attitudes toward life, which in turn, result in reduced psychological wellbeing over time. One explanation can be that sense of coherence may not be a stable trait as suggested by Antonovsky (1987). Smith, Breslin, and Beaton (2003) reported a lack of stability for sense of coherence over a 4-year study period. The authors suggested that sense of coherence may include a *state-type* component that is sensitive to variation in situational factors. For example, Carmel and Bernstein (1990) found that the higher the experienced distress, the higher the trait anxiety, and the lower the sense of coherence. Kivimaki, Vahtera, Elovainio, Lillrank, and Kevin (2002) found that major life events were associated with weakened sense of coherence about two years later. This suggests that changes in sense of coherence may be dependent on the stressful life situations, such as disease or ill health (e.g., Gustavsson-Lilius, et al., 2007). The same may hold true for positive life attitudes, although we found no evidence in literature to support the view that this variable as measured by LAP can be best conceptualised as a state as opposed to a trait component.

Limitations

There are several limitations that should be considered when interpreting the present findings. First, responses to the questionnaire indicate that our sample was relatively young and high functioning. Future research is required to determine whether our findings will generalise to more heterogeneous samples of older adults. Second, only two items, for example, 'having a confidante' and 'access to support groups' were used in the present study to assess perceived social support. Future research might use a more reliable measure of perceived social support (e.g., Medical Outcome Study Support Survey) assessing various aspects of social support, such as emotional, tangible, affective, and positive social interactions (Sherbourne & Stewart, 1991).

Implications and Conclusion

The results of the present study suggest that ageing-related decrements in physical health impact upon the psychological wellbeing over time. However, not all older individuals develop depressive symptoms and/or become psychologically distressed. Certain traits and attitudes (e.g., sense of coherence and positive life attitudes) have been found to operate as buffers, limiting the negative effects of stressors on mental health. In the present study, we failed to replicate these effects in a sample of older Australians. A promising finding was that perceived social support significantly attenuated the relationship between physical decline and reduced psychological wellbeing. Our findings suggest that individuals with stronger social ties/connections and support systems may have the ability to overcome negative effect of ageing-related changes in physical health on mental health. The results of this study may be of use to researchers and practitioners interested in better understanding and managing psychological wellbeing in an ageing population.

Endnote

1   We reanalysed data as a three-step hierarchical multiple regression with psychological wellbeing at T2 as the dependent variable. In Step 1, age, gender, psychological wellbeing at T1, and physical decline were entered. Three moderators (sense of coherence, positive life attitudes, and social support) were entered in Step 2, and the interaction between physical decline and each moderator was entered in Step 3. We found that interaction between physical decline and social support remained the same ($p < .05$).

References

Antonovsky, A. (1987). *Unravelling the mystery of health: How people manage stress and stay well.* London: Jossey-Bass.

Antonovsky, A. (1996). The sense of coherence: An historical and future perspective. *Israel Journal of Medical Science, 32*, 170–178.

Carmel, S., & Bernstein, J. (1990). Trait anxiety, sense of coherence and medical school stressors: Observations at three stages. *Anxiety Research, 3*, 51–60.

Cohen, J., Cohen, P., West, S.G., & Aiken, L.S., (2003). *Applied multiple regression/correlation analysis for the behavioural sciences* (3rd ed.). Mahwah, NJ: Lawrence Erlbaum Associates.

Dohrenwend, B.S., Krasnoff, L., Askenasy, A.R., & Dohrenwend, B.P. (1982). The psychiatric epidemiology research interview life events scale. In L. Goldberg & S. Breznitz (Eds.), *Handbook of stress: Theoretical and clinical aspects* (pp. 332–336). New York: Free Press.

Fry, P.S. (2001). The unique contribution of key existential factors to the prediction of psychological wellbeing of older adults following spousal loss. *The Gerontologist, 41*, 69–81.

Gustavsson-Lilius, M., Julkunen, J., Keskivaara, P., & Hietanen, P. (2007). Sense of coherence and distress in cancer patients and their partners. *Psycho-Oncology, 16,* 1100.

Hays, J.C., Saunders, W.B., Flint, E.P., Kaplan, B.H., & Blazer, D.G. (1997). Social support and depression as risk factors for loss of physical function in late life. *Aging and Mental Health, 1,* 209–220.

Hays, J.C., Steffens, D.C., Flint, E.P., Bosworth, H.B., & George, L.K. (2001). Does social support buffer functional decline in elderly patients with unipolar depression? *American Journal of Psychiatry, 158,* 1850-1855.

Johansson, I., Larsson, G, & Hamrin, E. (1998). Sense of coherence, quality of life, and function among elderly hip fracture. *Aging, 10,* 377–384.

Kivimaki, M., Vahtera, J., Elovainio, M., Lillrank, B., & Kevin, M.V. (2002). Death or illness of a family member, violence, interpersonal conflict, and financial difficulties as predictors of sickness absence: Longitudinal cohort study on psychological and behavioural links. *Psychosomatic Medicine, 64,* 817–825.

Kornblith, A.B., Herndon, J.E. II, Zuckerman, E., Viscoli, C.M., Horwitz, R.I., Cooper, M.R. et al. (2001). Social support as a buffer to the psychological impact of stressful life events in women with breast cancer. *Cancer, 91,* 443–454.

Larsson, G., & Kallenberg, K.O. (1996). Sense of coherence, socioeconomic conditions and health. *European Journal of Public Health, 6,* 175–180.

Maslow, A. (1955). Deficiency motivation and growth motivation. In M.R. Jones (Ed.), *Nebraska symposium on motivation* (pp. 1–30). Lincoln, NE: University of Nebraska Press.

Myall, B.R., Hine, D.W., Marks, A.D.G., Thorsteinsson, E.B., Brechman-Toussaint, M., & Samuels, C.A. (2009). Assessing individual differences in perceived vulnerability in older adults. *Personality and Individual Differences, 26,* 8–13.

Nygren, B., Alex, L. Jonsen, E., Gustafon, Y., Norberg, A., & Lundman, B. (2005). Resilience, sense of coherence, purpose in life and self-transcendence in relation to perceived physical and mental health among the oldest old. *Aging and Mental Health, 9,* 354–362.

Ranchor, A. (1994). *Social class, psychosocial factors and disease: From description towards explanation.* Groningen: The Netherlands: Stitching Drukkerij C. Regenboog.

Reker, G.T. (1992). *Manual of the life attitude profile-revised.* Peterborough, ON: Student Psychologists Press.

Reker, G.T. (2002). Prospective predictors of successful aging in community-residing and institutionalized Canadian elderly. *Ageing International, 27,* 42–64.

Reichstadt, J., Depp, C.A., Palinkas, L.A., Folsom, D.P., & Jeste, D.V. (2007). Building blocks of successful aging: A focus group study of older adults' perceived contributors to successful aging. *American Journal of Geriatric Psychiatry, 15,* 194–201.

Sherbourne, C.D., & Stewart, A.L. (1991). The MOS Social Support Survey. *Social Science and Medicine, 32,* 705–714.

Smith, P.M., Breslin, F.C., & Beaton, D.E. (2003). Questioning the stability of sense of coherence: The impact of socio-economic status and working conditions in the Canadian population. *Social Psychiatry and Psychiatric Epidemiology, 38,* 475–484.

van Gool., C.H., Kempen, G.I.J.M., Penninx, B.W.J.H., Deeg., D.J.H., Beekman, A.T.F., & van Eijk, J.T.M. (2003). Relationship between changes in depressive symptoms and unhealthy lifestyles in late middle aged and older persons: Results from the longitudinal aging study Amsterdam. *Age and Ageing, 32,* 81–87.

Westendrop, R.G.J. (2006). What is health aging in the 21st century? *The American Journal of Clinical Nutrition, 83,* 404S–409S.

Are You a Perfectionist and Does it Matter? Depression and Perfectionism in Australian University Students

Maryke R. Mead and Richard E. Hicks

This study examined the relationships that exist between depression and *adaptive* and *maladaptive* perfectionism among university students. There has been earlier evidence that depression in a general population is related to maladaptive perfectionism, but first, would this be the case among university students and second, would adaptive perfectionism be related positively to wellbeing (i.e., be related negatively to depression). This current study examined these questions in a sample of 215 university students across three Australian states. The links between maladaptive perfectionism and poorer mental health were confirmed, but there was *no significant relationship* found between adaptive perfectionism and depression or wellbeing. However, interestingly higher scores both on adaptive and on maladaptive perfectionism *were* related to higher stress levels for students. Implications are discussed.

'Getting things right' and preferably the first time round, is often a desired goal of employers and managers especially for their employees. But many individuals possess personal characteristics that can be described as 'perfectionist' also, especially in relation to their own work and actions generally. These attitudes about standards can be useful in many circumstances (if used appropriately or adaptively) but can also be detrimental to individuals (if used inappropriately or 'maladaptively'; e.g., Bieling, Israeli, & Antony, 2004; Enns & Cox, 2002). While perfectionism is seen as multidimensional (as having neurotic and normal, or maladaptive and adaptive, emphases), most studies have examined perfectionism overall rather than separately in terms of maladaptive and adaptive and have found negative links with wellbeing and positive mental health. As Blatt (1995) described it: perfectionism is characterised by the setting of high and unrealistic goals and standards combined with continuous self-scrutiny (with standards that virtually set the scene for failure). Aspects of 'adaptive perfectionism' (see later discussion) avoid some but not all of these attributes. Frost, Marten, Lahart and Rosenblate (1990) developed a multi-dimensional, six-scale model of perfectionism, involving concern over mistakes (CM), doubts about actions (DA), parental expectations (PE), parental criticism (PC), personal standards (PS) and organisation (OR). These elements were seen as either adaptive or maladaptive (and form the basis of the current research study being reported). The maladaptive components included four aspects but especially concern over mistakes and doubts about actions, and adaptive components included personal standards and perhaps organisation (cf. Frost, Heimberg, Holt, Mattia, & Neubauer, 1993). A total score on perfectionism from the FMPS can be obtained by summing five of the six components (organisation being seen separately), so that the adaptive and maladaptive components are seen to 'hang together' as part of the same overall construct of perfectionism. However, do these components (maladaptive and adaptive perfectionism aspects) operate in the same way in predicting depression and related variables? This current study examined this issue among university students.

Maladaptive Perfectionism
Maladaptive perfectionism is characterised by unrealistic goal setting, which inevitably leads to failure; this is often associated with poor strategies of self-regulation such as destructive coping mechanisms and cognitive schemas with negative ruminative styles (Blatt, 1995; Brown & Beck, 2002; Burns, 1980; Rice, Blair, Castro, Cohen, & Hood, 2003; Rice, Vergara, & Aldea, 2006). Maladaptive perfectionists are characterised by their doubts about their actions, concern over mistakes and pessimistic reactions to errors (e.g., Stoeber, Otto, Pescheck, Becker, & Stoll, 2007). Vulnerability to depression has generally been identified by researchers as associated with maladaptive perfectionism (Bieling et al., 2004; Flett, Besser, Hewitt & Davis, 2007; Grzegorek, Slaney, Franze, & Rice, 2004; Rice & Slaney, 2002; Stoeber & Rambow, 2007).

Most studies have examined the links between these adaptive-maladaptive perfectionist approaches and depression in the general population. Those few studies that have reported on samples of university and college students have also reported primary links between maladaptive perfectionism and depression (cf., Christopoulos & Hicks, 2008; Flett, Blankstein, Hewitt, & Koledin, 1992; Rice & Dellwo, 2002; Rice & Slaney, 2002). But what about adaptive perfectionism among university students?

Adaptive Perfectionism

Adaptive perfectionism is characterised by the setting of attainable and realistic goals and standards, driven by the need to succeed (e.g., Hart, Gilner, Handal, & Gfeller, 1998). Ghaly (2008) describes adaptive perfectionists as setting very high personal standards but not being excessively self-punitive when failures occur; their self-esteem helping them accept that they are 'less than perfect' (cf., Rice & Ashby, 2007; Rice & Mirzadeh, 2000). Frost et al. (1990) in their approach to assessing perfectionism saw high 'personal standards' as adaptive; and it is this aspect combined with 'organisation' (to yield a composite measure of adaptive perfectionism), that is examined in the current research on whether this apparently 'more positive' side of perfectionism is associated with lower levels of depression among Australian university students.

Adaptive perfectionists are seen as striving for perfection while enhancing self-esteem and satisfaction through achieving attainable goals. Adaptive perfectionism has been shown in a few studies to be unrelated to depression, anxiety or stress and to be related to enhanced adjustment to difficult situations (e.g., Lynd-Stevenson & Hearne, 1990; Stoeber & Otto, 2006), and to better academic adjustment (cf., Grzegorek et al., 2004; Rice & Dellwo, 2002). However, Christopoulos and Hicks (2008) in a recent study conducted as a precursor to the current study, examined responses of 116 students from one Australian university, with mixed findings. Further study of maladaptive perfectionism *and* adaptive perfectionism in relation to depression was needed.

The current study aimed therefore to investigate the relationship between adaptive and maladaptive perfectionism and depression in a somewhat wider Australian university sample. The sample included 215 students (56 males and 159 females, with ages ranging from 18 to 48 years — mean age: 23.15 years; $SD = 6.62$) from three states within Australia: Queensland, New South Wales and Victoria.

Two specific hypotheses were that:

1. individuals scoring higher in depression would score higher on maladaptive perfectionism (concern over mistakes and doubts about actions)

2. individuals scoring higher in depression would score lower on adaptive perfectionism (personal standards and organisation).

Method

The participants completed a range of questionnaires with good psychometric qualities. These questionnaires included the Depression, Anxiety and Stress Scale, 21-item version (DASS-21; Lovibond & Lovibond, 1995), the Multidimensional Perfectionism Scale (MPS, Frost et al., 1990) as well as a number of other measures not used within the current study. A Biodata questionnaire was also completed to obtain demographic information.

The current study thus included one criterion variable (depression) and four predictor variables. The predictor variables included DA and CM (combined to give a score on maladaptive perfectionism) and OR and PS (adaptive perfectionism). A number of studies have used other approaches to the maladaptive composite (summing four scales including parental criticism and standards) and to the adaptive 'composite' (some using just the one scale of Personal Standards as suggested by Frost et al., 1990). The four predictor variables were based on earlier studies and apparent conceptual linkages. All variables were measured using continuous scales of measurement. All scales have been reported in earlier research and the manuals as having high levels of reliability (or more strictly, homogeneity) of the items within the scales; these high levels, all above (Cronbach's alpha coefficients of) 0.70 were reflected also for the current sample.

Results

Two standard multiple regression analyses were performed to test the hypotheses.

Hypothesis 1, that depression would be predicted by scores on the variables Concern for Mistakes and Doubting of Actions (maladaptive perfectionism) was confirmed, using the standard regression analysis procedure ($F(2, 208) = 35.25$, $p < .001$, with $R^2 = .25$). The size and direction of the relationship indicated that individuals who scored higher on the DA and CM scales were more likely to report higher depression scores on the DASS-21. Doubting of actions was a stronger predictor of depression, but both DA and CM contributed significantly to the identified relationship.

Hypothesis 2, that depression would be negatively related to (predicted by) scores on the variables Personal Standards and Organisation (adaptive perfectionism) was *not* confirmed. No significant relationship, positive or negative, existed between depression and the two variables, either alone or combined.

That is, though the Frost et al. (1990) Multidimensional Scales are used in a way that sees both maladaptive and adaptive perfectionism as linked, there is a difference in how the two aspects predict depression and/or wellbeing (Hypothesis 1 was supported while Hypothesis 2 showed no significant links).

Discussion

The present study aimed to investigate the relationship between adaptive and maladaptive perfectionism and depression among Australian university students.

The confirmation of Hypothesis 1, that maladaptive perfectionism and depression would be positively correlated, is consistent with numerous empirical studies relating maladaptive perfectionism directly to depression (e.g., Bieling et al., 2004; Christopoulos & Hicks, 2008; Grzegorek et al., 2004; Hewitt & Flett, 1991; Rice & Slaney, 2002; Stoeber & Rambow, 2007). The current findings indicate that individuals higher in doubts about actions and concern over mistakes are more likely to suffer from depressive symptoms. The same results are evident for student samples as for general community and workplace samples. The implications for counsellors in universities are that building student self-confidence by replacing the doubts and concerns with more strategic and positive strategies would be helpful (see also Paspaliaris & Hicks, in press). Much work on depression includes the use of anti-depressant medication: but doubting of actions and concern over making mistakes relate to cognitive issues. Attention to these cognitive issues through appropriate strategies such as CBT and supportive therapies, may help reduce the depression levels of many affected students.

Hypothesis 2, that *adaptive* perfectionism would be related to lower levels of depression, was *not* supported. This finding is inconsistent with many previous studies. These studies had found that adaptive perfectionism was negatively related to depression — adaptive perfectionism was thought to contain protective characteristics, such as lowering stress levels, that would assist generally in mental health states (cf., Bieling et al., 2004; Enns & Cox, 2005; Stoeber & Rambow, 2007). However, the current finding is consistent with other previous studies, where adaptive perfectionism was also found not to be related to depression (cf., Blatt, 1995; Christopoulos & Hicks, 2008; Lynd-Stevenson & Hearne, 1999).

How can these differing results be explained? One suggestion is that many of the earlier studies with perfectionism as a predictor used summed combinations of scale scores to obtain a total score (e.g., the

Frost et al. [1990], MPS yields an overall score on perfectionism that is the sum of five of the six characteristics measured in the scale). Studies using such combinations as the measure of perfectionism may obscure the separate contributions of maladaptive and adaptive perfectionism. The current study unravelled this potential difference, and suggested that the two different aspects of perfectionism do in fact predict depression differently (although not quite as had been hypothesised). Another suggestion that could explain the differing results (between studies identifying adaptive perfectionism as predictive of positive outcomes, and our results showing no relationship) is that the relationship between depression and adaptive perfectionism may be curvilinear rather than linear, though this hypothesis has not been examined further in the current study. It could be, also, that there are differing cultural issues regarding the college and educational settings of the samples: mostly overseas and in the United States versus the Australian setting.

The current study replicated a similar finding from an earlier Australian study and confirmed for the larger more cross-sectional sample that adaptive perfectionism strategies did not lead clearly to positive mental health outcomes (though the maladaptive and the adaptive scales operated differently in prediction; the maladaptive scales were directly and clearly related to higher student levels of depression).

An Additional Note on Stress

There have been many studies indicating that depression and stress are related, though not completely: they are not the same concept. For example, Lovibond and Lovibond's (1995) Depression, Anxiety and Stress Scales (DASS) show considerable overlap among the three variables, while also differentiating among them. Because there have been growing reports of student (and staff) stress within universities, it was decided also to note *whether the current adaptive and maladaptive scales would predict experienced stress among students.* (For further information and comment on stress among university students, see Paspaliaris & Hicks, in press.)

The findings revealed that maladaptive perfectionism and stress levels were positively related. Thus maladaptive perfectionism (described as involving faulty thinking and perceptions, doubting of self, concern over actions, and lack of confidence) was found to be associated both with depression *and* with experienced stress among students. This finding concerning the relationship to stress is consistent with the bulk of earlier research (e.g., Bieling et al., 2004; Flett & Hewitt, 2002; Rice, Leever, et al., 2006; Rice, Vergara, et al., 2006). Giving attention to the faulty thinking involved in maladaptive perfectionism would clearly be beneficial not only in ameliorating the levels of depression but also levels of stress.

However, interestingly, it was also found that there was a direct positive association between adaptive perfectionism and stress. This is counter to research that has suggested for other general samples that adaptive perfectionism and stress levels are not related or are in fact negatively related (e.g., Rice, Leever, et al., 2006), but it is similar to research reported in another Australian study (Christopoulos & Hicks, 2008) which linked adaptive perfectionism to 'occupational stress' of university students (as assessed using as measures of stress role overload, role ambiguity, role insufficiency and role boundary). A possible reason for the different emphases found in different studies on adaptive perfectionism and stress may be the operational definitions of stress used, but the current study and that of Christopoulos and Hicks used different measures of stress: and the same direct relationship was found. It could be that stress is more ubiquitous among students than has been recognised in earlier studies. Or it could be that issues of definition of adaptive perfectionism need further attention. Regardless, it would seem there is room for further study in the areas of adaptive and maladaptive perfectionism and their relationships with mental health variables, and also with success, in today's changing climates within university and college classrooms.

Limitations and Future Research

The present research used a cross-sectional design and a correlational (regression) approach that does not allow causality to be concluded, even though a logical case may be made that it is the perfectionist ideas that come first or are likely to be a trigger for depression rather than that depression and stress 'cause' maladaptive perfectionist thinking (though this could be tested in subsequent research). The links, at least in the Frost et al. (1990) approach to perfectionism, to early parental criticisms and standards as part of perfectionist beliefs and approaches, suggest that the logic may be with the perfectionist beliefs as a causal link to depression and stress. This area may benefit from further research, especially given the importance to family upbringing.

Future research into this area of perfectionism, mental health and wellbeing and parental recollections concerning performance, seems warranted. Future studies could give special attention to clarifying *adaptive perfectionism* and its correlates. The currently available perfectionism measures generally address perfectionism as a whole, with a number of subdimensions. The development of a new measure addressing adaptive perfectionism in particular (with more attention to the adaptive perfectionism definitions across personal, social, and positive and negative contexts) could greatly aid in understanding and differentiating among the effects of both adaptive and maladaptive perfectionism in relation to depression, stress and wellbeing. Does it matter if you are a perfectionist? It certainly does if you are 'a maladaptive perfectionist'. The evidence is less clear at this point if you are 'an adaptive perfectionist'.

References

Bieling, P.J., Israeli, A.L., & Antony, M.M. (2004). Is perfectionism good, bad or both? Examining models of the perfectionism construct. *Personality and Individual Differences, 36,* 1373–1385.

Blatt, S.J. (1995). The destructiveness of perfectionism: Implications for the treatment of depression. *American Psychologist, 50,* 1003–1020.

Brown, G.P., & Beck, A.T. (2002). Dysfunctional attitudes, perfectionism, and models of vulnerability to depression. In G.L. Flett & Hewitt, P.L. (Eds.), *Perfectionism: Theory, research, and treatment* (pp. 231–251). Washington, DC: American Psychological Association.

Burns, D.D. (1980). The perfectionist's script for self-defeat. *Psychology Today, 14,* 34–52.

Christopoulos, M., & Hicks, R.E. (2008). Occupational stress, perfectionism and depression among university students. In S. Boag, (Ed.), *Personality down under: Perspectives from Australia* (pp. 201–209). New York: Nova Science.

Enns, M.W., & Cox, B.J. (2002). The nature and assessment of perfectionism: A critical analysis. In G.L. Flett, & Hewitt, P.L. (Eds.), *Perfectionism: Theory, research and treatment* (pp. 33–62). Washington, DC: American Psychological Association.

Enns, M.W., & Cox, B.J. (2005). Perfectionism, stressful life events, and the 1-year outcome of depression. *Cognitive Therapy and Research, 29,* 541–553.

Flett, G.L., Besser, A., Hewitt, P.L., & Davis, R.A. (2007). Perfectionism, silencing the self, and depression. *Personality and Individual Differences,43,* 1211–1222.

Flett, G.L., Blankstein, K.R., Hewitt, P.L., & Koledin, S. (1992). Components of perfectionism and procrastination in college students. *Social Behavior and Personality, 20*(2), 85–94.

Flett, G.L., & Hewitt, P.L. (Eds.). (2002). *Perfectionism: Theory, research, and treatment.* Washington, DC: American Psychological Association.

Frost, R., Heimberg, R., Holt, C., Mattia, J., & Neubauer, A. (1993). Comparison of two measures of perfectionism. *Personality and Individual Differences, 14,* 119–126.

Frost, R.O., Marten, P.A., Lahart, C., & Rosenblate, R. (1990). The dimensions of perfectionism. *Cognitive Therapy and Research, 14,* 449–468.

Ghaly,C. (2008). Depression and perfectionism. *Proprium Journal of Psychology* (Vol. 2).

Grzegorek, J.L., Slaney, R.B., Franze, S., & Rice, K.G. (2004). Self-criticism, dependency, self-esteem and GPA satisfaction among clusters of perfectionists and non-perfectionists. *Journal of Counseling Psychology, 51*, 192–200.

Hart, B.A., Gilner, F.H., Handal, P.J., & Gfeller, J.D. (1998). The relationship between perfectionism and self-efficacy. *Personality and Individual Differences, 24*, 109–113

Hewitt, P.L., & Flett, G.L. (1991). Perfectionism in the self and social contexts: Conceptualization, assessment, and association with psychopathology. *Journal of Personality and Social Psychology, 60*, 456–470.

Lovibond, S.H., & Lovibond, P.F. (1995). *Manual for the Depression Anxiety Stress Scales* (2nd ed.). Sydney: Psychology Foundation.

Lynd-Stevenson, R.M., & Hearne, C.M. (1999). Perfectionism and depressive affect: The pros and cons of being a perfectionist. *Personality and Individual Differences, 26*, 549–562.

Paspaliaris, T., & Hicks, R.E. (2010). Coping strategies employed by university students in handling their 'occupational role stress'. In R.E. Hicks (Ed.). *Personality and individual differences: Current perspectives.* Brisbane, Australia: Australian Academic Press.

Rice, K.G., & Ashby, J.S. (2007). An efficient method for classifying perfectionists. *Journal of Counseling Psychology, 54*, 72–85.

Rice, K.G., Blair, C., Castro, J., Cohen, B., & Hood, C. (2003). Meanings of perfectionism: A quantitative and qualitative analysis. *Journal of Cognitive Psychotherapy, 17*, 39–58.

Rice, K.G., & Dellwo, J.P. (2002). Perfectionism and self-development: Implications for college adjustment. *Journal of Counseling & Development, 80*, 188–196.

Rice, K.G., Leever, B.A., Christopher, J., & Porter, D.J. (2006). Perfectionism, stress and social (dis)connection: A short-term study of hopelessness, depression and academic adjustment among honors students. *Journal of Counseling Psychology, 53*, 524–534.

Rice, K.G., & Mirzadeh, S.A. (2000). Perfectionism, attachment, and adjustment. *Journal of Counseling Psychology, 47*, 238–250.

Rice, K.G., & Slaney, R.B. (2002). Clusters of perfectionists: Two studies of emotional adjustment and academic achievement. *Measurement and Evaluation in Counseling and Development, 35*, 35–48.

Rice, K.G., Vergara, D.T., & Aldea, M.A. (2006). Cognitive-affective mediators of perfectionism and college student adjustment. *Personality and Individual Differences, 40*, 463–473.

Stoeber, J., & Otto, K. (2006). Positive conceptions of perfectionism: approaches, evidence, challenges. *Personality and Social Psychology Review, 10*, 295–319.

Stoeber, J., Otto, K., Pescheck, E., Becker, C., & Stoll, O. (2007). Perfectionism and competitive anxiety in athletes: Differentiating striving for perfectionism and negative reactions to imperfection. *Personality and Individual Differences, 42*, 959–969.

Stoeber, J., & Rambow, A. (2007). Perfectionism in adolescent school students: Relations with motivation, achievement and well-being. *Personality and Individual Differences, 42*, 1379–1389.

Chapter

24

Measuring Adolescent Depression: The Adolescent Depression Scale

Mona Taouk and Mark Bahr

A new brief instrument for the measurement of adolescent depression is described. The instrument is the product of a systematic review of the factors currently considered to be salient to the investigation of adolescent depression. From an initial set of pilot investigations a 90-item test bank was constructed covering six domains of adolescent depression. The resultant instrument was administered to 263 adolescents, late adolescents and young adults. Factor analysis and item analysis reduced the item pool to a 20-item four-factor measure of adolescent depression, which correlates well with existing measures of depression.

Depression is acknowledged as a dominant factor increasing the disease burden, with young people in Australia aged 16 to 25 years having the highest prevalence of symptoms for mental health problems (Australian Department of Health and Aging, 2004). Furthermore, adolescence is a particularly stressful period in life in which depression is argued to have far reaching effects, impacting on the lives of families and the functioning of the community. Adolescent depression has been linked with heavy smoking, lack of closeness to parents, higher likelihood of school drop out, and deviant behaviour (Kandel & Davies, 1986). Research illustrates that there is a correlation between depression in adolescents and the likelihood of depression in adulthood (Robertson & Simons, 1989). A longitudinal study conducted by Kandel and Davies (1986) investigated depression in participants at ages 15 to 16, and nine years later at 24 to 25 years. Their findings revealed depression in adolescence was the strongest predictor of similar experiences in adulthood (Kandel & Davies, 1986).

Despite this, it has been claimed that the instruments currently used to assess depression in adolescence are insufficiently targeted to adolescent cohorts or inadequately cover the content domains of depression (Parker & Roy, 2001). An important consideration in test development is that it be created to target a specific population, including a specific age group, and using appropriate norms, which pertain to these specific groups in order for it to be interpreted accurately and without bias (Hogan, 2007). Where measures are not written for a particular audience, the language used and the items assessed may not be appropriate to that audience.

Given the significant cost to the individual and to society, more resources and greater research focus is needed in the area of adolescent depression. This paper describes a new instrument developed to provide broader coverage of adolescent depression than existing instruments. The current instrument was developed with the goal of developing an instrument specifically targeted at an adolescent population, which covered all of the domains associated with depression in the current literature.

Six domains are associated in the literature with depressive symptoms in adolescent populations (see Table 24.1). It is clear from Table 24.1, that while there is a degree of agreement that these six domains may reflect depression, few of the existing instruments appear to capture all six domains. For a depression tool to accurately assess the presence of depressive symptoms it should include items that address each of the domains described.

One domain affected by depression can be described as 'motivational'. When depression is present, an individual will frequently exhibit anhedonia, fatigue, and apathy, all of which display reduced responsiveness to

Table 24.1

Specification Table of Symptom Domains Associated with Depression

Depression scales/ researchers	Depression domains					
	Motivational	Cognitive	Physical	Behavioural	Emotional	Social
BDI-II (Beck, Steer & Brown, 1996)		X	X	X	X	
BDI-Youth (Beck, Beck, & Jolly, 2001)	X	X	X		X	
DSM-IV-TR (2000)	X	X	X	X	X	X
Gilbert (2007)	X	X	X	X	X	X
KDI (Kandel & Davies, 1982)	X			X	X	
World Health Organization (1993)	X	X	X	X	X	X

stimuli in the environment (Rottenberg & Gotlib, 2004). The motivational domain is inadvertently influenced by a person's emotional deficits, like negative mood and affect, commonly expressed through low self-esteem, shame and melancholy (Gilbert, 2007). The emotional aspects of depression are in some respects the most manifestly obvious and reflect changes in level of affect, feelings of sadness, loss or loss of interest in everyday activities. The emotional aspects of depression tend to covary with the other facets of depression such that the emotion content of depression often reflects the nature of the individual's cognitions and their motivation.

As emotional states are affected by thoughts (Seligman, 2006), much negative emotion may be attributed to an individual's cognitive information processing. This cognitive component of depression entails decreases in cognitive functioning, typified by memory and attention difficulties, and irrational negative beliefs (Seligman). A study conducted by Casper, Belanoff, and Offer (1996), using a student sample revealed 'school problems' accounted for 33% of the variance, with students reporting concentration difficulties, depressed mood, and reduced academic performance.

The physical domain explores the biological changes that typically accompany depression. These changes are usually evident in sleep and eating disturbances, decreased libido, and psychomotor changes (Avison & McAlpine, 1992). However, some researchers suggest that somatic symptoms are not as relevant to depression as they are for stress and anxiety (Lovibond & Lovibond, 1995). The behavioral domain of depression describes overt changes in behavior, such as an increased level of impulsivity, self-harm, and substance use. It has been suggested that depression is a predictor of adolescent initiation to elicit drugs, particularly where drugs are used as self-medication to relieve feelings of depression (Kandel & Davies, 1982). Finally, Ferster's (1973) model of depression proposes a social domain of depression, which describes an overall withdrawal from social and relational activities evident in people with depression.

A significant amount of overlap is evident between the domains of depression described, with many symptoms being potentially applicable to a combination of domains. This has resulted in some researchers combining domains to reflect this overlap, such as Rottenberg and Gotlib (2004), who describe the 'socio-emotional' domain.

The aim of the current study is to develop a scale measuring adolescent depression, The Adolescent Depression Scale (TADS), which has adequate symptom domain coverage, a representative adolescent sample, and contains sufficient items from each domain to establish some understanding of the reliability of the measures the instrument provides. It is expected that the TADS will demonstrate criterion-related validity by correlating strongly with related measures. It is expected that the new instrument will reveal multiple reliable domains of depression that closely reflect the domains of adolescent depression, in so doing the instrument will demonstrate construct validity, content validity, and internal consistency.

Method

Participants

Two hundred and sixty-three participants were recruited via convenience sampling from three main sites; a university, and two catholic secondary colleges. There were 188 females and 75 males, with ages ranging from 12 to 21 years ($M = 17.53$, $SD = 2.35$).

Materials: The 90-item The Adolescent Depression Scale (TADS) is a self-report measure created during the current study to measure depression in adolescents. The items are designed to assess six components that indicate presence of depression: motivational, emotional, cognitive, behavioral, physical, and social.

The Kandel and Davies Adolescent Depressive Mood Inventory (KDI; Kandel & Davies, 1982) is a six-item scale used to measure depressive mood in adolescents using a 3-point Likert index. Maximum Likelihood estimation of factor structure revealed that the items belong to one latent factor, with a Cronbach's alpha of 0.98, indicating high internal consistency.

The Adolescent Coping Orientation for Problem Experiences (A-COPE; Patterson & McCubbin, 1983) is a 54-item instrument used to assess coping strategies in adolescents. Factor analyses resulted in 12 factors accounting for 60.1% of the variance, with alpha reliabilities ranging from 0.50 to 0.76 (Patterson & McCubbin). Eight of the 12 factors describe positive or transformational coping behaviors (e.g. Factor 3: Developing self-reliance), while four factors describe negative or avoidance coping behaviors that are normatively evaluated as undesirable (e.g. Factor 6: Avoiding problems). Respondents are to indicate on a five-point Likert index how often they use each of the 54 coping behaviors when they face difficulties.

The Depression and Anxiety Stress Scale short form (DASS-21; Lovibond & Lovibond, 1995) is a subset of the 42-item self-report inventory comprised of three subscales, depression, anxiety, and stress. Internal consistencies of subscales were established using a sample of 717 psychology students at the University of New South Wales. Alpha coefficients for each subscale are: Depression 0.81; Anxiety 0.73; Stress 0.81 (Lovibond & Lovibond). The first 21 items of the full 42-item DASS were used as an alternate form of the DASS-21, since the item wordings were considered more applicable to the current sample. This is a common research practice and is psychometrically equivalent to the original DASS-21 (Lovibond & Lovibond).

Procedure

Items were written to assess each depression domain identified (motivational, emotional, cognitive, behavioral, physical, and social). Expert reviewers assessed these for content, face and construct validity, resulting in exclusion of 20 items considered to be ambiguously worded or assessing different constructs (i.e., anxiety). The refined TADS was then completed by a pilot sample to obtain feedback on readability, appropriateness of items, and comprehensiveness of instructions (Hogan, 2007). A further ten items were excluded.

The questionnaire was compiled, and participants were recruited from a university, a girl's Catholic secondary school, a co-education catholic secondary school, and a general cohort of students not belonging to the other groups ($N = 263$). Each university participant was given an explanatory statement and a consent form to sign prior to participation. Secondary school participants were given explanatory statements and parental consent forms to return two weeks prior to the scheduled testing date. The questionnaire was administered in a group format.

Results

Descriptive Statistics

Preliminary data screening was carried out and revealed that all assumptions for analyses were met. Table 24.2 displays descriptive statistics of sample.

Factor Analysis (Construct Validity)

An exploratory factor analysis was performed to examine the factor structure of the 90-item TADS. Assumptions regarding missing values, normality, linearity, and outliers were satisfied during initial data screening. Factor extraction was based on a priori conceptual beliefs about the number of dimensions of depressive symptoms, as well as visual inspection of the screeplot. The final principal axis factoring extraction of four factors with direct oblimin rotation provided the most parsimonious solution, with 20-items that had the greatest utility and interpretability.

Table 24.2

Frequencies and Descriptive Statistics with Respect to Sample Source

	Bond students N = 88	Co-ed. school N = 58	All girls' school N = 57	General students N = 60	Total N = 263
Age in years	19.38 (1.21)	16.41 (0.76)	15.05 (1.11)	18.25 (2.81)	17.53 (2.35)
Female	63	26	57	42	188
Male	25	32	0	18	75

Note: Standard deviations appear in parentheses following mean age.

This solution accounted for a total of 57.27% of the variance (see Table 24.3). The total scale had a Cronbach's alpha of 0.83, revealing satisfactory internal consistency. With the exception of Factor 3, each of the sub scales approached or exceeded an alpha of .80.

Bivariate Correlations (Criterion Validity)

The assumptions of linearity, normality, and skew were satisfied during initial data screening process. Table 24.4 lists the correlations between the TADS (total score and subscale scores) and the measures used to establish criterion validity: Convergent measures — Depression and Anxiety Stress Scale short version (DASS-21) total score and subscale scores, and Kandel and Davies Adolescent Depressive Mood Inventory (KDI); Divergent measure — Adolescent Coping Orientation for Problem Experiences (A-COPE) total score and subscale scores. These results suggest convergent validity for the TADS since it correlates most highly with other tests measuring the same construct (Hogan, 2007). The weakest observed relationships were those between the TADS factor 1 (Emotional) and A-COPE total, r (228) = 0.04, $p > 0.05$ (two-tailed). The relationship between the TADS and A-COPE, suggesting that the TADS has discriminant validity (see Table 24.4).

Discussion

The objective of this study was to develop and evaluate a multidimensional tool to measure adolescent depression that is appropriate and meaningful to an adolescent audience. The new multidimensional measure, the The Adolescent Depression Scale (TADS), was evaluated using a sample of 263 undergraduate and secondary school students. The main hypothesis of this study was that the TADS would reveal a factor structure comparable to the depression literature, and as such a priori

Table 24.3

Eigenvalues, Total Percentage of Variance Explained, and Reliabilities of Each Factor

	Factor			
	Emotional (negative affect)	Social/ relational	Cognitive– behavioural	Motivation and outlook
M	4.34	14.26	11.22	12.10
SD	4.30	3.27	3.41	3.43
Eigenvalue	5.76	2.26	1.93	1.50
Total variance accounted (%)	28.78	11.32	9.65	7.51
	0.86	0.77	0.49	0.82

definitions were given for six factors of adolescent depression (motivational, emotional, cognitive, behavioral, physical, and social; American Psychiatric Association, 2000; Gilbert, 2007). Four reliable factors were obtained from an obliquely rotated principal axis factoring extraction, which accounted for 57.27% of the variance, resulting in a 20 item TADS. The domains were named as follows: Factor 1 — Emotional (negative affect); Factor 2 — Social/Relational; Factor 3 — Cognitive–Behavioral; and Factor 4 — Motivation and Outlook. While the anticipated six-factor structure was not obtained the four factors extracted have good simple structure and reflect the structure of other existing depression measures, and demonstrated good coverage of depressive symptoms listed in the DSM-IV-TR (American Psychiatric Association) and ICD-10 (World Health Organization, 1993).

Factor 1 — Emotional (negative affect) accounted for most of the variance in the factor solution, and was in line with previous research indicating the significance of emotional changes in depression (Beck, Steer, & Brown, 1996). Crowe, Ward, Dunnachie and Roberts (2006) reported that the most frequently reported characteristics of depression in adolescent girls and boys were interpersonal symptoms (social withdrawal, irritability, and loneliness), and thought processing symptoms (concentration and indecisiveness). These observations are similar to the results of this study, and are reflected in Factor 2 — Social/Relational and Factor 3 — Cognitive-Behavioral. The Cognitive-Behavioral domain can be referred to as school related difficulties since each item addresses an issue that a student would face at school. It is consistent with previous research with adolescent samples that identify factors such as 'school problems' (Casper et al., 1996).

Table 24.4

Correlations between TADS and Measures to Assess Criterion-Related Validity

Subscales	TADS domains				TADS
	Emotional (negative affect)	Social / relational	Cognitive– behavioral	Motivation and outlook	Total
DASS-21 (total)	.62***	.25***	.22**	.49***	.62***
DASS-21 .52*** (stress items)	.21**	.20**	.37***	.50***	
DASS-21 (anxiety items)	.48***	.17**	.19**	.38***	.48***
DASS-21 (depression items)	.64***	.27***	.21**	.54***	.65***
KDI	.62***	.29***	.20**	.49***	.63***
A-COPE (total)	.04	–.32***	.10	–.27***	–.16*
A-COPE (transformational)	–.09	–.39	–.12	–.41***	–.36***
A-COPE (avoidant)	.20**	–.10	.41***	.09	.23***

Note: ***Correlations significant at the $p < .0001$ level (two-tailed).
　　　**Correlations significant at the $p < .001$ level (two-tailed).
　　　*Correlations significant at the $p < .05$ level (two-tailed).

Factor 4 — Motivation and Outlook, was also one of the hypothesised domains of depression, and is commonly assessed in other depression scales, such as the Beck Depression Inventory Youth (BDI-Y; Beck, Beck, & Jolly, 2001). The hypothesised physical/biological domain of depression was not reflected in the TADS since no interpretable solution could be found that contained somatic symptoms. However, it has been suggested in the literature that this domain may not be as relevant to depression as it is to other related constructs such as anxiety (Beck et al., 1996). Cronbach's alpha coefficients for three of the TADS domains exceeded 0.7 indicating that similar items are responded to consistently. Factor three (Cognitive-Behavioral) had a Cronbach's alpha coefficient of 0.49, and a reason for this is that, in effect, it is measuring two aspects of depression that are related to school difficulties, both cognitive and behavioral. Therefore, the items in this domain are more heterogeneous and will not have as much shared variance as other domains. Moreover, Boyle (1991) cautions against misinterpreting a moderate Cronbach's alpha as indicating reduced reliability.

The relationship between the TADS and various criterion measures was investigated to establish criterion-related validity. The TADS demonstrated a strong positive relationship with the convergent measures of depression (KDI; Kandel & Davies, 1982; DASS-21; Lovibond & Lovibond, 1995). The correlation coefficients for the stress subscale and anxiety subscale of the DASS-21 were moderate, and fell within the expected ranges, that is, they were lower than correlations observed between depression measures. Coping is a construct that is different to depression and therefore the A-COPE (Patterson & McCubbin, 1983) was used to evaluate discriminant validity of the TADS. As predicted, the TADS total scale and subscales had weaker correlations with the A-COPE, suggesting discriminant validity.

Although there are a number of factors that contribute to the strength of the current study, there are also limitations. One limitation is the exclusive use of self-report measures in obtaining data, which meant that participants could fabricate responses, because like other self-report symptom-based scales, the TADS is transparent and a respondent may disguise their symptoms (faking good or social desirability) or exaggerate their symptoms (faking bad or malingering; Lovibond & Lovibond, 1995). Another confounding variable was lack of supervision, since some participants completed questionnaires in their own time and in various environments. If all questionnaires were administered to participants in a standardized setting, researchers can more easily control for extraneous variables like noise and distraction (Shadish, Cook, & Campbell, 2002).

Directions for future research in this area include diversifying and expanding the current data set by recruiting participants from different geographic regions (e.g., another Australian state), recruiting a more representative sample to include as part of the norm group such as participants from different educational institutes, and investigating stability with test–retest reliability.

It is important to create a scale that is meaningful to an adolescent audience, which will assist in the assessment of adolescent adjustment in a variety of settings. The TADS has revealed that with further refinement and validation, it has high potential for utility as an adolescent depression screening tool. If this is achieved, the practical implications are that the TADS can be used in schools throughout Australia as part of a mental health program, whereby the TADS is administered to students on a large scale. Those students who score highly can then be given appropriate support. If adolescent depression is left untreated, it can have significant social, occupational, and psychological consequences (Crowe et al., 2006).

References

American Psychiatric Association. (2000). *Diagnostic and statistical manual of mental disorders* (4th ed. rev.). Washington, DC: Author.

Australian Department of Health and Aging (2004). *Responding to the mental health needs of young people in Australia.* Canberra: Author.

Avison, W.R., & McAlpine, D.D. (1992). Gender differences in symptoms of depression among adolescents. *Journal of Health and Social Behavior, 33,* 77–96.

Beck, J.S., Beck, A.T., & Jolly, J.B. (2001). *Beck Youth Inventories.* San Antonio, TX: Psychological Corporation.

Beck, A.T., Steer, R.A., & Brown, G.K. (1996). *Beck Depression Inventory-II Manual* (2nd ed.). San Antonio, TX: The Psychological Corporation.

Boyle, G.J. (1991). Does item homogeneity indicate internal consistency or item redundancy in psychometric scales? *Personality and Individual Differences, 12,* 291–294.

Casper, R.C., Belanoff, J., & Offer, D. (1996). Gender differences, but no racial group differences, in self-reported psychiatric symptoms in adolescents. *American Academy of Child and Adolescent Psychiatry, 4,* 500-508.

Crowe, M., Ward, N., Dunnachie, B., & Roberts, M. (2006). Characteristics of adolescent depression. *International Journal of Mental Health Nursing, 15,* 10-18.

Ferster, C.B. (1973). A functional analysis of depression. *American Psychologist, 28,* 857–870.

Gilbert, P. (2007). *Psychotherapy and counselling for depression* (3rd ed.). London: Sage Publications.

Hogan, T.P. (2007). *Psychological testing a practical introduction* (2nd ed.). NJ: John Wiley & Sons Inc.

Kandel, D.B., & Davies, M. (1982). Epidemiology of depressive mood in adolescents. *Archives of General Psychiatry, 39,* 1205–1212.

Kandel, D.B., & Davies, M. (1986). Adult sequelae of adolescent depressive symptoms. *Archives of General Psychiatry, 43,* 255–262.

Lovibond, S.H., & Lovibond, P.F. (1995). *Manual for the Depression Anxiety Stress Scale.* (2nd ed.). Sydney: Psychology Foundation.

Parker, G. & Roy, K. (2001). Adolescent depression: A review. *Australian and New Zealand Journal of Psychiatry, 35,* 572–580.

Patterson, J.M., & McCubbin, H.I. (1983). *A-COPE — Adolescent coping orientation for problem experiences (Research Instrument).* Madison, WI: University of Wisconsin.

Robertson, J.F., & Simons, R.L. (1989). Family factors, self-esteem, and adolescent depression. *Journal of Marriage and the Family, 51*(1), 125–138.

Rottenberg, J., & Gotlib, I.H. (2004). Socioemotional functioning in depression. In M. Power (Ed.), *Mood disorders: A handbook of science and practice.* New York: John Wiley & Sons, Inc.

Seligman, L. (2006). *Theories of counselling and psychotherapy* (2nd ed.). NJ: Pearson Merrill Prentice Hall.

Shadish, W.R., Cook, T.D., & Campbell, D.T. (2002). *Experimental and quasi-experimental designs for generalised causal inference.* Boston: Houghton Mifflin Company.

World Health Organization. (1993). *Mental Disorders: ICD-10 classification of mental and behavioral disorders. Diagnostic criteria for research.* Geneva: Author.

Applications in forensic psychology:
Risk assessment, aggression and malingering

The Importance of Ecological
Validity for Risk Assessment

Douglas P. Boer and Janine Blacker

Many of the commonly used risk assessment measures have little or no 'ecological validity' (EV). In psychological testing EV usually refers to the degree to which a test assesses (or estimates) a person's ability to do a 'real-life' task. In risk assessment, we argue that EV refers to the ability of the test to provide a contextualised analysis of a person's risk. That is, 'risk' (to reoffend) does not occur in a vacuum — risk is simply a reflection of an offender's propensity to reoffend, but the risky behaviour can only occur in his or her real-life context. Boer (2009) has argued that EV is generally lacking in most risk assessment strategies and noted that this is a critical oversight of such measures, particularly if the often-cited goal of risk assessment is to inform risk management. The final section of this chapter provides an overview of the environmental variables in the Assessment of Risk and Manageability in Intellectually Disabled Individuals who Offender — Sexually (ARMIDILO-S). Twelve of the 30 items in the ARMIDILO-S are comprised of environmental variables to help improve management strategies for ID offenders. Boer (2009) proposed that the EV of other risk measures could be enhanced by the inclusion of similar environmental variables.

The 'ecological validity' (EV) of a psychological test may be defined as the degree to which a particular test estimates (or assesses) using a proxy task a person's ability to do a 'real-life' task. For example, a subtest of an intellectual functioning test that designed to assess short-term memory should correlate with how well a student is able to recall telephone numbers or act on instructions in their everyday lives. While EV is an important aspect of neuropsychological testing (e.g., Burgess, Alderman, Evans, Emslie, & Wilson, 1998) and neuropsychological research (e.g., Chaytor, Temkin, Machamer, & Dikmen, 2007), there is little emphasis on this concept in the risk assessment literature. One could argue, that risk assessment is a new area of assessment compared to neuropsychological assessment, and therefore is would seem reasonable that the discussion of the methods, issues and research support would be weak by comparison. However, there is an extensive literature on risk assessment and it would seem that the issue of EV has simply been neglected and overlooked. Further, it would seem only reasonable that EV is as, if not more, important to risk assessment as it is to any other area of assessment — after all, is not society as a whole incredibly focused on sexual (and other violent) offenders and the risk they present to society upon release from custody?

The growth in types of risk assessment measures has been rapid in the past few decades. Nonetheless, there are still only two main types of risk measures, namely actuarial (or statistical) tests and structured clinical (or professional judgement) guidelines. Many 'new' tests, particularly of the actuarial sort, appear to be different combinations of variables already published by others. This book chapter will look briefly at two commonly used actuarial risk measures and two analogous structured clinical guidelines to illustrate a common failing: a dearth of EV in such measures. Finally, we discuss how the Assessment of Risk and Manageability of Intellectually Disabled IndividuaLs Who Offend — Sexually (ARMIDILO-S), has attempted to improve EV by including 12 environmental items (out of the total of 30 items) to enhance the usefulness of the measure in the risk management of intellectually disabled (ID) offenders.

Actuarial Tests

The two actuarial tests to be examined in this chapter include the Static-99 (Hanson & Thornton, 1999) and the Violence Risk Appraisal Guide (VRAG; Quinsey, Harris, Rice & Cormier, 2006). The Static-99 and the VRAG are arguably the most commonly used actuarial risk measures for sexual and nonsexually violent offenders respectively. The items that comprise these instruments are given in Appendix 25.A. The items that become part of most actuarial risk assessment measures are those that best postdict risk in a known sample of released offenders from a large pool of piloted variables. In the Static-99, the offender's score reflects his relative risk to the other men in the sample (and the resulting accuracy, in the individual case, would depend on the individual's similarity to the 'average' offender in the sample — analogous to the 'true score' of a person on an intelligence test). Although the Static-99 has relatively good predictive validity compared to other actuarial sex offender risk assessment tests (see the Hanson and Morton-Bourgon meta-analyses dated 2004 and 2007 for a review), the test does not contain any variables that change in response to (or, in turn, could effect change in) the environment. Essentially all the items of the Static-99 are de-contextualised — and are scored the same way regardless of personal circumstances of the offender being evaluated. The numbers can change — the offender can get older, live with someone for a sufficient time period to lower his score, or commit more and more varied types of sexual offences to increase his score — but none of these changes reflect EV.

The VRAG is similar in this respect. The majority of the items (see Appendix 25.A) have to do with the offender's behaviour — whether as an adult or a youth — but are essentially context-free. The second item (elementary school behavioural problems) is clearly context-dependent, but the context itself is not evaluated — just the offender's behaviour within that context. Thus, the 'school' in which an offender displays his behavioural problems remains unevaluated — and may range from a very good school with ample skills and resources, to a very deprived situation. One situation may work to eliminate behavioural problems, whereas the other may foster them — yet, the VRAG only evaluates whether or not behavioural problems were present.

In sum, it is our contention that EV can be compromised by the use of decontexualised risk variables. Many risk assessment tests are actuarial or statistical in nature — focusing on numbers as opposed to anything about the offender himself. The Static-99 and VRAG are two examples of actuarial tests that use primarily, if not exclusively, decontexualised items.

Structured Clinical Guidelines

The Sexual Violence Risk — 20 (SVR-20; Boer, Hart, Kropp, & Webster, 1997) and the Historical-Clinical-Risk-20 (HCR-20; Webster, Douglas, Eaves, & Hart, 1997) are arguably the most commonly used structured professional judgement or structured clinical guideline (SCG) instruments in use internationally at this time. There are other, closely related, instruments that include many of the same variables, some with similar purposes (risk assessment), but others with different strengths (e.g., treatment needs and measurement of change). A review of these is beyond the scope of this chapter. Nonetheless, all of the SCGs have a similar test construction philosophy — they are comprised of items that have varying degrees of empirical support and these instruments are constructed and then tested. This is the opposite strategy to that used in actuarial test construction. This difference in test construction is perhaps moot in the end

— both types of instruments have their uses and strengths. And, most of the literature comparing these types of tests is focused on which sort has the best predictive validity — and there is no clear winner (although the proposed victor seems to be depend on the allegiance of the author doing the particular comparison or meta-analysis).

As Boer (2009) has pointed out neither the SCG tests nor the actuarial tests have very good EV. The nature of the SCGs suggests these instruments should have more scope or promise for addressing EV. Indeed, some of the items (see Appendix 25.B) in the SVR-20 and HCR-20 are environmentally dependent, although some items have the same logistical problem described above in reference to youth behaviour. For example, in the HCR-20, item 8, 'early maladjustment' — the offender's behaviour is coded, not the problematic nature of the environment in which the behaviour occurred. Probably the best item in terms of EV from the HCR-20 is the second risk management item (item 17 overall), namely 'exposure to destabilisers' which 'is meant to refer to situations in which persons are exposed to hazardous conditions to which they are vulnerable and which may trigger violent episodes' (p. 64). Quite differently, the best item in terms of EV from the SVR-20 is the second psychosocial adjustment item (item 2 overall), namely 'victim of child abuse' which refers to the victimization of the offender when he was a child — that is, it is about what his environment did to him, not vice versa. Of course, the 'exposure to destabilisers' item is also about the effect of the environment on the offender — but given the immediate effects of the adult environment on the adult's behaviour (versus the more distal effects of child abuse on an adult's behaviour) the HCR-20's item would seem to have more immediate import in terms of EV.

Other HCR-20 and SVR-20 items have varying degrees of EV. 'Lack of personal support' (HCR-20, item 18) also has a moderate degree of EV, but is coded not only by the presence of absence of such support, but the offender's willingness to accept such support. Similarly, both instruments have items related to future plans and while the feasibility of such plans depends on opportunities in the EV, such items also depend on the individual's ability to assess the reasonableness of such plans. For example, an offender may have access to a University education because of the environment's support of 'mature students' (e.g., waiving academic prerequisites for older adult entrants), but such plans may not be responsible or realistic if he has dependent children or a criminal record for sexual offences against children.

Ecological Validity, Risk Management, and Current Test Technology

It is an oft-repeated phrase in many risk assessment manuals that the goal of risk assessment is to inform risk management (e.g., Boer, et al., 1997). Elsewhere, Boer (2009) argued that the ability of a risk assessment measure to aid in effective risk management is entirely dependent on the EV of that measure. Yet, it does not appear that any commonly used risk measures have made EV a priority by design. Boer (2009) argued that without adequate EV, there cannot be adequate risk management. Further, he noted that risk management occurs in the real world, not occur in a vacuum, and is much more than avoiding reoffending — it is the encouragement of positive changes in the offender's daily behaviour — whether the behaviour in question is offence-related or just part of his daily life.

If it seems reasonable that EV should apply to risk assessment, and theoretically it ought to, because offenders return to the community and risk measures, then we need to assess issues relevant to the community not just those issues that emanate from the offender himself. Therefore Boer (2009) suggested that 'the EV of a risk assessment test would be the degree that the score or risk level or risk concerns raised by that test would aid in determining how that offender would fare in the community and provide guidance as to how to improve his management'. Boer (2009) also noted that tests with greater EV may have to sacrifice predictive validity as environmental items may have limited predictive validity.

Towl (2005) and Boer (2009) suggested that the EV of actuarial tests in general (and the Static-99 in particular, and by extrapolation, the VRAG) can be improved by decreasing prediction timeframes. As Towl (2005) indicated, the longer the timeframe that a prediction uses, the more problematic because of the increasing likelihood of intervening variables affecting the predicted behaviour. The VRAG validation also suggests a further problem — the more defined the predictive outcome (e.g., 9 likelihood bins instead of 5 as in the Static-99), the more problematic — there are only 11 subjects in the 1st bin and 9 subjects in the 9th bin. How accurate can that be for violent offenders in general — in the short or long term — except for those 20 mentally disordered offenders?

Boer (2009) also discussed the fact that base rates of violent offending are dropping, there are age-related changes in reoffending, there is probably an effect of better interventions, and that these changes in offence predictors are best viewed in combination with other intervening variables. Therefore, shorter timeframes are more accurate and less contaminated by other variables other than the offender's risk propensities. Nonetheless, in our opinion, the best contribution of actuarial tests is the production of a risk profile — the higher one scores, the higher the likelihood (in general) of that person offending in the future. Focusing exclusively on percentage likelihood to reoffend ignores EV in the comparison of offenders to each other.

The EV of the SVR-20 and HCR-20 could be improved if the risk variables were defined more clearly in terms of their implications for risk management. Indeed, the new version of the SVR-20 (expected later this year) will have a chapter to this effect. However, the present item definitions are geared primarily towards risk assessment — not in terms of how the item can be reconceptualised to enhance risk management. Thus, while the more clinical nature of the SVR-20 would appear to have greater EV than the Static-99 (and the HCR-20 more so than the VRAG) it is not the case that the EV of the current SCGs is sufficient to facilitate in any comprehensive sense, risk management. Some research, notwithstanding, has shown that the clinical and risk management items of the HCR-20 have utility in the prediction of future risk of violent behaviour in the community (e.g., Strand, Belfrage, Fransson, & Levander, 1999; Gray, Taylor, & Snowden, 2008), suggesting that these items have some degree of EV relative to the purely historical or 'psychosocial' items of the HCR-20 and SVR-20.

In sum, both SCGs and actuarial tests would have better EV if relevant ecological variables were included in the assessment, albeit there would likely be a loss of statistical accuracy (i.e., predictive validity). This loss may be acceptable since the rationale for improving the EV of risk assessment is to try and realise the proposed reason for doing risk assessment in the first place — to inform risk management.

Improving Ecological Validity for the Risk Assessment of Intellectually Disabled Offenders — Sexually (ARMIDILO-S)

Boer, Tough and Haaven (2004) provided an initial overview of a risk assessment and management tool for use with intellectually disabled (ID) sex offenders. The Assessment of Risk and Manageability of Intellectually Disabled Individuals who Offend — Sexually (ARMIDILO-S) by Boer, Haaven, Lambrick, Lindsay, McVilly, and Sakdalan (in press), assesses environment risk factors related to risk along with the client risk variables to derive a 'risk picture' that would enhance the risk assessment and the risk manageability of ID sex offenders. The ARMIDILO-S contains 6 stable (slowly changing) and 6 acute (quickly changing) environmental variables and 10 stable and 6 acute client variables — all of which have varying degrees of literature support as related to risk (see Appendix 25.C).

The ARMIDILO-S contains a number of environmental variables related to the issue of risk manageability. Environmental variables that appear to affect the risk of offenders include housing, peers, intoxicants, support persons, medical staff, training sites and programs, staff members, employers, teachers, modes of transportation, potential victims, among many others. All of these variables can be offence-influencing — in either a risk-reducing or risk-increasing fashion — whether the variable is proximally or distally related to offending. For example, positive, pro-social peers can reduce risk and increase manageability while neglectful or abusive staff can increase risk and decrease manageability (and vice versa). As can be seen by Appendix C, over one-third of the items of the ARMIDILO-S are environmental, including supervisory and professional staff, and the living situation of the client. Preliminary (unpublished) data has shown that the ARMIDILO-S has better predictive validity — in the short term — than relevant actuarial tests for ID sex offenders. But the main benefits of the ARMIDILO-S seem to be linked to its enhanced EV. The examination of ecologically valid variables in the client's environment that adds complexity to the risk analysis found when using only the SVR-20 and Static-99 (or the HCR-20 and VRAG). However, it is Boer and colleagues' (2009) contention that the risk presented by the individual clients is more complex than a number or a list of risk-increasing variables. Boer (2009) noted that 'risk is the interplay of client factors and environmental factors that constantly changes over time'.

In the end, the problems with current risk measures is that the best (in terms of predictive validity) measures provide a sanitised, de-contextualised, picture that bears little reality to the dynamic risk picture the offender will present upon release to the community. The theory behind the ARMIDILO-S may appear sound, but the inclusion of more ecologically valid variables may result in a test that could have lower predictive validity overall as a result of the inclusion of more ecologically valid variables. That is, the inclusion of variables that have EV will simply add too much complexity for anyone invested in the supremacy of predictive validity of a measure over accuracy in the individual case. Of course, the only way to assess this issue is to study the ARMIDILO-S alongside the Static-99 and SVR-20 (and VRAG and HCR-20) using the same data sets. In the end, the scientist-practitioner model may have to put clinical utility ahead of scientific validity in order to do better work in the individual case.

References

Boer, D.P. (2009). Ecological validity and risk assessment: The importance of assessing context for intellectually disabled sexual offenders. *British Journal of Forensic Practice, 11*(2), 4–9.

Boer, D.P., Haaven, J., Lambrick, F., Lindsay, W.R., McVilly, K., & Sakdalan, J. (in press). *The Assessment of Risk and Manageability of Intellectually Disabled Individuals Who Offend — Sexually (ARMIDILO-S).*

Boer, D.P., Hart, S.D., Kropp, P.R., & Webster, C.D. (1997). *Manual for the Sexual Violence Risk-20.* Vancouver, BC: The British Columbia Institute Against Family Violence.

Boer, D.P., Tough, S., & Haaven, J. (2004). Assessment of risk manageability of intellectually disabled sex offenders. *Journal of Applied Research in Intellectual Disabilities, 17,* 275–283.

Burgess, P.W., Alderman, N., Evans, J., Emslie, H., & Wilson, B.A. (1998). The ecological validity of tests of executive function. *Journal of the International Neuropsychological Society, 4,* 547–558.

Chaytor, N., Temkin, N., Machamer, J., & Dikmen, S. (2007). The ecological validity of neuropsychological assessment and the role of depressive symptoms in moderate to severe traumatic brain injury. *Journal of the International Neuropsychological Society, 13,* 377–385.

Gray, N.S., Taylor, J., & Snowden, R.J. (2008). Predicting violent recidivism using the HCR-20. *The British Journal of Psychiatry, 192,* 384–387.

Hanson, R.K., & Morton-Bourgon, K. (2004). *Predictors of sexual recidivism: An updated meta-analysis.* Public Works and Government Services Canada. Cat. No.: PS3-1/2004-2E-PDF. ISBN: 0-662-36397-3.

Hanson, R.K., & Morton-Bourgon, K. (2007). *The accuracy of recidivism risk instruments for sexual offenders: A meta-analysis* (Cat. No.: PS4-36/2007E). Public Safety and Emergency Preparedness Canada.

Hanson, R.K., & Thornton, D. (1999). *Static 99: Improving actuarial risk assessments for sex offenders* (User report 1999-02). Ottawa: Department of the Solicitor General of Canada.

Quinsey, V.L., Harris, G.T., Rice, M.E., & Cormier, C. (2006). *Violent offenders: Appraising and managing risk.* Washington, DC: American Psychological Association.

Strand, S., Belfrage, J., Fransson, G., & Levander, S. (1999). Clinical and risk management factors in risk prediction of mentally disordered offenders — more important than historical data? *Legal and Criminological Psychology, 4,* 67–76.

Towl, G. (2005). Risk assessment. *Evidence-Based Mental Health, 8,* 91–93.

Webster, C.D., Douglas, K.S., Eaves, D., & Hart, S.D. (1997). *HCR-20: Assessing risk for violence (version 2).* Burnaby, Canada: Mental Health, Law, and Policy Institute, Simon Fraser University.

Appendix 25.A
Static-99 and VRAG items

Static-99

1. Prior sex offences (prior to current offence)
2. Prior sentencing dates
3. Any convictions for non-contact sex offences
4. Index (current offence) non-sexual violence (conviction)
5. Prior non-sexual violence (any prior convictions)
6. Any unrelated victims (in a sexual offence for which the offender was convicted)
7. Any stranger victims (in a sexual offence for which the offender was convicted)
8. Any male victims (in a sexual offence for which the offender was convicted)
9. Current age (at time of assessment)
10. Ever lived with a lover for at least two years (married or otherwise)

VRAG

1. Psychopathy Checklist-Revised score
2. Elementary School Behavioural Problems
3. Personality Disorder (using DSM III criteria)
4. Age at time of index (current) offence
5. Lived with both biological parents to age 16 (except for death of parents)
6. Ever failed on prior conditional release (e.g., bail, probation, parole)
7. Criminal history for non-violent offences (scored on a grid)
8. Ever married versus never married
9. Ever met DSM III criteria for schizophrenia
10. Degree of victim injury
11. History of alcohol problems (including parental alcoholism, teenage, adult, alcohol involved in prior offence, alcohol involved in current offence)
12. Female victim ever

Appendix 25.B
SVR-20 and HCR-20 items

SVR-20
Psychosocial items
Sexual deviation
Victim of child abuse
Psychopathy
Symptoms of mental illness
Substance use problems
Suicidal/homicidal ideation
Relationship problems
Employment problems
Past nonsexual violent offences
Past nonviolent offences
Past supervision failures
Sexual offences
High density sex offences
Multiple sex offence types
Physical harm to victim(s) in sex offences
Uses weapons or threats of death in sex offences
Escalation in frequency or severity of sex offences
Extreme minimisation or denial of sex offences
Attitudes that support or condone sex offences
Future plans
Lacks realistic plans
Negative attitude toward intervention

HCR-20
Historical items
Previous violence
Young age at first violent incident
Relationship instability
Employment problems
Substance use problems
Major mental illness
Psychopathy
Early maladjustment
Personality disorder
Prior supervision failure

Clinical items
Lack of insight
Negative attitudes
Active symptoms of major mental illness
Impulsivity
Unresponsive to treatment
Risk management items
Plans lack feasibility
Exposure to destabilisers
Lack of personal support
Noncompliance with remediation attempts
Stress

Appendix 25.C
ARMIDILO items

Stable Environmental Items (over the past year)

1. Attitude towards ID individuals
2. Communication among supervisory staff
3. Client-specific knowledge by supervisory staff
4. Consistency of supervision
5. Situational consistency
6. Unique considerations (e.g., parental support, access to specialised support services)

Acute Environmental Items (within 3 months)

1. Changes in social relationships
2. Changes in monitoring
3. Situational changes
4. Changes in victim access
5. Changes in access to intoxicants
6. Unique considerations

Stable Client Items (over the past year)

1. Supervision compliance
2. Treatment compliance
3. Sexual deviance
4. Sexual preoccupation/hypersexuality

5. Emotional coping ability
6. Self-efficacy
7. Relationships
8. Substance abuse
9. Impulsivity
10. Mental health
11. Unique personal considerations (e.g., self-harm tendencies, childhood abuse)
12. Unique lifestyle considerations (e.g., antisocial tendencies, peers, social vulnerabilities)

Acute Client Items (within 3 months)
1. Changes in attitude or behaviour towards supervision or treatment
2. Changes in sexual preoccupation
3. Changes in victim-related behaviours
4. Changes in emotional coping ability
5. Changes in ability to use coping strategies
6. Changes to unique considerations (e.g., mental illness, access to intoxicants)

Explaining Individual Differences in Physical Aggression Among a Community Sample

Bruce D. Watt, Erica Begelhole, and Nicole Guse

Violence poses an ongoing concern for society. Numerous risk factors have been implicated as contributors to individual differences in levels of physical aggression. The current study examined variations in physical aggression using a community sample in South East Queensland (N = 151). Self-report measures of alcohol misuse, retrospective conduct disorder, childhood victimisation, violent fantasies and attitudes to violence were examined in the prediction of involvement in physical aggression. Over half of the variance was accounted for by the combination of the independent variables. Cognitions justifying the use of violence and fantasies of aggressive actions emerged as the greatest contributors in explaining individual differences in physical aggression. The findings highlight the importance of addressing attitudes at the individual and societal level that convey pro-violence sentiments.

Violence in society poses an ongoing concern. Within Queensland, Australia, for the financial year 2007/2008, there were 31,702 incidents of violence reported to police (Queensland Police Service, 2008). The consequences of violence include physical, psychological and social harms to the victim, costs in responding to the perpetrator of violence, as well as the potential for fear among members of the community.

A central concern for efforts to prevent and reduce violence is understanding factors that contribute to individual differences in violent behaviour. Gender differences for involvement in violent behaviour have long been identified. Greater involvement in violence among males compared to females has been found for physical acts of aggression, although not necessarily for other forms of aggressive behaviour such as verbal aggression (Connor, Stenigard, Anderson, & Melloni, 2003). Childhood victimisation, involving physical, verbal and sexual abuse, as well as neglect, has been found in a number of studies as a significant precursor for adult involvement in violent behaviour (Widom, Schuck, & White, 2006). Furthermore, aggressive behaviour has been found to be a relatively stable characteristic, with individuals who engage in violence and antisocial behaviour in childhood being most likely to perpetuate acts of violence as adults (Huesmann & Eron, 1984).

While childhood victimisation and childhood history of antisocial behaviour are distal precursors for involvement in adult violence, proximal factors may be more pertinent predictors of individual differences in violence. Violent thoughts and violent fantasies, have been articulated within social-cognitive theory of aggression and the general aggression model as facilitating individuals propensity to be involved in violent behaviour (Anderson & Bushman, 2002; Grisso, Davis, Vesselinov, Applebaum, & Monahan, 2000). Cognitions involving violent content and attitudes that justify the use of violence may reduce individuals' inhibitions for engaging in violent behaviour in particular situations. Frequent recall of cognitions and fantasies with violent content may provide an opportunity to rehearse aggressive actions increasing the potential for subsequent aggressive actions. Intervention programs with adjudicated violent offenders often target such cognitions as well as other risk factors for continued violent behaviour (Howells, Watt, Hall, & Baldwin, 1997).

In contrast to the social-cognitive and general aggression model of violent thoughts and fantasies, a Cathartic view postulates that such cognitions may actually reduce the potential for later aggressive actions (Bushman, Baumeister, & Stack, 1999). The potential beneficial effects of cathartically fantasising about harming other, however, is not consistent with research from laboratory settings or surveys of individuals' involvement in aggressive actions (Goldstein, 1999).

The potential association between violent thoughts, violent fantasies and violent actions may reflect an additional factor contributing to the maintenance of all three constructs. Alcohol consumption and alcohol misuse have often been identified as increasing individuals' risk for involvement in violent behaviour (Luthra & Gidycz, 2006). Alcohol consumption has been found to have disinhibiting effects and increase the potential for violent actions, whereby an individual's information processing is effected with less responsiveness to prominent inhibitory cues. Individuals who consume alcohol at elevated levels may be prone to violent thoughts and fantasies, as well as violent actions. Consequently, research examining the contributions of violent cognitions on aggressive behaviours needs to include measurement of alcohol consumption. Previous research examining the relevance of violent cognitions and fantasies has primarily focused on forensic and psychiatric populations (Steadman, Mulvey, Monahan, & Robbins, 1998). Evaluating the contribution of proximal factors for violence among community samples is important for strategies to prevent and reduce further violence. Research is also required to further examine the role of cognitions and fantasies, beyond the contribution of alcohol misuse, as well as distal factors, such as gender, previous victimisation, and persistence of antisocial behaviour. As community research on involvement in violent behaviour may be biased by social desirability in responding, controlling for self-serving response sets is also indicated.

For the current study, it was hypothesised that (a) distal risk factors (childhood victimisation, childhood antisocial behaviour), proximal risk factors (alcohol misuse, violent thoughts, violent fantasies) as well as age and gender would correlate with involvement in physical violence among a community sample. Further it was hypothesised that (b) violent thoughts and fantasies would provide significant contribution to the prediction of violence beyond distal factors.

Method

Participants
Participants consisted of 151 respondents from 1000 randomly selected households in eight suburbs in the Gold Coast region of Queensland, Australia (response rate 15%). Over half of the participants were female (54.3%), one third male (34.4%) and the remainder of unreported gender (11.3%). The participants were aged between 18 and 65+ years (mdn = 36 to 40 years). Weekly income varied considerably across the participants from nil/negative income (8.2%) to $2000+ (4.1%) with median weekly income of $450 to $600 per week. The participants were of various educational backgrounds, with 36.4% reporting having a university education, 21.2% having TAFE qualifications and one quarter achieving less than a year 12 high school education (24.7%).

Materials
Self-report measures utilised in the current study included the Aggression Questionnaire (AQ, Buss & Perry, 1992), the Justification for Violence Scale (JFV; Kelty, 2006), the conduct disorder component of the

Composite International Diagnostic interview (CIDI; World Health Organization, 1990), the Alcohol Use Disorder Identification Test (AUDIT, Sitharthan, Sitharthan, Kavanagh, & Saunders, 2001), the Juvenile Victimisation Questionnaire (JVQ; Hamby, Finkelhor, Ormrod, & Turner, 2005), the Marlowe-Crowne Social Desirability Scale Short-Form C (MCSDS-C, Reynolds, 1982), and the Schedule of Imagined Violence (SIV; Grisso et al., 2000). Demographic questions inquired regarding participant gender, age, weekly income, occupation, educational level, religion and ancestry.

The AQ (Buss & Perry, 1992) is a widely used self-report inventory assessing individuals involvement in physical aggression, verbal aggression, anger and hostility. As the focus of the current study was violence, only the physical aggression subscale was used. The version of the AQ used in the current study had one item of the physical aggression scale missing due to administration error ('I have become so mad that I have broken things'). The internal consistency of the eight-item physical aggression with a Chronbach's alpha of .89, was comparable to the nine-item version of the physical aggression scale with a Chronbach's alpha of .85 (Buss & Perry, 1992). Validity for the AQ is indicated by significant correlations between AQ total scores, and peer-nominated ratings of aggressive behaviour (Buss & Perry, 1992).

Endorsement of attitudes favourable toward the use of violence was measured with the JFV scale (Kelty, 2006). Consisting of 14 pro-violence statements, the JFV was derived from qualitative interviews conducted with convicted violent offenders, and has been found to differentiate violent offenders from non-offenders.

Utilising the CIDI (WHO, 1990), items pertaining to Conduct Disorder were modified for use as a self-report inventory assessing participants involvement in behaviours consistent with the *Diagnostic and Statistical Manual of Mental Disorders*, fourth edition, text revised (DSM-IV-TR, American Psychiatric Association, 2000) diagnosis of Conduct Disorder.

The AUDIT is a widely used measure to screen individuals likely to be consuming alcohol at harmful levels (Stitharthan et al., 2001). The AUDIT inquires about the frequency, amount, tolerance and harms associated with an individual's alcohol usage.

The Juvenile Victimisation Questionnaire (Hamby et al., 2005) is a comprehensive retrospective questionnaire for gathering information about a broad range of childhood victimisations, including conventional crime, child maltreatment, peer and sibling victimisation, sexual victimisation, and witnessing and indirect victimisation. The JVQ's reliability and validity has been supported in large studies with youth up to 20 years of age, but not evaluated with older adults (Hamby et al., 2005).

Assessing individuals' tendency to respond in a socially desirable manner, the MCSDS-C consists of 13 true–false statements (Reynolds, 1982). Individuals obtaining higher scores on the MCSDS-C are more likely to be responding in a socially acceptable as opposed to truthful manner.

The SIV is an eight-item self-report inventory assessing an individuals endorsement of having experienced violent fantasies or daydreams (Grisso et al., 2000). Individuals answering affirmative to the first question, having had 'daydreams or thoughts about physically hurting other persons' are requested to answer subsequent questions qualifying the features of such fantasies, such as frequency, duration and intensity.

Design
The study utilised a between-subjects correlational research design, with physical aggression as the dependent variable. Predictors of physical aggression were entered in hierarchical regression in order of increasing proximity to aggressive actions. Step 1 entered participant gender; Step 2, age and social desirability (as a covariate); Step 3, childhood victimisation; Step 4, childhood conduct disorder symptoms; and at the final step, alcohol misuse, violent fantasies and attitude toward violence.

Procedure
Research procedures were conducted in accord with Bond University Human Research Ethics Committee Approval. Four higher socio-economic and four lower socioeconomic status suburbs were randomly selected from possible higher and lower status suburbs identified by the Australian Bureau of Statistics Census. Within each suburb, commencing with a randomly selected street, 125 questionnaires with response prepaid addressed return envelopes and explanatory statements were delivered. Instructions requested the youngest adult in the household to participate, to increase sampling of younger adults.

Results
Descriptive statistics for physical aggression and the predictor variables are reported in Table 26.1. Of note, 23% of the sample reported having had thoughts or daydreams involving harm toward other people. The mean for JFV is similar to the original means reported by Kelty (2006)

Table 26.1

Descriptive Statistics for Physical Aggression and Predictor Variables

	N	M	SD
Physical aggression	151	17.11	7.44
MCSDS	151	7.56	2.99
Justification for violence	150	28.21	11.34
Alcohol misuse	147	7.44	7.49
Conduct disorder	151	2.08	2.95
Total victimisation	151	25.96	23.90
		%	
Violent fantasy	151	23	

Note: MCSDS = Marlowe-Crowne Social Desirability Scale.

with a Perth nonoffender sample (Male $M = 28.62$, $SD = 6.94$, Female $M = 23.74$, $SD = 6.08$). Regarding the AUDIT, the mean is on the cut-off level for potential alcohol problems (6+ for females, 7+ for males; Sitharthan et al., 2001), indicating that approximately half of the participants were consuming alcohol at levels that may be harmful.

The results for the hierarchical regression and zero-order correlations with physical aggression are presented in Table 26.2. As hypothesised, the univariate correlation for each predictor with physical aggression was significant. Higher levels of physical aggression was associated with male gender, younger age, childhood victimisation and conduct disorder behaviours, greater alcohol use, violent fantasies and justification for violence.

For the hierarchical regression, each block of variables entered resulted in significant increments in explained variance, with the final model accounting for 55% of the variance (Adjusted $R^2 = .52$), $F(8,115) = 17.59$, $p < .001$. The distal variables of childhood victimisation in Step 3 and conduct disorder behaviours at Step 4 accounted for significant increments of variance beyond gender, age and social desirability, $F(1,119) = 9.48$, $p < .001$ and $F(1,118) = 17.00$, $p < .001$. Importantly, the addition of the proximal variables at Step 5 of alcohol use, violent fantasy and violent thoughts, enhanced the prediction beyond gender, age, social desirability, victimisation and conduct disorder, $F(3,115) = 12.80$, $p < .001$. At the final step, violent thoughts provided unique significant contribution in the prediction of physical aggression, $p < .001$, and violent fantasy approached significance, $p = .07$.

Table 26.2

Hierarchical Regression for Physical Aggression

Predictors	Step 1			Step 2			Step 3			Step 4			Step 5			Zero-order
	B	SEB	β	B	SEB	β	B	SEB	β	B	SEB	β	B	SEB	β	r
Gender	5.92	1.27	.39***	5.59	1.21	.37***	4.77	1.20	.31***	3.13	1.18	.22**	1.40	1.10	.09	.39***
Age				-0.30	0.21	-.12	-0.16	0.20	-.06	-0.02	0.19	-.10	-0.15	0.17	-.06	-.17*
Social desirability				-0.71	0.21	-.27	-0.53	0.21	-.21	-0.32	0.20	-.13	-0.22	0.19	-.08	-.35***
Victimisation							0.08	0.03	.26**	0.04	0.03	.14	0.03	0.02	.11	.42***
Conduct disorder										0.94	0.23	.37***	0.25	0.23	.10	.57***
Alcohol misuse													-0.02	0.07	-.24	.31***
Fantasy													2.40	1.34	-.14	.52***
JFV													0.29	0.05	.45***	.67***
Total R²			.15***			.26***			.31***			.40***			.55***	
Δ R²			.15***			.11***			.06**			.09***			.15***	

Note: B = Unstandardised Coefficient Beta; SEB = Unstandardised Coefficient Standard Error Beta; β = Standardised Coefficient Beta.
JFV = Justifications for Violence.
*p < .05, **p < .01, ***p < .001

Discussion

The present study examined predictors of physical violence among a community sample in South East Queensland. As hypothesised, distal factors including gender, age, childhood victimisation and conduct disorder behaviours were significantly associated with physical aggression, as were the proximal variables of alcohol use, violent thoughts and fantasies. The Marlowe-Crowne measure of social desirability response set also significantly correlated with aggression, underscoring the importance of measuring such potential sources of bias in community studies of violent behaviours.

The proximal predictors of physical aggression accounted for a significant proportion of variance beyond that accounted for by the distal factors. This was most evident for violent thoughts, and to a lesser extent, violent fantasy. The contribution of cognitions in understanding violence has been articulated by social–cognitive theory and the general aggression model. While previous research has found that cognitions regarding the use of violence predicts violent actions, the current research extends previous findings by controlling for childhood victimisation, child antisocial behaviours and alcohol misuse. This is important, as the connection between violent cognitions and actions could be explained by alcohol misuse and/or distal third factors.

The current findings are not consistent with a cathartic view. Thoughts, images and fantasies regarding violence do not appear to be beneficial, at least in relation to reducing potential for violent behaviour. Acceptance of individual's violent thoughts, and even encouraging violent cognitions as a self-regulation strategy are not recommended in light of previous research (Goldstein, 1999) and the current findings.

A number of limitations are evident for the current study. While the study utilised a procedure for randomly selecting participants in South East Queensland, the low response rate of 15% reduces confidence in generalisability of findings. Diversity in age, educational background and income provides some encouragement though in the interpretation of the results. The current study relied on self-report methodology, with the childhood indices requiring retrospective accounts of events and behaviours. The accuracy of recall was not evaluated in the current study, limiting the accuracy of reporting. The measurement of socially desirable responding was utilised to reduce one potential source of error among self-report measures, positively biased response set.

A further limitation pertains to the measurement of violent fantasies. The SIV inquires regarding various qualitative aspects of an individual's violent fantasies. Unfortunately only the first item involves a response by all participants (whether or not the respondent experienced violent fantasies or daydreams). To maintain sufficient sample size for analyses, only the first item was used. There is likely to be considerable heterogeneity in intensity and severity of violent fantasies. Refinement of approaches to measure violent fantasies is indicated for future research.

Notwithstanding the aforementioned limitations, the current study highlights the need to target proximal factors associated with violence, particularly violent thoughts and fantasies. Cognitive–behavioural approaches with violent adolescents and adults often identify thoughts and beliefs associated with aggressive incidents (e.g., Howells et al., 1997). Enhancement of such interventions could involve greater exploration and intervention with the fantasy component of cognitions, similar to approaches with sexual offenders' deviant sexual fantasies. At a public health level, messages that promote constructive and non-violent responses to manage interpersonal situations ought to be encouraged.

References

American Psychiatric Association (2000). *Diagnostic criteria from Diagnotic and Statistical Manual of Mental Disorders* (4th ed., rev.). Washinton DC: Author.

Anderson, C.A., & Bushman, B.J. (2002). Human aggression. *Annual Review of Psychology, 53*, 27–51.

Bushman, B., Baumeister, R., & Stack, A. (1999). Catharsis, Aggression and persuasive influences: Self-fulfilling or self-defeating prophecies? *Journal of Personality and Social Psychology, 76*, 367–376.

Buss, A.H., & Perry, M. (1992) The Aggression Questionnaire. *Journal of Personality and Social Psychology, 63*, 452–459.

Connor, D.F., Steingard, R.J., Anderson, J.J., & Melloni, R.H. (2003). Gender differences in reactive and proactive aggression. *Child Psychiatry and Human Development, 33*, 279–292.

Goldstein, A.P. (1999). Aggression reduction strategies: Effective and ineffective. *School Psychology Quarterly, 14*, 40–58.

Grisso, T., Davis, J., Vesselinov, R., Appelbaum, P., & Monahan, J. (2000). Violent thought and violent behaviour following hospitalisation for mental disorder. *Journal of Consulting and Clinical Psychology, 68*, 338–398.

Hamby, S., Finkelhor, D., Ormrod, R., & Turner, H. (2005). *The juvenile Victimization Questionnaire (JVQ): Administration and Scoring Manual* (Vol. 1). Durnham, NH: Crimes Against Children Research Center.

Hardt, J., & Rutter, M. (2004) Validity of adult retrospective reports of adverse childhood experiences: review of the evidence. *Journal of Child Psychology and Psychiatry, 45*, 260–273.

Howells, K., Watt, B., Hall, G., & Baldwin, S. (1997). *Developing programmes for violent offenders. Legal and Criminological Psychology, 2,* 117– 128.

Huesmann, L.R., & Eron, L.D. (1984). Cognitive processes and the persistence of aggressive behavior. *Aggressive Behavior, 10,* 243–251.

Kelte, S. (2005). *'You have to hit some people, it's all they understand!': Are violent sentiments more criminogenic than attributing hostile intent in the escalation of grievances?* (Doctoral dissertation). Murdoch University, Perth, Western Australia).

Kessler, R.C., & Üstün, T.B. (1989) The World Mental Health (WMH) Survey Initiative Version of the World Health Organization (WHO) Composite International Diagnostic Interview (CIDI). *International Journal of Methods in Psychiatric Research, 13,* 93–121.

Luthra, R., & Gidycz, C.A. (2006). Dating violence among college men and women: Evaluation of a theoretical model. *Journal of Interpersonal Violence, 21,* 717–731.

Queensland Police Service (2008). *2007–2008 Annual Statistical Review.* Brisbane, Australia: Author.

Reynolds, W.M. (1982). Development of reliable and valid short forms of the Marlowe-Crowne Social Desirability Scale. *Journal of Clinical Psychology, 38,* 119–125.

Sitharthan, G., Sitharthan, T., Kavanagh, D.J., Saunders, J.B. (2001). Brief opportunistic interventions: the role of psychologists in initiating self-change amongst problem drinkers. *Australian Psychologist, 36,* 219–226.

Steadman, H.J., Mulvey, E.P., Monahan, J., & Robbins, P.C. (1998). Violence by people discharged from acute psychiatric inpatient facilities and by others in the same neighbourhoods. *Archives of General Psychiatry, 55,* 393–401.

Widom, C.S., Schuck, A. M, & White, H.R. (2006). An examination of pathways from childhood victimization to violence: the role of early aggression and problematic alcohol use. *Violence and Victims, 21,* 675–690.

World Health Organization (1990) *The World Health Organization (WHO) Composite International Diagnostic Interview (CIDI).* Available at http://www.hcp.med.harvard.edu/wmhcidi/

Chapter

27

The Virus of Violence: The Relationship Between Victimisation and Aggression

Bruce D. Watt and Mattias J. Allard

Experiments for the relationship between victimisation and violence often do not include any mediation variables to account for the difference between victimised individuals that become violent in adulthood and those that do not. A model was proposed, using a Gold Coast community sample of 250 individuals (79 males, 138 females, 33 unspecified) with a median age range 41–45 years, that violent thoughts (measured as violent fantasies and permissive attitudes towards violence) mediate the relationship between victimisation (measured retrospectively) and aggression. The study consisted of distal factors (victimisation and gender), proximal factors (permissive attitudes towards violence and violent fantasies) and an outcome factor (aggression). The results indicated that the model's variables were all important in the prediction of aggression, though gender was no longer significant after all other variables were included.

Violence can be defined as the behaviour of inflicting harm upon another individual, whether the lasting effects are internal, external or both. Many theories have been developed and dismissed over the years regarding why some individuals act more violently than others.

Typically studies find that aggression is a fairly constant attribute in a person, remaining consistent in longitudinal studies from ages as low as 8 through to 30 (Heusmann, Eron, Lefkowitz, & Walder, 1984). Early aggressiveness was predictive of serious antisocial behaviour in adults, ranging from criminal behaviour and traffic violations to spouse abuse and self-reported physical aggression. Aggression has also been shown to be even more stable between generations in a family than across ages.

Over the years, much research has been conducted regarding the relationship of early childhood abuse and neglect with violent behaviour later in life (Widom, 2006). Some have postulated that the instilling of aggression occurs under appropriate learning conditions (Eron, Walder, & Lefkowitz, 1971), in which the child has many opportunities to observe aggression as the object of said aggression, reinforcing any aggression within the child. An implication of this is that the child's attitudes towards violence are changed in these circumstances, leading them to believe that aggression is a suitable means towards desired ends. In addition to this, more permissive attitudes towards violence have been associated with subsequent violence (Potegal & Knutson, 1994). A large study funded by the Italian government found permissive attitudes towards violence correlated highly with aggression and irritability (Caprara, Cinanni, & Mazzotti, 1989). As such, there is potential for a pathway from victimisation to aggression through permissive attitudes towards violence.

No clear line has been drawn regarding whether fantasising about or imagining violent acts should be considered an aggressive trait, in and of itself. While this study associates the two, it retains them as separate constructs. Very few studies have investigated the relationship of violent fantasies with other constructs. Despite this, it has been associated with higher rates of engaging in violent behaviours after discharge with hospitalised individuals, particularly among those who reported persistence of these fantasies (Grisso, Davis, Vesselinov, Appelbaum, & Monahan, 2000). However, other studies have found no relationship between violent fantasies and aggression (McNeil, 1962). These studies all fail to take into account any covariates, and treat violent fantasies and aggression as categorical variables, thus ignoring the continuous nature of these concepts. Despite similarities to attitudes towards violence and its relationship with appropriate learning conditions, the relationship between victimisation and violent fantasies, this relationship has never been tested. Due to the shortage of research pertaining to violent fantasies, this study will investigate its relationships with victimisation and aggression. Gender differences have also been found in the experiences of violent fantasies (Kenrick & Sheets, 1993), with women reporting lower levels of homicidal fantasies than men.

The idea behind the current common understanding of violence is that victimisation leads almost directly to violence in adulthood, with a general acceptance of gender as an influencing factor in the relationship. This understanding typically fails to take into account the aforementioned large number of individuals that find themselves falling into patterns of victimisation in adulthood after victimisation as a child rather than becoming aggressive themselves (Widom, Czaja, & Dutton, 2008). However, these models contain no transitional factor, which might indicate the aggressive tendencies have taken to the new individual after the initial abuse ceased. Nor, indeed, has any notable method of mediation, much less does the model itself suggest any means of intervention once the initial damage (for want of a better term) is done. Any model proposed should address these issues if possible.

These relationships are best put forward as a model. The model's variables exist in three major categories; the distal factors, the proximal factors and the outcome factors. The distal factors consist of retrospective victimisation and gender, being the variables decided earliest in the lifespan of an individual. The model then leads on to the proximal factors, which consist of attitudes towards violence (derived from justification for violence) and experience of violent fantasies. If the individual suffered victimisation as a child, then they would theoretically experience higher levels of violent fantasies and more permissive attitudes towards violence. The final category of the model, outcome, consists of any aggressive behaviours in adults.

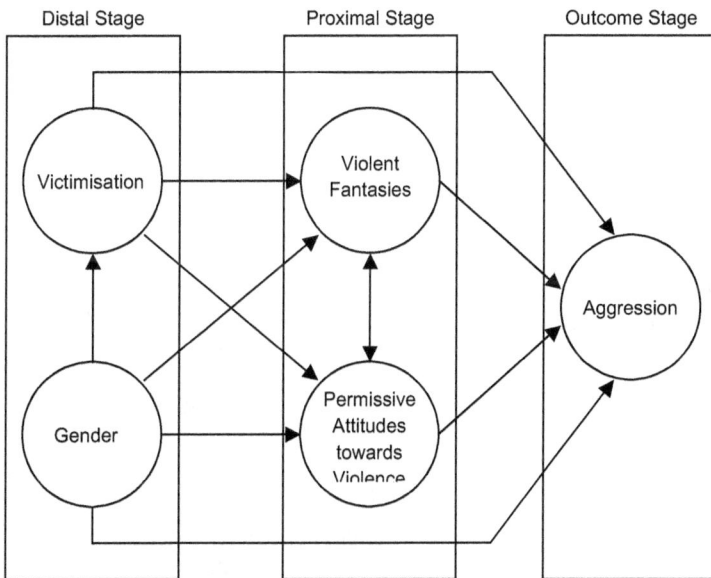

Figure 27.1
The relationships between the variables in the model.

The links between the variable are as shown in Figure 27.1. The core idea of the proximal factors is that only individuals who have taken up violent thought patterns will then lead to aggression from the proximal stage, measurable through the relationship between victimisation and aggression being attenuated by the pathway between the two through violent fantasies and attitudes towards violence.

Additionally, due to the related nature of violent fantasies and permissive attitudes towards violence, these variables are expected to correlate. Gender acts as a covariate in the model and is therefore expected to have some level of causal relationship with every other variable, including victimisation (Bergen, Martin, Richardson, Allison, & Roeger, 2004). Given that structural equational modelling typically requires very large sample sizes, it has been said that multiple regressions can be run instead, using the standardised beta weights to act as pathway coefficients (Billings & Wroten, 1978). As the sample size is inadequate to properly run structural equational modelling in this study, regressions were conducted to test the strength of the relationships within this model.

It was first hypothesised that participants that report higher levels of retrospective victimisation will indicate higher levels of aggression as adults.

Second, it was hypothesised that participants that reported higher levels of retrospective victimisation would also report more permissive attitudes towards violence and will be more likely to report higher levels of violent fantasies.

Third, it was further hypothesised that more permissive attitudes towards violence and stronger experiences of violent fantasies will be associated with higher levels of aggression.

Fourth, it was hypothesised that violent thoughts are an important part of the pathway from victimisation to aggression.

Fifth, it was hypothesised that female participants will show lower levels of violent fantasies, permissive attitudes towards violence and aggression than their male counterparts.

Method

Participants

Participants were sample of 250 adults that consisted of 79 males (31.6%) and 138 females (55.2%) plus 33 individuals that did not report their gender (13.2%) from 16 randomly selected Gold Coast communities of both higher and lower socioeconomic backgrounds. Ages of participants ranged from 18 to 61+ years (median = 41–45, mode = 18–25).

Materials

The Juvenile Victimisation Questionnaire (JVQ; Hamby, Finkelhor, Ormrod, & Turner, 2005) is a comprehensive retrospective 34-item questionnaire for gathering information about a broad range of childhood victimisations. Each item highlights a form of offence against a youth covering five general areas of concern: conventional crime, child maltreatment, peer and sibling victimisation, sexual victimisation, and witnessing and indirect victimisation. The internal consistency figure for the whole scale was measured at .80 (Finkelhor, Hamby, Ormrod, & Turner, 2005).

The Aggression Questionnaire (AQ; Buss & Perry, 1992) consists of 29 statements, which asked participants to rate their agreement on a 5-point Likert scale, measuring the participant's aggression. The questionnaire is made up of four subscales; physical aggression, verbal aggression, anger, and hostility. The subscales have consistency rated at .85, .72, .83 and .77, respectively with internal consistency for the scale as a whole of .89 (Buss & Perry, 1992). Due to a clerical error, one of the items was omitted from the physical aggression subscale, recalculation of internal consistency figures with the missing item yielded .82 for the subscale, and .90 for the overall questionnaire, which are both acceptable for research.

The Schedule of Imagined Violence (SIV; Grisso et al., 2000) is an eight-item scale to determine whether the respondent has experienced fantasies of a violent nature. The scale consists 12 items, including 4 new items for this study; only the second through fourth, and seventh through tenth items were used for calculations, being the ones that most logically contributed to the severity or strength of ideation of violence. As there are no norms, nor validity data pertaining to the SIV, internal consistency for the scale was calculated at .74 for the scale, which is acceptable for a scale with 7 items. The scale was shown to have predictive validity of engaging in violent acts within 20 weeks after discharge from the hospital in which the study took place for non-white patients, patients without major mental disorder but with substance abuse diagnoses, patients with high symptom severity, and patients whose reports of violent thoughts persisted after discharge.

The Justification for Violence Scale's responses (Kelty, Hall, and Watt, in press) was used as a measure of respondents' permissive attitudes towards violence. The scale consists of 14 items on a 5-point Likert scale. The Cronbach's alpha internal consistency score for the scale was rated at .88 for male and female university students, .92 for male high-risk offenders and .83 for male and female nonoffenders in the community in the original study.

Table 27.1

The Means and Standard Deviations for the Variables Used in the Aggression Regression

	M	SD	N
Aggression questionnaire total score	62.60	18.39	188
Gender	1.35	0.48	188
Victimisation total	29.62	24.50	188
Fantasies total	2.10	4.69	188
Attitudes towards violence total score	27.96	10.36	188

Demographic information was also obtained, including gender, occupation (open-ended), age (groups for 18–25, 61+, and intervals of five years in between), education level completed, average weekly income, religion, ancestry and an optional question as to whether the participant as a criminal record or not.

Design

This study used a correlational research design and explored Adult Recollection of Victimisation, Violent Fantasies and Justification for Violence scale scores as independent variables and Aggression Questionnaire Total Scores as the dependant variable; with gender was as a covariate.

A hierarchical linear regression was conducted using the aggression score as the dependant variable, and gender was entered as the sole variable of the second block (to act as a covariate for the remaining blocks). The second block consisted of the victimisation scores. The third block consisted of violent fantasies and the participants' scores for the justification for violence scale. This tests the first, third, fourth, and fifth hypotheses.

After this two additional regressions were run to investigate the relationship between victimisation and the proximal variables. The first used the justification for violence scores as the dependent variable. Gender was entered in the first block, and the victimisation scores in the second block. The next regression was identical, though replacing the attitudes towards violence scale with the violent fantasies measure. These test the second and fifth hypotheses.

Procedure

Participants were recruited for this study through a letterbox drop, consistent with Bond University Human Research Ethics Committee approval. Sixteen suburbs on the Gold Coast were randomly selected: eight of higher socioeconomic status, and eight of lower socioeconomic status selected from a report from the Australian Bureau of Statistics in

Table 27.2

The Correlations of the Items Used in the Regressions

	Aggression Questionnaire Score	Gender	Victimisation	Fantasies total
Gender	−.176*	1		
Victimisation	.460**	−.136*	1	
Fantasies	.494**	−.281**	.279**	1
Attitudes towards violence	.502**	−.356**	.254**	.515**

Note: * $p < .05$, ** $p < .01$
Listwise $N = 193$

order to maximise the diversity of the sample. In total, 2000 questionnaires were sent out at two separate times, 1000 in December of 2007 and 1000 in July of 2008, of which 151 were returned from the December drop, and 99 from the July drop.

Results

Aggression Hierarchical Regression

Descriptive statistics for the independent and dependent variables are displayed in Table 27.1. Hierarchical multiple regression was performed to test the ability of four blocks of independent variables, bias, gender, victimisation and violent thought variables to predict the participants' aggression scores which functioned as the dependent variable. Table 27.3 displays the unstandardised regression coefficients (Beta), standard error (SE), standardised regression coefficients (β) for each independent variable, along with R2, R2 change and significance for each stip (F change).

Before the inclusion of the violent thought variables the significant positive prediction of aggression by victimisation supports the first hypothesis, and as the weights for gender were nonsignificant, thus failing to support the fifth hypothesis.

After the inclusion of the violent thought variables the continued significant positive predictive validity of victimisation for aggression further supports the first hypothesis, and its small decrease in standardised beta indicates some support for the fourth hypothesis. Results for violent fantasies and permissive attitudes towards violence both supported the third hypothesis through positive significant beta-values of justification for both variables.

Violent Thoughts Hierarchical Regressions

Hierarchical multiple regression was performed to test the ability of the sum of the five child victimisation scores to predict justification for violence attitudes in adults. Justification for Violence scores were used as the

Table 27.3

Significance of the Blocks, and Beta Weights from the Aggression Regression

Block	R^2	R^2 change	F change	Variable	Beta	SE	β
1	.031	.031	6.11*				
2	.225	.194	47.50**	Gender	−4.40	2.46	−.12
				Victimisation	.33	.05	.44**
3	.419	.194	31.48**	Gender	1.86	2.28	0.05
				Victimisation	.24	.04	.32**
				Attitudes	.54	.12	.30**
				Fantasies	1.04	.26	.26**

Note: *$p < .05$, **$p < .01$
Listwise $N = 193$

dependent variable while gender was entered as the first block, with victimisation entered the independent variable in the second block. Contributions for independent variables and the overall models at each step predicting violent thoughts are displayed in Table 27.4.

The significant beta-value for victimisation's prediction of permissive attitudes towards violence supports the second hypothesis, while the negative beta-weights for gender indicate the females reported lower average levels of permissive attitudes towards violence than males, supporting the fifth hypothesis.

Hierarchical multiple regression was performed to test the ability of victimisation to predict violent fantasies in adults. Violent fantasies scores were used as the dependent variable while gender entered in the first block, and victimisation entered as independent variable in the second block. Due to the large number of zero responses to the violent fantasies scale, a more conservative alpha value of 0.005 was used for this test. Table 27.5 displays the coefficients for each independent variable and the overall model in predicting violent fantasies.

Table 27.4

Significance of the Justification for Violence Prediction Blocks, and Beta Weights

Block	R^2	R^2 change	F change	Variable	Beta	SE	β
1	.132	.132	29.92**				
2	.173	.040	9.53**	Gender	−7.28	1.41	−.34**
				Victimisation	.084	.03	.20**

Note: *$p < .05$, **$p < .01$
Listwise $N = 198$

Table 27.5

Significance of the Violent Fantasies Prediction Blocks, and Beta Weights

Block	R²	R² change	F change	Variable	Beta	SE	β
1	.081	.081	17.77**				
2	.150	.069	16.43**	Gender	−2.44	.65	−.25**
				Victimisation	.051	.01	.27**

Note. * p < .005, ** p < .001
Listwise N = 204

The positive beta-weights for victimisation's prediction of violent fantasies indicate a positive relationship between the two variables, supporting the second hypothesis. The negative beta-weights for gender indicated the females reported lower levels of violent fantasies than males, this supports the fifth hypothesis.

Discussion

The role of victimisation and its hypothetical appropriate learning conditions suggested in previous literature in which individuals are exposed to violent behaviours (Eron et al., 1971) was applied in testing the relationship. The relationships between victimisation and the proximal variables, in their power to predict aggression, were tested with regressions to understand their relationship with the model. The results supported the majority of the hypotheses without any notable violations of assumptions.

The first hypothesis that victimisation would predict aggression in adulthood was supported. This was observed in that the first regression with significant contribution of the victimisation retrospective scores to adult aggression scores, after accounting for gender. These results are congruent with numerous past studies including Widom (2006) and Eron and colleagues (1971) finding positive relationships between victimisation in childhood and aggression in adulthood, as with this study.

The second hypothesis regarding higher levels of retrospective victimisation being associated with more permissive attitudes towards violence was supported. The contribution of victimisation to permissive attitudes towards violence was significant after accounting for the variance explained by gender. These findings are congruent with the theories of 'appropriate learning conditions' in which the child is the object of the aggression (Eron et al., 1971) in altered attitudes towards violence.

The second hypothesis regarding higher levels of retrospective victimisation being associated with higher levels of violent fantasies was supported. However, there were likely some analysis difficulties due to the large number of 'zero' responses for the violent fantasies measure, due to a majority of people reporting no violent fantasies. This was something for which the study corrected in the use of a more conservative alpha value. In summary, the second hypothesis was supported.

The third hypothesis, that ingrained violence in the form of permissive attitudes towards violence and violent fantasies would lead to aggression, was supported. The fact that in the regression both violent fantasies and justification for violence made significant contributions towards the prediction of aggression, despite the model having already accounted for gender and victimisation, shows that these two variables still have an important predictive factor for which the other variables can not account. This indicates an importance in measuring violent fantasies and permissive attitudes towards violence in understanding the relationship between victimisation in childhood and aggression in adulthood.

The results for the fourth hypothesis regarding violent fantasies and permissive attitudes towards violence were also positive. The results indicated evidence for a relationship between victimisation and aggression, with strong ties between these and the violent thought variables. Additionally, it should be noted when comparing the beta values for victimisation's prediction of aggression before and after the inclusion of violent fantasies and permissive attitudes towards violence, points to a weakening of this relationship. This is positive evidence for the proximal factor variables mediating this relationship to support the model, suggesting that these variables do likely act as the midpoint.

The fifth hypothesis that females would show less aggression, violent fantasies and permissive attitudes towards violence than males, was partially supported. Gender was not a significant predictor of aggression once it was no longer the sole predictor, although it did significantly predict permissive attitudes towards violence and violent fantasies. This information contributes little to the model, beyond solidifying gender's place in the model as a covariate.

These results support arguments for all links within the model (except the vertical ones). With the beta-weights obtained from the analyses the model can be assembled, as shown in Figure 27.2.

Looking at the model and seeing the comparative relationships side by side it is clear that the direct predictive quality of victimisation towards aggression still narrowly surpasses the violent fantasies and attitudes towards violence pathways. With respect to the implications of these findings for the model, the signs are positive. All relationships suggested relationships were

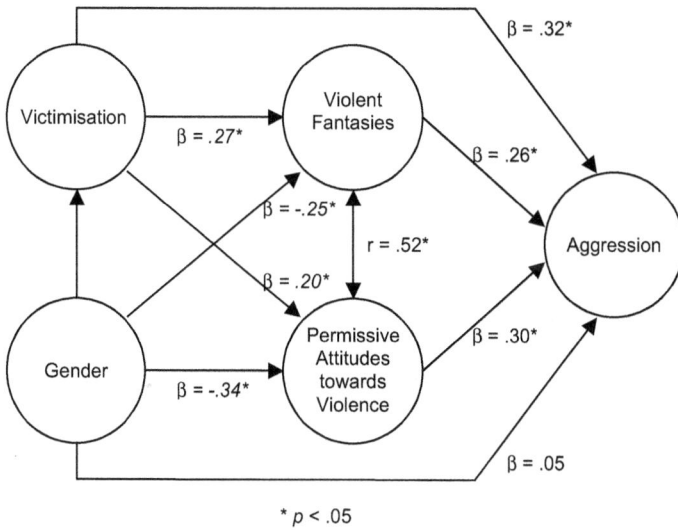

Figure 27.2
The relationships between the variables in the model as derived from regressions.

significant. Additionally, after the inclusion of all of the victimisation, violent thought data, this influence of gender attenuated to a point where it was no longer having an impact on the outcome of the model.

One potential limitation of the study was it did not account for potential inaccuracy of responses in the form of social desirability bias. This exception could be viewed as both notably pertinent and a potential confound based on the links to the sensitive topics of aggression, violent fantasies and attitudes towards violence. It is both possible that these topics would be too strongly influenced by accounting for social desirability bias, and that social desirability would notably improve the model. This could be addressed in future studies.

The implications of the supporting evidence for the model are rather positive. More research should be conducted examining the effects of the proximal variables on the relationship between victimisation and aggression, particularly the experiencing of violent fantasies and permissive attitudes towards violence and aggression as covered in this study. Additionally, and most importantly, the model lends itself well to understanding whether an individual has been infected with aggression violence, and allows a greater comprehension.

References

Bergen, H.A., Martin, G., Richardson, A.S., Allison, S., & Roeger, L. (2004). Sexual abuse, antisocial behaviour and substance use: Gender differences in young community adolescents. *Australian and New Zealand Journal of Psychiatry, 38*, 34–41.

Billings, R.S., & Wroten, S.P. (1978). Use of path analysis in industrial/organisational psychology: Criticisms and suggestions. *Journal of Applied Psychology, 63*, 677–688.

Buss, A.H., & Perry, M. (1992). Aggression Questionnaire. *Journal of Personality and Social Psychology, 63*(3), 452–459.

Caprara, G.V., Cinanni, V., & Mazzotti, E. (1989). Measuring attitudes toward violence. *Personality and Individual Differences, 10*(4), 479–481.

Eron, L.D., Walder, L.O., & Lefkowitz, M.M. (1971). *Learning of aggression in children.* Boston: Little, Brown.

Finkelhor, D., Hamby, S.L., Ormrod, R., & Turner, H. (2005). The Juvenile Victimization Questionnaire: Reliability, validity, and national norms. *Child Abuse & Neglect, 29*, 383–412.

Grisso, T., Davis, J., Vesselinov, R., Appelbaum, P.S., & Monahan, J. (2000). Violent thoughts and violent behavior following hospitalization for mental disorder. *Journal of Consulting and Clinical Psychology, 68*, 388–398.

Hamby, S., Finkelhor, D., Ormrod, R., & Turner, H. (2005). *The Juvenile Victimization Questionnaire (JVQ): Administration and scoring manual.* (Vol. 1). Durham, NH: Crimes Against Children Research Center.

Huesmann, L.R., Eron, L.D., Lefkowitz, M.M., & Walder, L.O. (1984). Stability of aggression over time and generations. *Developmental Psychology, 20*, 1120–1134.

Kelty, S. F., Hall, G., & Watt, B. D. (in press). You have to hit some people! Endorsing violent sentiments (Part 2: The measurement and criminogenic nature of justifications for violence). *Psychiatry, Psychology and Law.*

McNeil, E.B. (1962). Aggression in fantasy and behavior. *Journal of Consulting Psychology, 26*(3), 232–240.

Widom, C.S. (2006). Motivation and mechanisms in the 'Cycle of Violence'. *Nebraska Symposium on Motivation, 46*, 1–37.

Widom, C.S., Czaja, S.J., & Dutton, M.A. (2008). Childhood victimization and lifetime revictimization. *Child Abuse and Neglect, 32*, 785–796.

The Validation of a Screening Tool for the Assessment of Violence Risk Among Juvenile Offenders

Michelle A. Perrin, Bruce D. Watt, and Tasneem Hasan

Screening tools in forensic mental health settings are utilised to assess individual differences in risk for future violence. The Child and Youth Forensic Outreach Service Violence Screening Tool (CVST) was developed for use with juveniles referred to mental health and juvenile justice settings. The reliability and validity of the CVST was evaluated based on 156 consecutive referrals to a Youth Justice Service in South East Queensland. Data on future violence was obtained from official Youth Justice Service records as well as caseworker observations of youth violence. The CVST was found to have adequate inter-rater and test–retest reliability. Importantly, the CVST significantly predicted future violence over a 12-month period. The CVST has the potential to assist in differentiating individuals according to violence risk with implications for case planning and interventions.

The prevalence of youth violence is a growing concern worldwide. In Australia the number of assaults committed by juvenile offenders increased by 14% from 2005 to 2006 (Australian Institute of Criminology, 2008), with a further 2% increase in Queensland for juveniles aged 15 to 19 years of age from 2006 to 2007 (Queensland Police Service, 2007). In order to reduce the occurrence and subsequent impact of violence, appropriate interventions need to be implemented. Effective interventions require accurate assessment of risk factors for future violence for treatment planning and management (Andrews, Bonta, & Hoge, 1990; Meyers & Schmidt, 2008). Research indicates that the utilisation of violence risk assessment tools increases case management effectiveness, and prediction of future violence beyond assessments based on unstructured clinical judgement (Monahan et al., 2001).

Screening is the first stage in violence risk procedures. Risk screening refers to a brief process used to identify the presence or absence of key risk factors. It is generally applied to every individual within a service and is primarily focused on the identification of immediate concerns (Grisso, 2005). Screening tools aim to be efficient, cost effective, relatively quick to administer, require little data collection, and are usable by examiners with little or no specialised or clinical training (Grisso, 2005). Screening processes may result in the recommendation for a more comprehensive assessment.

In review of the literature on youth violence risk it is noted that there are a dearth of screening tools. Several comprehensive measures for youth risk assessment include the Youth Level of Service/Case Management Inventory (YLS/CMI; Hoge & Andrews, 1999), and the Structured Assessment of Violence Risk in Youth (SAVRY; Borum, Bartel, & Forth, 2002). Both instruments have been validated in a number of studies with juvenile offenders. However, use of the YLS/CMI and SAVRY requires completion by personnel who have been trained in the particular instrument, and involves a high level of clinician time. These requirements may prohibit their use for screening large numbers of youth being admitted to a mental health or juvenile justice service. Screening instruments may be a useful initial step prior to the completion of more comprehensive assessment instruments.

In 2002 a report on forensic mental health in Queensland, Australia, called for improved consistency and a more standardised approach to the assessment and management of violence risk (Mullen & Chettleburgh, 2002). The Child and Youth Forensic Outreach Service (CYFOS), a Queensland Health service developed to meet the needs of young people with mental health and offending behaviour concerns, responded to this report with the development of the CYFOS Violence Screening Tool (CVST). The CVST was developed to identify violence risk within the dual context of forensic and mental health services. The CVST was developed by CYFOS personnel based on an unpublished literature review conducted in 2002 and distributed via training to mental health and youth justice services throughout Queensland. The CVST was subsequently adopted by a youth justice service to assist caseworkers in measuring the level of risk to staff. The aim of the current study was to evaluate the psychometric properties of the CVST, which has not previously been conducted.

It was hypothesised that the CVST would be a reliable measure of violence risk whereby level of risk scores obtained by the first author would correlate with level of risk scores obtained by Youth Justice personnel (interrater reliability); and the first level of risk scores obtained by Youth Justice personnel would correlate with second level of risk scores (test–retest reliability). Second, it was hypothesised that the CVST is a valid measure of violence risk whereby individuals who are rated at high risk would have a higher level of involvement in physical aggression compared to youth rated as lower risk for violence.

Method

Participants

A file review was conducted on 156 files stored at a youth justice service centre, with 82.1% males and an average age of 16.32 years ($SD = 1.37$). The ethnic origin of the participants included, 20.5% Aboriginal and/or Torres Strait Islander, 50% Anglo-Australian, 20.5% Pacific Islander, and 9% of other ethnic origin. At the time the first CVST was completed 54.5% of participants had previous contact with a Youth Justice Service Centre.

Measures

The CVST contains 21 questions in a 'Yes/No/Unknown' response format, which address static and dynamic factors. Static items are historical or dispositional in nature whereas dynamic factors are amenable to change and indicate increased current risk. The static items include: male gender, previous incidents of violence, previous use of weapons, criminal history, previous dangerous and risk taking behaviour, childhood abuse, role instability, history of alcohol and/or drug misuse, and neighbourhood crime and violence. The dynamic items address antisocial attitudes, violent ideation, mental illness, misuse of drugs and/or alcohol, school problems, impulsivity, family stressors, antisocial peers and sexualised behaviour. The endorsement of items guides decision-making in regards to whether a young person is deemed to be at a low, medium or high risk of future violence.

The instrument is utilised by a youth justice service centre during intake and subsequent review processes. It is completed by using information gathered through initial interviews with the young person and their significant others, and through review of relevant documentation. The

308 | Personality and Individual Differences: Current Directions

outcome informs procedures in regards to the level and type of contact a case worker has with the young person.

The Modified Overt Aggression Scale (MOAS; Kay, Wolkenfiend, & Murrill, 1988) is an observational measure developed to assess the severity and frequency of aggressive behaviours in a mental health setting. It assesses four domains of aggression: verbal aggression; physical aggression against self; physical aggression against property; and physical aggression against others. Each domain contains a rating of increasing severity from 0 to 4. An observer is required to rate an individual's aggressive behaviour by recording the most severe rating in each domain based upon the domain descriptors (e.g., 'Shouts angrily, curses mildly, or makes personal insults' scores 1 on the verbal aggression domain). A total aggression score is obtained via the weighted addition of the four domains.

The MOAS has demonstrated reliability, including interrater reliability based on total scores, $r = .85 - .94$ and satisfactory internal consistency ($W = .68$). Further the MOAS has good criterion-related validity with a study demonstrating the MOAS's ability to distinguish between aggressive and non-aggressive individuals (Kay et al., 1988).

Procedure

The first author blindly coded 50 participant files with the CVST. The files for all participants for whom the CVST's were completed were then coded for incidents of aggression over a 12-month period on the MOAS. Demographics, additional CVST records and convictions for violence offences were also obtained.

Results

Analytic Plan

To assess interrater reliability the first CVST completed by Youth Justice personnel was compared with the first author's ratings. Interrater reliability was assessed on three levels, level of risk rating (low, medium, high), individual items using the Kappa coefficient Measure of Agreement (Sattler & Hoge, 2006 decision rules) and total scores for the dynamic items, static items and the overall total scores (sum of static and dynamic items) via Pearson correlation coefficient. To assess test–retest reliabilities the first CVST completed by Youth Justice personnel was compared with the second CVST completed by Youth Justice personnel.

The validity of the CVST was assessed regarding the prediction of violence 12 months post-completion of the instrument. Sequential logistic regression analysis was used to determine whether level of risk ratings could classify participants based on the presence or absence of future physical aggression. Receiver operating characteristic assessed the CVST's ability to differentiate violent from non-violent participants at a level greater than chance while accounting for differences in base rates.

Table 28.1

Reliability Coefficients for the Child and Youth Forensic Outreach Service Violence Screening Tool

	Interrater (n = 50)	Test–retest (n = 115)
	Kappa coefficients	
Static items		
Previous incidents of violence	.34**	.90***
Previous use of weapons	.51***	.73***
Male gender	1.00***	.89***
Criminal history	.50***	.63***
Previous dangerous/impulsive acts/violent ideation	.23*	.70***
Childhood abuse/maladjustment	.46***	.73***
Role instability	.60***	.73***
History of misuse of drugs and/alcohol	.46***	.80***
Neighbourhood crime and violence	.47***	.69***
Dynamic		
Expressing intent to harm others	.60***	.73***
Access to available means	.27**	.52***
Paranoid ideation about others	—	1.00***
Violent command hallucinations	.48***	.48***
Anger, frustration or agitation	.58***	.63***
Preoccupation with violent ideation	.35**	.65***
Inappropriate sexual behaviour	.11*	.51***
Misuse of drugs and/or alcohol	.58***	.62***
Reduced ability to control behaviour	.41***	.81***
Current family problems; e.g., conflict, violence	.60***	.69***
School problems — truancy, underachievement	.49***	.56***
Antisocial peers	.53***	.65***
Level of risk	.55***	.83***
	Pearson correlations	
Total static items	.58***	.90***
Total dynamic items	.73***	.82***
Overall total scores	.71***	.90***

Note: *p < .05, **p < .01, ***p < .001
Dash indicates that the correlation was not interpretable due to infrequent endorsement.

Reliability

Results of interrater and test–retest reliability analyses are reported in Table 28.1. Interrater data for the individual items revealed that only one static item fell within the excellent range, with the majority of static items considered fair to good reliability. Static items that fell within the poor range include previous incidents of violence, and previous dangerous/impulsive acts/violent ideation. No dynamic items fell within the excellent range with the majority of items evaluated as fair to good with the exception of access to available means, preoccupation with violent ideation, and inappropriate sexual behaviour, which fell within the poor range. Interrater reliability between the total scores for the dynamic and static items, and the total overall score on the CVST found moderately high levels of consistency for dynamic and overall total score, but lower for total static score.

Kappa coefficients for test–retest reliability indicated excellent consistency between time one and time two CVST ratings. All individual items fell either within the excellent or fair to good range. Analyses of all total scores found high levels of test–retest reliability. As expected, higher stability was found for the static scale compared to the dynamic scale.

Over the 12-month follow-up period, 29.30% of the overall sample had engaged in an act of physical violence based on the combination of MOAS and official offending records. Among the youth rated as high risk on the CVST 85.70% (6/7) had engaged in violence, compared to 46.50% (20/47) for the medium risk and 18.30% (17/93) for the low risk participants. Utilising sequential logistic regression, nine predictor variables were entered in four blocks. First, age, gender, and ethnicity were entered for the dependent variable of physical violence. Second, prior contact with youth justice was entered. Third, the first CVST level of risk rating was entered, and finally period of follow-up with youth justice was entered.

The full model containing all predictors was statistically significant, χ^2 (8, N = 146) = 25.14, $p < .001$, and explained between 15.80% (Cox & Snell R^2) and 22.60% (Nagelkerke R^2) of the variability in physical violence, correctly classifying 78.10% of participants. As displayed in Table 28.2 the strongest and only unique predictor of future violence was the CVST level of risk rating, recording an odds ratio of 4.43. Finally, receiver operating characteristics (ROC) for predicting physical violence over 12 month period revealed an area under the curve (AUC) for level of risk rating of .68 (95% CI = .58 to .78), .71 for total dynamic score (95% CI =

Table 28.2

Logistic Regression Predicting Likelihood of Engaging in Violent Behaviour: Block 4.

	B	SE	Wald	Odds ratio	95% CI for odds ratio	
					Lower	Upper
Age	−0.16	0.15	1.13	0.85	0.63	1.15
Gender	0.12	0.58	0.04	1.12	0.36	3.50
Ethnicity A/TSI	−0.39	0.77	0.25	0.68	0.15	3.07
Ethnicity Pacific Islander	−0.28	0.78	0.13	0.76	0.16	3.52
Ethnicity Anglo-Australian	0.44	0.71	0.37	1.55	0.38	6.24
Prior contact	−0.25	0.41	0.38	0.78	0.35	1.73
Level of risk	1.49	0.35	17.78***	4.43	2.22	8.85
Follow-up	0.26	0.23	1.33	1.30	0.83	2.03

Note: ***$p < .001$

.62 to .80), .64 for total static score (95% CI = .54 to .74), and .70 for the overall total score (95% CI = .60 to .79).

Discussion

The current study assessed the reliability and validity of the CYFOS Violence Screening Tool (CVST). Results provide preliminary support for the CVST's ability to measure future risk of violent behaviour in juveniles.

The interrater reliability of the CVST was supported with consistent level of risk scores obtained by independent raters across most of the items, level of risk, total dynamic and overall total scores. The reliability was lower, however, for the total static score. Stability for most items, level of risk and total scores was also obtained when participants were re-assessed within an average time period of 23 days, supporting test–retest reliability of the CVST. Higher stability was found for the static items compared to the dynamic items.

The predictive validity of the CVST was supported whereby juveniles deemed to be at a higher risk of future violence engaged in higher levels of subsequent physical aggression. For every level of risk increase on the CVST the participants were almost four and a half times more likely to engage in physical aggression. For example, a participant assessed at high risk was at least four times more likely to have engaged in physical aggression than a participant assessed at a medium risk of violence, and almost nine times more likely to have engaged in physical aggression than an individual assessed as a low risk of violence. Further the CVST was the strongest contributor in the prediction of future aggressive acts.

The predictive validity of the current study was also supported with findings from receiver operating characteristic analyses that evaluated the predictive accuracy of the level of risk ratings and total risk scores. The level of risk rating and overall total score was the most accurate predictor of future violence performing better than chance with an AUC deemed to be of a large effect size (Rice & Harris, 1995). However, the predictive accuracy of the CVST was at the lower end in comparison to the established assessment tools, the SAVRY and the YLS/CMI (AUC = .73; Catchpole & Gretton, 2003). This finding is not surprising, as the CVST was developed as a brief screening instrument that could be used quickly for all youth referred to mental health or juvenile justice services. Once screened, a comprehensive risk assessment should be conducted with individuals considered to pose a risk for future violence.

A number of limitations are evident in the current study. First, official offending records and recorded incidents of aggression were used to code violent behaviour using the MOAS. The MOAS provides greater depth of information than previous studies however information pertaining to unreported incidents of violence may still have been missed. Second, personnel within Youth Justice may record different levels and quality of information, and subjective opinions regarding aggression may have resulted in information being absent from files. The situation could be rectified with a prospective longitudinal research design whereby data accuracy is regularly checked. Finally, in completing the CVST the youth justice service utilised discretionary overrides. This application of discretion could have influenced findings as the CVST does not provide for the option, and as such, it was not used by the researcher.

Notwithstanding these limitations, the current study advances the field of research evaluating violence risk screening tools. The majority of previous research has examined violence risk in incarcerated youth. This study provides initial support for the use of a screening tool to provide reliable and valid classifications amongst offending youth in the community. The number of juveniles engaged with the juvenile justice system combined with limited resources highlights the need for an efficient and economical classification system to facilitate staff safety and the appropriate distribution of resources.

Further research on the CVST's reliability and validity is warranted to support its ongoing operational use. A number of the items had low interrater reliability. Operational definitions for individual items could increase reliability. Future evaluations of predictive validity could utilise prospective designs, whereby youth and carers are interviewed at regular intervals for further incidents of violence. Further, the predictive validity between the CVST and established risk assessment tools, such as the YLS/CMI and SAVRY could be compared.

In summary the CVST is currently used in juvenile justice and mental health settings to predict risk of violence among youth. Findings provide initial support for the CVST to predict future violence at a level above chance and inform decisions regarding interventions to minimise risk of violence. The overarching benefit of the validation of any screening or assessment tool is the wider benefit to the community. Violence has a far-reaching impact, including severe and negative consequences to many. As youth violence continues to be a prominent factor in our society the need to advance our ability to predict, and in turn prevent youth violence, remains vital for the safety and well being of all members of society. It is hoped that the current study contributes in part to this need.

Author Note

The content presented in this document results from Bond University research, with access to data granted by the Queensland Government, Department of Communities. The content is not intended to create, does not create, and may not be relied upon to create any rights, substantive or procedural, enforceable at law by any party in any matter civil or criminal. Opinions or points of view expressed in this document do not necessarily represent the official position or policies of the Queensland Government. The findings discussed in this document are presented for informational purposes only and do not constitute approval or necessary endorsement by the Queensland Department of Communities.

References

Andrews, D.A., Bonta, J., & Hoge, R.D. (1990). Classification for effective rehabilitation. *Criminal Justice and Behaviour, 17*, 19–52.

Australian Institute of Criminology. (2008). *Australian crime: Facts and figures 2007*. Canberra: Author.

Borum, R., Bartel, P., &, Forth, A. (2002). *Manual for the Structured Assessment of Violence Risk in Youth (SAVRY)*. Tampa, FL: University of South Florida.

Catchpole, R.E.H., & Gretton, H.M. (2003). The predictive validity of risk assessment with violent young offenders: A 1-year examination of criminal outcome. *Criminal Justice and Behaviour, 30*, 688–708.

Grisso, T. (Ed.). (2005). *Mental health screening and assessment in juvenile justice*. New York: Guilford Press.

Hoge, R.D., & Andrews, D.A. (1999). *The Youth Level of Service/Case Management Inventory (YLS/CMI): Intake manual and item scoring key*. Ottawa, Canada: Carleton University.

Kay, S.R., Wolkenfield, F., & Murrill, L.M. (1988). Profiles of aggression among psychiatric patients, I: Nature and prevalence. *The Journal of Nervous Mental Disorders, 176*, 539–546.

Meyers, J.R., & Schmidt, F. (2008). Predictive validity of the Structured Assessment for Violence Risk in Youth (SAVRY) with juvenile offenders. *Criminal Justice and Behaviour, 35*, 344–355.

Mullen, P.E., & Chettleburgh, K. (2002). *Review of Queensland Forensic Mental Health Services*. Retrieved from http://www.health.qld.gov.au/publications/corporate/mullenreview/

Queensland Police Service. (2007). *Annual Statistical Review 2006–07*. Retrieved from http://www.police.qld.gov.au/statsnet

Rice, M.E., & Harris, G.T. (1995). Comparing effect sizes in follow-up studies: ROC Area, Cohen's *d*, and *r*. *Law and Human Behaviour, 29*, 615–620.

Sattler, J.M. & Hoge, R.D. (2006). *Assessment of children: Behavioural, social and clinical foundations* (5th ed.). San Diego: Jerome M. Sattler Publisher, Inc.

Australian Psychologists' Beliefs and Practice in the Detection of Malingering

Jacqueline Yoxall, Mark Bahr, and Norman Barling

Malingering is a possibility in any assessment context where external incentive exists. However, it is not clear whether advances in malingering research over the last 10 years have translated to psychologists' assessment practices. There is limited Australian research regarding malingering base rates or psychologists' beliefs and practices in malingering detection (Sullivan, Lange, & Dawes, 2005). The current study surveyed Australian psychologists (n = 102), currently engaged in psycho-legal practice, in regard to their estimation of malingering base rates; their beliefs about malingering; and their assessment practices. Information gathered raises important matters to be considered in regard to the translation of research to practice in this area of deception detection.

Malingering is a deliberate behaviour that involves fabrication of symptoms for the purpose of attaining an desired outcome, usually financial gain (APA, 2000). Psychologists are frequently required to conduct psycho-legal assessments wherein clients have a vested interest in the diagnosis and the expert opinion regarding causality (Rogers & Payne, 2006; Rosen, 1995). Such circumstances are fertile ground for malingering.

Even a small incidence of successful malingering confounds the clinical database (Rosen, 2004); incurs substantial cost to the community; and creates obstacles to treatment for the clinical population (Rogers, 1997). Consequently, accurate detection of malingering is a crucial component of psychological assessment.

Calculation of the base rate of malingering in psycho-legal contexts is needed (Clifford, Byrne, & Allan, 2004; Sullivan, Lange, & Dawes, 2005).

Unfortunately, determination of base rates of malingering is inherently difficult because successful malingerers remain undetected. To date, retrospective estimation of malingering has been the predominant method of measurement (Mittenberg, Patton, Canyock, & Condit, 2002; Rogers, Salekin, Sewell, Goldstein, & Leonard, 1998; Rogers, Sewell, & Goldstein, 1994; Sharland & Gfeller, 2007; Slick, Tan, Strauss, & Hultsch, 2003). Using retrospective estimation, malingering base rates of 7–17% have been proposed for the malingering of psychopathology in forensic samples (Rogers, Salekin, et al., 1998; Rogers, Sewell, et al., 1994); and 1–39% of those presenting for assessment of neurocognitive dysfunction dependent upon presenting condition and the purpose of the assessment (Mittenberg et al., 2002; Sharland & Gfeller, 2007; Slick et al., 2003).

There has been only one study of retrospective estimation of neurocognitive malingering conducted in Australia. Although limited by a very small sample size ($n = 14$), Sullivan Lange & Dawes (2005) reported a malingering rate of 4–23% dependent upon presenting condition and purpose of assessment.

A substantial limitation of retrospective estimation is the impact of perceptual bias. Psychologists have to believe that malingering actually occurs before they are likely to look for it (Hickling, Blanchard, Mundy, & Galovski, 2002). Rogers (1997) warned that psychologists who do not look for evidence of malingering are unlikely to ever find it. Therefore, an individual's estimation of the base rate of malingering may be dependent upon their definition of malingering and their assessment practices.

Although most malingering surveys to date have attempted to elicit expert opinion regarding the indicators of malingering; assessment practices and reporting of malingering, there has been no focus on psychologists' beliefs about malingering. Exploration of these beliefs might provide some insight to subsequent estimations of malingering base rates.

Deconstructing psychologists' beliefs about malingering requires consideration of the possible reasons that a person might malinger. Rogers and colleagues posed three explanatory models of malingering which provide a basis for consideration of the beliefs that psychologists may hold (Rogers et al., 1998; Rogers et al., 1994). These are the pathogenic, criminological and adaptational models.

The *pathogenic model* considers malingering to reflect underlying psychopathology and proposes that the faking of symptoms ultimately results in the emergence of genuine symptoms. In contrast, the *criminological model* purports that all malingerers are fundamentally antisocial and are motivated to attain some unfair advantage(Rogers, 1990a, 1990b).

Like the pathogenic model, this model is substantially flawed. The assumption of a relationship between psychopathy and malingering is likely to be an artefact of research designs that have relied heavily upon forensic populations which by nature include a disproportionate number of psychopaths compared to the general population (Rogers & Cruise, 2000). Rogers found that the malingering rate in incarcerated individuals may be as low as 3–8% and that reliance on the criminological model in detecting malingering resulted in an unacceptable false positive rate of 79.9% (Rogers, 1990b). Overall, the assumption that malingering occurs because people are either 'mad' or 'bad' is not supported by the literature (Rogers, 1997).

A psychologist's adoption of either the criminological or the pathogenic explanatory model is likely to jeopardise accurate detection of malingering. Psychologists endorsing a pathogenic model are unlikely to explore the possibility of malingering if they believe that this behaviour is a merely a function of psychopathology. Psychologists endorsing a criminological explanatory model would be more likely to identify those with antisocial traits as malingerers, but remain blind to those malingerers who do not present with antisocial traits.

The *adaptational model* avoids the weaknesses of both former models because it is based upon decision theory (Rogers, 1990b). This model identifies malingering as a preferred behaviour in a circumstance that is perceived as adversarial and where an individual does not believe that honest responding would result in the desired outcome. It has been suggested that elements of the adaptational model are most applicable to malingering in a psycho-legal context (Rogers et al., 1998).

The explanatory beliefs held by a psychologist are likely to influence the manner in which that psychologists detect malingering (Rogers et al., 1994) and consequently, their estimation of malingering base rates.

The current study sought to (1) estimate the base rate of malingering in the Australian psycho-legal arena; and (2) to identify psychologists' beliefs and practices in regard to assessment and reporting of malingering and determine whether beliefs and practices influence estimation of the malingering base rate.

Method

Participants

Seven hundred and thirty-six psychologists engaged in psychological assessment were identified from public databases across all Australian states and territories. Psychologists who were not engaged in practice, or who had not conducted psycho-legal assessment in the prior 12 months were excluded. A total of 102 useable responses were attained (response rate of 13.8%). Although the response rate was low, it was similar to, if not higher than other surveys of psychologists' practice (Martin, Allan, & Allan, 2001; Sullivan et al., 2005). It is possible that the subject of malingering creates unease for some psychologists and this may explain the low response. Details of respondents are presented in Table 29.1.

The average age of respondents was 44.96 years ($SD = 12.10$); the average duration of psychological practice was 15.45 years ($SD = 9.27$); and the average number of adult psycho-legal assessments conducted by respondents in the prior year was 35.76 ($SD = 62.50$). The combined number of cases upon which the respondents based their answers upon was therefore approximately 3,070.

Materials

There is no established instrument for measurement of psychologist' beliefs or practices regarding malingering. Most studies have created a survey to address domains of interest. Slick and colleagues (2003) developed and administered a malingering survey to 30 Canadian forensic neuropsychologists to gain retrospective estimation of malingering and to explore malingering detection practices. The Slick et al. (2003) survey comprised of 42 items and presented a reasonable coverage of the domains of assessment practice; indicators of malingering; reporting and estimation of malingering. As is common with survey instruments, there

Table 29.1

Sample Demographics

Practice area and gender	Highest qualification				
	4th year + supervision ($n = 24$)	Masters degree ($n = 50$)	Psychology doctorate ($n = 4$)	PhD ($n = 18$)	Total
Primary area of practice					
Clinical	10	24	1	14	49***
Forensic	3	15	3	2	23
Neuropsychology	2	2	0	2	6
Counselling	6	9	0	0	15
Gender					
Male	14	32	2	7	58
Female	9	18	2	9	37

Note: ***$\chi^2(4,98) = 66.27$ $p < .001$

was no available information regarding the reliability or validity of the Slick et al. (2003) survey. However, the Slick et al. (2003) survey was succinct, clear in meaning and appeared relevant to the current research questions. With the authors' permission, this survey was adapted to suit Australian psychologists. Demographic items were retained and new items addressing years of practice and primary area of practice were added. Whereas the original survey addressed neurocognitive malingering, the adapted survey focused on malingering of psychopathology. New items were created to explore participants' attitudes and beliefs about malingering. Examples of items are presented in Table 29.2.

Respondents were required to complete items in reference to psycho-legal assessments that were conducted in the prior 12 months. Most items utilised a 5-point Likert scale of agreement or frequency (with 5 representing strong agreement or frequency and 1 representing strong disagreement or low frequency).

Procedure

The paper surveys were mailed to potential participants. Electronic invitations were sent via email to potential respondents with links to the online survey. Three reminder emails were sent to potential web survey participants over a 2-month period.

Table 29.2

Examples of Items

Domain	Example item	No. of items
Explanatory models	Most malingerers are likely to show features of antisocial personality disorder.	3
Beliefs about malingering	Malingering is a possibility in any psychological assessment	5
Assessment practices	I routinely screen for malingering	12
Indicators of malingering	Failure to respond to treatment is an indicator of malingering	6
Instruments used to detect malingering	I use the MMPI-II to detect malingering	13
Reporting of malingering	When suspicious of malingering I write, 'Test results are indicative of exaggeration'.	7
Confidence in detection of malingering	How confident are you in detecting malingering?	1
Estimation of malingering	My retrospective estimation of malingering in the last 12 months is ...	2

Results

Attitudes and Beliefs

While 82.6% of respondents agreed that malingering is a possibility in any psychological assessment ($\chi^2[4,100] = 116.6$, $p < .001$), 79.6% rejected the criminological explanatory model ($\chi^2[3,100] = 61.44$, $p < .001$) and 59.2% rejected the pathogenic explanatory model ($\chi^2[3,99] = 30.25$, $p < .001$). Interestingly, 37.9% rejected the adaptational explanatory model, 41.7% agreed with it, and 17.5% were neutral ($\chi^2[4,100] = 58.7$, $p < .001$). Similarly, no agreement was reached regarding behavioural indicators of malingering. Interestingly, many respondents (55.3%) did not believe that inconsistencies between reported symptoms and presentation are indicative of malingering, but 32% thought that this is an indicator of malingering ($\chi^2[4,93] = 57.70$, $p < .001$). Respondents were also divided as to whether lack of cooperation is an indicator of malingering with 29.1% of respondents rejecting disagreeing with this possibility and 38.8% agreeing ($\chi^2[4,92] = 52.02$, $p < .001$).

Testing Practices

Many respondents (61.1%) reported that they engage in routine screening for malingering ($\chi^2[4,97] = 28.52$, $p < .001$), but there was no clear outcome regarding the use of specialised detection instruments when external incentives are present ($\chi^2[4,60] = 2.17$, $p > .05$) or when malingering is suspected ($\chi^2[4,61] = 2.52$, $p > .05$). Interestingly, over a quarter of respondents (26%) reported that they often or very often issue warnings to clients about malingering indices within tests ($\chi^2[5,91] = 27,71$, $p < .001$).

Although many respondents reported that they screened for malingering, they were not in the practice of using malingering detection instruments. More than half (53.4) reported that they 'often' or 'very often' use the Personality Assessment Inventory (Morey, 2007) for detection of malingering ($\chi^2[4,96] = 30.45$, $p < .001$) and surprisingly few respondents (15.6%) 'often' or 'very often' use the Minnesota Multiphasic Personality Inventory-II (Butcher et al., 2001) ($\chi^2[4,93] = 105.65$, $p < .001$).

Of most concern however, was the finding that only a very small proportion of respondents reported that they use specialised malingering tests such as the Structured Interview of Reported Symptoms (Rogers, Bagby, & Dickens, 1992), which was used 'often' or 'very often' used by only 15.6% of respondents ($\chi^2[4,94] = 136.96$, $p < .001$).The Miller Forensic Assessment of Symptoms Test — MFAST (Miller, 1995) was used 'often' or 'very often' by 5.8% of respondents ($\chi^2[4,93] = 223.08$, $p < .001$) and the Test of

Memory Malingering (Tombaugh, 1996) was 'often' or 'very often' used by 16.5% of respondents ($\chi^2[4,94] = 87.92, p < .001$).

Reporting of Malingering

Although respondents did not routinely administer established malingering instruments, many (66.1%) reported that they would report any suspicion of exaggeration or malingering ($\chi^2[4,90] = 51.22, p < .001$). However, most (62.2%) said that they would 'rarely' or 'never' state that they suspected 'malingering' ($\chi^2[5,90] = 56.67, p < .001$), with 23.3% indicating that they would generally report that they suspected 'exaggeration' ($\chi^2[4,55] = 14.91, p < .005$). This indicated a general preference for a conservative or cautious approach to the reporting of potential malingering.

Confidence in Detection of Malingering

Despite the lack of consensus regarding beliefs about malingering, and the lack of use of malingering specific instruments, many respondents (41.7%), reported confidence in their capacity to accurately detect malingering ($\chi^2[3,82] = 46.49, p < .001$). Only 7.8% of respondents were 'not confident' and 30.1% were partially confident.

Estimations of Malingering

Estimations of malingering base rates were somewhat varied ($\chi^2(4,102) = 38.49, p < .001$). Overall, 36.9% of respondents retrospectively estimated malingering to be between 5–10% of psycho-legal cases assessed in the prior year. A very small proportion (9.7%) estimated malingering in psycho-legal cases to be 20% and a smaller proportion (2.9%) estimated the malingering base rate to be over 30%. Surprisingly, over a quarter of respondents (27.2%) reported a zero rate of malingering in psycho-legal assessment conducted in the prior 12 months and 22.3% did not complete the item. A direct discriminant function analysis (DFA) was performed using 6 variables (highest qualification; duration of practice; volume of assessments conducted in last year; endorsement of the criminological explanatory model of malingering; and belief that the incidence of malingering is low) as predictors of estimation of malingering (never occurs, occurs up to 10% of cases, occurs 20% or more). The discriminant function accounted for 76.4% of the between group variance ($\chi^2[12] = 37.29, p < .001$, Wilk's Lambda $\lambda = .56$, Canonical $R^2 = .34$). Sixty-seven per cent of original grouped cases were correctly classified (where chance would be 33.3%) indicating that the DFA solution has some utility for prediction. Table 29.3 indicates that duration of practice and practice area differentiates respondents' belief in malingering.

Table 29.3

Standardised Canonical Discriminant Function Coefficients

Predictors	Function 1
Number of assessments conducted in past year	.610*
Highest qualification attained	.469*
Years of practice	−.273
Practice area	.535*
Belief that malingering incidence is low	.664**
Endorsement of criminological model	.083

Note: *$p < .05$, **$p < .005$, ***$p < .001$

Those who believed that malingering had occurred at rate 10% or over 20% in the last 12 months tended to report a higher volume of psycho-legal assessments in same period, comparative to those who did not believe that malingering had occurred at all. Those that believed that malingering occurred at a rate of 10% generally held higher qualifications and were more likely to work in the forensic domain and did not believe that the malingering base rate is low. See Table 29.3 for details.

Discussion

In the current study, Australian psychologists retrospectively estimated malingering base rates in a psycho-legal context to be between 5–10%. This estimate is similar to that found by Sullivan et al., (2005), but lower than North American estimates. The reasons for this are not clear, but may relate to participants' beliefs and testing practices.

The current study found several inconsistencies between malingering research, malingering detection practices and psychologists beliefs about malingering.

An alarming finding was that nearly a quarter of respondents (who were identified as being involved in psycho-legal assessment), did not believe that malingering had occurred in the last 12 months of their practice. There are two potential explanations for this. The first is that there is substantial discrepancy between malingering research, which has clearly established that malingering occurs (Rogers, 1997), and the practice of some psychologists. The second possible explanation is that a substantial proportion of psychologists do not use effective strategies or instruments to detect malingering.

Of those that believe that malingering does occur, there was little consensus about the conceptualisation of malingering behaviour. While most

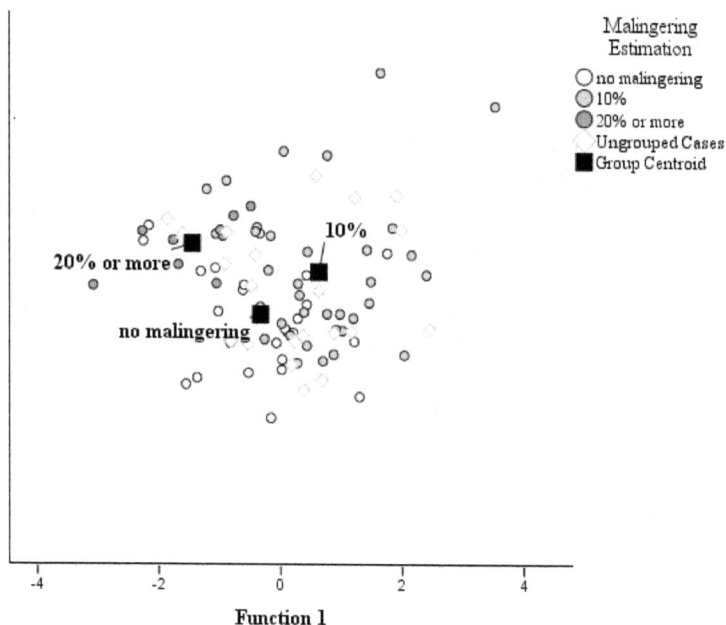

Figure 29.1
Canonical discriminant function.

rejected the idea that malingerers are likely to be antisocial, there was little agreement as to why some people feign psychological illness.

Regardless of their beliefs about why people malinger, most psychologists reported that they screened for malingering; and that they were confident in their capacity to detect malingering. Furthermore, they were prepared to report their suspicion of malingering. However, there appeared to be limited use of specialised malingering detection instruments, and a strong reliance upon multiscale self-report measures. This suggests that while malingering research is advancing, this progress is not transmitting quickly to practice.

These inconsistencies between research and practice prompt questions about the basis upon which many psychologists determine that malingering is present. If psychologists are not utilising specialised malingering detection instruments, it is not clear what form of detection they are relying upon.

Finally, this study found that psychologists who do not believe that malingering occurred in the past year, and those that believed that it did occur were somewhat distinguishable by their exposure to psycho-legal assessments, qualifications, area of practice and to a lesser extent, their beliefs about malingering incidence.

The limitations of this study relate predominantly to the sample, which didn't include many psychologists who were completing a high volume of psycho-legal assessment. This might explain some of the ambiguity in beliefs about malingering. Furthermore, the survey items used to tap into beliefs about malingering may not have comprehensively covered the respective concepts.

In future research it would be prudent to develop additional items to explore and differentiate the explanatory models that people hold. Furthermore, variation of some phrases and items may be beneficial in collecting more detailed data (e.g., questions about exaggeration or potential malingering may be less intimidating than asking about those that had definitely malingered).

Overall, the possibility of malingering must always be considered, particularly in psycho-legal assessment where substantial gains can be made from successful feigning of psychopathology. It appears that Australian psychologists have not reached consensus regarding conceptualisation of malingering and much work needs to be done in regard to the detection of malingering.

Author Note

This article describes a study conducted as ongoing work towards a doctoral dissertation by the lead author. Parts of this study have been presented at the APS Conference, 2008; the EAPL Congress, 2008; the ICP 2008 and the ACPID 2008.

References

American Psychiatric Association (APA). (2000). *Diagnostic statistical manual of mental disorders* (4th text rev. ed.). Washington, DC: Author.

Butcher, J.N., Graham, J.R., Ben-Porath, Y.S., Tellegen, A., Dahlstrom, W.G., & Kaemmer, B. (2001). *Minnesota Multiphasic Personality Inventory-2 (MMPI-2): Manual for administration, scoring and interpretation* (rev. ed.). Minneapolis: University of Minnesota Press.

Clifford, D., Byrne, M., & Allan, C. (2004). Getting caught in court: Base rates for malingering in Australasian litigants. *Psychiatry, Psychology and Law, 11*, 197–201.

Hickling, E.J., Blanchard, E.B., Mundy, E., & Galovski, T.E. (2002). Detection of malingered MVA related posttraumatic stress disorder: An investigation of the ability to detect professional actors by experienced clinicians, psychological tests and psychophysiological assessment. *Journal of Forensic Psychology Practice, 2*(1), 33–54.

Martin, M.-A., Allan, A., & Allan, M.M. (2001). The use of psychological tests by Australian psychologists who do assessments for the courts. *Australian Journal of Psychology, 53*(2), 77–82.

Miller, H.A. (1995). *M-FAST Miller Forensic Assessment of Symptoms Test professional manual.* Odessa, FL: Psychological Assessment Resources.

Mittenberg, W., Patton, C., Canyock, E.M., & Condit, D.C. (2002). Base rates of malingering and symptom exaggeration. *Journal of Clinical and Experimental Neuropsychology, 24,* 1094–1102.

Morey, L.C. (2007). The Personality Assessment Inventory professional manual (2nd ed.). Odessa, FL: Psychological Assessment Resources.

Rogers, R. (1990a). Development of a new classifactory model of malingering. [Review]. *Bulletin of the American Academy of Psychiatry and the Law, 18,* 323–333.

Rogers, R. (1990b). Models of feigned mental illness. *Professional Psychology: Research and Practice, 21,* 182–188.

Rogers, R. (Ed.). (1997). *Clinical assessment of malingering and deception* (2nd ed.). New York: The Guilford Press.

Rogers, R., Bagby, R.M., & Dickens, S.E. (1992). *Structured interview of reported symptoms: Professional manual.* Odessa, FL: Psychological Assessment Resources.

Rogers, R., & Cruise, K.R. (2000). Malingering and deception among psychopaths. In *Clinical and forensic assessment of psychopathy: A practitioner's guide* (pp. 269–284). New York: Lawrence Erlebaum.

Rogers, R., & Payne, J.W. (2006). Damages and rewards: Assessment of malingered disorders in compensation cases. *Behavioral Sciences & the Law, 24,* 645–658.

Rogers, R., Salekin, K.,L., Sewell, K.W., Goldstein, A.M., & Leonard, K. (1998). A comparison of forensic and nonforensic malingerers: A prototypical analysis of explanatory models. [Review]. *Law and Human Behavior, 22,* 353–386.

Rogers, R., Sewell, K.W., & Goldstein, A.M. (1994). Explanatory models of malingering: A prototypical analysis. [Review]. *Law and Human Behaviour, 18,* 543–552.

Rosen, G.M. (1995). The Aleutian Enterprise sinking and posttraumatic stress disorder: Misdiagnosis in clinical and forensic settings. *Professional Psychology: Research and Practice, 1,* 82–87.

Rosen, G.M. (2004). Malingering and the PTSD database. In G.M. Rosen (Ed.), *Posttraumatic stress cisorder: Issues and controversies* (pp. 85–99). New York: John Wiley and Sons.

Sharland, M.J., & Gfeller, J.D. (2007). A survey of neuropsychologists' beliefs and practices with respect to the assessment of effort. *Archives of Clinical Neuropsychology, 22,* 213–223.

Slick, D.J., Tan, J.E., Strauss, E.H., & Hultsch, D.F. (2003). Detecting malingering: a survey of expert's practices. *Archives of Clinical Neuropsychology, 19,* 465–473.

Sullivan, K.A., Lange, R.T., & Dawes, S. (2005). Methods of detecting malingering and estimated symptom exaggeration base rates in Australia. *Journal of Forensic Neuropsychology, 4*(4), 49–70.

Tombaugh, T. (1996). *Test of memory malingering.* Toronto, Canada: Multi-Health Systems.

Personality and Social Risk Factors for Driving Offences

Kate Fritzon, Carla Ferrari, and Laura Fleming

The aim of this study was to identify salient personality and social characteristics that are common to traffic offenders and may be predictive of the type of offences they commit and their risk of recidivism. A sample of *n* = 30 psychological assessment reports were subjected to a content analysis procedure to identify offender personal history variables, and these were entered into multidimensional scaling analyses to examine the structure among the variables. Three categories of driving offences were identified that each correlated with a specific set of background personality characteristics variables. Driving under the influence offences correlated with variables indicating substance addictions and poor coping skills; driving while disqualified offences correlated with previous traffic offences indicating a disregard for the law and needs based offending. Other traffic offences including not having a licence correlated with psychiatric history and lack of employment. Further study is necessary to understand the relationships among the variables but this study does provide some support for the possibility of creating a driving offender risk assessment instrument.

Road traffic and motor vehicle offences continue to be responsible for a large proportion of fatalities globally, and have been identified as one of the top three leading causes of death for individuals under the age of 45 (Peden, McGee, & Krug, 2002). In Australia in 2007, there were 1,616 deaths on the roads (DITRDLG, 2008) with Queensland Transport finding that 41% of all motor vehicle crashes were attributable to failure to obey traffic rules, 29% to inattention, 11% to drugs and alcohol and 5% each to speed and fatigue. In fatal crashes, the statistics for alcohol and drugs involvement increases to an alarming 38% and speeding accounted for 16%. In 2006–2007, road traffic and motor vehicle offences accounted for 43% of all defendants tried in the magistrates court, and 29% of these cases involved defendants under the age of 25 (Australian Bureau of Statistics, 2008). The prevalence of driving and traffic offence in courts, together with overrepresentation of psycho-legal issues such as substance use disorders among fatal crashes, indicates a serious problem worthy of investigation. The current literature on driving offenders has tended to focus on describing discrete categories of offences such as driving under the influence of drugs or alcohol (DUI; Leal, King & Lewis, 2006), driving without a licence or while disqualified (DWD; Watson & Steinhardt, 2002; Bakker, Hudson & Ward, 2000) or speeding (Tay, Watson & Hart, 2002). No study to date has examined variations among the different categories of driving offences and attempted to link these to psychosocial characteristics of the offenders.

Additionally, although research has found that personality factors together with gender account for 37.3% of the variance in risky driving practices (Oltedal & Rundmo, 2006), very limited research exists that specifies which sorts of personality characteristics might predict particular categories of driving offences. Risky driving in general has been linked with various personality traits including sensation seeking (Jonah, 1997), anger and hostility (Schwebel, Severson, Ball & Rizzo, 2006), impulsiveness (Renner & Anderle, 2000) and antisocial personality patterns (Andrews & Bonta, 2006). Furthermore, two high risk groups have been identified; one consisting of 81% males with high confidence in their driving skills, and the other consisting of 84% females who were not particularly confident in their driving skills (Ulleberg, 2002). Both groups had high levels of sensation seeking and aggression, but the females also had high levels of anxiety, whereas the males scored low on anxiety and altruism. These clusters were consistent with other studies that have used cluster analysis to classify offenders into high and low risk categories (Donovan & Marlatt, 1982; Dorn, 2005).

There is a wealth of information available on drink drivers in comparison to drivers affected by drugs other than alcohol. This may be due to the fact that there is more official information available on drink driving as this offender population is more easily caught via random breath testing procedures that have been established for a number of years, whereas random drug testing technology has only recently been introduced to police forces around Australia. Self-report studies have identified that a quarter of people who have used drugs have driven afterwards compared to only a sixth of people who have consumed alcohol and then driven (AIHW, 2005).

Driving without a licence or driving while disqualified can have severe consequences with 6–10% of fatal crashes in Queensland involving unlicensed drivers. Furthermore, unlicensed driving co-occurred with DUI in 23–33% of crashes (Watson & Steinhardt, 2007). A large proportion (30 to 70%) of disqualified drivers report that they maintain driving throughout their period of disqualification (Ferrante, 2003; Watson, 2004). A common reason to continue to drive is the need to get to work (Clark & Bobevsk, 2008; Watson, 2003) In a study of the effectiveness of licence disqualification, Ferrante (2003) discovered a number of protective factors accounted for people who did not reoffend. These were if the licence disqualification was a first offence (both traffic and nontraffic offences), if the offender was female, and if the offender was not of Indigenous heritage.

Despite the array of literature on personality and driving offences and the mounting interest in predicting risk of reoffending, research has tended to focus on just one or two categories of driving offenders, and there has been inadequate focus on developing risk assessment measures beyond the generic; for example, Level of Supervision Inventory-Revised (LSI-R, Andrews & Bonta, 2006). Given that this would currently be the most appropriate tool for assessing the risk level of a driving offender, the current study employs variables from the LSI-R in examining the offender characteristics of driving offenders. It is anticipated that the results of the current study will provide support for differentiating driving offenders into risk categories on the basis of the number of areas for intervention and management that are present in their profile. The LSI-R assesses offender risk levels on the basis of: antisocial personality factors and cognitions, substance use, social factors including family and peer group association, numbers of previous convictions, and lifestyle factors, including employment and leisure/recreation activities.

The hypotheses for the study were as follows:

Hypothesis 1. By examining correlations among offender background variables, it will be possible to differentiate groups of offenders based on those with a number of criminogenic needs (high risk), from those with few criminogenic needs (low risk).

Hypothesis 2. Personality features commonly associated with antisocial personality subtypes will be significant predictors of offending and traffic offenders in general. Antisocial personality patterns is characterised by traits such as impulsiveness, sensation-seeking, fearlessness, egocentrism, hostility and 'normlessness' or lawbreaking.

Hypothesis 3. DUI and DWD offences will have higher correlations with personality characteristics such as impulsivity, alcohol and drug dependence, aggression/hostility, sensation-seeking, and an interpersonal style that is low in empathy.

Hypothesis 4. It is expected that a number of social and personality variables will differentiate between high risk (10+ prior convictions) and low risk (one or no previous offences). In line with previous literature, it is specifically hypothesised that high risk offenders will be younger, single, with a lower level of completed education and with higher levels of drug and alcohol dependence.

Method

Data

The data for the study were a sample of $n = 30$ offenders who had been convicted of a driving related offence and referred by their legal representative to a psychologist for provision of an assessment report to be tendered to the sentencing judge. The reports were de-identified by the author. The cases consisted of 28 males and 2 females aged between 18 and 57 ($M = 26.3$) years of age. Twenty-five participants were employed at the time of offence with the majority ($N = 19$) employed in trade or manual labour settings. Only six participants had completed high school with most leaving school at some stage during Year 9 ($N = 13$) or 10 ($N = 10$). $N = 18$ participants were in a relationship at the time of the offences.

The most common type of driving charge for defendants to be facing was driving while disqualified ($N = 23$), with only $N = 12$ facing driving under the influence charges, $N = 8$ facing driving an unregistered car and $N = 13$ facing other traffic charges (e.g., speeding, not wearing a seatbelt, making excessive noise). These were the first traffic charges for only 5 participants, with most being repeat offenders ($N = 25$). For the repeat offenders the majority ($N = 11$) had been charged with various traffic charges on more than 10 occasions.

Materials

The reports in the current sample all contained a detailed psychosocial history, a personality assessment using the Personality Assessment Inventory (PAI, Morey, 1991) and a summary of risk of re-offending as well as a clinical opinion. The current research focuses on the information contained within the bio-psychosocial history section of the reports as well as the personality assessment. As the raw scores for the PAI were not provided due to confidentiality, the qualitative comments made in the interpretation section of the reports were used to code whether the offender had clinical elevations on particular scales, as well as clinical interpretations of these findings.

Content Analysis

A content analysis recording sheet was created and this acted as a template that would enable data to be extracted and organised from the presentence reports in a systematic way. The LSI-R (Andrews & Bonta, 2006) was used to guide the decision about what data would be extracted from the presentence reports.

Personality Assessment Inventory

The Personality Assessment Inventory (PAI; Morey, 1991) is a self-report objective personality measure designed to identify salient adult personality traits and screen for psychopathology. The PAI consists of 344 items and 22 scales; including four validity scales, 11 clinical scales, 5 treatment scales and two interpersonal scales. The PAI is a favoured measure of personality in clinical and forensic settings, as it requires a minimum reading level of fourth grade to complete the test, an important feature given the low education level of most offenders (Edens, Cruise, & Buffington-Vollum, 2001).

Design

The study employed a mixed design consisting of correlational analysis as well as a quasi experimental analysis involving risk group as the IV (high and low risk) and the various background and personality variables as the DVs.

Procedure

A sample of de-identified court reports was obtained from psychologists through personal contacts of the first author. Content analysis involved reading through the reports and listing descriptive variables that were frequently mentioned across the sample. For example, many offenders were referred to in the reports as engaging in offences after giving considered thought to their actions, while others were described as 'impulsive'. Thus, a variable 'impulsive' was created, with offenders in the former category scoring a 0, and those in the latter scoring a 1.

Interrater reliability was checked using Cohen's Kappa, which resulted in an agreement value of 1.00 for all but two of the variables. Number of previous offences was found to be $r = .286$ and childhood upbringing was $r = .688$. According to Krippendorf (2004) the alpha level is adequate for childhood upbringing but not for number of previous offences. The data were re-examined and it was identified that one rater had utilised the wrong definition for number of previous offences including only traffic offences. Once this error had been rectified the remaining reports were then split between the two raters for final coding.

Results

Initial Data Cleaning and Checking

After all information had been entered into SPSS version 16, frequencies were run on all variables to check for data entry errors. No out of range or missing values were found. Due to the small sample it was expected that the data would not form a normal distribution, which was supported by inspection of histograms for the descriptive data analysis. No univariate or multivariate outliers were found after inspection of boxplots.

Multidimensional Scaling Analysis of Driver Characteristics

In order to examine the structure among the variables and to test the hypothesis that the offender background variables would reflect a structure that relates to their criminogenic risk level, a multidimensional scaling analysis was undertaken. The resulting plot is presented in Figure 1 below. This represents the correlations among the 25 psycho–social variables coded dichotomously as either present (1) or absent (0). The plot in Figure 30.1 is a two-dimensional representation of a three dimensional plot. According to the principle of contiguity (Shye, 1985), the closer that two variables are the more often they co occur in the data. This solution had a Guttman-Lingoes coefficient of alienation of 0.16 indicating an acceptable level of stress between the original correlation matrix and the resulting plot (Donald, 1995).

This SSA was partitioned according to an axial facet (Canter, 1985) and according to a framework, which emphasised the level of intervention needs indicated by the combination of variables clustering into three distinct groups.

The first group contained a number of variables indicating that these offenders have multiple treatment needs, including psychiatric, social and functional needs. These offenders had been charged with driving unregistered vehicles as well as 'other' traffic offences including speeding and disobeying traffic rules.

The second group appeared to be offenders primarily charged with driving while disqualified, with previous traffic charges but whose motives for the current offence included prosocial motives such as trying to get to work. While this may indicate a level of post hoc justification, in

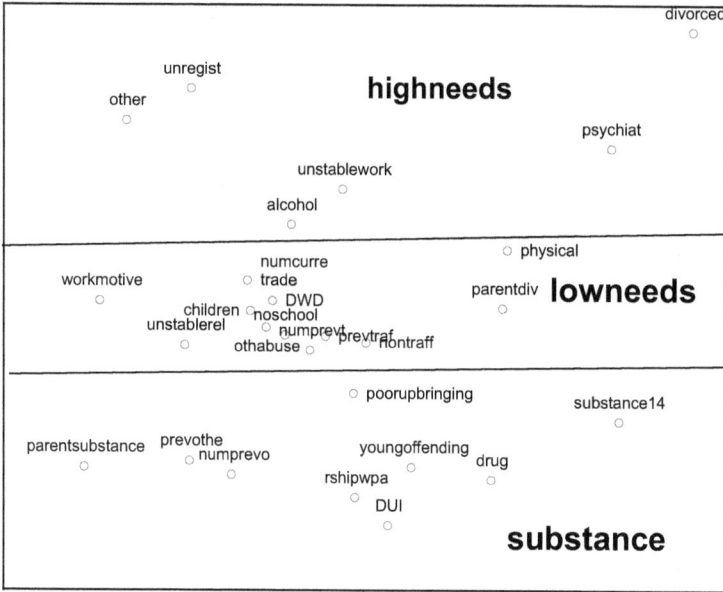

Figure 30.1
SSA of traffic offence variables.

terms of the criminogenic needs framework (Andrews & Bonta, 2006), these offenders' intervention needs appear to be primarily in the cognitive arena in terms of problem solving prosocial solutions to difficulties created by their previous offending history.

Finally, the third group of variables that correlated in the space indicated offenders with needs primarily relating to substance dependence. Their initial use of drugs was at an early age (less than 14) and followed a history of parental substance use as well as a generally poor relationship with parents and an abusive or dysfunctional childhood upbringing. These offenders had convictions for DUI.

Personality and Driving

A second MDS was undertaken to examine Hypotheses 2 and 3 relating to the personality characteristics of the driving offenders. The three dimensional MDS of 30 personality variables and offences had a Guttman-Lingoes coefficient of alienation of 0.20. The MDS in Figure 30.2 is a two-dimensional projection of the first two vectors of three-dimensional space.

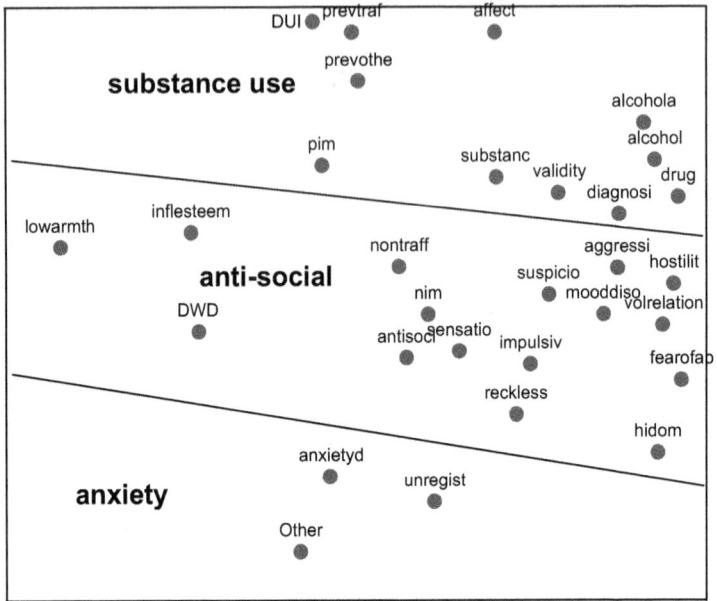

Figure 30.2
SSA of personality characteristics and driving offences.

This SSA was also partitioned according to an axial facet in a similar way to the previous. In the top region, variables indicate presence of substance use disorder as well as elevations of clinical scales on the PAI, and a high positive impression management score. The driving offence category contained within this region was driving under the influence, and these offenders also had previous convictions for both traffic and other offences.

The second region contained variables reflective of antisocial personality traits, including clinical elevations on the antisocial subscale of the PAI, as well as clinical descriptors contained within the text of the report consistent with this personality pattern. The driving offence contained within this region was 'driving while disqualified'. This supports Hypothesis 2, that variables associated with antisocial personality patterns would be present in the majority of cases, as this central region of the MDS contains the highest frequency variables.

Finally, the lower region contained just three variables. These included clinically elevated scores on the anxiety subscales of the PAI, as well as 'other' offences and the driving offence of 'driving an unregistered vehicle'.

Investigation of Risk

In order to test Hypothesis 4, an independent samples t tests was run to ascertain if there were differences between high risk (more than 10 previous traffic offenders) and low risk (first time traffic offender or one previous traffic offence) traffic offenders.

The results indicated that there were significant differences amongst the group means for the two risk groups for alcohol abuse dependence, $t(17)=2.21$, $p < .05$, 95% CI: 0.021–0.93 and the magnitude of this difference can be deemed as very large ($\eta^2 = 0.22$) (Cohen, 1988). There was also a significant difference in scores for substance abuse/dependence $t(10) = 2.39$, $p < .05$, 95% CI: 0.025.703. The magnitude of this difference was 0.25 indicating a large effect. There was also a significant difference found for relationship stability; $t(10) = 4.5$, $p <. 001$, 95% CI: –1.223 to –.413. The magnitude of this difference was large ($\eta^2 = .544$).

There were no differences observed for the static variables of age of level of schooling completed.

Discussion

This study aimed to collect information on psycho–social and personality correlates of driving offences and examine whether differing risk profiles existed for this category of offences. It was predicted that driving offenders could be differentiated according to their level of criminogenic risk (Andrews & Bonta, 2006). This hypothesis was supported by the results of the first MDS analysis, which found that the background and social history variables formed regions according to whether offenders had multiple risk needs, low level of risk needs, or risk needs primarily in relation to substance abuse.

It was further hypothesised that traits associated with antisocial personality types would be significant predictors of traffic offences and of offending in general. The results showed that antisocial personality features and pro-offending cognitive justifications were associated with repeat driving offending and in particular convictions for driving while disqualified (DWD).

A distinct category of offenders for whom the primary risk factor was substance use was identified by the MDS, and these offenders were found to have high numbers of previous convictions from a young age (first conviction under the age of 15), especially for nontraffic offences, sup-

336 | Personality and Individual Differences: Current Directions

porting research by Perrine (1990), McMillen, Adams, Wells-Parker, Pang, & Anderson (1992) and Clay, 1972.

The second MDS demonstrated that offenders with convictions for DWD had a range of elevations on the PAI, including inflated self-esteem, impulsivity, sensation-seeking, dominance, hostility and recklessness. Combining the results of the two MDS analyses together suggests that offenders with these personality features may consider themselves 'above the law' and justify their continued rule breaking as being part of their apparent efforts at 'doing the right thing' such as trying to get to work or meet parenting responsibilities.

The hypothesis relating to differentiating high-risk from low-risk driving offenders correctly predicted that high risk offenders were more likely to have alcohol and substance abuse or dependence issues that supports the findings of numerous previous studies (e.g., Aitken et al., 2000; Lapham et al., 2001; McMillen et al., 1992; Perrine et al., 1989; and Poyser, Makkai, Norman, & Mills, 2002). Relationship stability was also found to distinguish the two groups, with high risk offenders more likely to have unstable relationships. Combining the results from these *t* tests with the MDS analyses suggests that there may be two groups of high-risk offenders; those committing repeat offences of DWD, and those committing repeat offences of Driving While Under the Influence (DWUI). The treatment needs for these offenders appear to differ, with the former benefiting from increasing social support and providing social skills training to increase protective factors; while the latter primarily has treatment needs in the area of substance dependence.

The study was constrained by its sample size and sampling method. A further limitation was reliance on self-report from the offender to the psychologist, and the reporting of the findings of the PAI through narrative format rather than by direct access to the test results.

Conclusions

The results of the study demonstrated that personality and social factors are a key influence in offending and in particular traffic offences. Antisocial characteristics such as impulsivity, aggression, and sensation-seeking have been demonstrated to be predictive of an individual's propensity to engage in risky driving. Alcohol and substance abuse are also key targets for intervention, as are cognitive skills training to challenge their pro-criminal beliefs and encourage offenders to make prosocial choices.

It would be beneficial if future studies could include a large sample size as well as direct access to personality and other psychological test scores. Longitudinal studies are also needed to assess the predictive validity of identified risk factors, recognising that different driving offences may be associated with a slightly different set of risk factors. The results of this and future studies can enable more targeted interventions to focus on those risk needs that are most likely to reduce the likelihood of further driving offences being committed by the same individual.

Acknowledgments

The authors wish to gratefully acknowledge the assistance of QLD registered psychologists who provided de-identified reports for inclusion in this study

References

Aitken, C., Kerger, M., & Crofts, N. (2000). Drivers who use illicit drugs: Behaviour and perceived risks. *Drugs: Education, Prevention and Policy, 7,* 39–50.

Andrews, D., & Bonta, J. (2006). *The psychology of criminal conduct* (4th ed.). Newark, NJ: LexisNexis.

Australian Bureau of Statistics (ABS). (2008). *Criminal courts, Australia, 2006–2007.* Retrieved May 30, 2008, from http://www.abs.gov.au

DITRDLG. (Department of Infrastructure, Transport, Regional Development and Local Government). (2008). *Road deaths Australia: 2007 statistical summary.* Canberra, Australia: Author.

AIHW (Australian Institute of Health and Welfare). (2005). *2004 National Drug Strategy Household Survey: Detailed findings* (Drug statistics series, 16). Canberra, Australia: Author.

Bakker, L.W., Hudson, S.M., & Ward, T. (2000). Reducing recidivism in driving while disqualified — A treatment evaluation. *Criminal Justice and Behavior, 27,* 531–560.

Canter, D. (Ed.). (1985) *Facet theory approaches to social research.* New York: Springer Verlag.

Clark, B., & Bobevski, I. (2008). *Disqualified drivers in Victoria: Literature review and in-depth focus group study.* Melbourne, Australia: Monash University Accident Research Centre. Retrieved from from www.monash.edu.au/muarc

Clay, M.L. (1972, September). *Which drunks shall we dodge?* Paper presented at the 23rd Annual Meeting of the Alcohol and Drug Problems Association of North America, Atlanta, GA.

Cohen, J. (1988). *Statistical power analysis for the behavioral sciences* (2nd ed.). Hillsdale, NJ: Lawrence Erlbaum Associates.

Donald, I. (1995) Facet theory: defining research domain. In G. Breakwell, S. Hammond & C. Fife-Shaw, (Eds.), *Research methods in psychology*. London: Sage Publications.

Donovan D.M., Marlatt, G.A., & Salzberg, P.M. (1983). Drinking behavior, personality factors and high-risk driving. A review and theoretical formulation. *Journal of Studies on Alcohol, 44*(3), 395–428.

Dorn, L. (2005). Driver coaching: Driving standards higher. In L. Dorn (Ed.) *Driver behaviour and training* (Vol 2, 471–480). Aldershot, UK: Ashgate.

Edens, J.F., Cruise, K.R., & Buffington-Vollum, J.K. (2001). Forensic and Correctional Applications of the Personality Assessment Inventory. *Behavioural Sciences and the Law, 19*, 519–543.

Ferrante, A. (2003). *The disqualified driver study: A study of actors relevant to the use of licence disqualification as an effective legal sanction in Western Australia* (Report). Perth, Australia: Western Australia Crime Research Centre, University of Western Australia.

Jonah, B.A. (1997). Sensation seeking and risky driving: A review and synthesis of the literature. *Accident Analysis and Prevention, 29*(5), 651–665.

Krippendorff, K. (2004). *Content analysis: An introduction to its methodology* (2nd ed.). Thousand Oaks, CA: Sage.

Lapham, S.C., Smith, E., C'de Baca, J., Chang, I., Skipper, B.J., Baum, G. et al. (2001). Prevalence of psychiatric disorders among persons convicted of driving while impaired. *Archives of General Psychiatry, 58*, 943–949.

Leal, N., & King, M., & Lewis, I. (2006). *Profiling drink driving offenders in Queensland*. Paper presented at the Australasian Road Safety Research, Policing & Education Conference, Gold Coast, Australia.

McMillen, D.L., Adams, M.S., Wells-Parker, E., Pang, M.G., & Anderson, B.J. (1992). Personality traits and behaviors of alcohol-impaired drivers: A comparison of first and multiple offenders. *Addictive Behaviors, 17*, 407–414.

Morey, L.C. (1991). *Personality Assessment Inventory professional manual*. Odessa, FL: Psychological Assessment Resources.

Oltedal, S., & Rundmo, T. (2006). The effects of personality and gender on risky driving behaviour and accident involvement. *Safety Science, 44*, 621–628.

Peden, M., McGee, K., & Krug, E. (Eds.). (2002). *Injury: A leading cause of the global burden of disease 2000*. Retrieved from World Health Organization, http://whqlibdoc.who.int/publications/2002/

Perrine, M.W. (1990). Who are the drink drivers? The spectrum of drinking drivers revisited. *Alcohol Health and Research World, 14*(1), 26–35.

Perrine, M.W., Peck, R.C., & Fell, J.C. (2010). *Epidemiologic perspectives on drunk driving*. Retrieved from http://profiles.nlm.nih.gov/NN/B/C/X/Y/_/nnbcxy.pdf 8 August 2010.

Poyser, C., Makkai, T., Norman, L., & Mills, L. (2002). *Drug driving among police detainees in three states of Australia*. National Drug Strategy monograph series no. 50. Canberra, Australia: Commonwealth Department of Health and Ageing.

Renner, W., & Anderle, F. (2000). Venturesomeness and extraversion as correlates of juvenile drivers' traffic violations. *Accident Analysis and Prevention, 32,* 673–678.

Schwebel, D.C., Severson, J., Ball, K.K., & Rizzo, M. (2006). Individual difference factors in risky driving: The roles of anger/hostility, conscientiousness, and sensation-seeking. *Accident Analysis and Prevention, 38,* 801–810.

Shye, S. (1985). Nonmetric multivariate models for behavioral action systems. In D. Canter (Ed.), *Facet theory approaches to social research* (pp. 97–148). New York: Springer Verlag.

Tay, R.S., & Watson, B.C., & Hart, S. (2002, July). *Personal and social influences of speeding.* Paper presented at the International Conference on Traffic and Transportation Studies, Guilin, People's Republic of China.

Ulleberg, P. (2002). Personality subtypes of young drivers. Relationship to risk-taking preferences, accident involvement, and response to a traffic safety campaign. *Transportation Research Part F: Traffic Psychology and Behaviour, 4,* 279–297.

Watson, B.C. (2004, November). *How effective is deterrence theory in explaining driver behaviour: A case study of unlicensed driving.* Paper presented at the Road Safety Research, Policing and Education Conference, Perth, Australia.

Watson, B.C., & Steinhardt, D.A. (2007, August). *The long term crash involvement of unlicensed drivers and riders in Queensland, Australia.* Paper presented at hte International Council on Alcohol, Drugs and Traffic Safety (ICADTS), Seattle.

Closing Remarks

This is clearly not an ordinary book. There would be very few who would have read right through from the beginning to the end! But there would be many who have read one or two or three chapters at a sitting, or have sought to know what is happening in research today in personality and individual differences.

This text has given a picture of current thinking on theories and of practice in personality and individual differences. The subheadings within the two parts of this book reflect the many different areas of research that is ongoing: personality theory and contexts; education, personality and emotional intelligence; moral, social and individual aspects in personality psychology; performance aspects and personality; applications in organisational psychology; applications in clinical and health psychology; and applications in forensic psychology.

In each of these sections there is concern with theory and searching for answers that will in turn drive practice — affecting our lives at home, in leisure, at work and on the road. Part of the concern is also with not only understanding and explaining, but with effective assessment — and so we see many areas where improved effective measures are being considered (from risk assessment for violence or driving offences, to education and career assessment, workplace models and clinical health measures).

This research will be ongoing. In this regard, further publications, very likely annually, of the Australasian Personality and Individual Differences Interest Group will occur. Conferences of this interest group will continue, and there will be opportunity for many of you for collegial discussion and learning, and for making a contribution through your own research. We look forward to your participation in our shared adventures in this challenging and stimulating area, and welcome your interest.

We hope you have found this book useful and that you will watch out for further books in our series.

Richard E. Hicks
Editor

www.ingramcontent.com/pod-product-compliance
Lightning Source LLC
Chambersburg PA
CBHW072048020426
42334CB00017B/1426